NATO and the Warsaw Pact

NEW STUDIES IN U.S. FOREIGN RELATIONS

Mary Ann Heiss, editor

NATO and the Warsaw Pact

Intrabloc Conflicts

—◠◠◠—

EDITED BY MARY ANN HEISS AND
S. VICTOR PAPACOSMA

The Kent State University Press
Kent, Ohio

© 2008 by The Kent State University Press, Kent, Ohio 44242
ALL RIGHTS RESERVED
Library of Congress Catalog Card Number 2008001489
ISBN 978-0-87338-936-5
Manufactured in the United States of America

Library of Congress Cataloging-in-Publication Data
NATO and the Warsaw Pact : intrabloc conflicts /
edited by Mary Ann Heiss and S. Victor Papacosma.

p. cm. — (New studies in U.S. foreign relations)
Includes index.
ISBN 978-0-87338-936-5 (hbk. : alk. paper) ∞

1. North Atlantic Treaty Organization—History—20th century. 2. Warsaw Treaty Organization—
History. 3. Europe—Foreign relations—United States—20th century. 4. United States—Foreign
relations—Europe—20th century. 5. Europe, Eastern—Foreign relations—Soviet Union. 6. Soviet
Union—Foreign relations—Europe, Eastern. 7. Cold War. I. Heiss, Mary Ann, 1961–
II. Papacosma, S. Victor, 1942–

UA646.3.N2294 2008
355'.031091821—dc22
2008001489

British Library Cataloging-in-Publication data are available.

12 11 10 09 08   5 4 3 2 1

Contents

Introduction

S. Victor Papacosma

The essays in this volume are based on papers originally presented at Kent State University in an April 2004 conference, "NATO and the Warsaw Pact: Intra-bloc Conflicts." In what seemed like a natural melding of their missions, the Lemnitzer Center for NATO and European Union Studies hosted and cosponsored this gathering with the Parallel History Project on NATO and the Warsaw Pact (subsequently renamed the Parallel History Project on Cooperative Security).

The Cold War era has claimed no shortage of publications focusing on issues of interbloc conflict between NATO and the Warsaw Pact. Indeed, with the declassification of materials by NATO and member states of both blocs since the early 1990s, scholars have presented new information, insights, and interpretations. Contrastively, intrabloc conflicts, which plagued both alliances, have received generally extraneous attention. The fourteen essays in this volume, written by scholars from the United States and Europe, seek to fill this relative gap in the historiography. The volume is divided into two roughly equal sections, one on each alliance, with each introduced by an overview essay about the alliance's workings and general history.

"NATO United, NATO Divided: The Transatlantic Relationship" by Lawrence S. Kaplan provides the thematic backdrop for the coverage of intrabloc conflicts within NATO in the following essays. Differences among member states became evident from NATO's origins, but the reliance on consensus and common consent in the alliance's decision-making process somehow prevailed and is evident to the present. Kaplan refers to "the NATO method" for subsuming differences among allies and follows with several case studies embodying conflict and consensus.

Even before the signing of the North Atlantic Treaty (NAT) in April 1949, an unequal partnership between a dominant United States and its European allies surfaced and persisted to influence affairs in subsequent decades. It is this underlying theme that Kaplan emphasizes as he analyzes: NATO before the outbreak of war in Korea, the "special relationship" between the United States and the United Kingdom up to the 1956 Suez crisis, the challenges posed by France's Charles de Gaulle, and the Reagan administration's strident policies. In doing so, he lists a succession of intrabloc conflicts, concluding that no year during the Cold War passed without some indication of tensions in the relations between the United States and its European partners.

One might have speculated that with the demise of the Warsaw Pact, the "glue" supplied by the Soviet threat, now undone, would have led, along with mutual transatlantic resentments, to the dismantling of the Atlantic alliance. In his final case study dealing with Iraq, Kaplan maintains that even with the glaring divide in the policy positions of the Bush administration and most of its NATO allies, "the termination of the transatlantic alliance is not inevitable." He adds that despite a succession of intrabloc conflicts and despite the North Atlantic Treaty's provision for an alliance member to withdraw, no state has drawn on this option. Concluding, he argues that the great challenge for this long-lived alliance is to prove its ongoing relevance.

Although colonial issues hardly served as an impetus in the drafting of the NAT, they did surface after its signing largely because a number of its members were major colonial powers. Mary Ann Heiss in "Colonialism and the Atlantic Alliance: Anglo-American Perspectives at the United Nations, 1945–1963" analyzes the diverging stances of Britain and the United States on matters of non-self-governing territories in the United Nations, which, in turn, influenced NATO affairs. The UN General Assembly's composition and the Soviet Union's espousal of anticolonial positions in the UN assured that decolonization became another feature of Cold War confrontation. Washington found itself shifting from a customarily anticolonial position to a less critical one as it viewed the colonies of Western European allies as valuable bulwarks in the global struggle against communism. Concurrently, U.S. policymakers confronted the dilemma of containing the alienation of the growing list of nations supportive of anticolonialism. This two-pronged effort generated many complications and troubled ties between Washington and London at the United Nations.

The Eisenhower administration initially professed to shift from its predecessor's middle-of-the-road position but ultimately maintained, with some exceptions such as during the Suez crisis in 1956, the basic approach of not allowing anticolonialism to facilitate the advance of Communism in the developing world. The Kennedy administration followed and, with some variants, continued in this general direction. Throughout this earlier Cold War period, debates, votes, and resolutions at the UN posed problems for the United States and its colonial power allies. If these latter states weakened because of colonial problems, then their contributions in the Atlantic alliance would also falter. Intrabloc difficulties on colonial issues thus became another dimension of the Cold War, and Heiss contends that the general subject offers fertile ground for further research.

Article 2 of the NAT provides for advancing political cooperation among the signatories, an agenda not considered seriously in the alliance's first years when military priorities dominated. Winfried Heinemann reveals how political collaboration would become a critical component of NATO in "'Learning by Doing': Disintegrating Factors and the Development of Political Cooperation in Early NATO." He provides examples from the years 1953–56 to elaborate his position.

Behind-the-scenes efforts by the United States and Britain to impose a solution during the Trieste crisis of 1953 could well have set into motion a NATO military response if Yugoslavia attacked Italian forces—a situation no one desired. The need for consultation among all of the allies had become evident. Heinemann illustrates that such an approach could produce positive results in light of anticipated complications for the United States and NATO in 1956 with a Communist participation in Iceland's government and an associated call for the withdrawal of U.S. troops. He relates how concerted diplomatic action by NATO allies averted serious complications and brought on compromise.

In May 1956 the NATO Council assigned a three-man committee, subsequently dubbed the "Three Wise Men," to propose ways to extend political cooperation within the alliance. Confronting a number of difficulties from the start, the committee also had to contend with the budding crisis surrounding Franco-British policy toward the Suez crisis during the summer of 1956, which then exploded in late October. With Britain and France victimized by events, the call for intra-alliance political consultation and cooperation became paramount—and facilitated the acceptance, with minor alterations, of the report in December 1956.

The entry of Greece and Turkey into the ranks of NATO in 1952 constructed a "Balkan Front" for NATO, offering projected protection for its communication lines in the eastern Mediterranean and security to the two states. In "Failed Rampart: NATO's Balkan Front," John O. Iatrides relates how the original expectations for this region failed to materialize and instead introduced a succession of problems for the alliance and for its two newest members.

From the start, Greece's security objectives diverged from NATO's strategic priorities. A proposed NATO naval base on a Greek island positioned near the entry of the Dardanelles confronted the opposition of the Turks. Attempts to construct more substantive military cooperation with Yugoslavia, recently detached from the Soviet bloc, faltered by 1955. That same year, Turkey and Greece, two rivals who had shelved their centuries-old animosity for about two decades, reignited it with the advent of the Cyprus crisis—an ongoing dispute in variant forms up to the present. Turkey additionally registered complaints on how its strategic concerns were disregarded during the Cuban missile crisis. The Turkish invasion of Cyprus in July 1974 and resultant occupation of a large section of the island almost led to war between the two hostile allies. The ongoing feud over Cyprus would be complemented by Turkish challenges to Greek sovereignty rights in the Aegean, also intensifying to the brink of war on a couple of occasions—yet NATO as an institution failed to intervene positively. The narrow national interests of both states overrode broader NATO concerns, but in the final analysis, Iatrides points out that "the Balkan front was from the outset weak and expendable," representing one of the alliance's lowest priorities.

Gaullist France supplied many problems for NATO, and analysts have paid considerable attention to them. Anna Locher and Christian Nuenlist, however, focus on a generally neglected dimension of the conflict in "Containing the French

Malaise? The Role of NATO's Secretary-General, 1958–1968." Three NATO secretaries general, Paul-Henri Spaak, Dirk Stikker, and Manlio Brosio, served during these years, and the authors examine their policies toward France and other NATO states, evaluating their approaches and levels of success.

Spaak stood for the maintenance of increased consultation within NATO's ranks between the major powers and smaller states. However, Charles de Gaulle early in his tenure advocated a triumvirate composed of the United States, United Kingdom, and France for formulating political and military strategy. Such a stand sought to leverage the influence of Washington and London in the alliance but created diplomatic fissures among the various parties. Seeking to accommodate the headstrong de Gaulle, with whom he had a testy relationship, and several NATO factions proved a futile exercise for Spaak and contributed to his decision to step down in January 1961.

Spaak's successor, Dirk Stikker, fared no better in his dealings with de Gaulle, who initially blocked his appointment and who revived his call for tripartism. Attempts to arrive at a consensus response for the 1961 Berlin crisis found France generally at odds with the remaining fourteen members of NATO, a pattern that would continue in other issues. Stikker had hardly any contact with the French government, and when he announced that he would be departing from his position in the summer of 1964, de Gaulle did not permit a courtesy farewell visit.

Although initially received more favorably by de Gaulle, Manlio Brosio, the new secretary general, also ran into the stiff positioning of the French leader. The prospect of a French disengagement from the Atlantic alliance loomed possible and did occur in part in 1966 with the withdrawal of France's remaining troops from NATO's integrated command and the call for the closing of NATO headquarters in Paris. Institutionally, NATO weathered these storms and saw France approve the landmark Harmel Report the following year. The authors conclude that the three secretaries general collectively helped NATO withstand a number of internal challenges, overseeing in the process the alliance's reconfiguration.

Toward the end of the 1950s European members of NATO expressed concerns over the viability of the United States' nuclear guarantee. Ine Megens discusses a major effort to address these anxieties in "The Multilateral Force as an Instrument for a European Nuclear Force?" Robert Bowie, the head of the State Department's Policy Planning Staff, introduced a scheme in 1960 to establish a seaborne multilateral force (MLF) as part of a broader initiative to spawn a "partnership of equals" between the United States and Europe. The Kennedy administration continued internal discussions on the MLF proposal, determining to consult with European allies in early 1963.

From the start, however, issues of political control for a multilateral fleet with nuclear weapons complicated deliberations within the Kennedy/Johnson administrations and among European allies. Concurrently, public discussion of a European nuclear force began. Megens details the intra-European divisions, which included talk of advancing the cause of European political unity and U.S. positions in this debate. With no acceptable platform for the many parties to accept, momentum on the MLF and its variant forms fizzled during 1964.

Oliver Bange in "*Ostpolitik* as a Source of Intrabloc Tensions" approaches his subject by examining the impact of the initiative not only on NATO allies but also within the Soviet bloc. The *Neue Ostpolitik* of Willy Brandt and Egon Bahr, as it evolved from the mid-1960s, had the prime objective of German unification, which would be achieved by undermining Communism within the Soviet bloc (from the exposure of its citizens to Western ways) and by constructing an all-European security system.

Bange offers nine separate but interrelated arguments to present his findings. For example, he links *Ostpolitik* to earlier strategies forwarded by Washington on ideological competition. Concerns over German unification had spurred de Gaulle to call for an all-European security system, but Georges Pompidou, his successor, saw France's influence potentially undercut by German advances in Europe. Warsaw Pact states differed in their estimations of *Ostpolitik*, but the author reveals that Władysław Gomułka, head of Poland's Communist Party, perhaps alone among his peers saw through the cover of Brandt's policies and the inherent dangers to the existing system. According to the author, Moscow anticipated potential benefits for its agenda of realizing détente objectives while downplaying possible risks. In turn, considerable friction surfaced between the United States and West Germany during the Nixon-Brandt years, with the former suspicious of the chancellor's bold policies and even considering plots to overthrow his government. The Conference on Security and Cooperation in Europe (CSCE) sanctioned the Helsinki Accords in 1975, which, for the author, represented a natural culmination of the *Neue Ostpolitik*.

The manifold forces contributing to the close of the Cold War included the roles of prominent personalities. Charles Cogan has selected France's president for investigation in "The Florentine in Winter: François Mitterrand and the Ending of the Cold War, 1989–1991." He develops the case that Mitterrand attempted to restrain the momentum for German unification but had in due course to concede its inevitability. His public demeanor belied his behind-the-scene moves, which sought to contain a unified Germany. The French also envisaged a reformed NATO that would constrain the veto power of the United States in the alliance as Europeans constructed a new security architecture. Here, too, Mitterrand asserted French positions for a less dependent Europe but would accept some accommodation in accepting the carefully worded New Strategic Concept in 1991. Cogan demonstrates that France did not venture to separate itself from the decision-making process, an approach continued by his successors.

In "The Warsaw Pact: An Alliance in Search of a Purpose," Vojtech Mastny presents an overview of the now-defunct grouping of states lined up against NATO.

He stresses that a prime difference between NATO and the Warsaw Pact rested in their respective purposes: the former served to protect its members against the Soviet peril while the latter invoked uncertainty about its actual, rather than stated, purpose. According to Mastny, the "story of the Warsaw Pact is that of a search for its purpose, which kept changing over time." Distinguishing between political and military functions was among the divisive dimensions of the Soviet-dominated alliance. Thus, the Soviet Union acted to prop up regimes of member states, which relied on Soviet protection from internal threats rather than external attack. New research findings indicate that dissonance in the alliance was far more prevalent than outsiders originally realized. Perhaps this discord did not match the number of disputes within NATO, which institutionally could better withstand divergent positions, but opposition voices challenged to a greater degree the solidity of the Warsaw Pact. Mastny spans the Warsaw Pact's thirty-six-year existence with references to conflicts among its members, a number of which are detailed in the following chapters. Throughout his analysis Mastny draws comparisons with NATO's record to highlight the Warsaw Pact's limited accomplishments.

A prominent example of conflict within the Warsaw Pact is developed by Sheldon Anderson in "Polish–East German Relations, 1945–1958." He portrays the East Germans and Poles as quarreling siblings within the Soviet bloc, each pursuing distinctly incompatible national interests. As early as 1945 the mandated transfer to Poland of German territories up to the Oder-Neisse border precluded the spawning of civil relations between the two Communist parties. Because of the German refusal to acknowledge the historic claims of Poland to German lands, the Poles nurtured apprehensions of German designs to revise the new border.

Acrimonious sentiments failed to fade, and still other lines of division ensued. Thus, the two parties fell into ideological feuds, with the East Germans tending to adhere to more orthodox Marxist-Leninist positions against the reformist inclinations of the Poles. In particular, the very fresh memories of Germany's brutal occupation fed Polish aversion to German rearmament and then to the presence of East German forces in military exercises in Poland. East German officers came to question the loyalty and competency of their Polish counterparts in the Warsaw Pact. The two states also failed to coordinate positions on policy and proposals regarding possible German unification. Anderson concludes broadly that Eastern European Communist parties could not substitute Marxist internationalism for national loyalties.

In "The Warsaw Pact and the German Question, 1955–1970: Conflict and Consensus," Douglas Selvage extends analysis of issues discussed in Anderson's article. He approaches his subject by referring to the debate surrounding the Warsaw Pact's fundamental nature—that of a "transmission belt" for Soviet directives, an actual alliance, or something amid the two. The Warsaw Pact witnessed extensive deliberations on the issue of its policy toward the German problem, which, in turn, involved questions over the alliance's functioning in the political sphere. The Soviet Union, Poland, and, expectedly, the German Democratic Republic (GDR) would be the core states concerned with the problematic German issue.

The GDR pursued policy to enhance its international position and considered the transmission belt function the most efficacious route for achieving this objective. Under Władysław Gomułka's leadership, Poland supported a more consultative function for the Warsaw Pact to bolster the security interests of all the allies. Gomułka recognized that Poland could not receive Western recognition of the Oder-Neisse Line without allied help and that the Soviet Union had other priorities. Unwilling to acknowledge special consideration for the GDR, Gomułka advocated action toward the German question that would secure the interests of both states. Selvage points out that Moscow normally favored the transmission belt approach but found itself frequently assuming the role of arbiter until Leonid Brezhnev acted to reassert Soviet leadership in the late 1960s after the invasion of Czechoslovakia—a period that saw an acceleration of contacts with West Germany.

The Balkan front served up seemingly irresolvable disputes for NATO, and its eastern counterpart confronted related troubles, as Jordan Baev explains in "The Warsaw Pact and Southern Tier Conflicts, 1959–1969." In the late 1950s the Soviet Union appeared to have a firm grouping of allies in Albania, Bulgaria, and Romania. Yet in just a few years, this region evolved into a weak sector of the Warsaw Pact, a situation largely attributable to the wayward policies of two of the states.

Albania by the early 1960s turned into a vocal critic of "Soviet revisionism," as it sided with Maoist China in the widening ideological split with the Soviet Union. Tirana stopped participating in Warsaw Pact activities in 1961, although formal membership was not severed until 1968. On its part, Romania assumed an increasingly independent stance during the 1960s. Bucharest's policy drift troubled relations not only with Moscow but also with individual allies. Following the August 1968 invasion of Czechoslovakia, Romania would terminate field cooperation with the alliance. Bulgaria's Communist leadership in 1965 snuffed out an attempted military coup, reportedly inspired by pro-Maoist officers. Throughout the 1960s and in subsequent years, Sofia remained loyal to Moscow and the Warsaw Pact. Baev concludes that the Kremlin acted in a manner indicating it had more limited worries about NATO capabilities in the Balkans and greater concerns about the possible spread of Chinese influence and the formation of an "anti-Soviet" bloc among Albania, Romania, and Yugoslavia.

Bernd Schaefer continues analysis of China in "The Sino-Soviet Conflict and the Warsaw Pact, 1969–1980." He covers the transformation of an apparent intra-socialist ideological feud into a serious global conflict. Party and other relations between China and the Warsaw Pact states, apart from Romania's continued contacts, ceased during the 1960s. Actual fighting between Soviet and Chinese military units in 1969 solidified tensions and ill will. In the Warsaw Pact forum, maverick Romania blocked joint resolutions against China and possible military action against Moscow's Asian nemesis.

The rapprochement between the United States and China began in 1971–72 and introduced a new consideration for Soviet security policy, which now had two major foes with the potential of working together militarily. Much to Moscow's dismay, Beijing moved to improve economic ties with Eastern European states. By 1980 the security picture for Moscow had became quite gloomy with the collapse of détente, the impending morass in Afghanistan, and the ongoing threat of China.

In the years after the Cuban missile crisis, the Soviet Union had established regular procedures to inform its allies about international issues and policy. Moscow, however, dismayed Warsaw Pact states when it informed them of the Soviet intervention in Afghanistan on 25 December 1979 only after the fact, and Csaba Békés proceeds to detail important policy directions that followed in "Why Was There No 'Second Cold War' in Europe? Hungary and the East-West Crisis Following the Soviet Invasion of Afghanistan."

Budapest determined that the Soviet initiative in Afghanistan did not constitute an internal affair of the Warsaw Pact. But serious concerns set in when the United States responded with countermeasures against the Soviet Union, and Hungary and other allies feared that the positive returns from détente would stall or reverse. Consequently, the Hungarians reacted aversely to the Soviet request that they should "freeze" their high-level contacts with the West. Békés relates the sensitive diplomatic maneuvering that led Moscow to yield, allowing socialist states to maximize on the potential "contained in existing relations with Western European countries to counterbalance the United States's foreign policy line." Those ties with Western Europe had very critical returns and not just for Hungary's economy. Békés argues that small-state diplomacy had helped contain further deterioration in East-West ties, as had occurred between the United States and Soviet Union over Afghanistan, and averted a "Second Cold War."

In focusing on intrabloc conflicts, the studies in this volume collectively provide new insights into the Cold War and its dynamics from multiarchival research. Maintaining cohesion in light of the perceived enemy is a prime objective for alliances, and NATO and the Warsaw Pact confronted a succession of challenges in efforts to maintain relative unity and viability. Some conflicts were minor and others quite major, to the extent that they undermined the strategic capabilities of the two alliances. Interestingly, while some of the specific disputes assumed differing forms in the two blocs, others were rather similar in content and impact. The articles indicate that NATO generally seemed to accommodate diversity better than the Warsaw Pact and that the Soviet Union did not have the perceived all-powerful capacity to impose total discipline on its lesser allies. The two blocs, if anything, were certainly not able to operate as monolithic blocs.

And while NATO outlasted its now defunct rival, it has the difficult challenge of redefining its purpose and mission in a post–Cold War era. Lawrence S. Kaplan warns that not to do so might lead to "the possibility of NATO becoming as irrelevant as the League of Nations had been in the 1930s." In a related vein but from an alternate vantage point, Vojtech Mastny refers to the entry of former Warsaw Pact states into NATO's ranks and the concurrent need for the enlarged alliance to search for a clearly defined purpose. He reflects: "Until its new purpose has been found and clearly defined, NATO will court the fate of its former rival." History reveals that effectively accommodating intrabloc conflict is a related component for defining and maintaining purpose.

PART I

NATO

1

NATO United, NATO Divided

The Transatlantic Relationship

LAWRENCE S. KAPLAN

Published in 2001 by the NATO Office of Information and Press, the *NATO Handbook* tells its readers that the alliance's decision-making process is "dependent on consensus and common consent." If there should be differences between member governments, NATO will make efforts to reconcile them "in order that joint actions may be backed up by the full force of decisions to which all member governments subscribe. Once taken, such determinations represent the common determination of all the countries involved to implement them in full." This confident language suggests a history of relationships in which the alliance managed to confront "decisions which may be politically difficult," thereby adding "force and credibility" to the outcomes.[1] When those differences seemed impossible to keep within the confines of the North Atlantic Council, such as the withdrawal of France from the integrated military structure, the alliance could move on knowing that it was flexible enough to surmount such challenges.

The list of deviations for individual positions within the alliance, including those of Spain and the Scandinavian members as well as France, however, is long enough to raise a question about the meaning of "consensus." Were the allies as a body satisfied with France's decision to withdraw from the military structure of the alliance in 1966 or Denmark's and Norway's refusal in 1949 to allow stationing of foreign forces or nuclear weapons on their territories in peacetime? It would seem logical to find conflict rather than consensus to be the norm among twelve, then fourteen, fifteen, and sixteen nations during the Cold War. If so, extensive consultations in the North Atlantic Council and other NATO bodies were vital for the successful functioning of the organization. They were conducted behind closed doors where trade-offs were necessary to reach decisions acceptable to all. How the allies were able to subsume their differences under a common rubric, known as "the NATO method," is the subject of this chapter. Case studies during NATO's first fifty years illuminate both conflict and consensus.

NATO Before the Korean War

NATO's first year, before the outbreak of the Korean War in 1950, witnessed many of the problems that the alliance had to cope with in succeeding years. The allies had to deal with an unequal partnership in which the United States, the dominant figure, had the controlling vote behind the screen of consensus. This was hardly surprising. Western Europe was desperate for the kind of aid that only American power could provide—namely, the assurance that its economies would recover and its societies would remain free of the rising Communist menace. In the sweltering heat of a Washington summer, delegates from the five members of the western union met in July and August 1948 with U.S. and Canadian representatives for exploratory talks on European security.[2] The Europeans sought military aid (ultimately, article 3 of the North Atlantic Treaty) and a guarantee of America's commitment (article 5). After months of negotiations they received both, but at a price.

It took more than the summer of 1948 in Washington before the United States was prepared to break its long tradition of nonentanglement. The five signatories of the Brussels Pact reluctantly accepted language that did not quite fulfill the terms of the "pledge," as Canadian diplomat Escott Reid characterized the most important article of the treaty.[3] This, of course, referred to article 5—everything else was subordinate to this vital assurance in European eyes. The appropriate language in their view was available in article IV of the Brussels Treaty, which stated clearly and simply that an attack against one member "will . . . afford the Party so attacked all the military and other aid and assistance in their power." The State Department responded negatively to this wording in August 1948, asserting that "the United States could not constitutionally enter into any Treaty" that might place the nation "automatically at war as a result of an event occurring outside its borders or by vote of other countries without its concurrence."[4] That this contingency was unacceptable to the Senate Foreign Relations Committee became the nub of controversies that postponed signing of the treaty until April 1949.

A better choice of language had to be found to assure Congress that military action would not be an automatic response to an attack against an ally, yet this response was precisely what the allies required of the United States. The semantic agility of George Kennan, the father of containment but a skeptic about its military dimension, provided a suitable compromise. Instead of the allies taking "forthwith such military or other action . . . [as] may be necessary," the word "military" was finessed by replacing it with "including the use of armed force" to follow "such action as it deems necessary."[5] Individual members were free to fashion their responses according to their respective national interests.

The tortuous language of the article sharply contrasted with the spare terms of article IV of the Brussels Pact and certainly did not offer what the Europeans wanted. It was, however, the best they could get in 1949. What may have tipped the balance in favor of the American version of article 5 was a recognition that the president's powers as commander in chief could evade or at least dilute the constitutional prerogatives of the Congress. Sufficient precedents existed to give the allies confidence in the credibility of the American pledge. Thus, Woodrow Wilson in 1917 brought the nation into World War I despite a strong isolationist pull against involvement, and in the nineteenth century President James K. Polk manipulated Congress into declaring war against Mexico by dispatching troops into a disputed area in the expectation that the Mexican army would fire the first shots, thereby assuring passage of a declaration of war. Doubts about the viability of article 5 had to be weighed against the positive psychological impact on Europeans of the American guarantee. The image of U.S. B-29s, armed with atomic weapons, in the air twenty-four hours a day, and prepared to strike the Soviets in the event of an act of aggression, may have been an illusion, but it was a comforting one to the European allies in 1949.[6]

In article 5 the Europeans achieved almost all they wanted, while Americans could claim that constitutional procedures would be followed. There would be no automatic involvement in a European war if one of the allies were attacked. The Brussels Pact members were less satisfied with the enlargement of the prospective alliance to include such countries as Norway, Denmark, Iceland, Portugal, and even Italy. Adding these peripheral nations meant sharing American military aid with as many nations as comprised the Western union itself.[7] There was little choice. The United States needed Scandinavian and Portuguese bases in the North Atlantic to transport the aid abroad. Even more frustrating than having to settle for smaller pieces of an aid pie were the restrictions the United States placed on the activation of article 3, which would offer U.S. military assistance to alliance members under the rubric of "mutual aid." So urgent was this article that the Brussels core members presented a laundry list of items only one day after the signing of the treaty on 4 April 1949. It appeared that article 3 was almost as important to them as article 5.

Their démarche discomfited the Truman administration, which was reluctant to mix military aid with the principles of article 5. Washington felt that European requests were premature and perhaps somewhat unseemly by placing excessive emphasis on the military character of the alliance. It was as if the Europeans were too impatient in their race to avail themselves of American resources.[8]

The allies did receive congressional grants of military aid—$1 billion—before the end of the year, but not until the administration and the Senate had attached conditions that did not conform to the spirit of the alliance. NATO was intended to function as a multilateral institution, and the prospective recipients wanted to apply the principles of integration to the distribution of U.S. funds. Congress would take no action until the Senate ratified the treaty, and even then it took news of the Soviet detonation of an atomic device before a military assistance act could be passed in October 1949.[9] With its passage, the allies had to accept the bilateral nature of the grants: negotiations between the donor nation and the beneficiary determined the detailed arrangements of dollars to be dispensed rather than NATO as an organization. This bilateral approach, intended to ensure that the funds would be properly utilized, inevitably generated friction between the United States and its allies. Moreover, the American military advisory groups in European capitals proved too intrusive and frequently too numerous. For example, the mission in Oslo was larger than the entire Norwegian foreign office. In larger capitals the diplomatic status of the U.S. aid inspectors smacked of imperial arrogance. The sensitive French insisted that "advisory" be removed from the title of the mission, and the British insisted that military personnel wear civilian clothes.[10]

The military aid teams were embarrassments to European governments, as suggested by their efforts to disguise them. To add injury to insult, equipment was slow in arriving and often inadequate for a particular country's needs. In brief, the American tradition of nonentanglement in European affairs may have been breached by the signing of the North Atlantic Treaty, but old habits of unilateralism died hard, and new assumptions of superiority based on the prerogatives of power reflected an imbalance in the alliance that might have doomed it in its infancy. If it did not, Europe's sense of dependence on American support outweighed the resentment that American policies generated.

What helped preserve NATO in that first year was a fitful recognition on the part of the senior partner that it should repair damage to the relationship that it had unwittingly inflicted during the war. One instance grew out of the alliance's need to develop a strategic concept to cope with the adversary's aggressive actions. The distribution of forces in the concept displeased all the allies, large and small alike. The role of strategic air strikes would be filled by the United States, tactical air by Britain, and ground troops by the remaining member states. Logic dictated that strategic air power be placed in American hands, since only the United States possessed aircraft armed with atomic weapons. Nevertheless, the allies were unhappy serving as cannon fodder in the event of a Soviet attack when American airmen in the sky above the battleground would be less subject to casualties than the ground forces below. Echoes of dissent over this division of military labor could be found a half century later in Bosnia, Kosovo, and Afghanistan.

To calm some of the passions aroused by the unequal assignment of forces, the United States revised scenarios that the Joint Chiefs of Staff had drafted at the time of the treaty's framing. The predominant strategy after World War II had accepted the impossibilities of defending the European mainland from a Soviet attack. Their short-term defense plan postulated defense at the perimeters—the Pyrenees, the Suez, and the British Isles. From these bases NATO could mount an attack on Soviet Europe much as the allies of World War II had against Nazi Germany.[11] For Europeans, a defense plan of this sort evoked memories they preferred to forget. Liberation after another enemy occupation was unacceptable. Europeans, particularly the French, might opt for a pro-Communist neutralism rather than experience replication of World War II.[12] Responding to these concerns, the United States, at the meeting of NATO's Military Committee in March 1950, produced the medium-term defense plan, under which the blanket of NATO protection would be extended to the Rhine. This was not a wholly satisfactory solution, because it left the Netherlands, divided by the river, uncertain about its status, as well as Denmark and Norway closer to Soviet-dominated Europe.[13] Nevertheless, the continuing presence of allied occupation forces, particularly American, in divided Germany indicated responsiveness to European concerns. Trust in the senior partner's commitment to European security minimized transatlantic conflict in NATO's first year.

"The Special Relationship"

Of all the allies it was the United Kingdom that believed itself to be the most intimate partner of the United States. Foreign Secretary Ernest Bevin had taken the initiative in pushing the United States out of its isolationism after the collapse of negotiations at the foreign ministers meeting with the Soviet Union in London in December 1947. In his January 1948 speech before Parliament advocating a union of European nations, he sought to provide evidence of a serious break with their tradition of internecine conflict, thereby demonstrating that Western Europe was ready for a political counterpart to the economic reconstruction sponsored by the Marshall Plan.[14] Bevin's conception of the Brussels Pact two months later was to have the new western union serve as a vehicle for the United States to join the new organization.

The Truman administration's endorsement of the Brussels Pact did not include American membership, but the secret Pentagon conversations immediately after the signing of the treaty buoyed British hopes of engaging the United States in an Atlantic, if not a European, alliance,[15] resulting in a confidential understanding that an Atlantic security organization would follow in the near future. In the meantime, Britain dominated the negotiations in London that created the Western Union Defense Organization (WUDO) in the summer of 1948. It is worth noting that the British field marshal Bernard Montgomery, not the French general Jean de Lattre de Tassigny, became chairman of WUDO's Commanders-in-Chief Committee. France, excluded from the Pentagon conversations, appeared to play a secondary role in London as well as in Washington.

In this context it is understandable that British leaders would identify a special relationship with the United States, making it primus inter pares in Europe. Indeed, the sentiment prevailing in Britain in the 1950s, expressed by such influential pundits as Alastair Buchan, was that the British would serve civilization as Greeks to the American Romans.[16] In other words, Britain may have lost an empire but not the wisdom, as in the case of Greek slaves, to guide the powerful and relatively naïve Americans, the Romans of the twentieth century, in the ways of diplomacy.

Bevin and his colleagues were mistaken. The Americans had no intention of serving as surrogates for the strong but immature Romans. Their leaders, tested in World War II, came to the conclusion that Old World diplomats, especially the British in the 1930s, had failed to deal with the fascist menace. Americans could do better and did not need the discredited diplomacy of Europe to manage the Communist challenge. The British, after all, were the "Greeks," who successively departed India, Greece, and Palestine in the years immediately preceding the Atlantic pact. No American statesman expressed the devaluation of British statecraft more succinctly than former Secretary of State Dean Acheson, who outraged Britain in a 1962 speech at West Point when he observed that the British had lost an empire without finding a new mission.[17]

The "special" relationship obviously had its limits as became evident early in the history of the Atlantic alliance. The authority that the British felt they had exercised in 1948, when London hosted the Western union's headquarters, dimmed by 1952. American pressure to appease the French ally resulted in the transfer of NATO's headquarters to Paris. This was not a British proposal or in the British interest. Similarly, Britain was frustrated by its inability to secure a major command when NATO reorganized in 1951. With a long and distinguished naval tradition, its leaders assumed that the supreme command of the Atlantic would be assigned to a British admiral, a fitting counterpart to the American general as the supreme commander in Europe. To the dismay of the British government, the command went to a U.S. admiral with headquarters in Norfolk, Virginia, not Southampton, England. When an American was appointed supreme allied commander for the Atlantic, General Dwight D. Eisenhower ruefully, if belatedly, acknowledged that Americans should have learned from the experience in World War II of "the super-sensitiveness of the British public to anything and everything Naval . . . particularly as it may have an effect on the success of NATO."[18]

There was more frustration in store for the British when they were denied a Mediterranean command, under Admiral Lord Mountbatten in Malta, that might have had a standing only slightly inferior to Eisenhower's in Paris. Instead of enjoying an autonomous role in the Mediterranean, Mountbatten was required to report to Eisenhower through the southern command headquarters in Naples, headed by an American admiral. The most that the British could salvage from a distribution of commands was the assignment of the Channel command, an obvious sop to

British pride that also represented an accurate judgment of the disparity between the American and British military establishments.[19]

The "special" relationship suffered further setbacks in NATO's first decade, but none was more humiliating than the American reaction to Britain's effort to retake the Suez Canal by force in 1956. As defined in article 6 of the treaty, Egypt and the canal did not fall within NATO's area of responsibility. It became, however, one of the many "out-of-area" problems that influenced U.S. relations with its allies and occasionally even threatened the survival of NATO itself. The nationalization of the Suez Canal by Egypt's dictator, General Gamal Abdel Nasser, severely challenged the alliance. Asserting Egyptian nationalism in a bid for leadership of the Arab world, Nasser sought to control an operation that had been built and controlled for almost a century by Britain and France. For the British, the canal represented a vital link to what remained of their empire in Asia.

The Eisenhower administration had appeared to share the concerns of the allies, but when it came down to possible military action against Egypt, Secretary of State John Foster Dulles expressed the American position evasively. He wanted to work within the framework of the UN Charter to undo Nasser's seizure. Distrustful of Dulles's steadfastness, Britain and France joined with Israel in October 1956, without informing their American ally, to wrest the canal from Egyptian hands. Israel, under constant threat of Egyptian aggression, successfully crossed the Sinai Desert, defeating the Egyptian army as it moved swiftly toward the canal. The Anglo-French air and sea invasion, however, stalled before it could retake the waterway, allowing Egypt to appeal to the United Nations for support against aggression from two major NATO partners.

The result was the near destruction of the alliance as the United States sided with the Soviets in opposing the Suez operation. A painful moment for all the allies, the abortive invasion coincided with the Soviet suppression of the Hungarian revolt. Instead of marshaling world condemnation against the Soviets' brutal actions in Hungary, NATO found itself on the defensive as the Communist world directed attention in the United Nations to Anglo-French behavior toward a Third World victim. Given its strong position against the illegal use of force, the United States felt compelled to join the Soviet adversary in the United Nations' judgment against its NATO allies. America's condemnation proved all the more galling because it spoiled an opportunity to put the Soviet Union in the dock before the court of world opinion over its treatment of Hungary.

Both Britain and France succumbed to this combined pressure and retreated from the canal. Prime Minister Anthony Eden resigned under fire from liberals critical of gunboat diplomacy and from conservatives critical of the failure of that form of diplomacy, but Eden's successor, Harold Macmillan, repaired much of the damage done to the Anglo-American relationship, attributable in large part to his camaraderie with President Eisenhower during World War II. A case may be made that the relationship, having survived the Suez crisis, appeared stronger at the end of the 1950s than it had been at the beginning of the decade. The ongoing challenge of the Soviet Union, emboldened by its success with Sputnik, the first earth satellite, drew the two allies closer when they resisted Chairman Nikita Khrushchev's efforts to drive the Western allies out of Berlin in 1958. Yet the "special" relationship was never quite the same. The imbalance of power between the two nations never permitted the British to direct American NATO policy in the way the Greeks were said to have controlled imperial Rome's.

The Gaullist Challenge

That General Charles de Gaulle, president of France under the new Fifth Republic in 1958, became the leading European challenger to American primacy in NATO over the next decade is not open to doubt. De Gaulle's towering presence dominated Europe's relations with the United States, even as many of the European allies resented France's pretensions. His rise to power from the ashes of the Fourth Republic coincided with the perception, generated by the successful launching of Sputnik in October 1957, of American vulnerability to Soviet intercontinental ballistic missile attack. De Gaulle took advantage of the shock that this demonstration of Soviet power rendered to Europeans and Americans alike. Not even the quick dispatch of nuclear stockpiles to Europe or the assurance that American missile technology was actually more advanced than its Soviet counterpart proved sufficient to erase the trauma caused by the Soviet accomplishment.

Until 1957 the United States had been considered invulnerable to any Soviet aggression. Unlike Europe, its territory extended beyond the adversary's range, and its promise under article 5 to respond to an enemy attack was credible. The Soviet Union could not reach America, while U.S. nuclear power based in Europe restrained Moscow's allies. It was under this nuclear umbrella that the NATO allies had found a sense of security and achieved economic prosperity. Now the question was whether the American commitment would remain intact when the United States itself could be subjected to Soviet missiles. Repeatedly during his presidency de Gaulle answered this question negatively. It seemed illogical, he proclaimed, for any country to place the security of others, whether or not in an alliance, over its own. More specifically, he reminded the allies about America's interest in Asia being older and more constant than its involvement with Europe. He offered as his case in point the Vietnam War, in which the United States was increasingly entangled in the 1960s. Among its other instructive uses he cited this conflict to question the wisdom as well as the geographical direction of American policy. Given doubts about the credibility of the U.S. commitment to Europe's defense, de Gaulle envisioned France assuming the leadership of Europe, which the United States had held in NATO's first decade.[20]

De Gaulle's actions in the 1960s proceeded on the assumption that the Soviet threat of aggression had lessened. He considered the Soviet Union a nuclear power on a par with the United States with intentions no less hostile to the West than in the past, but at the same time he recognized that it was no longer the expansionist state it had been a decade before. Its retreat from belligerence over Berlin in 1959 and again in 1961, along with its literal retreat from Cuba in the missile crisis of 1962, encouraged de Gaulle not only to equate the two superpowers in their relation to Europe but also to claim that Europe under France's direction could play a significant role as mediator between the two superpowers. Although it was unlikely that he genuinely believed that the United States, given its history in NATO, posed the same kind of military threat, his image of the two adversaries suggested more similarities than differences.[21]

Gradually but inexorably, de Gaulle moved toward his goal in carefully calibrated steps. The first confronted the Anglo-Saxon powers with a plan for a triumvirate in which France would join the United States and the United Kingdom to direct NATO affairs. Presumably this would correct a situation in which the "NATO method" of consensus had given too much weight to the smaller allies. Not unexpectedly, the United States and Britain rejected the proposal on the grounds that it would distort the nature of the alliance, even if it improved its efficiency. Their reaction served to confirm de Gaulle's judgment that NATO was a ward of Anglo-America and that France could never achieve equality under this arrangement. He subsequently justified rejecting British membership in the European Economic Community on the premise that Britain would be America's Trojan horse in the European order he had in mind.[22]

Having failed to win over the United States to his version of a reorganized NATO, de Gaulle moved to accelerate the development of nuclear independence through a French *force de frappe*. Although France's nuclear program originated in the frustrations of the Fourth Republic, it was an important gauntlet thrown down before the senior partner. The United States reacted strongly, asserting that no other NATO member should find it necessary to have nuclear weapons; the American nuclear arsenal was more than sufficient to serve all the others. Secretary of Defense Robert McNamara irritated the French with his claim that smaller nuclear arsenals in the alliance would not only be needlessly expensive but also lack credibility as a deterrent.[23]

France made it clear that it would not accept American objections. Its military strategists rejected the notion that France's nuclear weapons would be quickly wiped out in the event of a nuclear war. On the contrary, they suggested that the prospect of destroying even a limited number of Soviet cities would serve as a force of disuasion.[24] National nuclear arms, no matter how small, would strengthen deterrence by instilling a sense of insecurity in the minds of a potential aggressor. At issue in French eyes was a transparent effort to block France from achieving an element of equality with the United States in NATO and undermine France's leadership in Europe.

America's failure to impress on the French the folly of their nuclear ambitions was only to be expected. Too much had been invested in their nuclear program. American opposition served up simply another piece of evidence in their case against the hegemony of the transatlantic partner. France's independence from the United States required keeping its nuclear weapons outside of NATO's integrated command.

It was only a matter of an appropriate time before de Gaulle detached France from the Supreme Headquarters, Allied Powers, Europe (SHAPE). He had begun the process by signaling to the Soviet Union that France would follow its own course when he removed the French fleet from the Mediterranean command in 1959. The slogan *Méditerranée aux Méditerranéens* was his assertion of preeminence in the area as well as an expression of his assumption that the warships of both superpowers would be excluded from the sea. Four years later he removed the French Atlantic fleet from the Supreme Allied Command, Atlantic (SACLANT). In refusing to allow France to participate in Fallex '66, NATO's annual military exercise, de Gaulle seems to have completed preparations for full withdrawal from the alliance's military structure.

By the end of 1965, conditions had ripened for such a move. The Cold War had sufficiently thawed for overtures to be made to the Soviets; the German neighbor had formally accepted France's leadership in NATO as a result of a special treaty of cooperation in 1963; and the Algerian war had been liquidated. In March 1966 de Gaulle sent a letter to President Lyndon B. Johnson demanding that all NATO installations on French territory be removed within a year's time and announcing that all French personnel would leave their SHAPE posts.[25] The deadline of a year appeared insultingly short for the United States to pick up its men and matériel and get out of France. At the same time, the French made it clear that they would not denounce the North Atlantic Treaty but would separate participation in the alliance from membership in its military organization.

There was shock and anger in Washington, although the former reaction was less understandable than the latter. The French president had supplied enough signals of his intentions over the years to cushion the surprise when the final action did occur. In fact, American reaction was mixed. The most vehement protests came from such Francophiles as Undersecretary of State George Ball, who felt personally betrayed by France's behavior. He wanted to challenge the legality of de Gaulle's cancellation of agreements that provided for two years' notice before termination. If Johnson had not restrained Ball, he would have had the United States retaliate by challenging the legality of its eviction from bases in France and denying the French access to NATO intelligence sharing.[26] The most serious NATO riposte was to remove its political, as well as military, headquarters from France to new homes in Belgium.

Undoubtedly, France did damage NATO's defense capabilities in the short run. The sheer physical effort to shift supply lines into Germany from an Atlantic route via France to North Sea ports in Germany was not only costly but also disruptive, yet it did not generate the kind of hostility that might have led to France's isolation, if not ejection, from the alliance. There was actually no mechanism to throw out a member. In fact, de Gaulle's posture always had admirers, particularly among Europeans sharing his resentment of American domination. Diplomats, such as NATO's secretary general, Manlio Brosio, had deep ties to France and were not anxious to move offices from Paris to Brussels. Ironically, Secretary of Defense McNamara welcomed de Gaulle's action as an occasion to reduce American obligations and place greater responsibility on Europeans for defense of their territories. He also saw an opportunity in France's departure to streamline the NATO defense system, to make it more efficient and less costly. President Johnson himself accepted de Gaulle's decision with equanimity, at least publicly, on the grounds that the French president was not going to change his mind, whatever arguments his allies might deliver.[27]

The alliance survived the French challenge, partly because de Gaulle, his grand gestures notwithstanding, maintained French forces in Germany, albeit not under NATO's provenance. He also kept French air space open to NATO aircraft. Moreover, France continued to be represented in every NATO military headquarters, though its representatives were identified as "missions" rather than "delegations."

In retrospect, de Gaulle's challenge failed to discredit America's leadership of NATO. Implementation of his aspirations to replace the United States as the paramount influence in Europe depended on Germany as a junior partner. Up to a point, the close links between the French president and German chancellor Konrad Adenauer, solemnized in the Franco-German treaty in 1963, gave substance to French hopes. But, while there was German dissatisfaction with America's management of the Berlin crisis in 1961 and with Secretary McNamara's preference for a high threshold of nuclear response to a Soviet attack, Germany was not prepared to substitute a less credible French leadership in place of the American. Nor were the smaller allies comforted by the prospect of a Gaullist Europe.

In some respects, NATO felt liberated by the departure of France from its military structure. Rarely in step with its allies, France absented itself from the new SHAPE headquarters in Mons and from meetings of the International Military Staff in Brussels (which had replaced the defunct three-nation Standing Group in 1966), freeing the alliance from deferring to its obstructive behavior at the meetings of the Defense Planning Committee. De Gaulle's self-propelled removal from SHAPE inadvertently opened the way for a more harmonious collaboration between the United States and the smaller nations of the alliance in the Nuclear Planning Group, established in the year France expelled NATO military bases from its soil.

Reagan and the "Evil Empire"

The Gaullist decade, not incidentally, witnessed a decline in U.S. authority in NATO, as exemplified by a new sense of Soviet power in the 1970s and a concomitant sense of relative weakness in America's response. Neither the Nixon-Kissinger approach to détente nor the Carter administration's efforts to defuse the Cold War satisfied the European partners, though they still depended upon America's nuclear deterrent, no matter how attenuated, and were concerned by the senior ally's apparent inability to cope with the Soviet Union's armory of medium-range nuclear missiles (SS-20) targeted against major Western European cities. Although the Carter administration did respond with a substantive increase in defense spending and the promise to deploy U.S. medium-range missiles in Europe, the allies continued to be worried about America's indecisiveness. NATO's dual-track initiative of 1979, which combined continued efforts toward détente with the promise of delivering to Europe sufficient medium-range cruise and Pershing missiles to cope with the Soviet threat, proved inadequate to dispel Europe's doubts. Excessive weakness, not excessive strength, was the major European grievance as the Reagan administration came to office in 1981.

President Reagan's simplistic vision of a world divided between good and evil and his determination to oppose unreservedly the Soviet evil empire should have been a tonic for the allies' morale. Intending to revive an unambiguous American primacy in the alliance, which had waned under his predecessor, Reagan delivered a strong message with the verve and polish apropos of a former Hollywood actor.[28] In light of the malaise associated with the Carter presidency, there was a hope in Europe that any change would be for the better, but to use an Aesopian image, Europeans soon wondered whether they had exchanged King Log for King Stork as leader of the alliance.

Conflict with European goals inevitably followed from the American perception under Reagan that détente was truly dead and that the Soviets could only be dealt with from a situation of strength. It was not that Europeans failed to appreciate Reagan's message: in view of the scare inspired by the Soviet missile threat, the clear promise of firm American guarantees was heartening. European appreciation, however, had distinct limits. Reagan's blood-curdling language lambasting the Soviets was difficult to overlook, particularly when administration officials saw no problem in surviving a nuclear war.[29] No matter how disturbing the Soviet intermediate-range missiles were to their sense of security, and no matter how much they deplored Soviet behavior in Afghanistan in 1979 or in Poland in 1981, Europeans had to share a continent with the Soviet Union and its Warsaw Pact allies. Détente could not be permanently scrapped.

The potential economic benefits of trade relations were a major element in the survival of détente for Europeans. They had never shared the American conviction, going back to the Mutual Defense Assistance Control Act of 1951, that trade relations with the Soviets would eventually defeat the Communist bloc. When the Polish military imposed martial law in 1981, the U.S. administration applied sanctions against Poland and the Soviet Union alike. Although there was considerable sympathy for Poland's resistance, just as there was revulsion against the Soviet invasion of Afghanistan, the more prevalent sentiment in Western Europe was that the United States had overreacted in both instances, at the expense of its allies. Their misgivings intensified when the Reagan administration, to put teeth into sanctions, suspended gas and oil technology sales to the Soviet Union and prohibited the export of technology manufactured by subsidiaries of American companies in Europe. These measures affected a planned pipeline designed to carry natural gas to the West. This apparently thoughtless automatic response to Soviet behavior did not sit well with the allies. Regulating European companies because of their American connections smacked of extraterritoriality, or at least of an infringement on the sovereignty of affected nations. The Europeans refused to abide by the American regulations, regarding economic connections of this sort as an occasion to revive détente as well as profit from the trade. After five months of wrangling with the United States, the Europeans prevailed.

Such mutual grievances never boiled over into transatlantic separation in these years. Other factors proved more important in keeping the alliance together. The ascent to power of Helmut Kohl in 1982 offered a source of comfort to American policymakers. The new chancellor firmly supported the deployment of American cruise missiles in Germany, a decision made in 1979 but requiring four years for enactment. The delay provided opponents with the opportunity to organize protests. Britain's Margaret Thatcher and Germany's Kohl stood firmly behind the decision and put the lives of their governments at risk in 1983 elections in their respective countries.

Britain and Germany experienced a wave of protest that, if successful in blocking deployment, would leave Europeans, not Americans, more vulnerable to Soviet attack. The European Left directed its anger against the United States and its European allies rather than against the source of the threat. The formerly centrist Laborites in Britain and Social Democrats in Germany had been radicalized by the 1980s, moving not merely toward opposition to the Atlantic alliance but also toward identifying the United States as the enemy of Europe. In both countries mass protests, which included pacifist and religious groups as well as Communist and pro-Communist elements, preceded elections. Moscow orchestrated many, but not all, of the demonstrations against deployment of the missiles. Communist arguments turned on the provocative nature of the missiles, with their ability to strike at the Soviet motherland. Peace demonstrators dwelled on the possibilities of a nuclear holocaust resulting from the emplacement of these missiles. Few opponents were willing to look at the Soviet role in raising the level of fear in Europe.

The protestors failed in their objectives. Soviet intimidation, which had accompanied the protests, united rather than divided the alliance over this issue. The Low Countries and Italy followed suit. The success of the conservative governments at the polls in Britain and Germany affirmed NATO solidarity both over the extent of the Soviet menace embodied in the SS-20s and over the need for cruise and Pershing missiles to counter them.

But if the deployment of missiles represented a centripetal force in transatlantic relations, the lack of progress in arms control—the other half of the dual-track decision in 1979—was a centrifugal force that had preceded and followed the NATO decisions on missile deployment.[30] The gratitude of the allies for the steadfast opposition of the Reagan administration to Soviet pressures coexisted with dismay, bordering on cynicism, at America's disinterest in working toward arms reduction, nuclear or conventional, with the Soviet adversary. Not until the arrival of Gorbachev to power in Reagan's second administration did a prospect for advancing arms control surface.

The Iraq Quandary, 2002–2004

The end of the Cold War only a few years later exacerbated rather than terminated fissures in the alliance. Without the Soviet menace to serve as glue, mutual transatlantic resentments could have spelled the end of NATO—and might yet in the near future. On the American side there was contempt for the minimal military capability of the European allies and a consequent temptation to go it alone outside NATO. For Europeans, the United States was the hyperpower, to use the French term, throwing its weight around in a manner dangerous to Europe's new sense of self, as reflected in the expanding European Union. Nowhere was the gulf more evident than in the U.S. war against Saddam Hussein's Iraq in 2003.

Throughout 2003 the Bush administration, led by its Pentagon planners, had linked the Iraqi dictator with the terrorist network of al Qaeda, which was responsible for the death of nearly three thousand Americans on 11 September 2001. Although proof of a clear link had not been made, Iraq fitted the image of a rogue state, part of the "axis of evil" that the president condemned in his 2002 state of the union address.[31] The Bush administration intended to strike down terrorists before they could strike, as the Islamic fanatics had done on 9/11, and as Saddam Hussein may have been preparing to do with biological and chemical, as well as nuclear, weapons.

The shifting emphasis from al Qaeda to Iraq in the war on terrorism opened a schism in the alliance that worsened when the United States prepared for war with a "coalition of the willing" or, if necessary, alone. Perhaps the unilateral stance was even preferable to some officials on the assumption that a Europe unwilling to raise its defense budgets would only be a drag on the American effort. The superpower could take on Saddam on its own. Weaker than it had been at the time of the Gulf War of 1991, Iraq should be an easier and more manageable target than the elusive al Qaeda.

Skeptical Europeans, along with some skeptical Americans, deprecated Bush's rush to war on a variety of grounds. Was the United States acting to gain control of Iraq's oil, or to complete what Bush *père* failed to do in 1991, or to display a presidential leadership that would assure Republican victory in the 2002 congressional elections, or to divert America's—and the world's—attention from the failure to rout the al Qaeda network? Or was the attack on Iraq simply a display of a superpower's ability to go its own way and expect its allies to follow?

European allies, aided by elements of the Bush administration, particularly Secretary of State Colin Powell, tempered the president's drive for immediate and unilateral action by working through the United Nations, even as he and administration hawks continued to say that they would not be bound by UN decisions. That Saddam Hussein was a persistent threat to stability in the Middle East was no more in question than his violation of UN resolutions since the end of the Gulf War. The allies recognized this challenge in their ultimatum to Iraq in November 2002 (Security Council Resolution 1441) to accept intrusive inspections of weapons of mass destruction or face the consequences of war.[32] Secretary Powell crafted this arrangement in a way that brought France, Russia, and China into agreement at the Security Council.

The apparent victory of diplomacy over military action, however, merely papered over divisions between the United States and Britain, on the one side, and France and Germany, on the other. The old NATO adversary, Russia, quietly opposed the American war but remained in the background as NATO allies separated over the wisdom of a forceful overthrow of Saddam Hussein. France and Germany had placed their faith in the inspection teams dispatched by the Security Council to investigate whether Iraq still possessed proscribed biological, chemical, or nuclear weapons. The Anglo-American allies, however, were convinced of the mission's futility, no matter how much more intrusive it would be compared with the failed inspections in the 1990s.

The suspicion of many in the West and in most of the Muslim world was that the United States had predetermined the failed outcome of inspections and only wanted to use the United Nations as a cover for its invasion. President Bush's insistence that the United States was justified in waging war unilaterally offered sufficient proof for critics to doubt America's good faith in accepting inspections while engaging in a military buildup on Iraq's borders.[33]

Anger over American behavior manifested itself on the European "street" and could be found in the editorials of most newspapers.[34] Germany vied with France to display its independence of the United States. Popular opposition to an American-led war supplied grist for Chancellor Gerhard Schroeder's election campaign in 2002, when he promised that under no circumstances would Germany provide troops or aid in the war, even if Turkey were attacked. In a sense, this was a reprise of a posture held in 1991.[35] But in 2002 antiwar and anti-American sentiments ran deeper. Schroeder's truculent position renounced Germany's habitual deference to the senior partner. World War II was long past, as was the feeling of gratitude for the sustenance America had provided to the fledgling democracy. Franz Munterfering, the general secretary of the Social Democratic Party, talked about a "German way" that resonated with voters unhappy with the American hegemon.[36] But it also could awaken memories of a "German way" in the Third Reich.

Problems with a newly assertive Germany, however, were relegated to the backburner in 2002. Europe's attention at this time centered on the American threat of a preemptive war against Iraq and its demands for allied compliance. A common anti-American posture solidified the Franco-German connection and clearly manifested itself in the inability of the North Atlantic Council to reach a consensus over an American request for support in the event of war.

American responses to European dissent were equally uncompromising when the administration accused the French and Germans of the kind of weakness that led to Munich in 1938. Secretary of State Powell suggested at one point that his French counterpart suffered from an attack of the "vapors."[37] Secretary of Defense Donald Rumsfeld went even further in suggesting that these two countries and their followers in the West represented "Old Europe." The NATO that had expanded eastward in 1999 and again in 2002 now included states comprising the "New Europe" with allies more understanding and more appreciative of American leadership.[38]

The war that seemed to have been won so easily in the spring of 2003 did not lead to a peaceful Iraq that would serve as a model for democracy in the Middle East and a warning to terrorists everywhere. Instead, the mounting occupation costs as well as the increasing opposition of remnants of the Saddam regime, augmented by Islamic militants, took American lives each day and impeded the country's reconstruction. By the fall of 2003 Europeans felt vindicated in their opposition to the Anglo-American war. There was a sense of schadenfreude on the part of the French and Germans, as the Bush administration was forced to turn to the United Nations and NATO for economic and military assistance. Unilateralism was discredited when the United States sought help from the very organizations that it had spurned the year before.[39] In light of the mutual resentments inflamed by the Iraq issue, the alliance appeared once again in danger of collapse.

The transatlantic division over Iraq actually was only the most dramatic occasion for an open break between Washington and Europe that had been in the making

since the end of the Cold War. The European Union under Franco-German domination had looked for opportunities to challenge U.S. hegemony. France's threatened
veto in March 2003 at the UN Security Council of any resolution authorizing the
use of force for the removal of Saddam Hussein symbolized the depth of European
alienation from America. President Bush's bellicose language seemingly reflected
values alien to the newly unified Europe. The war against Iraq that followed the
deadlock in the Security Council further estranged France and Germany as well as
the publics of those NATO partners accepting American leadership in the war.

After the sharp exchanges over Iraq in 2003, it was hardly surprising to find
speculation once again about NATO being at the point of dissolution. Or, if it should
survive, it might be a rump alliance of Central and Eastern European countries,
along with Italy and the Iberian members, as partners of the Anglo-Americans.
France and Germany might still lead the EU, but even here the admission of more
Eastern European countries into that organization could dilute the Franco-German
condominium. The end product may then be a return to the fractured Europe seen
before World War II and a NATO as powerless as the League of Nations, with the
United States permanently following a path of unilateralism.

Still, there are centripetal factors that work against the breakup of the alliance.
Some of them stem from ongoing transatlantic cooperation that has nonetheless
coexisted with the tensions of the last decade. No matter how badly the European
allies mismanaged the Bosnian crisis and subsequently hampered the conduct of the
Kosovo campaign, their role after both these conflicts was vital to the peacekeeping
process. Their numbers far exceeded those of the United States, whose contributions steadily decreased by the end of the 1990s. Europeans picked up a burden
that was appropriately theirs. Similarly, while the United States managed the war
against the Taliban in 2001, the postwar rebuilding of Afghanistan has been shared
by the allies. Even as Germany figuratively thumbed its nose at America over Iraq,
it sought to rebuild bridges by assuming cochairmanship in February 2003 with
the Netherlands of the International Security Assistance Force in Kabul. In April
2003 the North Atlantic Council formally approved a NATO role in Afghanistan.
For the first time in its history, NATO assumed command of a mission outside
the area covered by the terms of the North Atlantic Treaty.[40] Was it not possible,
as NATO supporters suggested in 2003, to place Iraq under a NATO command?
It would then have the authority of a Security Council mandate, as the allies have
long wanted, which through SHAPE would be under the operational control of an
American general reporting to the North Atlantic Council.[41]

In addition, Europeans have been supportive in the war against al Qaeda and
not simply as a service to the superpower. Their own security was at stake as Europe also appeared to be a target of the terrorist network and the site of terrorist
conspiracies. Here was an example of a war where transatlantic allies could fulfill
the mission of article 5. It is worth noting that high among the criticisms of U.S.

policy toward Iraq was the European complaint about the diversion of energy and resources from coping with the primary enemy, the al Qaeda network. Granted that Islamic fundamentalists have found safer havens in Western Europe than they have in the United States, credit should be given to those allies whose investigators have been increasingly active in rooting out terrorist networks as vigorously and, arguably, more effectively than their American counterparts. The termination of the transatlantic alliance is not inevitable.

In Retrospect

The North Atlantic Treaty Organization formed in 1949 to correct the inability of the United Nations to provide the security that the West had expected after the havoc of World War II. The Atlantic alliance drew its strength from a perceived need to contain the Communist threat to Western democracies and facilitate the political and economic integration of a divided Europe. By the end of the twentieth century, the implosion of the Soviet Union, the dissolution of the Warsaw Pact, and the advances of the European Union were tributes to the success of the common transatlantic effort.

Nevertheless, no year in the Cold War had passed without revelations of strains between the United States and its European allies. Some were minor, others serious. In most of the conflicts Europe stood relatively united against what the allies felt were acts of discrimination or neglect, of insensitivity or intimidation, committed by the senior partner. Occasionally, frictions within Europe manifested themselves, as, for example, between France and many of its allies in 1966, and between Greece and Turkey—though the United States was a principal player in both of these controversies. There were instances, too, where European governments lined up with the United States against their own citizens, as in their support of cruise missiles in the 1980s or of the war against Iraq in 2003. For the most part, however, Europeans could and did display common grievances against the United States and were ever ready to highlight them. Numerous congressional resolutions urging troop withdrawal from Europe suggested an American counterpart to Europe's grievances.

But the transatlantic bonds were never severed. Greece did remove itself from NATO's military structure but not permanently. France did not return to the military fold but made sure that its military was closely connected to SHAPE's command centers. For political reasons France has remained outside the integrated military structure, but its hostility to American leadership has never been as virulent as it was under de Gaulle. Although Britain has always chafed at its assignment as a junior partner in the Anglo-American relationship, its dissatisfaction, displayed in the command assignments of 1951 and the Suez adventure of 1956, never rose to the breaking point.

The United States growled periodically over its sense of unfair distribution of the military and financial burdens of the alliance, but its bark was always sharper than its bite. None of the many Senate resolutions contemplating withdrawal of American troops from Europe was ever implemented. A retreat into isolationism would have dangerous ramifications for the superpower, and a chaotic Europe would be as damaging to America's well-being as it had been between the two world wars. For its part, the European Union, absent a symbiotic relationship with NATO, could be as open to fratricidal disputes as the Brussels Pact powers were in 1948, when they had trouble deciding which member would exercise leadership.

In light of these constraints, it is not surprising that NATO and the EU have shown the possibilities of fruitful cooperation, as in the EU's assumption of NATO's peacekeeping mission in Macedonia in March 2003 and in its larger plans to take over the NATO mission in Bosnia in 2004.[42] The United States cannot manage world affairs alone. The partnership with the allies has been vital, if not always respected, for services provided in the Balkans, Afghanistan, and, more recently, Iraq. Granting the ongoing frustrations on both sides of the Atlantic, there is a mutual dependence that has kept NATO together in the past and should continue in the future as "out of area" missions promise to dominate NATO concerns. What is needed is mutual respect for the role each ally plays and a civilized rhetoric when tempers flare.

Arguably, the most compelling sign of transatlantic solidarity has been the allies' silence over terminating membership in the alliance. Under article 13 of the North Atlantic Treaty, any member can "cease to be a Party one year after its notice of denunciation." No member has chosen to take advantage of this exit from the alliance. The danger in the future, however, may lie not in the likelihood of an abrupt dissolution but rather in the possibility of NATO becoming as irrelevant as the League of Nations had been in the 1930s, if America and Europe fail to share the responsibilities of crisis management beyond the boundaries of the alliance.

Notes

An expanded version of the themes in this essay is in *NATO Divided, NATO United: The Evolution of an Alliance* (Westport, Conn.: Praeger, 2004).

1. *NATO Handbook* (Brussels: Office of Information and Press, 2001), 154.

2. U.S. Department of State, *Foreign Relations of the United States, 1948* (Washington, D.C.: G.P.O., 1974), 3:148ff (hereafter *FRUS,* with year and volume number). Achilles noted that "We met every day from the beginning of July to the beginning of September. That was before the days of air conditioning and we all worked with our coats off," in *Fingerprints on History: The NATO Memoirs of Theodore C. Achilles,* ed. Lawrence S. Kaplan and Sidney R. Snyder (Kent, Ohio: Lyman L. Lemnitzer Center for NATO and European Community Studies, 1992), 19.

3. Escott Reid, *Time of Fear and Hope: The Making of the North Atlantic Treaty, 1947–1949* (Toronto: McClelland and Stewart, 1977), 143ff.

4. State Department paper prepared for Working Group, Exploratory Talks, 10 Aug. 1948, Records of Interdepartmental and Intradepartmental Committees (State Department), Record Group 353, file 840 20/8–1048, Lot 53, D68, NATO, box 3, National Archives II, College Park, Md.

5. George F. Kennan, *Memoirs, 1925–1950* (New York: Bantam Books, 1969), 436; Nicholas Henderson, *The Birth of NATO* (Boulder, Colo.: Westview Press, 1983), 70; Alex Danchev, *Oliver Franks: Founding Father* (Oxford: Clarendon Press, 1993), 101.

6. Robert H. Ferrell, "Diplomacy Without Armaments, 1945–1950," in *The Romance of History,* ed. Scott L. Bills and E. Timothy Smith (Kent, Ohio: Kent State Univ. Press, 1997), 46–48.

7. See Ambassador Bonnet's comments at Fourth Meeting of the Washington Exploratory Talks, 8 July 1948, *FRUS, 1948* 3:165.

8. Requests from "Brussels Treaty Powers to the U.S. Government for Military Assistance," 5 Apr. 1949, *FRUS, 1949* (Washington, D.C.: G.P.O., 1975), 4:285–87; U.S. reply, 6 Apr. 1949, ibid., 287–88.

9. Lawrence S. Kaplan, *A Community of Interests: NATO and the Military Assistance Program, 1948–1951* (Washington, D.C.: Office of the Secretary of Defense Historical Office, 1980), 47–48.

10. Ibid., 61–62.

11. Kenneth W. Condit, *The Joint Chiefs of Staff and National Policy, 1947–1949, II,* in *History of the Joint Chiefs of Staff* (Washington, D.C.: Office of the Joint History, 1996), 156–57.

12. See Jean-Jacques Servan-Schreiber's editorial in *Le Monde,* 5 Apr. 1950, raising the possibility of neutralism in the face of NATO's failure to bring a sense of security to Europe.

13. Dutch foreign minister Dirk Stikker expressed shock over the allied strategy. See *Men of Responsibility: A Memoir* (New York: Harper & Row, 1965), 297.

14. Great Britain, *Parliamentary Debates* (House of Commons), 5th series, 446 (1048): col. 383ff.

15. Final Draft of United States–United Kingdom–Canada Security Conversations, Washington, D.C., undated [Apr. 1948], in *FRUS, 1948* 3:72–75; Cees Wiebes and Bert Zeeman, "The Pentagon Negotiations March 1948: The Launching of the North Atlantic Treaty," *International Affairs* 59 (summer 1983): 351–64.

16. Alistair Buchan, "Mothers and Daughters (or Greeks and Romans)," in *Two Hundred Years of American Foreign Policy,* ed. William P. Bundy (New York: N.Y. Univ. Press, 1977), 20ff.

17. Dean Acheson, "The Atlantic Alliance: The Political and Economic Strands," speech at U.S. Military Academy, West Point, 5 Dec. 1962, in *Vital Speeches of the Day*, vol. 29, no. 6, 1 Jan. 1963, 162–66.

18. Eisenhower to Harriman, 2 Mar. 1951, Pre-Presidential Eisenhower Papers, Harriman folder, box 55, 16–52, Dwight D. Eisenhower Library, Abilene, Kans.

19. Lawrence S. Kaplan, *The United States and NATO: The Formative Years* (Lexington: Univ. Press of Ky., 1984), 168–69.

20. "It is intolerable for a great State to leave its destiny up to the decisions and action of another state, however friendly it may be." From a press conference, 11 Apr. 1961, quoted in Charles G. Cogan, *Charles de Gaulle: A Brief Biography with Documents* (Boston: Bedford Books, 1996), 129; allocution prononcée à la réunion populaire de Pnom Penh, 1st septembre 1966, in *Charles de Gaulle a dit: L'essentiel de la pensée de Charles de Gaulle* (Paris: Presses Pocket, 1989), 330.

21. General Pierre Ailleret, "Défense 'dirigée' ou défense 'tous azimuts," *Revue de Défense Nationale* (Dec. 1967): 1923–32. See also Jean Lacouture, *De Gaulle*, t.3, *Le Souverain, 1959–1970* (Paris: Editions du Seuil, 1986), 483.

22. Michael Harrison, *The Reluctant Ally: France and Atlantic Security* (Baltimore: Johns Hopkins Univ. Press, 1981), 104. Harrison notes that de Gaulle makes this point in his *Memoirs of Hope: Renewal and Endeavor* (New York: Simon & Schuster, 1971), 200.

23. Remarks by Secretary of Defense Robert S. McNamara, 5 May 1962, NATO Ministerial Meeting, Athens, 12–13, *FRUS, 1961–1963* (Washington, D.C.: G.P.O., 1996), 8:278–81.

24. See view of General Pierre Gallois, *Stratégie de l'âge nucléaire* (Paris: Calmann-Levy, 1959); and Andre Beaufre, *Dissuasion et Stratégie* (Paris: Armand Colin, 1964).

25. De Gaulle to Johnson, 7 Mar. 1966, in *American Foreign Policy: Current Documents 1966* (Washington, D.C.: G.P.O., 1966), 316–17.

26. Oral History Interview with George Ball by Paige Mulhollan, 9 July 1971, 2, LBJ Library, Austin, Tex.; Lyndon B. Johnson, *The Vantage Point: Perspectives of the Presidency, 1962–1969* (New York: Holt Rinehart and Winston, 1971), 305.

27. Lawrence S. Kaplan, "The U.S. and NATO in the Johnson Years," in *The Johnson Years*. Vol. 3: *LBJ at Home and Abroad*, ed. Robert A. Divine (Lawrence: Univ. Press of Kans., 1994), 128–30.

28. Note president's news conference, 29 Jan. 1981, *Public Papers of the Presidents, Ronald Reagan, 1981* (Washington, D.C.: G.P.O., 1981), 57.

29. T. K. Jones, deputy undersecretary of defense for strategic nuclear forces, envisioned survival for anyone who would "dig a hole, cover it with a couple of doors, and then throw three feet of dirt on top." Quoted in Walter LaFeber, *America, Russia, and the Cold War, 1945–1984*, 5th ed. (New York: Alfred A. Knopf, 1985), 304.

30. Special meeting of foreign and defense ministers, Brussels, 12 Dec. 1979, *Texts of Final Communiqués* (Brussels: NATO Information Service, 1981), 2:121–23.

31. State of the union address, 29 Jan. 2002, text in *Facts on File*, vol. 62, no. 3190, 31 Jan. 2002, 43–44.

32. Text of ultimatum, UN Security Council Resolution 1441, 8 Nov. 2002, *Keesing's Record of World Events*, vol. 48, no. 11, Nov. 2002.

33. President's speech at West Point, *Washington Post*, 2 June 2002.

34. *International Herald Tribune*, 4 Sept. 2003.

35. Schroeder address to SPD, 5 Aug. 2002, *Facts on File*, 22 Aug. 2002, vol. 63, no. 3219.

36. *The Guardian*, 5 Aug. 2002. Munterfering told a press conference that the party leadership would have Germany go its own way: "Independently of what the UN decides, there must be a German way, that we must decide for ourselves what must be done."

37. *New York Times*, 7 Feb. 2002.

38. Jim Hoagland, *Washington Post*, 30 Jan. 2003.

39. *Defense News*, 16 Jan. 2003.

40. Ibid., 18 Apr. 2003.

41. Thomas Friedman, *New York Times*, 3 Mar. 2003; Frederick Bonnart, *International Herald Tribune*, 2 July 2003; Sen. Joseph Biden, *Washington Post*, 9 Nov. 2003.

42. *New York Times*, 15 Mar. 2003.

2

Colonialism and the Atlantic Alliance

Anglo-American Perspectives at the United Nations,

1945–1963

MARY ANN HEISS

At first blush, the topic of colonialism might seem out of place in a consideration of the Atlantic alliance. After all, the 1949 North Atlantic Treaty's sole reference to colonial territories is article 6's inclusion of "the Algerian Departments of France" under the alliance's military umbrella.[1] In addition, colonies (or non-self-governing territories) were not a main or even tertiary impetus behind the alliance's founding. Yet colonialism was an important subject for the members of the North Atlantic Treaty Organization (NATO), many of which constituted the world's leading colonial powers.[2] This chapter, which deals with colonial questions during 1945–1963 within the framework of the Anglo-American relationship, seeks to fill a gap in the scholarship on this important but heretofore relatively unexplored topic.[3] Rather than addressing colonial issues within overall diplomatic relations between Great Britain and the United States, however, it will explore Anglo-American positions on questions pertaining to non-self-governing territories at the United Nations and relate those positions to the Atlantic alliance itself.

Unlike the North Atlantic Treaty, the UN Charter contains specific and plentiful language regarding colonies and non-self-governing territories. In fact, chapter XI, titled "Declaration Regarding Non-Self-Governing Territories," is devoted exclusively to that topic, laying out in two relatively brief but important articles the responsibilities of administering nations and setting forth the hope of eventual self-government for nations that did not yet possess it. Article 73 affirmed that the interests of the non-self-governing territories were "paramount" and instructed the administering powers to foster "political, economic, social, and educational development" in their colonies. To ensure that such development was in fact being advanced, section (e) of article 73 called upon the administering powers to "transmit regularly to the Secretary-General . . . statistical and other information of a technical nature relating to economic, social, and educational conditions in the territories for which they are responsible."[4] Significantly, no provision was made for the transmission of information on political conditions or progress toward self-government.

Although the administering states had no quibble with the directive to provide the secretary-general with information on their colonies, they objected vociferously to the General Assembly's creation in 1946 of the Ad Hoc Committee on Information from Non-Self-Governing Territories.[5] This committee, to consist of one member from each of the eight administering nations and an equal number of nonadministering states, was empowered to examine and discuss the information that article 73(e) required the administering states to transmit to the secretary-general.[6] After its establishment in 1946, the committee was renewed annually until 1949 and then given three-year terms in 1949, 1952, 1955, and 1958.[7] Its creation and subsequent institutionalization signaled quite clearly that anticolonialism would be an important issue for the General Assembly and demonstrated the gradual emergence there of an anticolonial bloc, composed in large part by the 1950s and 1960s of countries themselves formerly classified as non-self-governing. The committee took its responsibility seriously. In addition to pressing for expansion of the types of information on the non-self-governing territories provided to the secretary general, the committee pushed successfully for the right to hear petitioners from those territories and to send fact-finding delegations directly to them. It also issued unrelenting calls for the administering states to set firm timetables for decolonization of their remaining territories.

The General Assembly's anticolonial crusade advanced further in December 1960 with passage of Resolution 1514 (XV) titled "Declaration on the Granting of Independence to Colonial Countries and Peoples." Approved with eighty-nine affirmative votes, zero nays, and nine abstentions, including the United Kingdom and the United States, the resolution dramatically expanded the United Nations' interests in the remaining colonial territories. In strident, almost messianic, language, it asserted, "All peoples have an inalienable right to complete freedom," "self-determination," and "the exercise of their sovereignty." It denounced "armed action or repressive measures of all kinds" designed to thwart nationalistic ambitions, and in complete contravention to prevailing British (and American) thinking it declared that "inadequacy of political, economic, social or educational preparedness should never serve as a pretext for delaying independence."[8] Resolution 1514 (XV) amounted to a declaration of war on colonialism and a de facto promise of UN support for indigenous independence drives. Furthermore, the lopsided margin by which it was approved indicated that the world's remaining colonial powers—and their supporters—faced an uphill battle where colonial issues were concerned at the United Nations.

The culmination of UN anticolonialism came almost a year later, in November

1961. Having added seventeen new states since 1960 alone, all of them in one way or another having been a non-self-governing territory, the General Assembly was now primed to play an even larger role in decolonization than had previously been the case.[9] Its members noted "with regret" that, contrary to Resolution 1514 (XV), "armed action and repressive measures continue to be taken in certain areas with increasing ruthlessness against dependent peoples." To remedy the situation and speed along the progress of non-self-governing territories to independence, the General Assembly created the seventeen-member Special Committee on the Situation with Regard to the Implementation of the Declaration on the Granting of Independence to Colonial Countries and Peoples to oversee implementation of Resolution 1514 (XV).[10] Later enlarged to twenty-four members (and referred to informally as the Committee of 24), the committee ultimately fell under the sway of the Asian-African bloc in the General Assembly and pursued an aggressive anticolonial course, including vocal demands for immediate decolonization of those territories still lacking self-government.[11] The Soviet Union's position as a leading backer of those demands politicized the United Nations' anticolonial charge and made decolonization a Cold War issue.

As one of the great powers responsible for drafting the UN Charter, Britain had played a key role in shaping its language, particularly regarding the potentially thorny issue of non-self-governing territories. At Dumbarton Oaks in 1944 and again in San Francisco the following year, the British had succeeded in limiting international supervision of non-self-governing territories to only those areas placed under the UN trusteeship system, which included the former League of Nations mandates and the colonies seized from the defeated Axis powers.[12] Conspicuously excluded from the trusteeship system were the colonies of the victorious Allies, and, although all of the Western colonial powers were invited to place their territories under UN supervision, not one did.[13] The UN Charter contained other limits on international involvement in the non-self-governing territories as well. Article 2(7) prohibited the United Nations from intervening in "matters which are essentially within the domestic jurisdiction of any state," a provision that British officials believed shielded the empire from UN supervision, since imperial matters clearly fell within Britain's domestic purview.[14] Moreover, chapter XI's references to administering states' responsibilities to the non-self-governing territories contained no standards for evaluating their performance and no guidelines for local administration. Perhaps more important, chapter XI referred only to the goal of "self-government" rather than outright independence, a crucial distinction for British policymakers, both in 1945 and thereafter.[15] Confident that these strictures regarding the United Nations' role in the non-self-governing territories would be followed, British officials approached the organization's inaugural session convinced that it would have little to do with those territories that were clearly within the empire.

British officials considered the Committee on Information an "unacceptable" intrusion into their internal affairs and opposed its creation from the start as an improper expansion of the General Assembly's authority.[16] To be sure, they conceded their obligation under the charter to transmit statistical and technical information to the secretary-general, but they adamantly denied that the General Assembly had the authority to discuss that information or to create a special committee to scrutinize it. They also resisted growing UN pressures to transmit political information to the committee, maintaining that the charter did not require it. In this instance, as in others, the British "found it difficult to accept fifty-eight 'back-seat drivers'" in matters that they believed fell within their own domestic jurisdiction. "According to the Charter," they intoned, "the United Nations was not a driver."[17]

Notwithstanding their misgivings about the United Nations' encroachment into colonial affairs, British officials cooperated with all but the most inappropriate demands for information on their colonies. (This position stood in marked contrast to that of some other administering states, most notably Portugal but also to some extent Belgium and the Netherlands, which refused full cooperation and, in the case of the former, withdrew entirely from participation in the Special Committee.) They provided the United Nations with innumerable reports on economic, social, and educational conditions in the territories they administered, so many, in fact, that in 1950 the UN Library asked them to scale back their submissions for lack of physical space for storage.[18] The British also provided information on these subjects to the secretary-general as provided for in article 73(e) of the Charter. They consistently drew the line, however, at sending information of a "political" nature or providing specifics on the development of institutions designed to foster territorial self-government. The charter, they repeatedly maintained, made no provision for the transmission of such information, and providing it would imply acquiescence to UN interference in Britain's internal affairs.

Britain's colonial troubles at the United Nations did not directly concern the United States, but they were troubling to policymakers in the Truman, Eisenhower, and Kennedy administrations nevertheless. In light of the priority all three placed on the Anglo-American relationship, they were keen to avoid anything that threatened Britain's international standing or weakened its potential contribution to Western defense, a contribution that depended at least in part on the empire. Yet, because these were precisely the potential results of disputes over colonial questions at the United Nations, it was essential that those disputes be resolved as amicably as possible, even if that eventuality necessitated U.S. involvement.

The United States, of course, had itself once been a non-self-governing territory and had historically supported such universal rights as self-determination and self-government. This long-standing antipathy toward colonies had helped inspire Woodrow Wilson's Fourteen Points and Franklin Roosevelt's push to apply the anticolonial principle of the Atlantic Charter universally, not just to the colonies of the Axis enemy.[19] It also helped shape U.S. aims in World War II, as expressed in an October 1942 *Life* magazine editorial that declared, "one thing we are *not* fighting for is to hold the British Empire together."[20]

It was clear even before the war had ended, however, that anticolonialism would not significantly influence U.S. policy in the postwar period. In April 1945, just ten days before Roosevelt's death, the Office of Strategic Services argued that U.S. interests lay in "the maintenance of the British, French and Dutch colonial empires," not in their destruction.[21] Although the principle of anticolonialism did remain an important ideological tenet for U.S. policymakers, by the late 1940s the Cold War with the Soviet Union came to overshadow it, and, as Communism, rather than colonialism, emerged as the number one enemy of the United States, official Washington came to see the colonies of the Western European nations as potential assets in the global struggle to protect the Free World rather than anachronistic remnants of a bygone era. The task for U.S. policymakers was supporting the colonial empires without alienating the growing segment of the world that was avowedly anticolonial in orientation.

It is clear that, whereas ideology and emotion seemed to dictate support for nationalistic movements—at least those that were non-Communist—security concerns put the brakes on wholesale endorsement of independence. Backing colonial drives for self-government could weaken the Western allies, which derived important economic benefits from their association with their colonies. U.S. officials, for example, found it "difficult to imagine how Britain could survive without such Colonial products as rubber, tin, sugar, cocoa and copper."[22] It might also jeopardize the international prestige of the colonial powers or alienate them at a crucial time in the solidification of the Western alliance. Forced to choose "between a . . . desire to help the colonial peoples toward independence and . . . strategic inter-dependence with the colonial powers which derived their strength from their colonies," security concerns dictated a tilt in the latter direction.[23] In fact, by 1950 U.S. officials were assuring their British counterparts that they were "not out to break up the British Empire" and in fact saw "it as a great force for stability."[24] To put it another way, U.S. policy may have been oriented toward the tripartite goals of strengthening the "Western European allies," maintaining "the continued friendship of the non-administering states," and ensuring "the alignment of dependent peoples with the democratic world," but for policymakers in the Truman administration, the first goal was paramount.[25]

If the Truman administration supported the maintenance of the British Empire, though, it did not always endorse Britain's reluctance to accede to UN supervision of the non-self-governing peoples. In principle, policymakers conceded Britain's assertions that the UN Charter contained nothing that would justify the organization's involvement in the Western European colonial empires. In practice, however, it worried that too rigid a British stand on colonial questions at the United Nations could have serious consequences. It might result in a dangerous loss of goodwill for the West at the United Nations, especially among newly independent nations such as India. It could fuel Soviet bloc propaganda about the rapacious nature of Western "imperialism" by giving the appearance that the British intended to hang onto their colonies forever, and it would definitely weaken the Western defense position by encouraging anti-Western nationalist movements in the colonies. To balance these two competing concerns, the Truman administration employed a middle-of-the-road approach to colonial questions at the United Nations that sought to moderate the British stand while simultaneously defusing anticolonial sentiment.

To accomplish the goal of moderating British policy on colonial issues at the United Nations, the administration relied on old-fashioned diplomacy, conducted most notably in regular bilateral discussions dealing exclusively with colonial topics, with the first such set of talks taking place in July 1950. Initially, British officials had sought to hold the talks in London in order to provide for the widest possible participation from their side, but they ultimately succumbed to U.S. pressure to hold them in Washington. Fully cognizant that the talks would generate global attention, U.S. policymakers worried about the unfavorable publicity that would stem from having American officials "going to capitals of 'colonial' powers to discuss 'colonial' issues." To avoid the impression that the United States was somehow supplicating the colonial powers, U.S. officials insisted that the talks be held in a more "neutral" venue.[26]

Both sides appreciated the chance to air fully their thoughts on dealing with colonial questions at the United Nations, and the talks proved to be a fairly free-wheeling exchange of ideas and perspectives. U.S. officials emphasized the need for cooperation at the United Nations, extolled the international benefits that would come from flexibility, and made clear on numerous occasions that a more cooperative British posture would make it easier for the United States to speak on Britain's behalf at the United Nations. Perhaps the best expression of the U.S. position came in Assistant Secretary of State for UN Affairs John D. Hickerson's simple declaration that "it did not embarrass the United States to transmit political information to the Special Committee." Why did it embarrass the British?[27] Refusing to submit that kind of information, the U.S. delegation maintained, would not prevent Britain's critics from "stirring up trouble," since information on political conditions in its non-self-governing territories was already available in the UN Library, but it could generate ill will and unfavorable publicity. Moreover, getting "hot under the collar" at criticism of British colonial policy, U.S. officials asserted, even when that criticism might be "intemperate and often unjustified," served no constructive purpose and, on the contrary, could do great harm. If the British would soften their stance on providing political information and somehow adopt a calmer, more measured response to their critics, the United States would then "be in a position to assist them in refuting unjustified attacks upon their colonial policy."[28] For their part, British officials emphasized the difficulties of "reconciling the responsibilities of colonial administration with the responsibilities of membership in an international body."[29] When push came to shove, they intoned, should those two responsibilities diverge, they would have no choice but to meet their responsibilities as colonial administrators first and let their obligations to the United Nations fall by the wayside.

Such rhetorical assertions aside, British officials acknowledged early on in the bilateral discussions that their handling of colonial questions at the United Nations had not been perfect. Perhaps, they conceded, it would be better to replace the "negative attitude" that had guided their policy at the United Nations since 1945 with a more flexible and accommodating approach.[30] In 1949, for example, of seventeen General Assembly resolutions on colonial and related questions, the British had voted in favor of one, abstained on four, and voted against twelve. The following year, after adopting the more flexible approach Washington had advocated, they supported twelve resolutions, abstained on three, and opposed three.[31] Similar voting records characterized subsequent years, proof positive for the Truman administration that the British attitude on colonial questions at the United Nations had dramatically improved.

By 1952, British officials had also adopted a more overtly propagandist posture at the United Nations, touting the positive attributes of their colonial policy in an effort "to refute the accusations sometimes levelled at the United Kingdom, particularly by those whose own records in such matters did not bear examination . . . that all colonial peoples lived in a state of slavery and had no hope for the future unless brusquely freed from their bonds."[32] This falsehood, and others like it, had to be dispelled through a positive public recitation at the United Nations of what the British saw as the significant and impressive accomplishments of their colonial administration. "The best colonial asset which the United Kingdom had—her record in the colonial territories"—had to be exploited if the British were to make headway against the "emotionalism and recklessness" that characterized discussion of colonial issues at the United Nations.[33] Mounting this sort of publicity campaign was another demonstration, at least to officials in the Truman administration, that the British had accepted U.S. advice about avoiding a negative approach to colonial questions at the United Nations and further proof that direct, bilateral diplomacy had succeeded.

British officials had been frank in admitting that in exchange for their greater flexibility and a more positive posture at the United Nations, they expected their "friends," key among them the United States, to work at "refuting unjustified and irresponsible attacks upon their colonial policy." "The isolated position in which the United Kingdom delegation found itself in the 1949 session of the General Assembly," British diplomats reported, "was not satisfactory," and it was hoped their greater efforts at flexibility would result in "more favorable publicity" for Britain in the United Nations. [34] In fact, stronger and more vocal U.S. support for Britain at the United Nations on colonial questions did follow from the bilateral consultations. Through them, U.S. policymakers gained a better understanding of what was at stake for Britain regarding the non-self-governing territories and repeatedly provided psychological reassurance to the British of the "U.S. desire to be helpful."[35]

To demonstrate their helpfulness, and to accomplish the Truman administration's other goal regarding colonial questions at the United Nations, U.S. diplomats there employed a variety of tools designed to soften or defuse anticolonial sentiment. During General Assembly debates, they took every opportunity to extol the virtues of responsible, non-Communist colonial administration of the sort they believed the British had generally practiced. They also warned of the dangers of haphazard, premature independence while preaching the wisdom of gradual progress toward responsible self-government. In other words, guided by Cold War considerations, the U.S. position on colonial questions at the United Nations favored continued subjugation for nations where independence movements were Communist or where an independent non-Communist government could not be guaranteed. Clearly, the Cold War came explicitly to color U.S. handling of colonial questions at the United Nations. U.S. diplomats at the United Nations also regularly abstained on controversial resolutions regarding colonial issues. Abstention, in fact, became a key U.S. tactic for dealing with colonial questions at the United Nations, although the noncommittal (some would say cowardly) fence-sitting that it implied probably satisfied neither side of the ideological divide.[36]

Although the Eisenhower administration eschewed its predecessor's middle-of-the-road efforts at the United Nations on colonial matters—efforts that Secretary of State John Foster Dulles called "unnecessarily ambiguous"—for all practical purposes it adopted the same strategy.[37] To be sure, U.S. rhetoric on colonialism stiffened after 1953, especially after 1956, when the Suez crisis laid bare the fallacy of staking the Free World's defenses on Western European ties to the colonial or developing states.[38] Yet there was never any thought within the administration of wholesale U.S. endorsement of anticolonialism for fear that such a step could encourage reckless or precipitate independence movements that might lead to Communist gains. The Soviet-American tensions that had been developing during the Truman years emerged full-blown during the Eisenhower era, and as the Cold War's battleground began shifting to the developing world, the Western European empires became hotly contested real estate for both sides. Accordingly, it became all the more important to control the pace and direction of independence movements so that only those likely to result in non-Communist governments achieved success.[39]

Again like the Truman administration, the Eisenhower team employed various strategies to accomplish U.S. goals regarding colonial questions at the United

Nations. It continued to push British officials to avoid excessively negative or antagonistic statements at the United Nations that might alienate the growing anticolonialist faction there or reflect poorly on the West in general. It continued to highlight the positive accomplishments of responsible colonial administration and to advise the anticolonial states to moderate their hostility toward the colonial powers and to limit anticolonial resolutions to only the most general of issues. And it continued to advise abstention on unacceptable General Assembly resolutions on colonial issues and to abstain itself as a symbol of U.S. displeasure at the Assembly's oftentimes emotional attitude when it came to colonial matters. The administration also relied on Secretary of State John Foster Dulles's expertise in international law to use the inherently conservative legal system to slow the anticolonial attack.[40]

A new twist at the United Nations when it came to colonial questions, however, was the Eisenhower administration's adoption of a campaign called "Communism—the New Colonialism."[41] This propaganda initiative reflected U.S. frustration with a perceived imbalance in the developing world's perceptions of the great powers: while Western European colonialism was widely condemned, Communism was not. To redress this imbalance, the administration sought to publicize the evils of Soviet repression throughout Eastern Europe as a direct counter to mounting Soviet charges at the United Nations about the insidious nature of Western European colonialism.[42] In taking the initiative in this way, the administration sought to give U.S. policy, and indeed, Western policy in general, a more positive spin and signal its refusal to surrender the initiative on colonialism at the United Nations to the Soviets. To be sure, this campaign did not go so far as to actually defend Western colonialism. It did, however, seek to portray in starkly black-and-white terms the differences between Soviet Communism, which offered no hope of independence or true self-government, and Western colonialism, which did offer such hopes and was, in fact, "transitory" by design. Simply put, nations colonized by the Western European powers generally gained independence. And by 1959, the emergence of twenty-one new nations proved it.[43] By contrast, as of that year, not one nation had ever emerged from Communism, and fifteen formerly independent nations were behind the Iron Curtain.[44] The "Communism—the New Colonialism" campaign painted in bold relief the intertwining of the issue of colonialism at the United Nations and the Cold War. (At the same time, the United States Information Agency was pursuing a campaign called "Exposing Red Colonialism.")[45] But its general lack of success revealed as well the deep-seated anticolonial sentiment that permeated much of the developing world and the difficulty the United States would have in winning the propaganda war in Asia, Africa, and other areas of the developing world.

The same may be said about the U.S. response to Resolution 1514 (XV), which constituted final proof of the Eisenhower administration's affinity for its European colonialist allies. As we have seen, the December 1960 resolution called for the speedy termination of all forms of colonialism. Ending colonial subjugation and granting all nations the right of political self-government were, of course, long-standing U.S. goals, and many members of the administration were sympathetic with the principles that Resolution 1514 (XV) embodied. Eisenhower himself, an avowed opponent of colonialism, especially after the Suez debacle of 1956, was ideologically inclined to endorse the resolution and contemplated a positive U.S. vote for it in the General Assembly.[46] Yet the specific wording of the resolution, introduced initially by the Soviet delegation, was dangerously strident and overtly anti-Western. It was an outgrowth of mounting Soviet propaganda at the United Nations against "imperialism" and, in the eyes of officials in Britain and the other Western European colonial powers, constituted nothing less than a shameless and transparent effort to embarrass them in the eyes of the rest of the world. At their behest, and especially after direct appeals from British prime minister Harold Macmillan, Eisenhower instructed the U.S. mission to the United Nations to join the other Western allies in abstaining.[47] In this way, the administration thus sustained a long-standing U.S. strategy for dealing with unacceptable UN resolutions on colonial matters and maintained the united Anglo-American front that was so important to the United States's transatlantic partner.[48]

By the time the Kennedy administration assumed office, the UN's stance on colonial questions was clearly reaching a head. The lopsided vote of approval on Resolution 1514 (XV) painted in bold relief the polarizing effect of colonialism in the General Assembly, as did the rhetoric that accompanied debate over the creation of the Special Committee. Although it was sympathetic with the desires of nations in Asia and especially Africa for independence and self-government, the Kennedy administration shared its predecessor's fears of the potentially disastrous consequences of premature independence, yet it was clear that past efforts to tame independence demands had not succeeded, in part because of the emotionalism that came to invest much of the UN debate over colonial questions. For this reason, the administration adopted a concerted campaign to approach such questions in a "responsible and moderate" manner devoid of the "unjustified doctrinaire extremism and impracticality" that it believed had dominated in the past, particularly during the initial work of the Special Committee. "Unrestrainedly criticizing all Administering Authority in advancing individual territories toward self-determination" and adopting "impractical and intemperate resolutions" had only negative consequences, officials in the administration believed, not only for the remaining administering states but also for the United Nations as a whole.[49]

In the eyes of administration officials, the blame for investing colonial questions with unfounded and dangerous emotionalism rested solidly with the Soviet Union. Soviet premier Nikita S. Khrushchev had himself appeared at the United Nations in the fall of 1960 to solicit support for Soviet efforts to place colonialism on the Fifteenth General Assembly agenda, efforts that had led to the passage of Resolution 1514 (XV). In the second of his two speeches, both of which inspired spirited attacks by the Western nations, he railed against the "disgraceful colonial regimes" and their "plunder[ing]" leaders and appealed to Asian and African nations that had recently gained independence to join the Soviet condemnation of all remaining forms of colonialism.[50] The same sort of hyperbole continued in general discussions at the United Nations once the new Kennedy administration had assumed office. "While posing as the most ardent champion of dependent peoples, the Soviets [had] attempted to lump the United States with European colonial powers allegedly following 'aggressive and repressive' policies."[51] Moreover, they sought "to exploit the colonial question by every means" possible in an effort "to enhance their ability to influence neutralist opinion while at the same time attacking and if possible embarrassing the West."[52] To regain the initiative, salvage the U.S. reputation, and ensure that the United Nations remained capable of playing the "vital and constructive role in the liquidation of colonialism" that U.S. officials were confident it could play, the administration embarked on an even more aggressive propaganda campaign against Soviet imperialism than its predecessor.[53]

In keeping with the administration's general emphasis on information policy, the U.S. delegation to the United Nations worked assiduously to parry Soviet assaults against Western colonialism with thrusts against what U.S. officials variously called "Soviet colonialism," "Red Colonialism," or "Soviet imperialism." Whatever the nomenclature involved, the gist of the propaganda remained the same as that put forth in the Eisenhower administration's earlier "Communism—the New Colonialism" campaign.[54] This time, however, other Western nations, most notably, Britain and Canada, joined the administration's efforts. The British, much stung by what they considered unfair attacks on their colonial record, appeared to relish the opportunity to paint Soviet imperialism in a bad light. They were particularly active when it came to publicizing the abuses of Soviet Communism.[55] Canadian prime minister John Diefenbaker also contributed to the U.S. campaign against the Soviet Union. On 22 November 1961, he denounced as "a complete travesty" the Soviet Union's efforts "to pose as the champion of human liberty and the liberator of captive peoples." With its own "awful record for denying national freedom, self-determination, and independence" to "so many peoples behind the iron curtain," it was a "monstrous . . . hypocrisy" for the Soviet Union to endorse, as it had, immediate independence for all peoples still lacking it. "He who accuses another man of shameful conduct," Diefenbaker warned, "should take care to keep himself blameless."[56]

Developments during the last year or so of the Kennedy administration revealed some successes when it came to dealing with colonial issue at the United Nation. Although the general tenor of the UN General Assembly remained anticolonial, there was evidence that efforts to moderate anticolonial sentiment had at least partly succeeded. Secretary of State Dean Rusk, for example, proudly reported that at the Seventeenth General Assembly, which concluded in the autumn of 1962, "some

ten delegations made a point of referring to the dependent status of Soviet satellites, and to the subject people inside the Soviet Union itself."[57] U.S. officials were
also heartened that the initial meetings of the Committee of 24 failed to live up to
their dire predictions of negativity and anti-Westernism. To be sure, members of
the committee continued to exhibit a "lack of realism."[58] They had, however, been
unable to win approval of a resolution granting it the power to set "target dates for
the achievement of independence by the remaining dependent territories," which
U.S. officials considered a singular and important achievement.[59]

Amid these positives, though, colonial issues at the United Nations also manifested a number of looming problems by 1963 and suggested new challenges for
the Kennedy and then Johnson administrations. Mounting African opposition to
"the hard-core racial issues in the southern third of [the continent]," for example,
was a serious concern. Officials in Washington feared that U.S. reluctance to apply
sanctions to racist regimes like South Africa and Portuguese Angola might cost
the United States African backing on other questions at the United Nations, such
as the admission of Communist China.[60] Growing support within the General
Assembly for universal human rights—and indeed, for a UN convention on racial
discrimination—was another potential problem for U.S. officials. Human rights
had been a UN concern from the start, and U.S. officials had always offered tepid,
if not enthusiastic, support for human rights measures. They remained moderately
supportive of such initiatives in the early 1960s but feared, probably with more than
a little justification, that any UN-sponsored campaign against racial discrimination
would complicate "the domestic debate on civil rights legislation." In the end, the
U.S. delegation did support the Universal Declaration against All Forms of Racial
Discrimination but made clear in the process that the United States intended "to
carry out its terms in accordance with [its] constitutional processes."[61] Although
only 2 percent of the world's population remained in dependent status by 1963,
the question of colonialism, and its legacies, continued to cast a shadow over U.S.
policymakers.[62]

Despite the slightly different tactics pursued by the Truman, Eisenhower, and Kennedy administrations when it came to colonial questions at the United Nations, all
sought the same overall objectives: avoiding a rift between the administering and
nonadministering states; preventing the defection of recently independent states to
the "wrong" side of the Cold War divide; assuaging the Western European colonial
states; defending Western security. It was the linkage between these last objectives
that tied the issue of colonialism to the Atlantic alliance. The formation of NATO
itself had not been popular with the emergent nations, as it fueled their suspicions
that the Western powers were joining forces in a concerted campaign to thwart
independence movements and maintain the colonial status quo. In a way, these
suspicions were correct, though again it is worth reiterating the absence of any

sustained discussion of colonies or colonialism in the North Atlantic Treaty. What the treaty did contain, though, was the implicit U.S. admission that the Western European colonial powers were essential to the security and survival of the Free World, and this conviction meant ipso facto that anything that weakened those colonial powers—such as unchecked nationalism in the colonies or unbridled criticism of Western colonial policy at the United Nations—threatened Western security.

Because their primary concern was protecting the Western security position, policymakers in the Truman, Eisenhower, and Kennedy administrations concluded that they had no real alternative but to throw their weight behind the colonial powers, both in general practice and in diplomatic language. To be sure, the degree of overt U.S. backing of the colonial empires, including Britain's, diminished over time, especially after the Suez debacle of 1956, but at the United Nations U.S. officials were unwavering in defending responsible colonial administration, warning against the dangers of premature independence drives, and, beginning in 1954, mounting a propaganda campaign designed to expose the evils of Communism. The general lack of success of these initiatives demonstrated the strength of anticolonialism, laid bare the growing isolation of the colonial powers on the world stage, and served as a harbinger for a widening global divide between the developed North and the developing South.

Throughout the period 1945–1963, Cold War concerns and especially the goal of containment came to dominate virtually every aspect of U.S. foreign policy. NATO, of course, was a child of the Cold War and was designed with the goal of containment in mind. The U.S. attitude toward the rise of anticolonial sentiment around the world was also shaped by the Cold War, though perhaps in less obvious ways. As this brief chapter has suggested, colonialism did become a Cold War issue for the United States after 1945, and it was inextricably linked to the Atlantic alliance. Exploring the links between that issue and the alliance, links that heretofore have gone largely ignored, would provide scholars with a number of very profitable research agendas and allow them to link the history of the alliance with larger international developments. It is hoped that this chapter will inspire such exploration.

Notes

1. See article 6 of the North Atlantic Treaty, 4 Apr. 1949, in North Atlantic Treaty Organization, *NATO Handbook: Fiftieth Anniversary Edition* (Brussels: NATO Office of Information and Press, 1998), 397.

2. For colonialism as a factor at the Alliance's founding, see Lawrence S. Kaplan and Sidney R. Snyder, eds., *Fingerprints on History: The NATO Memoirs of Theodore C. Achilles* (Kent, Ohio: Lyman L. Lemnitzer Center for NATO and European Community Studies, 1992), 23–24.

3. Notable exceptions are two chapters by Scott L. Bills: "The United States, NATO, and the Colonial World," in *NATO After Thirty Years,* ed. Lawrence S. Kaplan and Robert W. Clawson (Wilmington, Del.: Scholarly Resources, 1981), 149–64, and "The United States, NATO, and the Third World: Dominoes, Imbroglios, and Agonizing Reappraisals," in *NATO After Forty Years,* ed. Lawrence S. Kaplan, S. Victor Papacosma, Mark R. Rubin, and Ruth V. Young (Wilmington, Del.: Scholarly Resources, 1990), 149–77.

4. UN Charter in *The Charter of the United Nations: A Commentary,* ed. Bruno Simma (New York: Oxford Univ. Press, 1995), xxxi–xxxii.

5. See Resolution 66 (I), "Transmission of Information Under Article 73(e) of the Charter," 14 Dec. 1946.

6. UN Charter in *Charter of the United Nations,* ed. Simma, xxxii. The eight administering powers were Australia, Belgium, Denmark, France, the Netherlands, New Zealand, the United Kingdom, and the United States. The eight nonadministering powers elected to the committee were Brazil, China, Cuba, Egypt, India, the Philippines, the Soviet Union, and Uruguay.

7. See Senate Committee on Foreign Relations, *The United Nations and Dependent Territories,* 84th Cong., 1st sess., 1955, Staff Study No. 9, 14; and Edward T. Rowe, "The Emerging Anti-Colonial Consensus in the United Nations," *Journal of Conflict Resolution* 8 (Sept. 1964): 219, 220.

8. UN General Assembly Resolution 1514 (XV), "Declaration on the Granting of Independence to Colonial Countries and Peoples," 20 Dec. 1960.

9. Arnold V. Kunst, "The United Nations and Dependent Peoples," in *Annual Review of United Nations Affairs, 1961,* ed. Richard N. Swift (New York: Oceana Publications, 1962), 104.

10. UN General Assembly Resolution 1654 (XVI), "The Situation with Regard to the Implementation of the Declaration on the Granting of Independence to Colonial Countries and Peoples," 27 Nov. 1961.

11. See UN Office of Public Information, *The United Nations and Decolonization: Highlights of Thirty Years of United Nations Efforts on Behalf of Colonial Countries and Peoples* (New York : United Nations, 1977), 4, 14; and UN Office of Public Information, *The United Nations and Decolonization: Summary of the Work of the Special Committee of Twenty-Four* (New York: United Nations, 1965), 4–5.

12. Early British efforts to limit international supervision of the colonies may be followed in Ernest B. Haas, "The Attempt to Terminate Colonialism: Acceptance of the United Nations Trusteeship System," *International Organization* 7 (Feb. 1953): 15–16.

13. Chapter XII of the UN Charter, "International Trusteeship System," in *Charter of the United Nations,* ed. Simma, xxxii–xxxiv.

14. UN Charter, in *Charter of the United Nations,* ed. Simma, xx. See Rupert Emerson, "The United Nations and Colonialism," in *The Evolving United Nations: A Prospect for Peace?* ed.

Kenneth J. Twitchett (New York: St. Martin's Press, 1971), 88–89, for a discussion of article 2(7)'s relevance to the colonial question.

15. UN Charter, in *Charter of the United Nations,* ed. Simma, xxxi.

16. Sir Hilton Poynton (UK) remarks, 36th meeting of the Fourth Committee of the UN General Assembly, 3 Oct. 1947, Official Records of the United Nations, A/C.4/SR.36, Cleveland Public Library, Cleveland, Ohio.

17. "Summary Record of Colonial Talks with the United Kingdom (11:00 A.M.–1:00 P.M.)," 6 July 1950, General Records of the State Department, Record Group 59, Records of the Office of Assistant Secretary and Under Secretary of State Dean Acheson, 1941–1948, 1950, box 13, folder: Colonial Talks (British), National Archives II, College Park, Md.

18. "Summary Record of Colonial Policy Talks with the United Kingdom (11:00 A.M.–1:00 P.M.)," 5 July 1950, RG 59, Records of the Office of Dean Acheson, box 13, folder: Colonial Talks (British).

19. See Haas, "The Attempt to Terminate Colonialism."

20. *Life* editorial quoted in A. P. Thornton, *Doctrines of Imperialism* (New York: Wiley, 1965), 211–12. Additional discussion of anti–British Empire sentiment may be found in, among other sources, Roy Fraser Holland, "Mobilization, Rejuvenation, and Liquidation: Colonialism and Global War," in *World War II,* ed. Loyd Lee (Westport, Conn.: Greenwood Press, 1999), 159–91.

21. OSS memorandum, 2 Apr. 1945, cited in Christopher Thorne, "Indochina and Anglo-American Relations, 1942–1945," *Pacific Historical Review* 45 (Feb. 1976): 96. See also Tony Smith, *The Pattern of Imperialism: The United States, Great Britain, and the Late-Industrializing World Since 1815* (New York: Cambridge Univ. Press, 1981), 172.

22. U.S. embassy, London, despatch 3293 to State Department, "The British Situation," 20 Jan. 1953, RG 59 (General Records of the Department of State), 741.00/1–2053, National Archives II.

23. "Minutes of the Twenty-fifth Meeting of the United States Delegation to the Third Regular Session of the General Assembly, Paris, Hotel d'Iéna, Nov. 3, 1948, 9:15 A.M.," 3 Nov. 1948, *FRUS, 1948* (Washington, D.C.: G.P.O., 1975), 1:284.

24. "Summary Record of Colonial Talks with the United Kingdom (11:00 A.M.–1:00 P.M.)," 5 July 1950, RG 59, Records of the Office of Dean Acheson, box 13, folder: Colonial Talks (British). See also Henry Shullaw (BNA) memorandum to William P. Snow (BNA), "United States Relations with the British Commonwealth: Comments on Paper Drafted by Mr. Satterthwaite," 2 Feb. 1950, RG 59, 611.41/2–250; Henry R. Labousisse Jr. (BNA) memorandum to George W. Perkins (EUR), "US-British Relations," 27 Feb. 1950, RG 59, 611.41/2–2750; and Theodore C. Achilles (BNA) memorandum to Perkins, 1 Mar. 1950, RG 59, 611.41/2–2850.

25. "Department of State Policy Statement Regarding the United Nations," 18 Sept. 1950, *FRUS, 1950* 2:40.

26. Dean Acheson (secretary of state) tel. 2631 to U.S. embassy, London, 2 June 1950, RG 84, London Embassy Classified General Records, box 208, file 322 A-Z 1950, National Archives II.

27. "Summary Record of Colonial Talks with the United Kingdom (3:00 P.M.–5:00 P.M.)," 5 July 1950, RG 59, Records of the Office of Dean Acheson, box 13, folder: Colonial Talks (British).

28. "Summary Record of Colonial Talks with the United Kingdom (11:00 A.M.–1:00 P.M.)," 5 July 1950, RG 59, Records of the Office of Dean Acheson, box 13, folder: Colonial Talks (British).

29. "Summary Record of Colonial Talks with the United Kingdom (11:00 A.M.–1:00 P.M.),"
7 July 1950, RG 59, Records of the Office of Dean Acheson, box 13, folder: Colonial Talks
(British).

30. "Summary Record of Colonial Talks with the United Kingdom (11:00 A.M.–1:00 P.M.),"
6 July 1950, RG 59, Records of the Office of Dean Acheson, box 13, folder: Colonial Talks
(British).

31. See "Anglo-American Discussions of the Handling of Colonial and Trusteeship Questions in the United Nations," 10–12 Oct. 1951, CO 537, 7157.

32. Hopkinson remarks, 251st meeting of the Fourth Committee of the UN General Assembly, 23 Oct. 1952, Official Records of the United Nations, A/C.4/SR.251.

33. "Summary Report on Anglo-American Conversations on Treatment of Colonial Affairs in the United Nations," 26–27 July 1954, CO 936, 317.

34. "Summary Record of Colonial Talks with the United Kingdom (11:00 A.M.–1:00 P.M.),"
6 July 1950, RG 59, Records of the Office of Dean Acheson, box 13, folder: Colonial Talks
(British).

35. William Sanders (UNA) to John D. Hickerson (UNA), "Report on the Talks on Colonial
Policy Held in London and Paris, October 10 to October 16, 1951," 7 Dec. 1951, FRUS, 1951
(Washington, D.C.: G.P.O., 1979), 2:652.

36. For the Truman administration's policy see, for example, Sir Alan Burns, In Defence
of Colonies: British Colonial Territories in International Affairs (London: George Allen &
Unwin, 1957), 122–33; and Robert C. Good, "The United States and the Colonial Debate,"
in Alliance Policy in the Cold War, ed. Arnold Wolfers (Westport, Conn.: Greenwood Press,
1959), 224–70.

37. Dulles in "Report on the Near East," U.S. Department of State Bulletin 28 (15 June 1953):
833–34.

38. Eisenhower's sentiments may be followed in Eisenhower to Winston S. Churchill, 22 July
1954, Ann Whitman File, International Series, box 19, folder: Churchill, July–Dec. 1954 (1),
Dwight D. Eisenhower Library, Abilene, Kans.; and Eisenhower to General Alfred M. Gruenther
(Supreme Commander, SHAPE), 30 Nov. 1954, Whitman File, DDE Diary, box 8, folder: DDE
Diary—Nov. 1954 (1).

39. For the competing pressures on the Eisenhower administration in the area of colonial
policy see Pruden, Conditional Partners, 178; and Lawrence D. Weiler and Anne Patricia
Simons, The United States and the United Nations: The Search for International Peace and
Security (New York: Manhattan Publishing, 1967), 388–95.

40. The Eisenhower administration's handling of colonial questions at the United Nations
is covered in Pruden, Conditional Partners, 173–97.

41. For a concise outline of the campaign see Henry A. Byroade (assistant secretary of state
for Near Eastern, South Asian, and African affairs) address before the World Affairs Council
of Northern Calif., "The World's Colonies and Ex-Colonies: A Challenge to America," 31 Oct.
1953, Department of State Bulletin 29 (16 Nov. 1953): 655–60. Many of the ideas of the new campaign were foreshadowed in a speech by Ambassador at Large Philip C. Jessup, "The Problem
of Dependent Peoples" to the Ottawa Women's Canadian Club, 25 Sept. 1952, Department of
State Bulletin 27 (13 Oct. 1952): 571–75.

42. The "Communism—the New Colonialism" campaign was pursued especially vigorously
by U.S. ambassador to the United Nations Henry Cabot Lodge II. See Pruden, Conditional
Partners, 176.

43. See address by Francis O. Wilcox (assistant secretary for international organization affairs), "The United States and the Challenge of the Underdeveloped Areas of the World," *Department of State Bulletin* 40 (25 May 1959): 750–58.

44. For these kinds of arguments see address by John Foster Dulles (secretary of state), "The Moral Initiative," *Department of State Bulletin* 29 (30 Nov. 1953): 741–44; and Irving Solomon (US) remarks, 824th meeting of the Fourth Committee of the UN General Assembly, 1 Dec. 1958, Official Records of the United Nations, A/C.4/SR.824.

45. The Eisenhower administration's propaganda campaign is thoroughly covered in Kenneth Osgood, *Total Cold War: Eisenhower's Secret Propaganda Battle at Home and Abroad* (Lawrence: Univ. Press of Kans., 2006). See also Osgood, "Words and Deeds: Race, Colonialism, and Eisenhower's Propaganda War in the Third World," in *The Eisenhower Administration, the Third World, and the Globalization of the Cold War,* ed. Kathyrn C. Statler and Andrew Johns (Lanham, Md.: Rowman and Littlefield, 2006), 3–25.

46. See, for example, record of telephone calls between Secretary of State Christian A. Herter and Eisenhower, 8 Dec. 1960, and between Herter and British ambassador Harold Caccia, 8 Dec. 1960, Christian A. Herter Papers, Miscellaneous Memorandums Series, box 10, folder: Presidential Telephone Calls, 7/1959–1/20/1961, Eisenhower Library.

47. Eisenhower's decision in favor of abstention may be followed in record of telephone call between Herter and Eisenhower (10:50 A.M.), 9 Dec. 1960, between Herter and General Andrew Goodpaster, 9 Dec. 1960, and between Herter and Eisenhower (6:15 P.M.), 9 Dec. 1960, Herter Papers, Miscellaneous Memoranda Series, box 10, folder: Presidential Telephone Calls, 7/1959–1/20/1961.

48. For the Eisenhower administration's approach to decolonization, particularly domestic affairs, see Thomas Borstelmann, *The Cold War and the Color Line: American Race Relations in the Global Arena* (Cambridge, Mass.: Harvard Univ. Press, 2001).

49. Circular airgram CA-2368 from the Department of State to certain posts, "Committee of 17 in the Seventeenth United Nations General Assembly," 30 Aug. 1962, RG 59, 320/8–3062.

50. Khrushchev, "Speech at the General Assembly on Colonial Freedom," 12 Oct. 1960, in N. S. Khrushchev, *Disarmament and Colonial Freedom: Speeches and Interviews at the United Nations General Assembly, September–October 1960* (Westport, Conn.: Greenwood Press, 1975), 170, 174. Khrushchev's first speech, delivered on 23 September, was bombastically anti-Western in tone and language, so much so that it reads in spots as deliberate exaggeration. See ibid., 13–63.

51. Circular airgram CA-2368 from the Department of State to certain posts, "Committee of 17 in the Seventeenth United Nations General Assembly," 30 Aug. 1962, RG 59, 320/8–3062.

52. Bureau of International Organization Affairs memorandum for the president, "United States Strategy at the Sixteenth General Assembly," undated [late summer 1961], *FRUS, 1961–1963* 25: no. 174, www.state.gov/r/pa/ho/frus/kennedyjf/xxv/6012.htm, accessed 22 May 2006; Bureau of Intelligence research memorandum, RSB-148, "Soviet Tactics on Some Major Issues at the 17th UN General Assembly," 27 Aug. 1962, *FRUS, 1961–1963* 25: no. 219, www.state.gov/r/pa/ho/frus/kennedyjf/xxv/6015.htm, accessed 22 May 2006.

53. Circular airgram CA-2368 from the Department of State to certain posts, "Committee of 17 in the Seventeenth United Nations General Assembly," 30 Aug. 1962, RG 59, 320/8–3062.

54. See, for example, Secretary of State Dean Rusk memorandum for the president, "The 17th General Assembly: A Summary Round-Up," undated [late 1962], *FRUS, 1961–1963* 25: no. 232, www.state.gov/r/pa/ho/frus/kennedyjf/xxv/6016.htm, accessed 22 May 2006.

55. Among the British propaganda pamphlets issued as part of this campaign are "The World's Newest Colonies," Jan. 1961, FO 371/160907; "The Soviet Central Asian Republics: A Model for Africa?" May 1961, FO 371/172593; and "Soviet Imperialism," Oct. 1962, FO 371/172593.

56. Office of the High Commissioner for Canada press release, 27 Nov. 1961, FO 371/166822.

57. Rusk memorandum for the president, "The 17th General Assembly: A Summary Round-Up," undated [late 1962], *FRUS, 1961–1963* 25: no. 232, www.state.gov/r/pa/ho/frus/kennedyjf/xxv/6016.htm, accessed 22 May 2006.

58. Department of State tel. 422 to U.S. mission at UN, 13 Aug. 1963, *FRUS, 1961–1963* 25: no. 261, www.state.gov/r/pa/ho/frus/kennedyjf/xxv/8679.htm, accessed 22 May 2006.

59. William H. Brubeck (executive secretary of the Department of State) memorandum to McGeorge Bundy (president's special assistant for national security affairs), "U.S. Participation in the UN Committee of 24," 18 Mar. 1963, *FRUS, 1961–1963* 25: no. 247, www.state.gov/r/pa/ho/frus/kennedyjf/xxv/6016.htm, accessed 22 May 2006.

60. Harlan M. Cleveland (assistant secretary of state for international organization affairs) memorandum to the secretary of state, "Current Issues Before the United Nations," 27 Nov. 1963, *FRUS, 1961–1963* 25: no. 282, www.state.gov/r/pa/ho/frus/kennedyjf/xxv/6017.htm, accessed 22 May 2006.

61. Ibid.; George Ball (acting secretary of state) memorandum to the president, "The Current Session of the United Nations General Assembly," 13 Dec. 1963, *FRUS, 1961–1963* 25: no. 289, www.state.gov/r/pa/ho/frus/kennedyjf/xxv/6017.htm, accessed 22 May 2006.

62. Department of State tel. 422 to U.S. mission at UN, 13 Aug. 1963, *FRUS, 1961–1963* 25: no. 261, www.state.gov/r/pa/ho/frus/kennedyjf/xxv/8679.htm, accessed 22 May 2006.

3

"Learning by Doing"

Disintegrating Factors and the Development of Political Cooperation in Early NATO

Winfried Heinemann

No Unnecessary Luxury

In his memoirs, Dean Acheson criticizes Lester "Mike" Pearson, the Canadian minister for foreign affairs, and article 2 of the North Atlantic Treaty: "Article 2 has continued to bedevil NATO. Lester Pearson has continually urged the Council to set up committees of 'wise men' to find a use for it, which the 'wise men' have continually failed to do."[1] Acheson made clear that he did not like article 2, did not like the obligation to conduct political consultations, an obligation the United States evaded from the start with all its might, and did not like Pearson for being one of the leading exponents of a political role for the alliance.

Nevertheless, the founding fathers of NATO did include the subject of political cooperation in the text of the treaty, and this was by no means done thoughtlessly or out of pure naiveté. The rapid militarization of the North Atlantic alliance as a result of the Korean shock often obscures the fact that, initially, the threat to the West was perceived to be political as much as military.

Common efforts to contain expansionist Soviet ambitions necessarily required that the members of the alliance be willing to subordinate their sometimes conflicting national interests to the common interests of the alliance to make the pledge of mutual military assistance in the event of an external attack credible. At the same time, it was important to keep the burdens of collective defense within reasonable limits. In addition, the populations of each individual member state had to be convinced that the burden imposed on it was not considerably heavier than that imposed on the others.

Only if the alliance succeeded in maintaining a united defensive front against Communism would it be able to serve its purpose. Hence, a minimum of political cooperation constituted no superfluous luxury but was, rather, an urgent necessity for achieving the specific aim of the alliance. How international politics came to understand these new thoughts, even against the reluctance of classic diplomats such as Acheson,[2] will be the subject of this chapter, illustrated by two examples from the years 1953–54 and 1956.

Trieste

At the end of the Second World War, Trieste was a free territory, divided into two zones of occupation. U.S. and British troops controlled Zone A, and the Yugoslavs occupied Zone B.[3] Both Italy and Yugoslavia laid claim to the whole territory.

As long as Yugoslavia had formed a solid part of the Communist bloc, everything seemed clear. During the Italian election campaign in 1948, the United States, Great Britain, and France had officially confirmed Italy's claim on the territory.[4] But the more Yugoslav leader Josip Broz Tito distanced himself from Josef Stalin and instead pursued a rather Western-oriented foreign policy, the more the Western powers had to take a mediating position. On the one hand, they wanted to deepen the split in the Communist bloc evidenced by the Yugoslav breakaway, even going so far as to give substantial military aid to Yugoslavia, a process in which U.S. Army General Lyman L. Lemnitzer was prominently involved. On the other hand, the West sought Italy's ratification of the European Defense Community and Rome's approval of U.S. naval bases in Naples.

In the autumn of 1953, the situation seemed to have reached an impasse. Neither Italy nor Yugoslavia was willing to give in. On top of that, Italy and Yugoslavia sent troops to their common frontier after a diplomatic misunderstanding, the Italian troops normally being assigned to NATO. The threat from this hot spot became all too obvious. In this situation, London remembered that, on the occasion of his visit in March 1953, Tito had indicated his willingness to accept a solution imposed by the Western powers.[5]

In early October 1953, London and Washington were in agreement to leave Zone A to Italy and silently accept Yugoslavia's de facto annexation of Zone B. Moreover, the two also agreed to make this move without France because they were worried that the French would inform their friends in Rome prematurely and thus scuttle the whole idea of an imposed solution from the very start.[6]

Because not even France had been informed in advance, NATO participation had to be ruled out even more. Denying the council prior consultation would foreseeably incur the displeasure of some alliance members. The U.S. State Department brushed aside these objections and told its permanent representative in the council that the reasons why the NATO Council could not be involved in advance should be obvious to all members. In case some would still grumble, the permanent representative should furnish them with copies of the British-U.S. press release, which, in turn, he could pick up from the embassy.[7] Four years after the signing of the North Atlantic Treaty, this showed a remarkable view of political cooperation!

On 8 October 1953, the United States and Great Britain confronted the governments in Rome and Belgrade with their joint decision. From the beginning, neither Yugoslavia nor Italy embraced the idea. Tito publicly declared that Italy's occupation of Zone A would have to be interpreted as an "aggressive action" and that Yugoslav troops had already been moved into Zone B.[8] Should Italy enter Zone A, Yugoslavia would do the same.[9] If the Anglo-American plan were implemented, a war between Italy and Yugoslavia would become a distinct possibility. Moreover, the two states that had brought the alliance into this situation had not consulted any of their allies in advance. Even days after the incident, the Trieste issue was not raised in the NATO Council.[10]

The Foreign Office had acted lightly on the assumption that Trieste was situated outside the "NATO area." A few days after the Anglo-American statement, however, the Danish foreign ministry asked the British ambassador in Copenhagen whether Denmark might get involved in a conflict under the NATO treaty if Yugoslav units attacked Italian troops in Zone A.[11] Whitehall's legal branch came to a surprising conclusion: Actually, article 6(2) of the North Atlantic Treaty, as amended in 1951, had to be interpreted in such a way that an attack on Italian troops in Trieste would invoke the mutual defense clause of article 5.[12] Soon afterward, Washington, too, concluded that a Yugoslav attack on Italian troops in Trieste would invoke the mutual defense clause in accordance with the text of the North Atlantic Treaty.[13]

In view of this development, the NATO partners pressed even harder for adequate information. Pearson in particular took offense: although it might be understandable why the news should not have become public knowledge prior to 8 October, the lack of any kind of consultation after the event was incomprehensible. Regardless of the individual case, it would be necessary to maintain the principle of prior consultation, especially for any action that might lead to hostilities: "acquiescence in by-passing the Council cannot but have a bad effect on the future of the organization."[14]

Pearson had found the alliance's vulnerable spot: in a question that might well develop into the *casus foederis*, the United States had intentionally excluded all its partners, with the exception of the United Kingdom, from the decision-making process. "Crackpot idea" was the comment of the German representative in New York, and he may not have been entirely wrong.[15]

Iceland

There is, however, a counterexample from 1956 that demonstrated how to play skilfully with the diplomatic rules of the alliance. Such occurred in the manner NATO dealt with the Communist participation in the Icelandic government and the Icelandic demand for withdrawal of U.S. troops.[16] Iceland, then a country with a population of around one hundred thousand, had no armed forces. The problem was of some relevance for the alliance. On a practical, military level, there was a real risk that Iceland might fall victim to a swift Soviet attack if it was left completely defenseless.

More fundamentally, Iceland openly defined the U.S. troop presence as a "burden." Several other allies had to carry similar burdens on top of maintaining their own military. Suddenly, Iceland seemed to be the ultimate "free rider," a member that wanted to profit from the security created by the alliance but did not want to shoulder its fair share of the cost.[17]

On 28 March 1956, the Icelandic parliament adopted a resolution demanding the withdrawal of U.S. forces from the island.[18] If the United States did not agree to the bases being taken over by Icelandic civilian personnel, the U.S.-Icelandic Defense Agreement of 1950 would be terminated. What seemed especially disturbing from NATO's perspective was the fact that all parties but the Conservatives had voted with the Communists and, therefore, made them "socially acceptable" in a certain way. The *Neue Zürcher Zeitung* described the decision as a "major setback for the policies of the United States and the Western Defence Alliance in general."[19]

Scandinavia was especially concerned. Norway and Denmark also did not tolerate any stationing of foreign troops on their territory in peacetime, but at least both countries maintained their own armed forces, and they had already given in to some extent. Norway had accepted NATO Headquarters Europe North (AFNORTH) in Kolsaas, and Denmark had agreed to the U.S. presence in Greenland. The military security of Norway and Greenland would depend on a fast and undisturbed reinforcement of forces via the North Atlantic—that is, past Iceland—in case of war, especially in view of their low military peacetime operational readiness. Therefore, the international public was speculating that the Scandinavian NATO partners might bring their traditionally good connections to Iceland into play.[20]

From the outset, the U.S. president and his secretary of state emphasized the necessity of dealing with this question within the NATO framework, which finally happened on 11 April. Contrary to its publicly demonstrated calmness, the United States was greatly concerned about Iceland's Althing Resolution and demanded support from all other NATO governments.[21]

The Althing Resolution became, of course, part and parcel of the Icelandic election campaign that was reaching its peak in mid-June 1956. The election result was ambiguous: the opponents of the U.S. troop presence had lost some votes but had won some seats.[22] On 24 July 1956, the first NATO government with Communist participation was formed in Reykjavik.[23] Now, the alliance had two questions to answer: what was to become of the bases, and how would the NATO Council deal with a Communist-influenced government within its own ranks?

Washington cleverly managed to involve its allies in the bases question. The Scandinavian partners, above all Halvard Lange, the Norwegian foreign minister, but also his Canadian counterpart Lester Pearson, asserted their influence. In a concerted campaign, the United States cut off the Icelandic government from all foreign currency supplies. In early summer, Bonn, for example, had promised Reykjavik a loan. Now, suddenly, Germany reversed its position after the U.S. embassy in Bonn dropped a broad, though secret, hint.[24] Because of a "cod war," there were no earnings from fish sales in the United Kingdom. France was visibly annoyed about the way Iceland had voted when North Africa had been debated in the United Nations. So, apart from the Soviets, nobody was willing to provide funds. In the autumn of 1956, the new Icelandic government demonstrated its willingness to compromise. A slightly modified defense agreement was signed and sealed in November 1956, guaranteeing the presence of U.S. forces indefinitely.[25]

On the question of how to handle a Communist-influenced government, it was NATO Secretary General Lord Ismay who took the initiative. He knew full well that, above all, the United States would express security concerns—how could one prevent secret information from being leaked to Moscow via Reykjavik? But how could a solution be found that would not suggest Iceland had become a second-class member? Ismay suggested a gentlemen's agreement. The Icelandic representative would be invited to all meetings. He would also be provided with all documents, but he would be expected not to participate in meetings dealing with truly secret subjects and would simply not collect classified documents.[26] Certainly, this solution was only feasible because Hans G. Andersen, the Icelandic permanent representative, had a high reputation as being absolutely trustworthy.[27] All partners approved the procedure, and it thus became the basis for later action in similar cases. The alliance's diplomatic machinery was by now well coordinated, and together with a clever combination of classic bilateral negotiations and a very modern multilateral diplomacy it had helped to defuse a crisis before it could turn into a real threat to alliance cohesion.

The Three Wise Men

As Dean Acheson had pointed out, the question of political cooperation had repeatedly been a central issue in NATO deliberations. In September 1951, the Temporary Council Committee (TCC) was appointed to improve economic cooperation within the alliance.[28] Simultaneously, another, less well known committee was to discuss political cooperation. It consisted of five foreign ministers, Halvard Lange (Norway), Alcide de Gasperi (Italy), Mike Pearson (Canada), Dirk U. Stikker (the Netherlands), and Paul van Zeeland (Belgium), and its task was to develop options for implementing the "Canadian" article 2 of the North Atlantic Treaty referring to an "Atlantic Community."[29] The committee came to the conclusion that, at the time being, member states were unwilling to deepen their economic or cultural cooperation.[30] In contrast to the TCC, this committee soon fell into oblivion.[31] Immediately after the Korean shock, the major powers were interested not in creating an Atlantic community but in improving the collective defense.

In May 1956, only a short time after the Icelandic parliament's resolution, the NATO Council again appointed a similar committee on political cooperation. This time, it consisted of the foreign ministers of Canada, Norway, and Italy: Pearson, Lange, and Gaetano Martino, who ultimately succeeded de Gasperi. Its composition was very reminiscent of the Committee of Five of 1951–52, especially if one took into account Martino as the successor to de Gasperi, and considered that Stikker had not held office since 1952.

In a way, it was a warning sign that Paul-Henri Spaak, the Belgian foreign minister, did not participate in the committee. He was one of the most prominent supporters of Atlantic and European integration, as his term as NATO secretary general from 1957 until 1961 would eventually show. Spaak, however, was skeptical of the prospects of the committee appointed in May 1956.[32]

Nonetheless, the members of the Committee of Three were a fortunate choice in many respects. The council had garnered a Liberal (Pearson), a Social Democrat (Lange), and a Conservative (Martino), and, at the same time, a North American, a northern European, and a southern European. Above all, though, the council had engaged three men with previous practical experience in political cooperation within the alliance. The Italian foreign minister stood for the successful Trieste solution, his Norwegian colleague stood for careful consideration among Scandinavian states, and Pearson had made a name for himself as the keeper of the political dimension of the alliance, as Acheson had rightly emphasized. The fact that, unlike Spaak, the three foreign ministers were again willing to make the effort and run the risk of failure, however, reveals that, based on their experience with political cooperation in the alliance, they saw realistic chances of a successful outcome.

One main disadvantage in the composition of the committee immediately struck all participants: not one of the "Big Three" was willing to participate.[33] Obviously, Washington's main intention was to prevent the other alliance members from pursuing goals that might have a potentially damaging effect on the alliance without losing much of its own freedom of action as a leading power. The U.S. government preferred to influence the work of the "Three Wise Men" without being automatically identified with the results. Therefore, President Dwight D. Eisenhower appointed Walter F. George, a Democratic senator from Georgia and

chairman of the Senate Committee on Foreign Affairs, as his personal commissioner for cooperation with the Committee of Three.[34] This appointment gave
Eisenhower several advantages. It took the question of NATO policy out of the
upcoming presidential election campaign and provided bipartisan backing in the
Senate. At the same time, George was "top-class" enough to counter any accusations that the United States was seeking to back out of its responsibilities.

Senator George immediately made clear to Pearson the limits within which the
work of the Three Wise Men should take place: the United States was unwilling
to accept any expansion of NATO activities into the economic field or into Third
World policies and would not agree to obligatory consultations limiting long-term
American freedom of action. From the perspective of the smaller partners, the
purpose of the whole exercise, to integrate the United States, had been thwarted
from the start.[35]

As a result, the three foreign ministers abandoned any hope of achieving essential changes in the area of cooperation under article 2 and concentrated on
proposals on article 4.[36] In this area, progress had to be possible. The credibility
of the United States, which had already suffered much by the Radford Plan for a
partial withdrawal of forces from Europe, was bound to decrease even more with
a too obvious disinterest in alliance political cooperation.[37]

But whereas the committee consulted with the governments of the member
states on this issue and still analyzed the results, the Suez crisis brought political
cooperation to the brink of failure.[38] As early as the end of July, the NATO Council
had demanded appropriate consultation or, at least, information on British and
French intentions.[39] On 6 August 1956, the British and the French permanent
representatives informed the council that both states intended to withdraw troops
from Central Europe as a result of the Suez crisis. The information only referred
to Central Europe; there was no mention of what was going to happen to those
forces once they had deployed to the eastern Mediterranean.[40]

Eisenhower was not willing to identify himself with an act of violence, and
especially not with a measure supporting European colonialism.[41] On 1 August,
acting on advice from the State Department, General Alfred Gruenther postponed
a meeting with senior British military representatives, just to preclude the impression of U.S. approval.[42]

France and Britain demanded consultation with the NATO Council on the Suez
issue before the end of August. The United States would have preferred bilateral
contacts to avoid the impression that Suez was an alliance issue. At minimum, the
council was to limit its handling of Suez to the barest minimum—that is, a simple
report without any discussion.[43] British foreign minister Selwyn Lloyd arrived
from London, and, under British pressure, Pearson and Spaak participated in the
meeting. Dulles, however, decided not to fly to Paris. Despite high expectations,
neither London nor Paris intended to become involved in real consultations. Selwyn

Lloyd provided only minimal information, explicitly without "asking the Council for its intervention or the passing of a resolution."[44] To London and Paris it was important to give the impression publicly that their allies were backing them but without intervening in their policy.

The aggravating crisis now also began to affect the military structure of the alliance. In early September, the State Department considered whether the planned participation of U.S. units in the NATO exercise code name WHIPSAW in the East Mediterranean could go ahead without the United States identifying itself too clearly with the United Kingdom's position. It was typical of the U.S. attitude at this point to be willing to risk participation because the refusal to send U.S. units would have publicly revealed the alienation in the special relationship between both powers.[45]

In fact, the special relationship had already been greatly damaged when Eisenhower's demand to refrain from the use of force failed to change British and French intentions. The only consequence was that the United States was not informed about the true intentions of the two countries. On 29 October, Israeli forces crossed the Sinai Peninsula to attack the Egyptian army at the Suez Canal. Two days later, British and French aircraft bombed the canal. On the same day, 31 October, the NATO Council convened a crisis meeting in which all partners sharply criticized the lack of consultation within the alliance framework.[46] U.S. criticism referred not to the NATO dimension of the issue but rather to the fact that not even Washington had been informed. Washington already knew that the Israeli attack and the "neutral" intervention of Great Britain and France had been a put-up job and saw itself as having been intentionally and deliberately deceived. Eisenhower was particularly hurt by Britain's commencement of military action in the middle of the decisive phase of his reelection campaign.[47] Consequently, it was no surprise that the United States denied the two allied powers any support and forced Britain to abandon the operation by refusing financial backing. The conflict was settled in the forum of the United Nations with the considerable assistance of Pearson, who was awarded the Nobel Peace Prize in 1957 for his efforts. Troops from several countries under the command of the Canadian lieutenant general E. L. M. Burns (the first "blue helmets" in the history of the United Nations) were deployed to separate the combatant parties. It was the unloved United Nations and not NATO that had turned out to be the appropriate forum for crisis management.

Pearson was aware that the prospects of the smaller partners to influence the United States politically were quite low. If any members of the alliance had a certain influence on Washington at all, they were France and, above all, the United Kingdom. Even worse, these two states had refused any political consultation in a decisive situation, also within the framework of the Commonwealth, which had been to their own detriment in the end.[48] Flagrant British and French violation of all principles meant to guide the work of the Three Wise Men nearly resulted in Lange's resignation from the Committee of Three.[49]

Nevertheless, NATO was still the basis for Western security, and the crisis had shown that it was necessary to make efforts to save the alliance. For the United States, the Suez crisis had been virtual proof of the fact that the variant of political consultation they had demanded was more necessary than ever.[50] On all sides, attempts to construct a new solidarity quickly after the debacle were perceptible. Following the Suez crisis, the report of the Three Wise Men, which for the most part had already been finished, naturally had to be redone. Under Pearson's stewardship, the document was finished in mid-November 1956, and the committee submitted its report to the NATO Council on the seventeenth.[51]

The report explicitly mentioned the "events of the last few months" and the "severe strains" the alliance had undergone.[52] The introduction stressed that, although the alliance from the beginning had been founded as a reaction to the Soviet threat, it was not simply designed for the purposes of defense.

The chapter on political cooperation was subdivided into different sections: "Consultation on Foreign Policies," "Peaceful Settlement of Inter-member Disputes," and a short passage on parliamentary cooperation. The section on foreign policy started with a longer quotation taken from the 1951 report of the five foreign ministers, in which they had demanded early informal consultations prior to the formal procedures under article 4. The report from 1956 emphasized once again the importance of this cooperation and, in case of its absence, predicted that "the very existence of the North Atlantic Community may be in jeopardy" (para. 44). Yet the report itself already restricted the obligation for timely prior consultation by conceding that "a situation of extreme emergency may arise where actions must be taken by one government before consultation is possible with the others" (para. 48). This was more than just a "practical limit to consultation." It was, above all, meant for the United States, which wanted to keep its political freedom of action.

U.S. reservations about obligatory procedures for political consultation were nothing new. They had lasted from 1953[53] through 1955 until May 1956.[54] The fact that the smaller partners could not achieve more was not surprising. The report, however, also mentioned that "on all occasions and in all circumstances member governments, before acting or even before pronouncing, should keep the interest and the requirements of the Alliance in mind" (para. 50). This was an important change compared with 1951. The way the United States had phrased its national policy in the years since the earlier report increasingly showed its will to consider the interests of the alliance. The action Washington had taken on Trieste in October 1953 was no longer to be feared in December 1956. The Iceland crisis had also shown how skillfully the State Department could use the mechanisms of the alliance. The United Kingdom and France had foundered on their antialliance attitude in Suez in the autumn of 1956.

To improve foreign policy cooperation, the Committee of Three recommended the regular stocktaking of the foreign policy situation by the secretary general and the foreign ministers at their spring meetings (paras. 52ff.). The parallel to the

Annual Review was obvious. At the end, the report demanded a council resolution by which the member states undertook to settle disputes within the framework of the alliance first (para. 57). Thus, NATO took the de facto place of the United Nations for its members, though the United Nations should have been the forum for the settlement of intergovernmental conflicts.

The NATO foreign ministers meeting in Paris in mid-December 1956 took place against the background of damage limitation after the Suez debacle. On the one hand, this fact made it easier for the council to accept the report and make only minor alterations, even though it wanted the statements on political consultation to be understood as "recommendations" only. On the other hand, it expressly adopted the "resolution on the peaceful settlement of disputes" suggested by the Three Wise Men.[55] This had been the aim of U.S. policy: to maintain political consultation as noncommittal as possible but to keep the creation of unity between the partners, the commitment to a joint anti-Communist line, as explicit as possible.[56]

From the point of view of those who expected a decisive step toward an "Atlantic Community" of partners with equal rights by the project of the Three Wise Men, the result was disappointing. For them, only the conflict between national freedom of action and consideration of comprehensive alliance interests seemed to have been solved.[57] NATO would not become the basis for such a community, as Pearson himself recognized.[58]

Nonetheless, political cooperation within NATO may not be lightly regarded as failed or futile. The hopes of the Three Wise Men from December 1956 did remain unfulfilled, but, compared with the expectations that the members of the alliance had for article 4 in April 1949, a more positive picture emerged. Organizations and mechanisms had developed, had been improved, and were functioning rather well, which made the alliance "workable."[59] Even Pearson, who deeply regretted the failure of article 2 and, thus, the failure of the concept of a comprehensive Atlantic community, explicitly points in his memoirs to this benefit despite all bitterness. The permanent exchange of political information and points of view was new in political life, as was the exchange of economic data and armaments data in the *Annual Review*.[60]

There may also have been reflection on the basic reality that the obvious failure of efforts for political cooperation would have caused lasting damage to the alliance's good reputation and that it was, therefore, necessary to maintain the "myth" that NATO was more than just a military alliance.[61] Through the present, political coherence in the alliance has surprised all its critics, and this coherence may not be explained solely by the necessity of military cooperation.[62]

The positive conclusion that the 1956 report of the Three Wise Men is still the "gospel" of NATO[63] is, therefore, definitely justified, especially if it is seen as the result of prior achievements. The years from 1949 until 1956, and particularly the events of the autumn of that final year, had made perfectly clear to all members of the alliance the necessity of dealing consciously with conflicts that might threaten the cohesion of the alliance at risk. This was also the reason why the report of the Three Wise Men demanded no fundamentally new procedures or institutions in the field of political consultation but instead expressly described the structures that had developed to this point as appropriate (para. 88) and called for only their increased use by the member states that implied a change of views in the respective national policies (para. 44).

To burden NATO with economic, social, and propagandistic tasks in accordance with article 2 would probably have been an excessive demand. Inevitably, the failure of transatlantic economic integration within the framework of NATO made European economic cooperation seem all the more necessary. The signing of the Treaty of Rome in 1957 signified a response to this development. In the end, it also met the ideas of the United States, because it favored the politico-economic balancing of U.S. interests between the Atlantic and the Pacific areas.[64] The years until 1956, as summarized in the report of the Three Wise Men, had demonstrated possibilities of and limits to nonmilitary cooperation in the alliance. Through trial and error, NATO had found the appropriate degree of cooperation and had established itself as an independent authority on the international scene.[65]

Notes

This chapter is an updated version of my article "Politische Zusammenarbeit im Bündnis, in Von Truman bis Harmel. Die Bundesrepublik Deutschland im Spannungsfeld von NATO und europäischer Integration," ed. Hans-Joachim Harder, Munich, 2000. For the translation, I would like to thank Herr Steffen Krüger, Potsdam.

1. Dean Acheson, *Present at the Creation: My Years in the State Department* (New York: Norton, 1969), 277.

2. For further detail please refer to my book, *Vom Zusammenwachsen des Bündnisses: Die Funktionsweise der NATO in ausgewählten Krisenfällen 1951–1956* (Munich: Oldenbourg, 1998), upon which this chapter draws.

3. Only a few of the many analyses of the Trieste crisis can be listed here. The two standard works are Jean-Baptiste Durosell, *Le Conflit de Trieste 1943–1954* (Brussels: Institut de Sociologie Bruxelles, 1966); and Bogdan C. Novak, *Trieste, 1941–1954: The Ethnic, Political, and Ideological Struggle* (Chicago: Univ. of Chicago Press, 1970). For the early history Walter Hildebrandt, *Der Triest-Konflikt und die italienisch-jugoslawische Frage: Eine soziologisch-zeitgeschichtliche Untersuchung* (Göttingen: AG für Osteuropaforschung, 1953), is very good. Diego de Castro, *La questione di Trieste: L'azione politica e diplomatica italiana del 1943 al 1954*, 2 vols. (Trieste: Lint, 1981), does not refer to original sources. Roberto G. Rabel, *Between East and West: Trieste, the United States, and the Cold War, 1941–1954* (Durham, N.C.: Duke Univ. Press, 1988), relies heavily on U.S. sources and tends to neglect the British and French roles. John C. Campbell, ed., *Successful Negotiation: Trieste, 1954: An Appraisal by the Five Participants* (Princeton, N.J.: Princeton Univ. Press, 1976), relates the London talks on Trieste from the participants' point of view—a good example of "oral history." Like all the other books, Giampaolo Valdevit, *La questione di Trieste, 1941–1954: Politica internazionale e contesto locale* (Milan: Angeli, 1986), does not see the NATO dimension.

4. Beatrice Heuser, *Western "Containment" Policies in the Cold War: The Yugoslav Case, 1948–1953* (London: Routledge, 1988).

5. Harrison memorandum to Harrison about meeting with Ruddock, 1 Oct. 1952, and Dixon minutes, 3 Oct. 1952, Record Class FO 371 (Foreign Office Political Correspondence), 102181, Public Record Office, Kew, England; Anthony Eden, *Full Circle*, vol. 1, *1945–1957* (London: Cassell, 1960), 181; Valdevit, *La questione di Trieste*, 252.

6. Makins tels. 2078 and 2083 to Foreign Office, 1 Oct. 1953, FO 371, 107378; Cheetham-Barbour memorandum of conversation, 1 Oct. 1953, Record Group 59 (General Records of the State Department), DF 1950–54, 750G.00/10–153, National Archives II, College Park, Md.

7. State Department tel. PRIORITY TOPOL 316 to Embassy Paris, 6 Oct. 1953, RG 59, DF 1950–54, 750G.00/10–653.

8. Wallner tel. 447 NIACT to State Department, 10 Oct. 1953, RG 59, DF 1950–54, 750G.00/10–653.

9. Wallner tel. 451 NIACT to State Department, 11 Oct. 1953, RG 59, DF 1950–54, 750G.00/10–1153; Novak, *Trieste, 1941–1954*, 432.

10. UK Delegation NATO tel. to Foreign Office, 12 Oct. 1953, FO 371, 107404.

11. Berthoud tel. to Foreign Office, 12 Oct. 1953, FO 371, 107404.

12. Foreign Office tel. to Berthoud, 18 Oct. 1953, FO 371, 107404.

13. Hughes tel. POLTO 688to State Department, 28 Oct. 1953, RG 59, DF 1950–54, 740.5/10–2853.

14. Department of External Affairs tel. to Embassies Washington (EX-1776) and London (1644), 22 Oct. 1953, RG 25, Acc. 1991–92/109, vol. 92, 50233–40, pt. 4, National Archives Canada, Ottawa.

15. Consulate General New York tel. to Auswärtiges Amt Nr. 166 (Obs), 16 Oct. 1953, Pol Abt 3, 213–00 Band 4, Politisches Archiv des Auswärtigen Amtes, Berlin, Germany.

16. For Iceland see Donald E. Nuechterlein, *Iceland: Reluctant Ally* (Ithaca, N.Y.: Cornell Univ. Press, 1961); Elfar Loftsson, *Island i NATO: Partierna och Försvarsfragan* (Göteborg: Författares Bokmaskin, 1981); Heinemann, *Vom Zusammenwachsen des Bündnisses*, chap. 6, which also updates my earlier publication on the subject, "Die NATO und Island. Kommunistische Regierungsbeteiligung und Stützpunktfrage," *Militärgeschichte* 3 (1993): 6–13.

17. Memorandum, "Iceland, Canada and NATO," 10 May 1956, RG 25, Acc. 1991–92/109, vol. 177, 50373–40, pt. 1; note d'Information, 24 June 1956, EU44–60, Islande 15, Direction Générale des Affaires Politiques—Europe—S/Direction d'Europe du Nord, Archives du Ministère des Affaires Étrangères, Paris.

18. For the text of the resolution see encl. 1 of Embassy Reykjavik despatch to State Department, 28 Mar. 1956, RG 59, DF 1955–59, 740B.5/4–456.

19. *Neue Zürcher Zeitung*, 3 Apr. 1956.

20. Ibid.

21. Embassy Washington tel. 694 to Department of External Affairs, 11 Apr. 1956, RG 25, Acc. 1990–91/008, vol. 53, 50030-AB-5–40, pt. 1; secretary of state for external affairs tel. to NATO-Delegation Paris, 2 May 1956, RG 25, Acc. 1990–91/008, vol. 53, 50030-AB-5–40 pt. 2.

22. Muccio tel. 500 to State Department, 25 June 1956, RG 59, DF 1955–59, 740B.00/6–2556.

23. Elbrick memorandum for Under Secretary (Hoover), 30 July 1956, RG 59, DF 1955–59, 740B.00/7–3056.

24. Memorandum of conversation Maenss and memo Welck memo to D2 and D4 300–210–01/94.11/689/56, 2 Aug. 1956, Ref. 301–94 Band 67.

25. Muccio tel. NIACT 373 to State Department, 23 Nov. 1956, RG 59, DF 1955–59, 740.5/11–2356; Muccio tel. 375 to State Department, 24 Nov. 1956, RG 59, DF 1955–59, 740.5/11–2456.

26. Ismay to Andersen, 24 July 1956, P.A. 7–8-01 (no further call sign), NATO Brüssel.

27. Muccio tel. 161 to State Department, 27 Aug. 1956, RG 59, DF 1955–59, 740.5/8–2756. Then British permanent representative to NATO, Sir Frank Roberts, to author, 18 Oct. 1991.

28. For the TCC, see now Helmut R. Hammerich, *Jeder für sich und Amerika gegen alle? Die Lastenteilung der NATO am Beispiel des Temporary Council Committee, 1949–1954* (Munich: Oldenbourg, 2003).

29. Communiqué of NATO Council meeting Sept. 15–20, 1951, in *Texts of Final Communiqués 1949–1974, issued by Ministerial Sessions of the North Atlantic Council, the Defence Planning Committee, and the Nuclear Planning Group*, ed. NATO Information Service, Brussels [n.d.]; High Commissioner London tel. 2113 to Department of External Affairs, 22 Aug. 1951, RG 25, Acc. 1990–91/008, vol. 50, 50030-V-40, pt. 3.

30. Robert S. Jordan, with Michael W. Bloome, *Political Leadership in NATO: A Study in Multinational Diplomacy* (Boulder, Colo.: Westview Press, 1979), 36; Joseph P. Sinasac, "The Three Wise Men: The Effects of the 1956 Committee of Three on NATO" (M.A. thesis, Univ. of Waterloo, 1989), 28.

31. Communiqué of NATO Council meeting, 20–25 Feb. 1952, in *Texts of Final Communiqués*, 69; Acheson, *Present at the Creation*, 731.

32. Alger tel. 1043 to State Department, 9 May 1956, RG 59, DF 1955–59, 740.5/5–956; Embassy Brussels tel. to Auswärtiges Amt Nr. 227, 9 May 1956, Ref. 301–80.04 Band 1.

33. Sinasac, "The Three Wise Men," 30f.

34. U.S. Delegation memorandum to Executive Secretary NATO including copy of letter Eisenhower to George, 11 May 1956, NISCA 4/5/1, NATO Brussels.

35. Bruno Thoss, "Bündnissolidarität und Regionalkonflikt. Die Suche der NATO nach einem System gegenseitiger Konsultation und die Suez-Krise (1955–1956)," *Acta No. 14. Commission Internationale d'Histoire Militaire, XIVe Colloque International d'Histoire Militaire, Montréal 1988: "Conflicts of High and Low Intensity Since the Second World War,"* vol. II (Ottawa: Commission Internationale d'Histoire Militaire, 1989), 699f; John Milloy, *The Formation and Work of the 1956 Committee of Three on Non-Military Cooperation in NATO,* Oxford (Research Paper) 1991, 20f; Sinasac, "Three Wise Men," 33; Embassy Washington tel. WA 1134 to Department of External Affairs, 13 June 1956, RG 25, Acc. 1990–91/008, vol. 247, 50105-F-40, pt. 2.

36. Sinasac, "The Three Wise Men," 33f.; Bruno Thoss "Der Beitritt der Bundesrepublik Deutschland zur WEU und NATO im Spannungsfeld von Blockbildung und Entspannung (1954–1956)," *Anfänge westdeutscher Sicherheitspolitik.* Vol. 3: *Die NATO-Option* (Munich: Oldenbourg, 1993), 213f.; Lester B. Pearson, *The International Years* (London: Gallancz, 1974), 96.

38. For Suez see Winfried Heinemann and Norbert Wiggershaus, eds., *Das Internationale Krisenjahr 1956: Vorgänge—Perzeptionen—Auswirkungen* (Munich: Oldenbourg, 1999), particularly Detlev Zimmermann, "Frankreich und die Suezkrise 1956," 395–420; and Isabel Warner and Richard Bevins, "Das Foreign Office und der ungarische Volksaufstand von 1956," 374–94.

39. Pearson, *The International Years*, 229.

40. Thoss, "Bündnissolidarität," 703; Milloy, *The Formation and Work*, 32f.

41. Wm. Roger Louis, "Dulles, Suez, and the British," in *John Foster Dulles and the Diplomacy of the Cold War*, ed. Richard H. Immerman (Princeton, N.J.: Princeton Univ. Press, 1990), 135.

42. Lyon tel. 571 to State Department , 1 Aug. 1956, RG 59, DF 1955–59, 740.5/8–156; State Department tel. TOPOL 191 to Embassy Paris, 7 Aug. 1956, RG 59, 740.5/8–756.

43. State Department tel. TOPOL 305 PRIORITY to Embassy Paris, 29 Aug. 1956, RG 59, DF 1955–59, 740.5/8–2956; Murphy memorandum to Dulles, 28 Aug. 1956, U.S. Department of State, *Foreign Relations of the United States, 1955–1957* (Washington, D.C.: G.P.O., 1990), 16:309f; Martin tel. POLTO 418 to State Department, 30 Aug. 1956, RG 59, 740.5/8–3056; Dulles tel. to Embassy London, 30 Aug. 1956, *FRUS, 1955–1957* 16:339ff.

44. Thoss, "Bündnissolidarität," 704.

45. Elbrick memorandum to MacArthur, 7 Sept. 1956, RG 59, DF 1955–59, 740.5/9–756; Henderson (Naples) tel. 107 to State Department, 10 Sept. 1956, RG 59, 740.5/9–1056.

46. Pearson, *The International Years*, 237f; Thoss, "Bündnissolidarität," 705.

47. Memorandum of discussion at the 302d Meeting of the National Security Council, 1 Nov. 1956, *FRUS, 1955–1957,* 16:902–16; Louis, "Dulles, Suez, and the British," 152ff.; Ritchie Ovendale, "Britische Aussen- und Bündnispolitik 1949–1956," in *Nationale Aussen- und Bündnispolitik der Mitgliedstaaten,* ed. Norbert Wiggershaus and Winfried Heinemann (Munich: Oldenbourg, 2000), 129–51.

48. Michael B. Oren, "Faith and Fair-Mindedness. Lester B. Pearson and the Suez Crisis," *Diplomacy and Statecraft* 3 (1992): 56f.; Geoffrey A. H. Pearson, *Seize the Day: Lester B. Pearson and Crisis Diplomacy* (Ottawa: Carleton Univ. Press, 1993), 160.

49. Perkins tel. POLTO 986 to State Department, 3 Nov. 1956, RG 59, DF 1955–59, 740B.5/11–356.

50. State Department circular telegram 362 to Embassies in NATO countries, 6 Nov. 1956, RG 59, DF 1955–59, 740.5/11–656.

51. Pearson, *Seize the Day*, 29; letter of transmittal of the Report of the Committee of Three, 17 Nov. 1956, NISCA 4/5/8 C-M(56)126, NATO Brüssel.

52. As quoted in www.nato.int/docu/basictxt/b561213a.htm, accessed 25 July 2007.

53. Pearson, *Seize the Day*, 96f.

54. Milloy, *The Formation and Work*, 19.

55. Thoss "Der Beitritt der Bundesrepublik Deutschland," 230.

56. For a differing interpretation see Milloy, *The Formation and Work*, 20.

57. Cees Wiebes and Bert Zeeman: "'I don't need your handkerchiefs': Holland's Experience of Crisis Consultation in NATO," *International Affairs* 66 (1990): 95.

58. Pearson, *The International Years*, 97.

59. Maria Helene Schlösser, *Die Entstehungsgeschichte der NATO bis zum Beitritt der Bundesrepublik Deutschland* (Frankfurt: Lang, 1985), 699.

60. *Politische Konsultation*, ed. NATO-Informationsdienst (Paris: NATO, 1962); Pearson, *The International Years*, 69f.

61. Sinasac, "The Three Wise Men," 45.

62. Peyton V. Lyon, *NATO as a Diplomatic Instrument* (Toronto: Atlantic Council of Canada, 1970), 3f.; Robert E. Osgood, *Alliances and American Foreign Policy* (Baltimore: Johns Hopkins Univ. Press, 1968), 22, 51.

63. Lyon, *NATO as a Diplomatic Instrument*, 13.

64. Gustav Schmidt, "Vom Nordatlantischen Dreieck: Grossbritannien—USA—Kanada zum Trilateralismus: EG—USA—Japan. Der Strukturwandel der westlichen Welt und die politische Gestaltung der Dreiecksbeziehungen im Überblick," *Geschichte und Gegenwart* 7 (1988): 28.

65. Thoss, "Der Beitritt der Bundesrepublik Deutschland," 230.

4

Failed Rampart

NATO's Balkan Front

JOHN O. IATRIDES

The decision of the Atlantic Council in October 1951 to admit Turkey and Greece into its ranks ostensibly represented a significant expansion of the defense community's capabilities and, at the same time, a boon to its two new members. The enlargement made possible the protection of NATO's vitally important communication lines in the entire Mediterranean and established for the alliance a "Balkan front," extending its southern flank eastward from the Adriatic to the borders of Soviet Armenia and Georgia. For their part, Turkey and Greece, both recent targets of direct or indirect Soviet pressures, were brought behind NATO's nuclear security shield and provided with access to the vast economic, industrial, and military resources of the Atlantic community, especially those of the United States.[1] Thus, membership in NATO secured their place in the Western world and extended to them enormous benefits. Real protection from external attack, however, remained problematic.

Under NATO plans, the principal mission of the Balkan front was to block or at least impede the advance of Soviet forces into the eastern Mediterranean overland through Thrace or the breaching of the Turkish Straits. In addition, Turkey and Greece could assist in securing shipping lanes and communications in the eastern Mediterranean and in supporting operations of the U.S. Sixth Fleet in that area. In the event of a Soviet attack on West-Central Europe, the two Balkan allies were expected to enhance NATO's operational capabilities by strengthening its southern flank, forcing the dispersion of enemy troops and threatening to exact a heavy price from the left flank of the invading armies. Finally, and most important, the Balkan front was responsible for the defense of Greece and Turkey, specifically against attack from or through Bulgaria.

According to regional military authorities, the tasks outlined above could be achieved if certain key prerequisites were put in place. First, the adoption in the Balkans of a forward defense strategy (defense at the border), which NATO had already instituted for Western Europe, would enable Greece and Turkey to hold western (Greek) and eastern (Turkish) Thrace, the narrow strip of land along the Aegean linking the two neighbors. Second, the establishment of a major NATO naval base in the Aegean would facilitate the ability of fast patrol and torpedo boats to intercept Soviet warships attempting to enter the eastern Mediterranean. Third, in the event of attack through Bulgaria, the cooperation of Yugoslavia's armed forces would be needed to assist Greece and Turkey in holding the line in Thrace by forming a strong and continuous front.[2]

As students of NATO know, none of these essential prerequisites materialized. Consequently, almost from its inception the Balkan front consisted of periodic planning sessions and impressive-sounding allied headquarters commanding mostly inadequate and unintegrated national forces. The reasons for this failure are many and can only be briefly outlined here.

No Forward Defense

In 1952 Greek military planners sought NATO's formal approval to advance the country's main defense line closer to the Bulgarian border (along the Nestos River) and implement the strategy of forward defense. Such a move would enable Greece and Turkey to coordinate their efforts closely in defending all of Thrace and protecting the western flank of the Turkish Straits. It would also compel the enemy to concentrate troops on Bulgarian soil in preparation for attack, making them attractive targets for NATO's air power and projected tactical nuclear weapons. Otherwise, if the Greek defense line remained at its designated position (the Struma River), defending Thrace and eastern Macedonia would be impossible and any nuclear explosions would devastate Greek territory.

At the regional level NATO planners were receptive to Greek arguments for the adoption of forward defense in the Balkans and for a concerted allied effort to defend all of Thrace. Preoccupied with other priorities, however, higher authorities would not agree to supply Greece with the requisite weapons for such a difficult undertaking: large numbers of medium tanks, heavy artillery, fighter-bombers, and modern warships. In NATO's original plans, which adopted American strategic considerations, the primary mission of the Greek armed forces was to provide for internal security; defense against external attack ("repelling an attack by satellite forces augmented by guerrillas") was viewed as a secondary task.[3] From the outset, Greek defense capabilities against external attack (forward defense) required substantial support from NATO. Although the Greek armed forces improved greatly over the years, forward defense remained beyond their capabilities. By contrast, the much larger but poorly equipped Turkish army's principal responsibility was to defend the country's long borders against Soviet attack while maintaining contact with allied forces in the Mediterranean. This was to be a veritable "mission impossible."

For the Greek military forces, compelled to retain their principal defense line on the Struma River, the failure to adopt forward defense in the Balkans clearly indicated that NATO's strategic priorities differed substantially from Greece's defense needs. In 1956, Prime Minister Constantine Karamanlis, a staunch supporter of NATO, complained bitterly that four years of membership in the alliance had done virtually nothing to improve his country's defenses. Specifically, he asserted that, in the event of an attack through Bulgaria, the Greek army would be forced to abandon eastern Macedonia and western Thrace to the enemy, thereby breaking off contact with the Turkish forces and destroying NATO's Balkan front.[4]

No NATO Naval Base in the Aegean

An important element of the Balkan front was the chain of Greek islands in the Aegean that could be used as a barrier to harass and slow down an advancing Soviet fleet. In 1953, after careful study, CINCMED (Commander in Chief Mediterranean) planners selected Leros as the location of a proposed major NATO naval base. After first trying to have the base built on its own coast, however, Turkey opposed the plan for the Leros base on the grounds that it represented a security concern for Turkey and would compromise Greek-Turkish relations. As the Turkish ambassador to the United States put it, the fortification of Leros "might start a Greek campaign to fortify the rest [of the Dodecanese islands, demilitarized in 1947]. Turkish public opinion would be convinced that this was only another step in Greece's ambitions and Turkey would strongly oppose such a move. The Greek press would launch another campaign vilifying the Turks. Inflamed public opinion on both sides might wreck Greek-Turkish cooperation and threaten a breach too wide to heal."[5] In view of Turkey's objections, SHAPE (Supreme Headquarters Allied Powers Europe) instructed NATO's Standing Group to reexamine the issue from a political point of view. Nevertheless, NATO's military planners continued to insist that Leros was the best location.[6] At the December 1954 session of the Atlantic Council, Turkey's representative restated his government's objections, in effect vetoing the Leros project. When the representatives of the United States and Britain expressed concern that the issue would damage Greek-Turkish relations, the project was derailed and NATO did not acquire a naval base in the Aegean.

The controversy over Leros brought to the surface the deep-seated resentment felt by many Turks that virtually all the Aegean islands, some very close to the Asia Minor coast and once Turkish possessions, were now Greek. In 1947, as the Dodecanese islands (which had fallen under Italian control in 1911–12) were about to be ceded to Greece by the victorious Allies, the Turkish foreign ministry approached the British Foreign Office, inquiring "if it were not possible for Turkey to regain control of those islands whose coastal waters overlapped with Turkey's coastal waters and which can be clearly seen from the [Turkish] mainland." According to the Turkish diplomat involved, the "personal response" from Foreign Secretary Ernest Bevin was that "the UK felt Turkey had a good case but the time for discussion of this matter was not propitious."[7] In the 1950s, demands that British-controlled Cyprus be united with Greece revived in Turkish minds the perception of yet another of their former territories coveted by the Greeks. In later years, friction over the islands would assume a new dimension when both Greece and Turkey became involved in oil exploration in the Aegean, raising thorny questions about maritime boundaries, economic zones, and the limits of the continental shelf.[8]

No Military Cooperation with Yugoslavia

Following the outbreak of the Korean conflict and as Cold War tensions mounted, Bulgaria emerged as a potential spearhead for a probing Soviet attack in southern Europe and the eastern Mediterranean. Bulgaria's armed forces were strengthened and placed under Soviet commanders, while Soviet troops in Romania and Hungary were reinforced in numbers and firepower. In view of such ominous signs, the advantages of military cooperation among Greece, Yugoslavia, and Turkey became all too obvious.[9] During 1950–52 secret Greek proposals to the Tito regime for bilateral military cooperation in the event of Soviet aggression through Bulgaria received favorable responses, and Turkey soon joined in negotiations for a tripartite military pact. Progress proved slow and arduous, in part because the Greek and Turkish governments felt compelled at every step of the way to secure the consent of the United States and, ultimately, of NATO.

This was to prove a difficult task. On the one hand, although the United States, Britain, and France expressed support for the proposed tripartite cooperation, they opposed any concrete military commitments to Yugoslavia that might expand or complicate NATO's responsibilities in the Balkan region. On the other hand, Italy, then involved in a bitter dispute with Yugoslavia over Trieste, sought to derail tripartite military cooperation altogether and threatened to veto any NATO ties to Yugoslavia. The Italians were also determined to prevent Greece and Turkey from sharing intelligence obtained through NATO channels with Yugoslavia.[10]

Despite the less than propitious diplomatic environment, negotiations for a tripartite pact moved forward, with Belgrade at times taking the lead. On 20 February 1953 the Yugoslavs proposed that the soon-to-be-signed treaty contain explicit provisions for military cooperation. Although the Greeks were inclined to agree, the Turks reserved judgment pending Washington's position on the matter. They did not have long to wait.

The Department of State advised the Greek and Turkish governments: "In order to avoid NATO and other implications, commitment must in our view go no further than commitment to consult as to such common measures as might be required, and not extend to commitment to lend assistance."[11] Accordingly, under the Treaty of Friendship and Collaboration, formally concluded in Ankara on 28 February 1953, the three signatories pledged to cooperate through regular consultation in preserving their freedom, independence, and territorial integrity against outside aggression. In short, although consultations and planning were to continue, Greece and Turkey could not commit themselves to military cooperation with Yugoslavia without NATO's prior approval.[12]

Before the end of 1953, the Greek general staff, preoccupied as always with the defense of Thrace against attack through Bulgaria, proposed to incorporate in the Treaty of Ankara a new agreement providing for automatic activation of plans for military cooperation in the event any one of the three partners were attacked in their "common space" along their borders with Bulgaria. If the attack originated elsewhere but was carried out through Bulgaria, the signatories not attacked would be committed to take "expediency measures" and would consult with NATO before resorting to military action. Once again, however, Washington would give its consent only if tripartite military planning remained "on a contingent basis to become binding only if and when political commitment [is] given." Moreover, in any military arrangements SACEUR (Supreme Allied Commandor Europe) was to serve as "the channel for Greeks and Turks to coordinate with NATO their planning with Yugoslavs."[13] When it appeared that U.S. concerns might not be receiving proper attention, the three Balkan governments were warned that their "over-hasty furtherance of this cooperation at this time might well upset the very delicate Trieste negotiations."[14]

For all its concerns, the United States did not wish to stop all progress or to see other NATO allies interject themselves too forcefully in the tripartite negotiations. The Department of State advised the British and French governments to "carefully avoid giving impression [of] interference which might well be resented and jeopardize present opportunity we have for moderating development." Specifically, it pointed out that the North Atlantic Treaty did not prohibit alliances between NATO and non-NATO states nor grant NATO members veto power over an alliance negotiated by other NATO members. Moreover, a "Greek-Turkish-Yugoslav military alliance [is] inevitable and not likely [to] be delayed indefinitely." Therefore, "development [of] alliance terms should be closely followed with a view to corrective action in event of (a) any possible conflict with NAT and (b) any possible imbalance of obligations especially relative to NATO implications." Finally, "Greece and Turkey should present alliance plans in fullest possible detail to NAC sufficiently in advance of signature to give NATO partners feeling their views, if any, will be given friendly consideration."[15]

On 29 July 1954 Greece and Turkey submitted to the North Atlantic Council the text of their new agreement with Yugoslavia. The Greek representative explained that the new pact committed Yugoslavia to side with the Western alliance if a NATO member were attacked but that NATO assumed no formal obligation to defend Yugoslavia. Turkey's representative expressed the hope that Italy would join the Balkan pact. After much discussion the council members voiced their approval of the new tripartite agreement.[16]

Despite its bolder title, the Treaty of Alliance, Political Cooperation and Mutual Assistance signed at Bled, Yugoslavia, on 9 August 1954 added little of substance to the Treaty of Ankara.[17] Plans for tripartite military cooperation against attack from or through Bulgaria were finalized, yet Greece and Turkey could not activate them without NATO's prior approval. Moreover, the lingering reluctance of most NATO members to support allied entanglements in the Balkans, combined with NATO's rule of unanimity, made it anything but certain that such approval would be forthcoming. In any event, the 1954 Balkan alliance was virtually stillborn. Following Stalin's death and Nikita Khrushchev's dramatic visit to Yugoslavia in May 1955, Tito's government lost interest in military cooperation with NATO members.[18] The dramatic deterioration in Greek-Turkish relations in the fall of 1955, however, delivered the deathblow to the tripartite pact.

AFSOUTH: NATO's Soft Underbelly

The fragility of the Balkan front also reflected the weaknesses of AFSOUTH (Allied Forces Southern Europe), to which Turkey and Greece were assigned. From the outset, the ability of AFSOUTH's national components to function as a team in the event of war was dubious at best. The southern flank, whose members had no tradition of military cooperation, lacked continuity on land and defense in depth. It was little more than a patchwork of national forces nominally integrated under regional allied commanders in headquarters created to accommodate political sensitivities as much as military strategy. Its only powerful element that could provide strength and continuity at sea, the U.S. Sixth Fleet, lay outside NATO's command structure. Moreover, in the event of imminent hostilities the Sixth Fleet was to withdraw west of Malta in preparation for a massive counterattack against Warsaw Pact targets. This move would leave Turkey and Greece, and possibly Italy as well, to fend for themselves, since reinforcing or supplying them during wartime was expected to be all but impossible. Simply put, NATO could possibly avenge, but could not defend, Turkey and Greece against Soviet aggression.

It can, of course, be argued that NATO's principal value has been its role as a deterrent against aggression, but to be credible deterrence must be based on the capability to deliver to the aggressor a punishing counterblow. That was the significance of stationing American troops in Western Europe as an extension of American power. In the absence of such capacity to retaliate, deterrence can be little more than dangerous self-deception. In the case of the Balkan front, NATO's counterblow was almost certain to come only after Greece and Turkey had been effectively annihilated.

After other organizational options were found to be unsatisfactory, a separate command for the armies of Turkey and Greece, LANDSOUTHEAST (Land Forces Southeastern Europe), was established in Izmir under an American officer with a Turk and a Greek as deputies, with an advance (later "rapid deployment") post in Thessaloniki. The Turkish and Greek air forces and navies were placed under already existing and much stronger regional commands both headquartered in Naples, AIRSOUTH and NAVSOUTH.[19] These allied commands functioned as planned only until the fall of 1955, when, for all practical purposes, the Balkan front ceased to exist.

Greek-Turkish Disputes and NATO

Insecure and vulnerable to the Soviet menace, NATO's new members appeared eager to move beyond their age-old conflicts and build a new relationship based on cooperation and trust. With American support and guidance the regional commands in Izmir and Thessaloniki were set up and functioning in 1953, and NATO's Balkan front became a reality. But the signs of trouble were unmistakable. The decision of the Greek government in 1954 to bring the Cyprus issue to the United Nations put Greece on a collision course with three of its most important allies: Britain, Turkey, and the United States. Turkey's veto of a NATO base on Leros angered Greek political and military authorities. In 1954, even as the tripartite pact was receiving favorable publicity, relations between Athens and Ankara showed signs of severe strain over Cyprus and would soon lead to violence.

On 6 September 1955, bloody anti-Greek riots in Istanbul and Izmir, which years later were shown to have been instigated by the Turkish authorities, decimated Turkey's Greek minority. Especially disturbing to Greek officials was the attack on the Greek consulate in Izmir and the physical abuse of Greek officers serving in the NATO headquarters, soon followed by the burglarizing of the Greek embassy in Ankara, in which classified documents and code books were taken.[20] Athens lodged strong protests with Ankara and NATO and announced that its armed forces would not participate in NATO exercises until those responsible for the riots were punished and their victims compensated. On 18 October Athens withdrew its officers in Izmir and recalled the Greek contingent in Korea.[21]

Despite the setbacks, Prime Minister Karamanlis remained determined to improve Greece's position in NATO and repair relations with Ankara. In particular, he hoped to persuade the United States to support the enlargement of the NATO Council's authority to include mediation in disputes between allies. He missed no opportunity to present his arguments to American and European leaders, but to no avail. Washington's position remained that it could not dictate to its allies and that the solution of Greek-Turkish disputes could be achieved through informal and friendly negotiations among the parties directly involved rather than through the rigid procedures of the Atlantic Council.[22]

Karamanlis's disappointment with NATO would be all too evident during the rest of his political career. In late 1961, when the Kennedy administration informed the Greek prime minister that the United States would consider a Soviet or Bulgarian attack on Greece as falling under article 5 of the North Atlantic Treaty, he inquired whether the message constituted a "direct US assurance" or a NATO guarantee. Told that it was the latter, he replied dismissively that "he frankly lacks confidence in ability of NATO to come immediately to aid of Greece" in view of the "pulling and hauling involved in all NATO decisions."[23] More than a decade later, following Turkey's invasion of Cyprus during the summer of 1974, the prospect of full-scale war between Greece and Turkey would once again cause Karamanlis to express bitterness over NATO's failure to intervene.

Turkey's Grievances Against NATO

Turkey had its share of problems with the United States and NATO, especially over issues of financial assistance for defense and the modernization of its armed forces. In 1962, the Cuban missile crisis severely tested Turkey's confidence in its allies, and especially the United States. In the complex U.S.-Soviet negotiations to defuse the crisis, the presence in Turkey of fifteen Jupiter intermediate-range ballistic missiles became a sticking point when Chairman Nikita Khrushchev demanded their removal in exchange for the withdrawal of the Soviet missiles from Cuba. Although the nuclear warheads had remained under American control, the missiles themselves were under Turkish command and integrated into NATO plans for the defense of Turkey. Thus, the removal of the Jupiters was bound to be resented by Turkey and might lead other NATO allies to fear that in another U.S.-Soviet crisis they might have to surrender some of their NATO-provided weapons. According to Ankara's representative on the Atlantic Council, "Turkey regards these Jupiters as symbol of alliance's determination to use atomic weapons against Russian attack on Turkey whether by large conventional or nuclear forces." For his part, President Kennedy feared that if the United States invaded Cuba to remove the Soviet missiles, the Soviet Union might retaliate by attacking Jupiter missiles in Turkey and Italy. He therefore ordered that the Jupiters in Turkey were not to be fired without specific authorization from the White House; if they came under

Soviet attack, they were to be destroyed or made inoperative. The order was to be kept secret from all NATO allies.[24]

In place of the Jupiters, in December 1962 the United States proposed the creation of a pilot multilateral sea-based nuclear force for AFSOUTH, using Polaris submarines in whose targeting Turkey, Italy, and Greece might participate. Unimpressed by the proposal, Ankara's representative declared that the "substitution of more secure weapon system for Jupiters must take into account all political and military factors" and that Turkey's confidence in its allies was at stake.[25] In the end, no new multilateral nuclear force was created. Instead, a Polaris submarine from the Sixth Fleet took up station in the eastern Mediterranean.

Turkey's frustration with the United States and NATO intensified in June 1964 when, reacting to renewed violence in Cyprus, the government of Prime Minister İsmet İnönü prepared to invade the troubled island and asked for Washington's "understanding attitude." An American official characterized President Lyndon B. Johnson's response as "the most brutal diplomatic note I have ever seen . . . the diplomatic equivalent of an atomic bomb."[26] Johnson pointed out to İnönü that the invasion of Cyprus would spark war between Turkey and Greece and that membership in the Atlantic alliance "in its very essence, means that NATO countries will not wage war on each other." Moreover, an invasion could lead to a direct Soviet involvement, and "your NATO Allies have not had a chance to consider whether they have an obligation to protect Turkey against the Soviet Union if Turkey takes up a step which results in Soviet intervention without the full consent and understanding of the NATO Allies."[27] Unwilling to defy Washington, the İnönü government called off the operation.

Greece Withdraws from All NATO Commands

In an ironic twist, the coup of 21 April 1967 that imposed a military dictatorship on Greece was carried out by activating a NATO-approved contingency plan, code-named Prometheus, for dealing with an internal upheaval. Although the Atlantic Council remained silent, individual members denounced the junta and urged that a scheduled allied exercise in Greece be canceled in protest. Suggestions that the junta be ostracized were deflected by the Department of State, which took the position that "[i]t is essential that we maintain Greece as an active and functioning member of NATO . . . [and] avoid pressing Greece in the direction of the French with their lukewarm and unhelpful posture in a NATO context."[28] For its part, under Colonel George Papadopoulos the junta missed no opportunity to proclaim its loyalty to the Western alliance and to the United States, which was granted important home-porting privileges, as well as missile storage facilities and early warning radar and communications stations. Greek officers, however, did not return to NATO's command posts in Izmir.

In July 1974, Turkey's invasion of Cyprus caused the collapse of the Greek junta, brought Greek-Turkish relations once again to the brink of war, and led to the hasty recall of Karamanlis from self-imposed exile. It also revealed the sorry condition to which the military dictatorship had brought the Greek armed forces. Orders to mobilize reserves turned into fiascoes as weapons and equipment of every kind could not be found and the army's command structure disintegrated. When Karamanlis asked whether the navy and air force could strike at Turkish targets in Cyprus, he was told that they could not. As Turkish troops in Cyprus continued their advance, in the process decimating the small contingent of Greek troops, he requested an emergency meeting of the Atlantic Council, only to be told that Secretary General Joseph M.A.H. Luns and council members were about to begin their summer holidays or were otherwise too busy to meet on short notice.[29] For years afterward Karamanlis would complain bitterly that while Turkey was invading Cyprus, Greece's NATO allies chose to go on vacation.

When Luns finally offered to mediate, the Turkish government would not receive him. Thereupon, Karamanlis ordered the recall of Greek representatives from NATO commands. In a letter to all NATO governments he charged that in the ongoing crisis in Cyprus the alliance had failed to live up to its obligations and had demonstrated a "strange and surprising indifference, confining itself to the role of a simple spectator." He added, "When the Atlantic Alliance is unable to avert the armed clash between two of its members, it is even more incapable of protecting them against possible external aggression." Accordingly, to defend its independence, Greece was restoring to national command its armed forces assigned to NATO and would henceforth exercise full sovereignty over its airspace and territorial waters. Greece, he declared, would return to NATO's military structure only when Turkish troops had been removed from Cyprus.[30] Three years later, at the 1977 NATO summit, Karamanlis warned his counterparts that the "pro-Turkish disposition" of Luns and of "certain defense ministers" could damage the southeastern flank of the alliance.[31] The following year he again chided the NATO Council members: "We cannot be talking of world order and peace when we cannot secure peace within the ranks of the Alliance."[32] When Luns proposed that the final communiqué of the 1978 NATO summit include a paragraph opposing the American embargo on military assistance to Turkey, a furious Karamanlis sent word to President Jimmy Carter that such a statement would force him to withdraw from the summit and terminate Greece's membership in NATO. In the end, the communiqué made no mention of the embargo.[33]

Although Karamanlis's sense of frustration and disappointment with NATO's reaction to his difficulties was genuine, it is safe to assume that he never seriously considered pulling out of the alliance altogether. He believed to the end that NATO membership was essential not only for the security of the country but also for positive confirmation of Greece's proper place among the nations of the Western world. Thus, in September 1958, when Makarios III, archbishop and later president of Cyprus, suggested to him that Greece might threaten to leave NATO, Karamanlis cut him short: his government was "not prepared to pursue a policy of getting out of NATO. . . . It would be unpardonable to endanger the security of free Greece in order to expedite the solution of the Cyprus [problem]. . . . [I]f Greece abandons its alliances, it will risk extinction as a free country. But without a free Greece there can be no thought of freedom for Cyprus."[34]

As the Turkish occupation of northern Cyprus continued, Greek officials realized that withdrawing from NATO's military structure had, if anything, placed Greece's interests in the Aegean in greater danger. Specifically, in the absence of Greek representatives, command of LANDSOUTHEAST and SIXATAF (Sixth Allied Tactical Air Force) was assumed by Turkish officers (with American deputies). In place of the naval headquarters (COMEDEAST, Commander Eastern Mediterranean), previously under Greek command, NATO planners proposed to create an integrated task force in which Turkey's role was bound to emerge predominant. In the meantime, tensions between Greece and Turkey mounted, forcing commercial carriers to discontinue flights over the Aegean.

Reversing course, in October 1975 the Karamanlis government offered to reintegrate Greece's armed forces in NATO on the basis of the pre-1974 division of operational responsibilities in the Aegean. In addition, during peacetime Greek armed forces would remain exclusively under national authority, while in the event of a general war there would be full cooperation with NATO through mechanisms to be put in place in advance. Also, in all circumstances NATO activities on Greek territory would require the prior consent of the Greek government, and American bases in Greece would be placed under Greek command.[35] While not pleased with the Greek terms, NATO authorities were willing to discuss them further. Turkey, however, took the position that Greece would not be allowed to return before new arrangements for operational responsibilities in the Aegean had been agreed upon.[36] For the next five years Greece's return to NATO would, in effect, be vetoed by Ankara.

At the urging of Secretary General Luns, SACEUR, General Alexander Haig during 1977–1979 and then General Bernard W. Rogers in 1979–1980, sought to negotiate with Athens and Ankara several complex formulas for the reintegration of the Greek armed forces into NATO's military command structure. The Greek and Turkish governments took turns rejecting the final products of these negotiations.[37] At one point, on a visit to Washington for a meeting of the Atlantic Council, Karamanlis warned the American government that if Ankara continued to veto Haig's proposal, Greece would be compelled to withdraw its offer to return to NATO's military structure, "in which case, the next step would be the complete departure of Greece" from the alliance.[38] As it turned out, the last two proposals made under Haig and two more by his successor, Rogers, were rejected by the Karamanlis government as the terms contained in each new plan were increasingly less favorable to Athens. In February 1980, a Greek official disclosed that the latest NATO proposal was unacceptable because it was "based on the assumption that a permanent military solution for the complete reintegration of Greece in NATO's military structure is neither possible nor desirable until the disputes between Greece and Turkey on political issues have been resolved."[39]

Greece Returns to NATO's Commands

The break in the impasse came unexpectedly and from the Turkish side. In September 1980, following the overthrow of the Ankara government by military coup, and possibly concerned over the Soviet invasion of Afghanistan and renewed tension in the Middle East, the new Turkish foreign minister signaled his government's willingness to accept temporary arrangements that would facilitate the reintegration of Greece in allied commands before disputes over operational boundaries in the Aegean were resolved.[40] General Rogers, who had continued his mediation efforts, visited Ankara on 17 October and secured the approval of General Kenan Evren, the head of the military government, of a vaguely worded and elastic formula for the return of the Greek armed forces to NATO's military command structure. The Greek parliament approved the Rogers Plan on 24 October 1980, thereby formally ratifying the agreement.

A key element in the Rogers Plan, first proposed under the Haig-Davos agreement of May 1978 but rejected by Turkey, was the establishment in Larissa (in central Greece) of new allied headquarters for land forces (LANDSOUTHEAST) and for air forces (SEVENATAF, Seventh Allied Tactical Air Force), to share command and control responsibilities with the already existing headquarters in Izmir. Pending a permanent settlement of Greek-Turkish disputes concerning the Aegean, however, AFSOUTH was to determine the operational authority of the two Balkan allies in that region.[41] The vagueness of the Rogers Plan, whose terms were not made public, was indicated by remarks to parliament by the new Greek prime minister, George Rallis: "[I]t is clear that the provisions [of the Rogers Plan] suit us completely because, without saying so verbally, we return to NATO under the regime of 1974, and all the unresolved issues would be discussed and no decision can be taken if we do not agree since, as is known, if we cast a 'veto' a decision cannot be taken."[42]

The Rogers Plan defused the most volatile element in the Greek-Turkish conflict but also highlighted the urgent need for a more durable settlement of outstanding differences. Because neither side was prepared to yield on the key issues, the dispute over operational control in the Aegean remained unsolved and the newly created NATO headquarters in Larissa, intended to serve as the twin to that in Izmir, were "allied" in name only. Greece and Turkey continued to behave as adversaries, and the possibility of violence between them remained real. Moreover, Greece's estrangement from the Atlantic alliance intensified following the electoral victory of the socialist PASOK Party in October 1981. The new prime minister, Andreas Papandreou, had come to power largely on a strongly anti-American and anti-NATO platform. In December 1981, at his first appearance at a NATO summit, Papandreou challenged the alliance to guarantee the territorial integrity of its members against "every threat, from whatever side it emanates." When Turkey blocked the proposal, Greece vetoed the meeting's traditional final communiqué.[43] In November 1982, effectively denouncing the Rogers Plan, Papandreou announced his government's intention "to disengage ourselves from NATO's military wing. . . . We do not feel there is a danger for us from the [Communist] north, unless of course there is a world war in progress. Our problem lies in the east [Turkey]. . . . And NATO cannot help us. Therefore, Greek national strategy is clearly different from that of NATO."[44] The following year, Papandreou declared that Greek membership in NATO had been rendered "inactive," limited to meetings of special concern to the Greek government.

Squaring Off Between NATO Allies

By the mid-1980s the confrontation between Greece and Turkey had become formalized in ways that rendered virtually meaningless their status as NATO allies. In January 1985 the Papandreou government announced a new defense doctrine whose declared objective was to strengthen and redeploy its armed forces so as to assure the country's defenses against Turkey. The primary mission of the new "defensive-offensive strategy" was to protect Greek Thrace and all Greek-inhabited islands from Turkey: an attack on even the smallest inhabited island would trigger full-scale war. Although Greece would not strike first, in the event of war the Greek armed forces would attempt to inflict the heaviest possible damage to Turkey's military and war-making capabilities. The employment of surface-to-surface missiles and of large-scale raids on the Turkish coast was to be an integral part of the new strategy. The concept of "Total Peoples' Defense" was also introduced, coupled with an expansion of the domestic arms industry so as to reduce drastically the country's dependence on foreign supplies.[45] In September 1986 Papandreou visited Bulgaria, and the two governments signed a declaration of friendship, good neighborliness, and cooperation under which the two sides agreed to consult in the event of threats of aggression against one of them. There was speculation that the agreement included a secret understanding on military cooperation.[46] Greek defense commitments were formally expanded in 1994 under the "Doctrine of the Joint Defense Area" concluded with the Republic of Cyprus. Under that agreement, a Turkish attack on the Republic of Cyprus would constitute for Greece a casus belli.[47] According to Greek Ministry of Defense publications, the primary mission of the nation's armed forces was to deter "the Turkish threat and, secondarily, dangers from other directions."[48]

As for Turkey, according to reports published in the 1980s, its four army corps were deployed as follows: the Third, with a 50 percent level of readiness, was positioned to protect the border with the Soviet Union; the Second was employed in the occupation of northern Cyprus, while the First, with an 80–100 percent level of readiness, was deployed in eastern Thrace; the Fourth, named the "Army of the Aegean" and retained outside NATO's military structure, was positioned along the country's coast facing the nearby Greek islands.[49]

In December 1996, the serious confrontation over the barren and uninhabited Imia islet (in the Dodecanese) demonstrated how quickly an otherwise insignificant incident could escalate to serious violence. For several tense days and nights, units of the navies and air forces of Greece and Turkey circled the barren rocks, their weapons trained on each other, while ultranationalist sentiment in both countries demanded satisfaction. Although American pressure on Athens and Ankara, including calls from President Bill Clinton, compelled the two sides to back down, tensions remained high.[50] In June 1996 Ankara's representative at AFSOUTH followed with a request that Gavdos, a small Greek island south of Crete, be excluded from a planned NATO exercise because it constituted "disputed area."[51]

In recent years, although their principal disputes remain unresolved, tensions between NATO's Balkan allies have eased considerably and the threat of armed confrontation has all but disappeared. Greece and Turkey played modest roles in NATO operations in Kosovo, Albania, and Macedonia. Despite the setback in April 2004, when a UN plan for the reunification of the island was rejected by the Greek Cypriots, there is still hope that the Cyprus problem will continue to inch its way toward some form of accommodation. Turkey's desire to join the European Union, of which the Republic of Cyprus is now a member, could have a calming effect on relations between Athens and Ankara. Equally important, political developments in East-Central Europe, especially the entry of former Warsaw Pact members into the Atlantic alliance, have rendered almost irrelevant questions of NATO's Balkan-Aegean headquarters and delimitation of operational responsibilities. NATO's Balkan front, in a state of virtual paralysis for almost thirty years, shows no signs of life and there is good reason to believe that the alliance is content to leave matters as they are.

Conclusions

NATO's intrabloc feuds were, of course, not confined to the Balkan region. Nor were Greece and Turkey the only members for whom narrowly defined national interests and clashing aspirations overshadowed support of the alliance's strategic goals and unity of purpose. The behavior of other allies—and of France in particular—was more damaging to NATO's military capabilities than Greek-Turkish confrontations. In the final analysis, the Balkan front was from the outset weak and expendable, representing one of SACEUR's lowest priorities.

What made the disputes between Greece and Turkey unique was the fact that they periodically brought the two neighbors perilously close to the brink of war while as an institution NATO appeared helpless to the point of distraction. That war did not occur was due partly to the determination of both Greek and Turkish governments to avoid it if at all possible, as well as to the direct intervention of the United States. In fact, the formal collapse of NATO's Balkan front commands was averted by the continued presence of American military personnel and of the U.S. Sixth Fleet. Since bringing Turkey and Greece into NATO, Washington has been playing the role of Dutch uncle, keeping its two quarreling wards from going too far in their periodic slugfests.

Despite the obvious need to develop mechanisms for the resolution of conflicts between member states, the Atlantic Council made no attempt to establish them. While most NATO members had no wish to become involved in regional disputes, such as those dividing Greece and Turkey, the United States preferred to deal with them directly, without the meddlesome influence of allies or of international bodies. The occasional experiments in mediation undertaken by the secretary general and SACEUR were narrowly confined to technical issues and produced modest results despite the obvious identification of the United States with such efforts.

Thus, having been built atop the fault line of clashing Greek-Turkish interests, historical claims, and mutual suspicions, the Balkan front remained a shaky and ineffective structure that the Atlantic alliance could not repair. To be sure, on balance, Greece and Turkey benefited greatly from their status as NATO members. Nevertheless, the inability of the alliance to provide them with credible protection against the Soviet bloc and to assist them in reconciling their differences perpetuated their sense of insecurity and isolation. In turn, the persistent feeling of vulnerability and victimization in their bilateral relations strengthened their attachment to traditional concepts of territorial imperatives and self-imposed national security priorities. Their leaders, political and cultural elites, and the media made no attempt to lift the two nations above their history's poisonous legacy. On the contrary, they very often added fuel to the fire with their irresponsible rhetoric and distortion of the facts. The result was a power struggle that acquired its own dynamics and a contest that neither could win.

Greece and Turkey are hardly unique in their inability to resolve, peacefully and on their own, clashing interests, age-old disputes, and historical antagonisms. NATO's difficulties with its Balkan members offer lessons that are significant, particularly in the context of the ongoing enlargement of the Atlantic community.

Notes

1. On the entry of Turkey and Greece in NATO see U.S. Department of State, *Foreign Relations of the United States, 1951* (Washington, D.C.: G.P.O., 1982), 3:460–61 (hereafter *FRUS*, with year and volume number); Ekavi Athanassopoulou, *Turkey. Anglo-American Security Interests, 1945–1952: The First Enlargement of NATO* (London: Frank Cass, 1999); Yiannis Stefanidis, *Apo ton Emfylio ston Psychro Polemo* (Athens: Proskinio, 1999), 53–91.

2. The author served with the Hellenic National Defense General Staff as liaison officer with NATO (1955–1956) and with the press and information department of the prime minister's office (1956–1958). In part this chapter is based on personal notes and recollections. The author is grateful to Professor Evanthis Hatzivassiliou of the University of Athens for his constructive criticism.

3. National Security Council (NSC) 103/1, 14 Feb. 1951, "The Position of the United States with Respect to Greece" (partially declassified 19 Sept. 1977).

4. *Constantinos Karamanlis. Archeio. Gegonota kai Keimena* (hereafter *Karamanlis Archive*), II, 198.

5. General Records of the Department of State, Record Group 59, file 781.022/11–1554 CSEM, National Archives II, College Park, Md.

6. Ibid., aide memoire attached (emphasis added). Detailed discussion in Yiannis Stefanidis, *Asymmetroi etairoi* (Athens: Pataki, 2002), 231–33.

7. Department of State, RG 59, file 781.022/1554. Lord Bullock, Bevin's biographer, wrote: "My guess is that Bevin did not take the matter all that seriously, and that his remarks were intended simply as a polite way of shelving the question." Letter to the author, 23 Sept. 1986.

8. See the collection of essays in Theodore C. Kariotis, ed., *Greece and the Law of the Sea* (The Hague: Martinus Nijhoff, 1997).

9. John O. Iatrides, *Balkan Triangle: Birth and Decline of an Alliance Across Ideological Boundaries* (The Hague: Mouton, 1968), 52–85.

10. *FRUS, 1952–1954* (Washington, D.C.: G.P.O., 1988), 8:590–91.

11. Ibid., 624.

12. Text of the treaty and analysis in Iatrides, *Balkan Triangle*, appendix A, 104–13.

13. *FRUS, 1952–1954*, 8:636–39.

14. Ibid., 644.

15. Ibid., 653–54.

16. Ibid., 671–73.

17. For the text of the treaty and analysis see Iatrides, *Balkan Triangle*, appendix B, 138–42.

18. Ibid., 163.

19. Lord Ismay, *NATO. The First Five Years: 1949–1954* (NATO publication, n.d.), 73.

20. Iatrides, *Balkan Triangle*, 67–71; *Karamanlis Archive* II, 501.

21. *Karamanlis Archive* I, 280.

22. *Karamanlis Archive* II, 194–99; *FRUS, 1955–1957* (Washington, D.C.: G.P.O., 1989), 24:577–78.

23. *FRUS, 1961–1963* (Washington, D.C.: G.P.O., 1994), 16:616–17.

24. Graham Alison and Philip Zelikow, *Essence of Decision* (New York: Longman, 1999), 197–201.

25. *FRUS, 1961–1963*, 16:738–41.

26. Thomas Schoenbaum, *Waging Peace and War: Dean Rusk in the Truman, Kennedy and Johnson Years* (New York: Simon & Schuster, 1988), 419.

27. *FRUS, 1964–1968* (Washington, D.C.: G.P.O., 1999), 15:107–11.

28. *FRUS, 1964–1968* (Washington, D.C.: G.P.O., 2002), 16:624–25.

29. *Karamanlis Archive* VIII, 89.

30. *Karamanlis Archive* VII, 131.

31. *Karamanlis Archive* X, 64.

32. Ibid., 238–39.

33. Ibid., 240–42.

34. *Karamanlis Archive* III, 227–29.

35. *Karamanlis Archive* IX, 77.

36. S. Victor Papacosma, "Greece and NATO," in *NATO and the Mediterranean,* ed. Lawrence S. Kaplan, Robert W. Clawson, and Raimondo Luraghi (Wilmington, Del.: Scholarly Resources, 1985), 204.

37. On the Haig proposals and their fate see *Karamanlis Archive* X, 228–29, 353, 363, 383, and XI, 58–59, 113–19. On the Rogers proposals see *Karamanlis Archive* XI, 285, 390.

38. *Karamanlis Archive* X, 353.

39. *Karamanlis Archive* XI, 390.

40. Tozun Bahcheli, *Greek-Turkish Relations Since 1955* (London: Westview Press, 1990), 149; Papacosma, "Greece and NATO," 206.

41. Bahcheli, *Greek-Turkish Relations,* 149.

42. *Karamanlis Archive* XII, 50.

43. John O. Iatrides, "Papandreou's Foreign Policy," in *The Greek Socialist Experiment. Papandreou's Greece, 1981–1989,* ed. Theodore C. Kariotis (New York: Pella, 1992), 153.

44. Ibid., 154.

45. Thanos P. Dokos, "Greece in a Changing Strategic Setting," in *Greece in the Twentieth Century,* ed. Theodore A. Couloumbis, Theodore Kariotis, and Fotini Bellou (London: Frank Cass, 2003), 54; George J. Tsoumis, "The Defense Policies of PASOK," in *Greece Under Socialism: A NATO Ally Adrift,* ed. Nikolaos A. Stavrou (New Rochelle, N.Y.: Caratzas, 1988), 102–11.

46. Iatrides, "Papandreou's Foreign Policy," 141.

47. Dokos, "Greece," 54.

48. *Lefki Vivlos gia tes Enoples Dynameis, 1998–1999* (Athens: Ministry of National Defense, 2000), 34–35.

49. Athanassios Platias, "High Politics in Small Countries: An Inquiry into the Security Policies of Greece, Israel and Sweden" (Ph.D. diss., Cornell Univ., 1986), 240–41.

50. Evangelos Raftopoulos, "The Crisis Over the Imia Rocks and the Aegean Sea Regime: International Law as a Language of Common Interest," in *The Aegean Sea After the Cold War: Security and Law of the Sea Issues,* ed. Aldo Chircop, Andre Gerolymatos, and John O. Iatrides (London: Macmillan, 2000), 134–51.

51. *Greece,* June 1996, vol. 2, no. 6. Greek embassy, Washington, D.C.

5

Containing the French Malaise?

The Role of NATO's Secretary General, 1958–1968

ANNA LOCHER AND CHRISTIAN NUENLIST

Intrabloc relations in East and West during the Cold War gain momentum in the current historical analysis. Among the strains that have loomed large throughout NATO's existence, the foreign policy of Gaullist France (1958–1968) was the most intense. Yet, the often-told story about France and NATO in the 1960s misses an important institutional and personal dimension—that of NATO's secretaries general. How did Paul-Henri Spaak, Dirk Stikker, and Manlio Brosio assess France's NATO policies and what active measures did they take to influence Paris and other NATO capitals? By comparing the interactions between each of these three secretaries general and NATO governments, differences in their approaches and success levels come to light.[1]

Spaak's Efforts to Counter de Gaulle's Challenge to NATO in 1958

In a speech on 27 September 1958, Paul-Henri Spaak praised NATO's flexibility and achievements in the political field. Since his assumption of the NATO chairmanship in May 1957, the major Western powers had increasingly consulted their smaller allies in the North Atlantic Council (NAC) on East-West relations. Spaak characterized this development as a "revolution in international diplomacy" and was confident that the West could calmly face the Soviet challenge of peaceful coexistence.[2]

Spaak's speech also attempted to counter another challenge to NATO. Three days earlier, Charles de Gaulle had given Spaak a copy of his memorandum of 17 September 1958 to U.S. president Dwight D. Eisenhower and British prime minister Harold

Macmillan.[3] To account for the changing nature of the Cold War, de Gaulle suggested establishing permanent U.S.-UK-French consultations to determine Western political and military strategy.[4] Spaak was "stupefied," for he understood that the French proposal contradicted his understanding of NATO as an alliance of equals and that his summer efforts to mediate between de Gaulle and NATO had failed.[5]

Spaak had tried to establish a working relationship with the new French leader from the very beginning. In their first meeting, de Gaulle had assured Spaak on 23 June 1958 that France in no way opposed NATO but that it wished to play a more important role to outbalance the influence of Washington and London within the alliance.[6] Spaak was supportive of such a move and in a long memorandum encouraged France to play a more active role within the alliance. As an example, he mentioned NATO's preparatory work for a possible East-West summit in early 1958, where he had missed U.S. leadership. France could have filled this gap by taking an initiative, Spaak speculated, and he asked de Gaulle to show "more eagerness and imagination" regarding the NATO machinery.[7]

Anticipating a fissure within NATO, Spaak asked West German chancellor Konrad Adenauer to convince de Gaulle that Bonn would not accept a U.S.-UK-French directorate within NATO, but when Adenauer and de Gaulle met on 14 September, neither broached the topic.[8] Three days later, de Gaulle's memorandum triggered a prolonged crisis within NATO and prompted a round of informal high-level intrabloc consultations.

In this situation, U.S. secretary of state John Foster Dulles and Adenauer asked the NATO secretary general to mediate between France and the rest of the alliance. In Boston, Dulles encouraged Spaak to prepare an answer to de Gaulle with the aim of bringing the discussion back into the NATO forum. Germany's NATO ambassador, Herbert Blankenhorn, recommended that Spaak react to the French challenge with a comprehensive review of both the alliance's political consultation procedures and its strategic planning.[9]

On 15 October, Spaak replied to de Gaulle with a memorandum of his own. While expressing sympathy with most of de Gaulle's concerns, he completely opposed installing a tripartite directorate, an idea that he characterized as "neither pragmatic nor fortunate," because it would mean the end of the Atlantic alliance. Spaak emphasized that Germany, Italy, and NATO's smaller countries also had major interests in developments in Africa and elsewhere outside of NATO territory. They would never accept tripartism, but instead choose neutralism.[10] He intended to write a report with his own ideas for improving political consultation in the alliance and discuss the problem at NATO's December ministerial meeting.[11]

Revelations in the German press of de Gaulle's memorandum in late October, however, ruined Spaak's plan to launch an alliance-wide debate on the future of NATO. Upon learning of the memorandum, NATO ambassadors in Paris judged de Gaulle's proposal a "great mistake." The Norwegian and Danish ambassadors in particular decried that they had not been informed.[12]

In his *Interim Report on Political Cooperation*, Spaak only hinted at de Gaulle's memorandum between the lines. For him, restricted consultations among some member states were acceptable as long as NATO was informed of any results. When NATO foreign ministers met in Paris in mid-December, no multilateral discussion on the matter took place. Rather, de Gaulle's memorandum had been the subject of an informal, sub–foreign minister trilateral meeting in Washington earlier that month.[13]

Spaak's mediation efforts contributed to prevent the reintroduction of official U.S.-UK-French trilateral meetings into international diplomacy. In a meeting with de Gaulle on 15 December 1958, Dulles in clear terms rejected establishing a formal permanent organization *à trois*. De Gaulle repeated his own unsettling message: if tripartism could not be organized and NATO reformed, France would begin to reappraise its whole attitude to the alliance.[14]

Fighting for NATO's Relevance in East-West Relations

A new development indirectly helped de Gaulle's demand for a tripartite directorate. When Soviet leader Nikita Khrushchev launched the Berlin crisis in late 1958, the views of de Gaulle and Spaak on consultations over Berlin differed in two aspects. First, France was of the opinion that only the three Western powers with special responsibilities for Germany had to consult each other concerning a response to the Soviet challenge in Berlin. Spaak, however, strongly opposed the formation of an "inner circle" within NATO. In his view, all NATO countries had a legitimate interest in the German problem and all had committed themselves to defend against a Soviet attack on West Berlin. Second, while de Gaulle in principle refused to negotiate with Khrushchev under the pressure of an ultimatum, Spaak favored talks with Moscow.[15]

Meeting with Spaak on 28 February 1959, de Gaulle assured him that France would not deepen the NATO crisis parallel to the Berlin crisis.[16] Thus, in 1959, Spaak still stood up for many of de Gaulle's demands. In a July memorandum on French relations with NATO, he argued that U.S. nuclear sharing policy toward France should be similar to that toward Britain.[17] Discussing his ideas with de Gaulle on 16 July, Spaak was ready to debate the contested issues of Africa, nuclear weapons, and military integration within NATO. In retrospect, he described the lack of such a discussion as a "missed opportunity."[18] Working relations between the NATO secretary general and the French government were still good at that time. Spaak successfully intervened in an intrabloc quarrel of France with Norway and the United States, whose arms sales to Tunisia irritated the French.[19]

Moreover, Eisenhower's détente policy and his surprising invitation for Khrushchev to visit the United States without prior NATO consultation irritated Spaak almost as much as de Gaulle's isolation within NATO. In Spaak's view, the three major Western allies increasingly neglected the habit of consultation. He was also troubled that Eisenhower had not used his September and December 1959 meetings with de Gaulle to seek a confrontation over the importance and role of NATO. Finally, he was concerned about an apparent French-German rapprochement. At an informal lunch in northern Italy, Adenauer shocked Spaak with a radical volte-face regarding tripartite consultations. When the chancellor unexpectedly gave his assent to France guarding the interests of continental Europe, Spaak protested forcefully. In the end, Adenauer revised his opinion, but his mistrust of the Anglo-Saxons remained.[20]

In 1960, Spaak's (and NATO's) voice was heard less and less in international issues. His idea to establish a five-power NATO steering committee—following the example of the UN Security Council—to harmonize the Western position for East-West conferences was rejected by both major and smaller allies.[21] Spaak's fear of a directorate still provided for "very animated" NATO discussions. When U.S. NATO ambassador Randolph Burgess informed his colleagues of early June 1960 trilateral foreign minister talks in Washington, Belgium's André de Staercke bashed this new trend toward accommodating de Gaulle by establishing inner-circle consultations among NATO "senior partners": in his view, "it was better to be a neutral than an unconsulted ally." Spaak, himself a "radical opponent" of a directorate, warned the Big Three that they were playing with fire.[22]

Referring to a U.S. report on "NATO in the 1960s," Spaak warned Secretary of State Christian Herter that studies about the future of NATO should not become an alibi exercise to distract attention from current problems.[23] When Spaak met with de Gaulle on 21 July 1960 and asked whether delivery of U.S. missiles would help the French atomic program, de Gaulle agreed that it would reduce financial costs considerably. Spaak later regretted that Washington had not responded with more sympathy to de Gaulle's ambition for a national atomic capability.[24]

When Spaak seriously considered retiring from his post in August 1960, British NATO ambassador Frank Roberts explained Spaak's lack of favor with the French administration: "This is mainly because NATO is not popular with them and he is Mr. NATO."[25] After a rambling discussion at the December ministerial meeting in Paris, Spaak resigned on 31 January 1961. De Gaulle cynically embraced his decision to return to Belgian politics "as there was nothing for him to do in NATO."[26]

On his way out, Spaak in "absolute frankness" and "disregarding diplomatic form" bitterly complained to the new U.S. president, John F. Kennedy, about the French attitude toward NATO, which he summarized as "silence and abstention." Frustrated, he stated that "the General does not like NATO . . . and does not see in NATO a solution to the political problems." To counter the French malaise, Spaak asked that the United States strengthen political consultations within NATO to set an important precedent for London, Bonn, and smaller allies—and maybe even for Paris.[27]

Stikker's Role in the Berlin Wall Crisis of 1961

For Spaak's successor Dirk Stikker, former Dutch foreign minister and ambassador to NATO, cooperation with de Gaulle proved difficult. With the support of Italy and Greece, France blocked Stikker's candidacy for more than two months. De Gaulle then waited another three months before receiving him—and only after Adenauer intervened personally. Their first (and only) meeting on 12 July 1961 lasted for a mere thirty minutes. The French president made clear that, although he still wanted to cooperate with NATO, the demands of his 1958 memorandum remained.[28]

While de Gaulle practically ignored Stikker, the new secretary general, a NATO insider, entertained friendships with Adenauer, Spaak, de Staercke, NATO supreme commander Lauris Norstad, and Kennedy's NATO advisor, Dean Acheson, all of whom often visited him at his Italian villa.[29] In May 1961, Stikker expressed pessimism that de Gaulle's ideas on NATO would change and suggested instead "to find solutions so that other countries can go ahead with essential steps in the integration field." For Stikker, NATO's air defense served as a good model. Here, the other fourteen countries went ahead, and the French were more or less forced to go along.[30]

As Washington, Paris, and London tried hard to come up with a joint reaction to Khrushchev's challenge in Berlin, Stikker reflected on the task and location of the NATO Council in time of war. He thought that present arrangements, which meant incorporation into the French government, were "illogical" and "unsatisfactory" since de Gaulle's attitude toward NATO would "completely paralyze" the work of the council.[31] Kennedy asked Stikker to inquire whether Washington's European allies were ready to go to war for Berlin. Stikker reluctantly agreed to this mission, but as he told Macmillan, he normally "did not wish to get into the position of 'go-between' between governments."[32]

After his reconnaissance mission, Stikker warned the United States in late June that the European allies feared a war over Berlin, disagreed with the tough Berlin policy of the Kennedy administration, and preferred negotiations with Moscow.[33] The NATO Council, however, had not yet started discussing the political ramifications of the Berlin crisis. In July, Stikker thought "it would be a mistake to have a substantive discussion in NATO on Berlin" before the German elections in September, as Bonn would be forced to assume a rigid position. He therefore recommended postponing discussion.[34]

Following the border closure and the beginning of wall construction in Berlin on 13 August 1961, Stikker was in a "very pessimistic mood" and, in a reversal of his earlier position, now demanded meaningful consultation on East-West negotiations.[35] At a highly restricted council session on 2 September, NATO ambassadors unanimously agreed to seek talks with Moscow.[36] In Washington and Ottawa a few days later, Stikker maintained that he had initiated considerable consultation, in which the NATO ambassadors worked out basic objectives that all could accept.[37]

Stikker's optimism proved premature. De Gaulle remained skeptical toward the Anglo-American push for détente, even with Adenauer supporting negotiations after his electoral success in September. The French could not be convinced of the value of talks with Moscow. At the December ministerial meeting in Paris, Stikker maintained that a NATO vote on the issue of Berlin negotiations would result in a "14 to 1 favor of the US/British/German position."[38] After spirited debates, Stikker had to acknowledge that France still strictly opposed negotiations.[39] He was very concerned about the fact that "the Council came as near as in my memory it has ever come to a public breakdown over a major issue" and feared that "the fabric of the Alliance will not stand many more [such] scenes."[40]

Thereafter, Stikker remained unable to establish a working relationship with de Gaulle or with anyone else from the French government. His work increasingly focused on NATO's nuclear strategy, particularly in the run-up to the Athens ministerial meeting in May 1962.[41] NATO's role in East-West relations had suffered from discord between France and the other fourteen. For Stikker, the December 1961 meeting had revealed that "too many members of NATO attached greater value to certain political principles than to the overriding idea of the Alliance, which implied a give and take."[42] In early September 1962, Stikker became severely ill, and during the subsequent Cuban missile crisis and through the rest of the year he was absent from Paris and NATO.

Working Around the General: Stikker's Policy of "Mutual Forbearance"

Stikker was still very much recovering when Kennedy and Macmillan met at Nassau in December 1962, and when de Gaulle staged his press conference and the French-German Elysée Treaty in January 1963.[43] To help calm things down, Stikker at the 30 January council meeting urged that there be "no repercussions" affecting alliance unity and denied the existence of a crisis in NATO.[44] Trying to get in touch with the French government, Stikker received no response whatsoever. "For France, NATO almost does not exist," he told his predecessor and current Belgian foreign minister Spaak.[45]

In early 1963, Stikker traveled to NATO capitals urging "positive action," including nuclear cooperation in NATO, and seeking to avoid a split in the alliance.[46] He was determined to sell the Nassau provisions for a NATO nuclear force as "not bad" and "realistic."[47] Meeting with Adenauer on 4 January, Stikker unsuccessfully defended the Anglo-American idea of a NATO nuclear force as protecting European interests—although he admitted in talks with Henry A. Kissinger that he had not yet really understood the implications of the Nassau agreements.[48]

Despite two high-level council meetings in March and April meant to reassure allies, the January events still reverberated heavily in ministerial contributions at

NATO's meeting in Ottawa in May. Stikker pushed military rather than political measures and promoted especially his ideas on NATO defense planning and an interallied nuclear NATO force. Indeed, ministers, with the abstention of France, decided to continue discussions on the force and force planning and to appoint a European nuclear deputy to SACEUR.[49] The difficulties of coordinating policies between France and NATO, however, increased in late July. After French NATO ambassador François Seydoux had officially buried any hopes that Paris might agree to the defense planning project, Stikker met with him bilaterally to inquire about French readiness for exploratory talks with NATO's international staff, but Seydoux responded that the Quai d'Orsay wished no such contacts. This stance did not soften when an upset Stikker recalled a basic NATO document from 1952 stipulating that the secretary general "should have direct access to all NATO agencies and to Governments."[50] With France's unyielding opposition, discussion of NATO strategy was basically delayed until after the French withdrawal from NATO's integrated command in 1966.

The "only answer" to de Gaulle's unchangeable policies, Stikker maintained in 1963 and 1964, was to reach "a position of 'mutual forbearance' with the French." This meant that de Gaulle should no longer be allowed to prevent the other allies' efforts toward integration.[51] Washington objected that the recommended procedure would reduce France's role in NATO to an observer status, thereby "only playing de Gaulle's game," and asked about French reactions. Stikker had to admit he had "virtually no contact with the French Government."[52] To overcome the rule of unanimity within NATO, Stikker in the spring of 1964 suggested that a full-fledged "abstention doctrine" following the Organization for Economic Cooperation and Development pattern be deliberated at the ministerial meeting in May in The Hague.[53] He envisaged a "real discussion" to establish "where NATO is going."[54] The restricted debate that eventually took place against U.S. objections cleared the air but could not fundamentally affect relations between France and NATO.[55]

Stikker's long-announced departure from Paris in the summer of 1964 resembled his arrival at the Seine. De Gaulle denied receiving him for a farewell courtesy call, but the original French fear that Stikker "would be a 'strong' Secretary General"[56] had not materialized.

Avoiding Confrontation with France: Brosio and de Gaulle

Manlio Brosio's election as Stikker's successor and his subsequent introduction to de Gaulle went off smoothly.[57] Washington had explicitly looked for someone "who will not be anathema to the French."[58] As Italian ambassador to France in 1961–64, Brosio was, as the *Times* of London emphasized, "very much *persona grata* in Paris."[59] Many evaluated the new secretary general in comparative terms: "Like

Spaak, Brosio is politically minded. We can expect him to place more emphasis on the political side of NATO than his predecessor, Stikker, who really never put his heart in the non-military side of NATO."[60]

In office from 1 August 1964, Brosio had a substantive fifty-minute discussion with de Gaulle on 3 September.[61] Inquiring about French plans to revise the alliance, de Gaulle replied that "denouncing the treaty" was "a quite big word," but things could not remain the way they were.[62] NATO's new secretary general came away with the impression that France was likely to leave the alliance in 1969. U.S. ambassador to France Charles Bohlen thought Brosio's assessment was wrong but considered de Gaulle's exposition "more brutal and specific" than his previous statements.[63] Indeed, Brosio had in this first meeting with de Gaulle experienced "a baptism of fire."[64]

The French attitude caused a sense of alliance turmoil among many allies. German foreign minister Gerhard Schröder in July 1964 believed that "we have to attempt to keep France in a kind of 'co-existence' with NATO to avoid dangerous tensions," and Chancellor Ludwig Erhard promoted the idea of a NATO summit to counter the perception that "NATO was running out."[65] The U.S., Belgian, and Dutch foreign offices explored measures for concerting policy within NATO and the Canadians launched a multilateral initiative to counteract the decreasing sense of purpose within the alliance.[66] To Brosio's eyes, however, the future of the alliance could not meaningfully be discussed until after the French and German elections at the end of 1965. He opposed particularly Ottawa's initiative because "NATO is not out of date."[67]

In the United States and Canada, Brosio discussed in detail de Gaulle's positions—namely, continued support for the alliance, opposition to the organization, rejection of a change of military strategy, and—quite in contrast with his earlier views—unwillingness to extend Western consultations to out-of-area questions. In the latter point, the otherwise Francophile Brosio sided with the United States and favored "full solidarity" on issues outside the treaty area.[68] Given the situation in Vietnam, intimate consultation increasingly mattered to Washington.[69]

Regarding a tentatively scheduled meeting between Lyndon B. Johnson and de Gaulle, Brosio admitted he preferred no such meeting because the U.S. president was "the hundred percent American politician, and General de Gaulle the one hundred percent sophisticated European."[70] Brosio skeptically viewed all attempts to push relations between France and NATO and maintained that an expansion of NATO's integration was subject to the "unanimous consent of all concerned."[71] Singling out the plans for a NATO nuclear force, Brosio stressed the "limitations" of Stikker's doctrine of flexibility. Throughout 1964, Brosio preferred harmony to divergences.[72]

On 27 February 1965, de Gaulle received Brosio with all military honors and invited him to call on him whenever he wished. He insisted, however, that by 1969 the West needed an "alliance of the classical type," freed of the current political and military organization. The secretary general concluded from the discussion that France would not attack NATO's organization before 1969, provided the organization was not strengthened by a multilateral or an interallied nuclear force.[73] Even in the spring of 1965, when the pace of French disengagement sped up, Brosio still thought it best to avoid anticipatory moves antagonizing Paris.[74] He therefore advised against nuclear proliferation within NATO and favored U.S. secretary of defense Robert McNamara's 31 May proposal for a select committee of NATO defense ministers, designed to share nuclear knowledge rather than nuclear weapons because it was "less unpalatable to France."[75]

Facing France's Withdrawal and the Harmel Report

During 1965, Brosio became increasingly annoyed with the French attitude. On the scope and duration of the select (now special) committee, in which the French questioned his role, Brosio eventually resorted to the doctrine of flexibility he had qualified a year before. The French themselves could abstain, but they could not prevent others from moving ahead with the project for Atlantic nuclear consultation.[76] As for the bourgeoning war in Vietnam, Brosio came out against the French call for peace at any cost.[77]

In addition, Brosio did not support de Gaulle's post-1964 turnabout on East-West relations.[78] He deplored that "France was now more friendly to the Soviet Union than to the FRG" and worried about a Franco-German split. For Brosio, détente fundamentally endangered the alliance: "If we were to conclude that the Soviet threat was not the main problem, we had to ask ourselves what was the meaning of NATO."[79] In his eyes, French ideas projecting the dissolution of blocs endangered peace and had the potential to lead to anarchy.[80]

An atmosphere of expectation prevailed at the ministerial meeting in December 1965. Couve de Murville had told Brosio in the run-up that his government would "not accept that France should be called into court before a North Atlantic Council divided 14–1."[81] After contradictory signals to Brosio and the NATO governments, de Gaulle in a 21 February press conference and in more detail on 7 and 9 March 1966 announced that France would withdraw its remaining forces from NATO's integrated command and that allied troops and facilities would have to leave French soil.[82]

At this time, Brosio privately noted that Washington and London had no right to accuse France of questioning the alliance because their policy of détente promoted its weakening just as well. Brosio's feeling that he was not able to change the course of action reinforced this malaise. In April, while desperately seeking to retain a crucial role for the NATO Council, he recognized with resignation, "In the very moment of crisis my function is that of a walk-on, with no authority and no power."[83]

In his *Annual Political Appraisal* of May 1966, Brosio sought to avoid exaggerating the situation and expressed confidence not only in NATO's continuation but also in its vitality: "The facts are that all Allies accept the Alliance, that fourteen of them consider the military organization to be indispensable, and that one member no longer wishes to participate in it. If the Alliance is to be maintained, we cannot but accept these different elements of the situation and attempt to make the necessary adjustments through pragmatic approach and practical cooperation."[84]

Still, throughout 1966, Brosio feared a complete French break with the alliance and considered it "most unwise and dangerous to push a showdown" with France. At the same time, he registered with concern Paris's now very offensive East-West policies, culminating in de Gaulle's visit to Moscow in late June 1966. His feelings contrasted with NATO allies' assessment that by December 1966 they had not only clearly determined to maintain NATO but also "sorted out the France-NATO relationship."[85]

Brosio's rejection of openings to the East rendered him suspicious of Belgian foreign minister Pierre Harmel's initiative to address NATO's future tasks in the fall of 1966. The idea responded to the need for an "up-to-date role" for NATO in view of détente, the out-of-area question, and the blocked military strategy discussion. Although it was also presented as a means of reacting to the French move, Brosio initially opposed the proposal for fear of alliance disintegration and decreasing defense readiness.[86]

At the December ministerial meeting, though, Harmel obtained ministerial support to study the future tasks facing the alliance.[87] In the spring of 1967, Brosio came to chair the exercise's special group of representatives, which decided to set up four subgroups dealing with East-West relations, interallied relations, defense policy matters, and out-of-area issues.[88] As the work within the groups proceeded over the summer, Brosio's skepticism mounted in relation to French reluctance to cooperate. In September, Couve de Murville told Brosio that Paris was ready to accept the challenge if the Harmel exercise was "used to corner the French." Having consented to the exercise out of goodwill, Paris could not accept the projected political role for NATO.[89] In the end, however, to avoid foreseeable political costs, even the French approved the final Harmel Report on 14 December 1967.[90] By that time, Brosio agreed that it offered the advantage of preventing a showdown with France by providing for NATO's survival in a "more or less illusory but more or less decorous" manner.[91] Ironically, his assessment of the exercise was at odds with his function as "clearing house" for the interests of member governments in 1967.[92]

During de Gaulle's last year in power, Brosio remained concerned about outbalancing NATO's drive for détente by emphasizing especially its defense efforts. He was—rightly—confident at least to the point that he no longer expected anyone to denounce the North Atlantic Treaty.[93]

Conclusions

Cooperation and coordination between France and the other fourteen member states within NATO was increasingly difficult in the decade between 1958 and 1968. For Paul-Henri Spaak, Dirk Stikker, and Manlio Brosio, Charles de Gaulle's alliance policies constituted a major source of concern, but the expression "French malaise" does not sufficiently reflect the understanding of these three secretaries general, who at times supported French policies or at least placed them into perspective. This is remarkable because they all faced the same fundamental obstacle in their ability to influence the French: from de Gaulle's perspective, the NATO secretary general was inherently part of the NATO problem.

Not surprisingly, therefore, de Gaulle's NATO policies caused Spaak, Stikker, and Brosio to fear for NATO's future. All three worked against small-circle ideas that would depreciate the council, the office of the secretary general, and NATO as such. Each in a different manner looked for ways to cope with the multiple French "no-go policy." Whereas Spaak actively sought a confrontation with de Gaulle and tackled key controversies, Stikker and Brosio tried to minimize the (appearance of a) crisis within the alliance.

The merits of the three secretaries general in dealing with de Gaulle, then, have to be assessed by taking into account this structural factor. Against this background, they did make a difference in containing French obstructionism. With his outspoken criticism of a tripartite directorate, Spaak in 1958 prevented the "death of the alliance." As "Mr. NATO," he continuously and with some success urged NATO consultations on the Berlin crisis. Given his nonexistent contact with de Gaulle, Stikker introduced "mutual forbearance" as a viable concept for handling the French problem. Brosio decisively facilitated "coexistence" between France and NATO before and after France's withdrawal as well as during the Harmel exercise.

Thus, despite the bleak prospects for NATO's survival in the 1960s, the efforts of the secretaries general supported the larger process of alliance reconfiguration. Struggling for political cooperation and consultation, Spaak, Stikker, and Brosio significantly contributed to the transformation of NATO from a defense organization into an instrument for managing collective security.

Notes

1. See Frédéric Bozo, *Deux stratégies pour l'Europe: De Gaulle, les Etats-Unis et l'Alliance atlantique 1958–1969* (Paris: Plon, 1996); Maurice Vaïsse, *La grandeur: Politique étrangère du général de Gaulle, 1958–1969* (Paris: Fayard, 1998); Erin Mahan, *Kennedy, de Gaulle, and Western Europe* (Houndmills: Palgrave, 2002). For a biographical approach toward the first four secretaries general, see Robert S. Jordan and Michael W. Bloome, *Political Leadership in NATO: A Study in Multilateral Diplomacy* (Boulder, Colo.: Westview, 1979). On Spaak, see Michel Dumoulin, *Spaak* (Brussels: Racine, 1999). A full political biography of Stikker remains a desideratum. See Christian Nuenlist and Anna Locher, "Dirk Stikker," *North Atlantic Treaty Organization: An Encyclopedia of International Security*, ed. Craig T. Cobaine (Santa Barbara: ABC Clio, 2008). For an assessment of Brosio's role, see Bruna Bagnato, "NATO in the mid-1960s: The View of NATO Secretary General Manlio Brosio," in *Transatlantic Relations at Stake: Aspects of NATO History, 1956-75*, ed. Christian Nuenlist and Anna Locher (Zurich: ETH Zurich, 2006), 165–88. This chapter draws mainly on documents from the NATO archives, the Spaak and Stikker Papers in Brussels and The Hague, respectively, and on sources in the United States, Britain, Germany, and Canada.

2. Spaak speech at Atlantic Treaty Association, Boston, 27 Sept. 1958, Fondation Paul-Henri Spaak, Brussels (FPHS), 294/5508. On the evolution of political consultation in NATO from 1955 to 1958, see Christian Nuenlist, *Eisenhower, Kennedy, and Political Cooperation within NATO: Western Reactions to Khrushchev's Foreign Policy, 1955-64* (London: Routledge, 2008).

3. Memorandum of conversation (memcon), Spaak–de Gaulle, 24 Sept. 1958, FPHS, 294/5479; *Documents Diplomatiques Français* (DDF) 1958 2:430.

4. De Gaulle to Eisenhower, 17 Sept. 1958, U.S. Department of State, *Foreign Relations of the United States, 1958–1960* (Washington, D.C.: G.P.O., 1993), 7:81ff. On the background of the memorandum, see Vaïsse, *La grandeur*, 114–23.

5. De Staercke to Wigny, 7 Oct. 1958, FPHS, 294/5496.

6. Spaak note, 23 June 1958, FPHS, 294/5471; Paul-Henri Spaak, *Memoiren eines Europäers* (Hamburg: Hoffmann & Campe, 1969), 381, 386.

7. Spaak to de Gaulle, 3 July 1958, FPHS, 294/5472.

8. Blankenhorn diary entry, 9 Sept. 1958, German Federal Archives, Koblenz (BA), NL Blankenhorn, vol. 90; Hans-Peter Schwarz, *Adenauer II: Der Staatsmann, 1952–67* (Stuttgart: DVA, 1991), 455ff.

9. Memcon, Spaak-Dulles, 27 Sept. 1958, FPHS, 297/5507; Blankenhorn diary entries, 3 and 9 Oct. 1958, BA, NL Blankenhorn, vol. 91; Herbert Blankenhorn, *Verständnis und Verständigung* (Frankfurt: Propyläen, 1980), 324–29.

10. Memcon, Couve de Murville–Spaak, 15 Oct. 1958, DDF 1958 2:523–27. See also de Staercke to Wigny, 25 Oct. 1958, FPHS 294/5482. Spaak's eight-page memorandum from 15 Oct. 1958 is in FPHS 294/5483.

11. Blankenhorn diary entry, 24 Oct. 1958, BA, NL Blankenhorn, vol. 91.

12. Blankenhorn diary entries, 29 Oct. and 4 Nov. 1958, BA, NL Blankenhorn, vol. 91.

13. Spaak, interim report on political cooperation, 28 Nov. 1958, NATO Archives, Brussels (NA), C-M(58)138, 7a; summary record of NATO ministerial meeting, Paris, 16 Dec. 1958, NA, C-R(58)61–62; memcon, 4 Dec. 1958, *FRUS, 1958–1960* 7:128–37.

14. Memcon, Dulles–de Gaulle, 15 Dec. 1958, *FRUS, 1958–1960* 7:146–53.

15. See Marc Trachtenberg, *A Constructed Peace: The Making of a European Settlement,*

1945–1963 (Princeton, N.J.: Princeton Univ. Press, 1999), 251–82; Rolf Steininger, *Der Mau-erbau: Die Westmächte und Adenauer in der Berlinkrise 1958–63* (Munich: Olzog, 2001), 21–54. For Spaak's thinking, see Roberts to Foreign Office (FO), 17 Nov. 1958, Public Record Office, Kew/London (PRO), FO 371/137335; memcon, Dulles-Spaak, 13 Dec. 1958; Burgess to Department of State (DoS), 15 Dec. 1958, USNA, RG 59, Conference Files (CF), box 163. For the NATO debates in Dec. 1958, see summary records of NATO ministerial meeting, Paris, 16 Dec. 1958, C-R(58)60–62-E, NA. For NATO's Berlin declaration, see www.nato.int/docu/comm/49–95/c581216b.htm, accessed 21 June 2007.

16. Memcon, Spaak–de Gaulle, 28 Feb. 1959, DDF 1959 2:247f.

17. Spaak, *Memoiren*, 399–401.

18. Talking points for meeting with de Gaulle, 16 July 1959, FPHS, 295/5524; memcon Spaak–de Gaulle, 16 July 1959, FPHS, 295/5523. See also Spaak, *Memoiren,* 402.

19. Spaak, *Memoiren,* 410.

20. Spaak to Adenauer, 21 Aug. 1959, FPHS 295/5533; summary record of NATO ministerial meeting, Paris, 15 Dec. 1959, NA, C-R(59)44-E; Palliser (Spaak's son-in-law) note, 28 Dec. 1959, "Monsieur Spaak's Views on Recent NATO Meeting," PRO, FO 371/154552; Nolting to Herter, 19 Aug. 1959, DDEL, Norstad Papers, Policy Files, box 90, declassified on 8 Aug. 2001.

21. Spaak memorandum, 5 Feb. 1960, "The Preparation of Future Summit Meetings," NA, PO(60)139-E; Herter to Burgess, 11 Feb. 1960, USNA, RG 59, DF, 396.1-PA / 2–1160.

22. Roberts to FO, 8 June 1960, PRO, FO 371/152099. For Spaak's bitter complaints in the aftermath of the meeting, see Roberts to FO, 10 June 1960, PRO, FO 371/152099; Blankenhorn diary entry, 9 June 1960, BA, NL Blankenhorn, vol. 101.

23. Spaak, *Memoiren,* 403f. Spaak to Herter, 6 July 1960, FPHS, 297/5565.

24. Memcon, Spaak–de Gaulle, 21 July 1960, FHPS, 297/5561; Spaak, *Memoiren,* 406f.

25. Roberts to Shuckburgh, 10 Oct. 1960, PRO, FO 371/154553.

26. Memcon, Spaak-Kennedy, 21 Feb. 1961, *FRUS, 1961–1963* (Washington, D.C.: G.P.O., 1994), 13:260–66.

27. Spaak to Kennedy, 13 Feb. 1961, FPHS, 298/5581; memcon, Spaak-Kennedy, Washington, D.C. 21 Feb. 1961.

28. On Stikker and Kennedy, see Christian Nuenlist, "Into the 1960s: NATO's Role in East-West Relations, 1958–1963," in *Transforming NATO in the Cold War: Challenges Beyond Deterrence in the 1960s*, ed. Andreas Wenger, Christian Nuenlist, and Anna Locher (London: Routledge, 2007), 67–68. The discussions on Spaak's successor can be traced in detail in USNA, RG 59, CDF, 740.5. For de Gaulle's antipathy toward Stikker, see Dirk U. Stikker, *Bausteine für eine neue Welt: Gedanken und Erinnerungen an schicksalshafte Nachkriegsjahre* (Vienna/Düsseldorf: Econ, 1966), 418–32; memcon, Stikker–de Gaulle, 12 July 1961, Dutch National Archives, The Hague (NLNA), Stikker Papers, box 56. Vgl. Stikker, Bausteine, 429, 444f.

29. See Stikker, *Bausteine*, 321f., 379f. See memcon, Stikker-Adenauer, 13 May 1961, NLNA, Stikker Papers, box 56.

30. Memcon, Stikker-Rusk, 7 May 1961, USNA, RG 59, CF, box 248.

31. Memcon, Stikker-Adenauer, 27 June 1961, NLNA, Stikker Papers, box 56; memcon, Stikker-Macmillan, 14 July 1961, NLNA, Stikker Papers, box 58.

32. Memcon, Stikker-Macmillan, 14 July 1961, NLNA, Stikker Papers, box 58.

33. Finletter to Rusk, 24 June 1961, John F. Kennedy Library (JFKL), NSF, box 220a; memcon, Stikker-Home, 13 July 1961, PRO, FO 371/161283.

34. Memcon, Stikker-Macmillan, 14 July 1961, NLNA, Stikker Papers, box 58; memcon, Stikker-Home, 13 July 1961.

35. Durbrow to Kohler, n.d. [Aug. 1961]; memcon, Durbrow-Stikker, 19 Aug. 1961, DDEL, Norstad Papers, box 90.

36. Finletter to Rusk, 4 Sept. 1961, USNA, RG 59, CDF, 740.5/9–461.

37. Memcon, Stikker-Green, 11 Sept. 1961, NLNA, Stikker Papers, box 55.

38. Memcon, Stikker-Kohler, 12 Dec. 1961, USNA, RG 59, EUR/RPM, NATO Records, 1957–64, box 6.

39. Summary record of NATO ministerial meeting, 15 Dec. 1961, NA, C-R(61)71e.

40. Stikker to Rusk, 18 Dec. 1961, FRUS, 1961–1963, 13:340f.

41. In the so-called Stikker exercise, the secretary general discussed NATO strategy with NATO ambassadors in early 1962. See Jordan and Bloome, Political Leadership, 145f.

42. Memcon, Stikker-Adenauer, 11 Jan. 1962, NLNA, Stikker Papers, box 56.

43. Trachtenberg, Constructed Peace, 367–79; Christof Münger, Kennedy, die Berliner Mauer und die Kubakrise: Die westliche Allianz in der Zereissprobe, 1961–63 (Paderborn: Schöningh, 2003), 214–63.

44. Summary record of NAC meetings, 30 Jan. and 20 Mar. 1963, NA, c-r(63)4e and 14e; Howe to Rusk, 7 Feb. 1963, USNA, RG 59, Alpha-Numeric File (ANF) 1963, DEF 4 NATO, box 3697.

45. Memcon, Stikker-Lefevre-Spaak, 1 Feb. 1963, NLNA, Stikker Papers, box 55.

46. Memcon, Stikker-Home-Thorneycroft, 24 Jan. 1963, NLNA, Stikker Papers, box 54; memcon, Stikker-Lefevre-Spaak, 1 Feb. 1963; memcon, Stikker-Kennedy, 6 Mar. 1963, FRUS, 1961–1963, 13:518–23. See also Stikker, Bausteine, 433–46.

47. Memcon, Stikker-Lefevre-Spaak, 1 Feb. 1963.

48. Memcon, Stikker-Adenauer, 4 Jan. 1963, NLNA, Stikker Papers, box 56; memcon Stikker-Kissinger, 12 Jan. 1963, JFKL, NSF, box 321.

49. Annual Political Appraisal 1963, 6 May 1963, NA, c-m(63)29e.; Rusk to NATO missions, 29 May 1963, FRUS, 1961–1963, 13:587–90. See also Stikker, Bausteine, 476; and Jordan and Bloome, Political Leadership, 149.

50. Memcons, Stikker-Seydoux, 26 and 30 July 1963, NLNA, Stikker Papers, box 56. See also Le Figaro, 24 July 1963.

51. Memcon, Stikker-Rusk, 16 Oct. 1963, NLNA, Stikker Papers, box 58.

52. Memcon, Tyler-Stikker, 16 Oct. 1963, USNA, RG 59, ANF 1963, DEF 4 NATO, box 3696. See also memcon, Stikker-Butler-Thorneycroft, 7 Nov. 1963, NLNA, Stikker Papers, box 58. "Contacts with France were non-existent," Stikker told Adenauer in August 1963: memcon, Stikker-Adenauer, 22 Aug. 1963, NLNA, Stikker Papers, box 56.

53. In his memoirs, Stikker explained he never considered the rule of unanimity to be a valid NATO concept: Stikker, Bausteine, 331ff.

54. Memorandum, "Hague Ministerial," 19 Mar. 1964, CNA, RG 25, 27–4-NATO-12–1964-Spring; memcon, Stikker-Popper, 20 Feb. 1964, NLNA, Stikker Papers, box 58; memcon, Stikker-Rusk, 18 Mar. 1964, NLNA, Stikker Papers, box 58.

55. For an analysis of the ministerial discussions, see Anna Locher, Crisis—What Crisis? The Debate on the Future of NATO, 1963–66 (London: Routledge, 2008).

56. Background paper, "Status of NATO," [Oct. 1963], USNA, RG 59, EUR/RPE 1948–63, box 2.

57. Stikker had repeatedly expressed his concern over Brosio's unfamiliarity with NATO. He "doubted that Brosio is a real fighter" and insisted that his selection would "play into French hands." Memcon, Stikker-Rusk, 18 Mar. 1964, NLNA, Stikker Papers, box 58.

58. Draft memorandum, [2 Dec. 1963], Lyndon B. Johnson Library (LBJL), NSF International Meeting and Travel File, box 34.

59. *Times* (London), 14 May 1964.

60. Briefing memorandum, "Ways of Improving Political Consultation," 23 Sept. 1964, LBJL, NSF Agency File, box 38.

61. Bohlen to Tyler, 14 Sept. 1964, *FRUS, 1963–1968* (Washington, D.C.: G.P.O., 1994), 13:71–73.

62. Memcon, Brosio–de Gaulle, 3 Sept. 1964, DDF 1964 2:208.

63. Bohlen to Tyler, 14 Sept. 1964; briefing memorandum, "France and NATO," 24 Sept. 1964, USNA, RG 59, EUR/RPM, Records Relating to NATO Affairs 1959–66, box 5; memcon, Brosio-Martin, 2 Oct. 1964, CNA, RG 25, 27–4-NATO-1.

64. Memorandum, "December Ministerial Meeting," 23 Sept. 1964, USNA, RG 59, CF, box 358.

65. Schröder speech manuscript for 1 July 1964, "Problems of NATO," 4 Aug. 1964, *Akten zur Auswärtigen Politik der Bundesrepublik Deutschland* (AAPD) 1964 2:927–938, 936, 938; McGhee to Rusk, 17 Sept. 1964, *FRUS, 1963–1968*, 13:73–75.

66. See Ignatieff to Pearson, 10 Mar. 1964, CNA, MG 26-N3, vol. 273, 832. Policy; editorial note, *FRUS, 1963–1968*, 13:90. See also Anna Locher and Christian Nuenlist, "Reinventing NATO: Canada and the Multilateralization of Détente, 1962–66," *International Journal* [Toronto] (spring 2003): 283–302.

67. Memcon, Rusk-Brosio, 28 Sept. 1964; memcon, Rusk-Brosio, 13 Dec. 1964, LBJL, NSF International Meetings and Travel File, box 33.

68. Briefing memorandum, "France and NATO," 24 Sept. 1964; defense background brief, "Brosio's Discussion with de Gaulle," 16 Sept. 1964, USNA, RG 59, CF, box 358.

69. Van Hollen to Bowie, 14 July 1964, USNA, RG 59, EUR/RPM, Records re: Political Affairs 1957–66, box 6.

70. Memcon, Brosio-Martin, 2 Oct. 1964, CNA, RG 25, 27–4-NATO-1.

71. Rusk to U.S. missions, 8 Oct. 1964, *FRUS, 1963–1968*, 13:83–89; memcon, Rusk-Brosio, 28 Sept. 1964.

72. Finletter to Rusk, 18 Nov. 1964, Bohlen to Rusk, 17 Nov. 1964, both in LBJL, NSF Agency File, box 37. See also Jordan and Bloome, *Political Leadership*, 181–82.

73. De Staercke to Spaak, 1 Mar. 1965, FPHS, 32/302/5670.

74. See speeches by de Gaulle, 4 Feb. and 27 Apr. 1965, DM, 325–42, 354–58; Bohlen to Rusk, 4 May 1965, *FRUS, 1963–1968*, 13:206f.

75. Finletter to Rusk, 5 June 1965, LBJL, NSF Country File, box 171; briefing paper, "Nuclear Sharing: ANF/MLF," [n.d.], LBJL, NSF Agency File, box 35; Schaetzel memorandum, "France and NATO," 13 May 1965, LBJL, NSF Country File, box 171; Rusk to Johnson, 5 Oct. 1965, LBJL, NSF Agency File, box 35; memcon, Rusk-Brosio, 7 Oct. 1965, LBJL, NSF Agency File, box 36.

76. Cleveland to Rusk, 16 Dec. 1965, LBJL, NSF Country File, box 172. See also Bozo, *Deux stratégies*, 146–48.

77. Bohlen to Rusk, 30 Nov. 1964, *FRUS, 1963–1968*, 13:122–26; Vaïsse, *La grandeur*, 527–32.

78. For the changing French concept of détente, see Vaïsse, *La grandeur*, 419–25; Bozo, *Deux stratégies*, 133–37.

79. Martin to Ignatieff, 5 Oct. 1965, CNA, MG 31-E83, vol. 22, 13; Brosio address to Eleventh NATO Parliamentarians' Conference, 4 Oct. 1965, in *The Atlantic Alliance: Allied Comment* (Washington, D.C.: G.P.O., 1966), 53–64.

80. Ibid.

81. *Washington Post,* 17 Dec. 1965.

82. De Gaulle to Johnson, 7 Mar. 1966, *FRUS, 1963–1968,* 13:325f.

83. Brosio diary entries, 1 Mar. and 15 Apr. 1966, quoted in Bagnato, "NATO in the mid-1960s," 173.

84. Brosio annual political appraisal, in Ignatieff to Martin, 5 May 1966, CNA, RG 25, vol. 10301, 27-4-NATO-12–1966-Spring, pt. 1. See also Jordan and Bloome, *Political Leadership,* 199.

85. Scope paper, 7 Dec. 1966, LBJL, NSF International Meetings and Travel File, box 35.

86. Position paper, 6 Dec. 1966, LBJL, NSF International Meetings and Travel File, box 35; talking points, "Meeting with Secretary-General Brosio," [13 Dec. 1966], USNA, RG 59, CF, box 431; Helga Haftendorn, "Entstehung und Bedeutung des Harmel-Berichtes der NATO von 1967," in *Vierteljahrshefte für Zeitgeschichte* 40, no. 2 (Apr. 1992): 169–220.

87. Summary record of NATO meeting, 15 Dec. 1966, NA, c-r(66)68, 69 (NISCA 4/10/1). NATO's subject files on the Harmel exercise have recently been published by the Parallel History Project on NATO and the Warsaw Pact (PHP) at www.php.isn.ethz.ch, accessed 21 June 2007.

88. Andreas Wenger, "Crisis and Opportunity: NATO's Transformation and the Multilateralization of Détente, 1966–68," *Journal of Cold War Studies* 6, no. 1 (2004): 22–74; Haftendorn, "Entstehung," 177–84.

89. Memcon, Brosio-Brandt, 9 Oct. 1967, NA, DPA/67/213 (NISCA 4/10/6).

90. For the French turnaround, see Rusk to NATO posts, 16 Nov. 1967, *FRUS, 1963–1968,* 13:640f.; Wenger, "Crisis and Opportunity," 68; Frédéric Bozo, "Detente vs. Alliance: France, the United States and the Politics of the Harmel Report, 1964–1968," *Contemporary European History* 7, no. 2 (1998): 343–60, 358–60; Haftendorn, "Enstehung," 215.

91. Brosio diary entry, 23 Nov. 1967, quoted in Bagnato, "Handling the Alliance," 13.

92. Haftendorn, "Entstehung," 177; Wenger, "Crisis and Opportunity," 68–71.

93. Memcon, Johnson-Brosio, 19 Feb. 1968, *FRUS, 1963–1968,* 13:667f.; Rusk to Cleveland, 22 Feb. 1968, *FRUS, 1963–1968,* 13:670–73.

6

The Multilateral Force as an Instrument
for a European Nuclear Force?

INE MEGENS

The Atlantic Alliance as a Partnership of Equals

At the end of the 1950s, the European allies began to question the effectiveness of the American nuclear guarantee. The successful launch of the Soviet Sputnik satellite in 1957 fueled European fears of abandonment by the United States as it made U.S. territory vulnerable to Soviet nuclear attack, and discussion of Atlantic policy intensified within the U.S. government.

Robert Bowie addressed political, economic, and military aspects of U.S. relations with Europe in a 1960 report on long-term planning. He recommended different kinds of actions in each field, the best known of which is his proposal for the creation of a seaborne multilateral force (MLF). At the same time, Bowie argued that the nature of the relationship was in transition as the Europeans had regained their economic strength and aspired to a role reflecting that strength. "A Europe able to act as an effective entity would deserve and could exercise comparable influence on common policy and action. Disposing resources much nearer to those of the US, such a Europe could join in the genuine partnership of equals."[1] The idea of an Atlantic community as a partnership of equals assumed new significance when the Kennedy administration made it one of the key elements of its foreign policy. President Kennedy stated in July 1962 that the United States was prepared "to discuss with a united Europe the ways and means of forming a concrete Atlantic partnership, a mutually beneficial partnership between the new union now emerging in Europe and the old American Union founded here 175 years ago."[2]

Kennedy's views were very much in sympathy with those expressed in Europe by Jean Monnet.[3] This should come as no surprise to those who are acquainted with the intimate relationship between Monnet and some officials in the then new administration, notably George Ball. Jean Monnet was the founder of the Action Committee for the United States of Europe, which promoted European integration[4] and was made up of individuals from political parties and trade unions in Belgium, France, Germany, Italy, Luxembourg, and the Netherlands. During its annual session, the Action Committee adopted resolutions, presented positions on current issues, outlined specific principles, and formulated demands for further integration. The June 1962 declaration is the first one to mention the idea of a partnership of equals between Europe and the United States,[5] stating that the current relationship should be gradually transformed into a partnership between a united Europe and the United States. François Duchêne, one of Monnet's closest associates, has argued that for Monnet the principle of an Atlantic partnership was both an attempt to prevent a split between European countries and a license to develop the community in cohabitation with the United States.[6] Accordingly, the establishment of a political union, a United States of Europe, was a prerequisite if Europe was to be on equal terms with the United States of America.

British accession to the European Economic Community rather than a political union was the first priority for Europeanists on both sides of the Atlantic in the early 1960s. Although the prospects of Britain joining the community fluctuated, Charles de Gaulle's veto on British entry in January 1963 seems nonetheless to have taken many by surprise. The French veto came in the wake of the Nassau conference where President John F. Kennedy had offered Polaris missiles to British prime minister Harold Macmillan. The United States tendered the same missiles to France on equivalent conditions, but de Gaulle declined the offer. This was yet another instance of French and American policies clashing on nuclear weapons. The Franco-German treaty of the same month worsened the situation and created a tense atmosphere between the Atlantic partners. De Gaulle's veto added urgency to the negotiations about the trade expansion act, while the proposal for a MLF took on new importance in the military field.

The MLF as a Panacea for All Problems

It was Bowie who first put forward a plan for a seaborne MLF to be assigned to the Supreme Allied Commander Europe. In his view, both sea basing and mixed manning were essential features, designed to ensure joint control, prevent the national withdrawal of units, and reduce vulnerability of the force. A proposed first step called for the United States to commit Polaris atomic missile submarines to the Atlantic alliance.[7] Outgoing secretary of state Christian Herter had presented this proposal to the North Atlantic Council in December 1960, while Kennedy reaffirmed it in a speech to the Canadian parliament in May 1961. Thereafter, the administration took its time examining the feasibility of the proposal, and both the Policy Planning Staff of the State Department and the Pentagon issued studies and reports. The MLF concept was thus kept under discussion, but the debate lingered on without reaching any conclusion.

In an attempt to take the initiative and alleviate tensions between the Atlantic partners after de Gaulle's veto, Kennedy authorized Ambassador Livingstone Merchant to consult the European allies on the MLF proposal. The plan now called for the creation of a fleet of twenty-five surface vessels equipped with a total of two hundred Polaris missiles. The Polaris A-3 was a ballistic missile with a range of twenty-five hundred miles, armed with a one-megaton nuclear warhead. Management, control, and financing of the fleet would be the joint responsibility of the participating countries. Joint manning, another essential element in the proposals, planned for each ship to carry a crew consisting of at least three nationalities. The fleet was expected to cost approximately $500 million per year over the next decade.[8] The choice of surface ships—which were less costly, could be built more quickly, and would be easier to operate and maintain—rather than submarines was a major change from the initial plans.

The proposal for a MLF received a warm welcome in Germany, but elsewhere the reaction was at best lukewarm. Whereas some of the smaller countries, notably Greece and Turkey, displayed some interest, Great Britain in particular remained cool to the proposal while France was not even consulted. Military leaders everywhere expressed serious reservations. Surface vessels were vulnerable to attack, and the control mechanisms as suggested were too complicated and therefore unreliable during a crisis.[9] It also became obvious from the beginning that the issue of control was one of the crucial elements in the concept of a multilateral fleet, and the one that received most criticism. A U.S. veto over the launch of the commonly owned missiles was not very different from the existing situation where the United States held sole responsibility for launching the nuclear weapons deployed in Europe, as well as its own strategic missiles.

In the spring of 1963, Kennedy was reluctant to apply pressure on the European allies and hesitated to make the MLF the core of his European policy. MLF adherents within the administration—the most influential among whom were George Ball, Walt Rostow, Henry Owen, and Robert Schaetzel—were to be found in the State Department. Pascaline Winand has argued that the MLF served many overlapping goals for these policymakers. It was both "a means of strengthening the Atlantic Alliance, reducing the pressures of proliferation by giving Germans and Italians alike some kind of participation in managing nuclear weapons, and an educational tool to coach those Europeans who did not possess a nuclear capability on the responsibilities of nuclear sharing, while also encouraging them to move towards unity."[10]

After preliminary talks in Washington in October 1963, a working party was created in Paris to discuss the political aspects of the MLF plan.[11] A subcommittee in Washington dealt with military aspects. West Germany, Italy, Greece, and Turkey participated in these talks, joined later by Great Britain, Belgium, and the Netherlands. The Paris working group of ambassadors created five subgroups of experts whose task was to study the technical and legal aspects. At the start, the working party accepted a program of fifteen items requiring further discussion. The ambassadors made steady headway in systematically elaborating these items and putting them into "treaty-like language." Internal developments in some countries at the end of 1963, however, shelved the project for some months. In the United States, the assassination of John F. Kennedy brought Lyndon B. Johnson to the White House, and in West Germany, Ludwig Erhard succeeded Konrad Adenauer. Johnson committed himself to the MLF project in early April 1964 after a new round of consultations in the administration.

Political Control as the Essential Issue for the MLF

The most controversial issue with respect to a multilateral fleet was the arrangement for political control, an issue that cropped up again and again throughout discussions within the U.S. administration. State Department officials held out the prospect of a greater European say in the launching of missiles, referring in public speeches to the possibility that the partners in the project could be jointly responsible for the control of the force. At a meeting in Copenhagen in September 1962, McGeorge Bundy, for example, said that "if it should turn out that a genuinely multilateral European deterrent, integrated with ours in NATO, is what is needed and wanted, it will not be a veto from the administration in the United States which stands in the way."[12] Secretary of Defense Robert McNamara, by contrast, held serious misgivings about decentralizing control. In fact, he and the Joint Chiefs of Staff were skeptical about the whole project because they wanted to give priority to conventional defense forces for Europe. They disputed the need for new nuclear forces in the alliance and definitely wanted to retain complete control over the nuclear warheads.[13] Kennedy endorsed their view and expressed serious reservations about relinquishing control when the MLF proposal came up for discussion in the National Security Council in February 1963. State Department officials urged the president to leave open the question of control while presenting the proposal to the European countries.[14] In the end, Merchant was instructed to present the concept of a committee made up of at least the larger participants in the MLF. This committee would decide on the launching of the missiles by unanimity, and each major participant would thus have a veto. If the allies favored some other system of control, the United States was willing to discuss these alternatives. Merchant was also to point out that the initial arrangements could be reexamined in due course.[15]

In Europe, Dirk Stikker, secretary general of NATO, considered the idea of unanimity to be a poor one and hoped that a system of weighted voting could be developed.[16] The German and Italian representatives also questioned the unanimity principle. The Germans favored the adoption of some kind of majority vote system, first, because they thought France more likely to join on this basis and, second, because a veto might prove to be disastrous if a European country, such as Italy, elected a left-wing government.[17] The Italians' hope was that the proposal would instill new vigor to Europe's role in the alliance and, therefore, the European members should be able to decide whether and when to use it. They did realize themselves that if all the contributing countries were to have a veto, the force would cease to be a credible deterrent, but they had no ready-made solution at the time.[18] A few months later, the issue resurfaced in talks between U.S. and Italian representatives. In a meeting with American diplomats, the secretary-general of the Italian Foreign Office, Attilio Cattani, raised the question of whether the MLF could be transformed into a European force if the European Economic Community succeeded in advancing to political unity. In this way, the MLF could provide greater responsibility for the Europeans in the field of security and also encourage European integration. According to Cattani, the Americans responded positively.[19]

A European Nuclear Force

The problem of nuclear control and sharing was the most prominent one in the public debate on the future of the Atlantic alliance that was rekindled in Europe during 1963. Frequent references to the idea of a European nuclear force are to be found in speeches and debates of that time. This idea had been brought up for discussion in government-level talks on Franco-German military cooperation in the preceding years,[20] but until then it had never been a major political issue in Europe.

It is true that the Assembly of the West European Union (WEU) had called for the creation of a joint European strategic nuclear force as a complement to the U.S. strategic force in 1959. This could be interpreted as a bold statement, but the explanatory memorandum and the speech of the rapporteur, the British Labour representative Fred W. Mulley, suggest that this was not deliberate. The idea was put forward as a matter of principle, not as a program of action, and there was no follow-up.[21] The WEU Assembly was one of the few places in Europe where Western defense was under close scrutiny and discussed in public. Every year the defense committee conducted a review of the state of European security, and subsequently the assembly formulated political recommendations addressed either to the Council of Ministers or to the member countries.

The WEU Assembly in 1962 discussed once more the issue of a European nuclear force. Some members of the defense committee considered the establishment of a European nuclear force, based on existing French and British nuclear resources, a logical corollary to the creation of a European political union. Others opposed such a force on purely political grounds. The majority believed that a nuclear force for the alliance as a whole was required. The resolution called upon the member governments to make proposals to the United States "to secure the integration of allied nuclear forces into a single NATO nuclear force, possibly based on a European and an American component."[22] This procedure, however, points to a distinguishing feature of the discussions in the assembly. The debates often centered on issues of topical interest, most often as a result of U.S. initiative. This holds true for the debates in the national parliaments as well: official statements from the U.S. government on nuclear sharing within the alliance invariably elicited some debate in Europe.

The public interest in the idea of a European nuclear force increased early in 1963. Frans-Jozef Strauss, who had recently resigned as the West German minister of defense, was among the first to put forward a proposal to merge the French and British nuclear forces. The French *force de frappe* in particular should become the nucleus of an independent European nuclear force.[23] Other conservative German politicians, such as Baron von Guttenberg, shared Strauss's critical attitude toward the MLF and his support for a European force around the French deterrent. Assenting voices could be heard from one or two British Conservatives, and even in de Gaulle's France some politicians spoke in favor of European nuclear cooperation.[24] Maurice Schumann, at the time president of the Foreign Affairs Commission in the French Assemblée Nationale, contended that it was necessary to end the U.S. monopoly and transform the whole of Western Europe into a "partner" and therefore into a nuclear power.[25] Schumann issued his statement at a conference in Cambridge attended by many high-level civil servants, military representatives, and scholars from different countries. Many of those present expressed serious reservations about whether Europe should become a third superpower. Some doubted whether it would be able to build a credible deterrent, while others considered such a force neither feasible nor desirable. The main potential obstacle to a European nuclear force was a lack of political unity. Many potential participants readily agreed that Europe would have to achieve a greater degree of political unity and establish political institutions before acquiring nuclear weapons.[26]

A similar discussion took place at the meeting of the WEU Assembly in December of the same year. The defense committee had submitted a report calling for a NATO political executive "to be the sole authority on the use of nuclear weapons by forces assigned to NATO."[27] The assembly, however, refused to adopt the draft resolution and voted in favor of a revised statement proposed by George Brown, Labour member of the British Parliament. The text, as amended by the assembly, called for a unified planning system aimed at the development of a common strategy instead of a political executive. The draft resolution had also welcomed the mixed-manned NATO nuclear force as the nucleus around which integrated NATO forces could be built in the future. This, however, was taking things too far for many parliamentarians. At the end of 1963 there had been no substantial discussions on the MLF in the national parliaments, and many countries had only reluctantly agreed to participate in the international working group. It should come as no surprise, therefore, that every reference to the mixed-manning proposal was deleted from the final statement of the WEU Assembly.

In political circles, a European nuclear force was a topic for debate, but not a well-argued demand or a major political issue. Vague ideas about a European nuclear force were formulated only in the context of a more general discussion on nuclear sharing or in response to U.S. policy statements. There were no genuine desires to move forward with a European initiative or to formulate an elaborate plan to establish a European nuclear force, no outspoken proponents or political parties that identified with the demand for a European nuclear force, and no lobby groups actively working in this field. Most politicians speaking out in favor of a European nuclear force did so mainly for the purpose of pointing to the necessity of a greater voice for the European allies. For many others, it was just a prospect for a distant future when political unity in Europe might have come about.

A European Clause to the MLF Treaty

At the meeting of the WEU Assembly in December 1963, the members had also listened to a speech by Robert Bowie arguing that an integrated nuclear NATO force would limit the further proliferation of nuclear weapons and offer a possibility for absorbing the French and British national nuclear forces. The MLF might evolve in different ways: either as an Atlantic force controlled with less than unanimity, or a European force that European members would control according to whatever formula they might decide among themselves. According to Bowie, the United States was willing to revise control mechanisms in the future, and he pointed to an early November official statement from then vice president Johnson to reinforce his argument.[28] It was up to the Europeans to elaborate this scheme.

The working group of ambassadors in Paris discussed the matter of political control frequently over the next six months but could not come to a definitive conclusion. The final document of the working group on 1 September 1964 therefore lists seven alternative voting arrangements ranging from unanimity to a simple majority. Most of the alternatives distinguish between the member states by some form of weighted voting.[29] Assigning equal weight to the U.S. vote on one side and a European vote on the other was not included in the proposal. The same document contains a very general formula with respect to a future review with a note that additional paragraphs were being considered.

Officials in the Italian Foreign Ministry had given much thought to how the MLF treaty should take into account future changes in Europe. As early as July 1963 they had proposed a plan for a European vote in the political control of the MLF. Italian representatives discussed this idea with the German government in Bonn and presented a draft amendment for a future review to the MLF treaty should a European union emerge, the so-called European clause. The Germans supported the proposal as such but considered the wording of the relationship of future European elements with other parts of the MLF force too weak, because it was raised only as a matter of coordination. In that case, a European clause, as suggested by the Italians, might lessen the political impact of a multilateral fleet and weaken the bonds between the United States and Europe. Moreover, the draft text laid down the principle of "Europeanization" in case a European union was established that the Germans thought too compelling. They favored a short and generally worded formula, which would make the acceptance of such a clause much easier.[30]

After several months of bilateral talks between the Italian and German delegations, the European clause was presented to the Paris working group in June 1964, which examined it in three subsequent meetings.[31] The political implications of the amendment were far reaching. In case a European union having authority in the field of defense would be established, the clause envisaged a review of the treaty to meet the new political circumstances. It meant that a European union, in which France took part, might lead to adaptation in the MLF treaty to which France— or for that matter any other nonparticipating country—was not a member. The most critical comments came from the Dutch and the British representatives, who expressed doubts as to whether it was appropriate to refer to future developments that might necessitate bringing about changes in the treaty if the aim of the MLF project was to strengthen transatlantic ties. This transatlantic cooperation might crystallize into two pillars in the future, but this was not yet the case. They argued that European integration in the field of defense was a distant prospect at best and that to refer to these issues in the treaty was premature. Other representatives had fewer objections or believed that it might be important to refer to closer European cooperation in order to sway public opinion in Europe. During the discussions, the German ambassador Wilhelm Grewe and the Italian Ambassador Adolfo Alessandrini made it clear that their support for a European clause was partly brought about by internal political considerations. Both ambassadors also pointed out that they had been guided by a recent resolution of the Action Committee for the United States of Europe.

Monnet Comes to Support the MLF

The Action Committee had accepted a resolution in June 1964 whereby the members supported the MLF project under certain conditions. During the previous year, Monnet himself had gradually arrived at the conclusion that Europe could afford to neither turn its back on issues on which the survival of the West might depend nor remain aloof from attempts to achieve nuclear disarmament. Europe should therefore contribute to nuclear armament, although he believed that the proliferation of national nuclear armaments endangered European unity. These national nuclear powers would diverge, instead of unite, and create dangerous inequalities among European nation-states. A joint effort by the European countries was needed if Europe wished to become an equal partner of the United States. As new initiatives toward further integration in Europe seemed unlikely, Monnet considered the MLF acceptable as a temporary solution. It was, in his opinion, however, at best an incomplete solution, because the United States would keep a preferential position within the force and because the majority of the U.S. nuclear weapons would be left out of the multilateral arrangement.[32]

The statement of the Action Committee of June 1964, the most extensive declaration ever published by it, provoked much discussion among its members. During their meeting in Bonn, Monnet emphasized the importance of agreeing on a point of view as the committee members could then try to influence the international negotiations taking place in Paris. MLF opponents argued that such a force endangered transatlantic cooperation as it called the U.S. nuclear guarantee into question. Some of the members present feared that the MLF could become a divisive element among the European countries instead of bringing European unity closer. Those in favor of the MLF described the force as essentially a temporary solution, and some explicitly opposed an independent European nuclear force. An amendment put forward by four of the participants that emphasized the enduring necessity of the Atlantic alliance was accepted.[33] The resolution called for political cooperation in Europe because this would contribute to the power and coherence of the West and enable the European countries to deal with the nuclear issue in close cooperation with the United States. In this way, the nuclear issue could be a means of bringing political unification of Europe a step further. Seen in this light, the MLF proposal was at best half-hearted, because no common European agency was provided for the force and participation was on a national basis only. Although it could form the beginning of a joint organization and had the support of the Action Committee, its members wanted to ensure that the new organization would adapt to future changes and that the treaty would contain a possibility for future review. If a European organization was established, the European countries participating in the MLF should be able to decide "'to transform their national participation into joint participation."[34]

Lobbying for a European Vote Within the MLF

Immediately after the meeting in Bonn, Monnet embarked on implementing the resolution and intensified his contacts with officials of different nationalities to this end. He dispatched a telegram to Attilio Cattani, one of the most ardent supporters of European integration in Italy, with whom he discussed the voting formula and the European clause to the MLF during a subsequent meeting in Rome. Cattani promised to bear in mind the conditions of the Action Committee for the MLF.[35] Apparently he was successful, because a month later the Italians put forward a new draft of the European clause that included two elements to which the Action Committee attached great value for discussion in their talks with the Germans. First of all, reference was made to a partnership between the United States and the European union and, second, the draft included a demand that national participation in the MLF be transformed into a joint participation in the European union. German ambassador Grewe correctly termed this demand the Monnet clause, as the words used were precisely the same as in the resolution of the Action Committee.[36]

The Action Committee also lobbied actively for its cause among the diplomatic representatives in the Paris working group. During June and July, Jacques van Helmont, one of Monnet's associates, had at least five meetings with members of the U.S. delegation that definitely went beyond the informative contacts he had established before. At one point, for instance, he discussed the precise wording of the European clause in order to meet the wishes of the Action Committee. Van Helmont argued that it was necessary to find a formula that was acceptable to the committee, because it was the only European organization that endorsed the MLF.[37]

Monnet himself left for Washington in mid-July, where he talked to several U.S. officials and friends, the most important of whom was Robert Bowie. During the summer, Monnet and his staff members discussed points that should be included in the MLF charter with Bowie, both in person and in writing.[38] At the time, Bowie was working on a report on Atlantic collaboration under the authority of Secretary of State Dean Rusk. As a by-product of this study, he submitted a long memorandum to the department on the best approach to the MLF and draft language for a treaty.[39] Bowie was also instrumental in arranging contacts for Monnet with American representatives in the MLF working group. The two then went to see Ambassador Thomas Finletter, and one of his assistants, Philip Farley, in London on 15 September.[40] The discussion concentrated on institutional aspects of the treaty and issues of tactics. The participants agreed that it was essential to underline the political importance of the MLF proposal and made agreements on the next steps to be taken. Monnet took it upon himself to discuss the MLF with his German friends and acquaintances, and these discussions ultimately continued at his country house. Much thought was devoted to the question of the decision-making process. In a memorandum, Van Helmont had suggested giving one vote to the United States and one vote to Europe, the latter cast by a majority defined on the basis of the existing practice within the European Community. The participants agreed that this "partnership formula" represented the best scheme yet proposed. The formula met the U.S. need for a veto and the German concern that no one other than the United States have a veto. It also provided a rationale in terms of past European practices for giving the Italians equal status with the Germans and offered a practical majority voting system. Last but not least it symbolized the evolving U.S.-European relationship of partnership and equality.[41] This idea so charmed Finletter that he discussed it with the Germans and the Italians in the following months. It was also mentioned in high-level discussions between U.S. ministers and their European colleagues.[42]

By late 1964, however, the tide for achieving the treaty was turning. The German government began to encounter growing internal criticism. The French dropped their aloofness and started an actual counteroffensive, while the Russian government warned of the negative effects the MLF treaty might have on talks about nuclear arms control in Geneva. There had never been much enthusiasm for a multilateral fleet among the smaller NATO countries either, and from the beginning several military experts had taken exception to the surface ships as suggested by the Americans. The newly elected British Labour government also commented unfavorably on the MLF plan and made a proposal for an Atlantic Nuclear Force. The American administration, which also had to take into account serious opposition in Congress, thereupon decided to wait and see in order to avoid the impression that the United States wished to impose the multilateral fleet on its European allies.

The MLF as a First Step Toward a European Nuclear Force?

Researchers who have analyzed U.S. nuclear policy are convinced that the United States would never have relinquished the veto over the firing of nuclear weapons and see the MLF as an inadequate solution to the problem of nuclear sharing in the alliance. Some authors do mention in passing that the United States was willing to reconsider the veto in the future, but they qualify this offer as an illusion, or even a bribe.[43] The concept of an Atlantic Community is likewise poorly received by researchers. They claim that the U.S. government employed the rhetoric of partnership but showed no genuine interest in a two-pillar structure for the Atlantic institutions. "The Kennedy Administration talked community, but practised hegemony."[44] By late 1963, with Kennedy dead and Adenauer in retirement, there was much less momentum for reorganizing Atlantic relations and the prospect of ever establishing the MLF appeared unlikely.

Nevertheless, the MLF was kept on the agenda of international meetings and was even endorsed by President Johnson in mid-1964. The advocates of a European political union and equal partnership with the United States seized the opportunity to introduce their ideas and made proposals for discussion at various levels. They ably used the possibilities made available to them by the ambivalence of the American policy regarding the abandonment of the veto. Even more remarkable in this diplomatic fencing is the close cooperation between U.S. officials at the

State Department, Italian and German diplomats, and officials and the Action Committee for the United States of Europe, in the person of Jean Monnet. These talks also show how much weight Monnet's views and the support of the Action Committee carried in these discussions. In retrospect, it is easy to conclude that the confirmed believers in European political unity and Atlantic partnership were fighting a rearguard action, but in mid-1964 that was not yet a foregone conclusion. The partnership voting formula and a European clause would have made it possible to transform the MLF into a two-pillar force—the nucleus of an Atlantic community of equals. In fact, the partnership formula ended up as one of many proposals on voting and the status of the European clause was nothing more than an amendment for future review to a draft treaty that never materialized.

Notes

1. Robert Bowie, *The North Atlantic Nations Tasks for the 1960s* (1960; repr., College Park, Md.: Nuclear History Project, 1991), 98.

2. Address at Independence Hall, Philadelphia, 4 July 1962, *Public Papers of the President: John F. Kennedy, 1962* (Washington, D.C.: Government Printing Office, 1962–64), 539.

3. Although I readily agree with Monnet himself and others who assume there is a close connection between the ideas of Monnet and Kennedy, I think Douglas Brinkley exaggerates Monnet's influence when he states that the resolution "resurfaced in a slightly revised form" in Kennedy's speech. See Douglas Brinkley, *Dean Acheson: The Cold War Years, 1953–1971* (New Haven, Conn.: Yale Univ. Press, 1992), 188. See also Jean Monnet, *Memoirs* (Garden City, N.Y.: Doubleday, 1978), 466–67; Walt Rostow, "Kennedy's View of Monnet and Vice Versa," in *John F. Kennedy and Europe,* ed. Douglas Brinkley and Richard Griffiths (Baton Rouge: Louisiana State Univ. Press, 1999), 281–88; Eric Roussel, *Jean Monnet, 1888–1979* (Paris: Fayard, 1996), 761–62; and Klaus Schwabe, "Jean Monnet, die Vereinigten Staaten und die Rolle Europas in der atlantischen Völkergemeinschaft," in *Interessen verbinden. Jean Monnet und die europäische Integration der Bundesrepublik Deutschland,* ed. Andreas Wilkens (Bonn: Bouvier, 1999), 225–53.

4. Francois Duchêne, *Jean Monnet: The First Statesman of Interdependence* (New York: W. W. Norton, 1994), 284–88; Pascal Fontaine, *Le Comité d'Action pour les Etats-Unis d'Europe de Jean Monnet* (Lausanne: Centre de Recherches Européennes, 1974).

5. "Joint declaration, 26 June 1962," in Action Committee for Europe, *Statements and Declarations, 1955–1967* (London: Chatham House, 1969), 64–65.

6. Duchêne, *Jean Monnet,* 327.

7. Bowie, *North Atlantic Nations.* Older but still relevant books are John Steinbruner, *The Cybernetic Theory of Decision: New Dimensions of Political Analysis* (Princeton, N.J.: Princeton Univ. Press, 1974), and David Schwartz, *NATO's Nuclear Dilemmas* (Washington, D.C.: Brookings Institution, 1983). Recent publications include Marilena Gala, "The Multilateral Force: A Brief History of the American Efforts to Maintain the Nuclear Status Quo Within the Alliance," *Storia delle Relazioni Internazionali* 13, no. 1 (1998): 121–51; and Helga Haftendorn, "Das Projekt

einer multilateralen NATO-Atomstreitmacht (MLF): Vademecum für die Glaubwürdigkeit der nuklearen Strategie?, *Militärgeschichtliche Mitteilungen* 54 (1995): 417–50.

8. Kennedy memorandum to the members of the MLF negotiating team, 12 Feb. 1963, U.S. Department of State, *Foreign Relations of the United States, 1961–1963* (Washington, D.C.: Government Printing Office, 1994), 13:509–11.

9. Head of the MLF negotiating delegation memorandum to Secretary of State Rusk, 20 Mar. 1963, *FRUS, 1961–1963*, 13:529–37.

10. Pascaline Winand, *Eisenhower, Kennedy, and the United States of Europe* (New York: St. Martin's Press, 1993), 242.

11. In his Ph.D. thesis, Robert von Pagenhardt, special assistant to U.S. ambassador Finletter, provides detailed but not always accurate information about the Paris working group. See Robert von Pagenhardt, "Toward an Atlantic Defense Community: The First Effort, 1960–1966" (Ph.D. diss., Stanford Univ., 1970). There is no single repository for the files of the Paris working group; documents were found in various archives.

12. McGeorge Bundy speech at the general assembly of the Atlantic Treaty Association, 27 Sept. 1962, *Department of State Bulletin* 1962, 604–5. For the speeches of George Ball (Mar. and Nov. 1962) and Robert Schaetzel (Aug. 1962) see *Department of State Bulletin* 1962, 353–54, 364–70, 385.

13. Steinbruner, *Cybernetic Theory*, 319. Lawrence S. Kaplan even argues that McNamara's support of the MLF was never more than a tactical move. Kaplan, "The MLF Debate," in *Kennedy and Europe*, ed. Brinkley and Griffiths, 51–66.

14. Proposed memorandum Merchant to Bundy for the president on control, 15 Feb. 1963, National Archives and Records Administration (NARA), College Park, Md., RG 59, MLF Negotiating Team, box 2, Control Issue.

15. Summary record of NSC executive committee meeting number 41 on Multilateral Nuclear Force, 12 Feb. 1963, memorandum of conversation re Merchant mission and the MLF, 18 Feb. 1963, Kennedy memorandum to the members of the MLF negotiating team, 12 Feb. 1963, *FRUS, 1961–1963*, 13:494–502, 502–6, 509–11.

16. Memcon, Rusk-Stikker, 6 Mar. 1963, *FRUS, 1961–1963*, 13:518–23.

17. Head of the MLF negotiating delegation memorandum to Rusk, 20 Mar. 1963, *FRUS, 1961–1963*, 13:529–37; note of discussions between the British minister of defense, Peter Thorneycroft, and the German minister of defense, Karl Uwe von Hassel, 18 Mar. 1963, Public Record Office, Kew (PRO), Prime Minister files (PREM) 11/4150, 8136.

18. British Embassy Rome tels. to Foreign Office, 203 and 204, 6 Mar. 1963, PRO, PREM 11/4148, 3793

19. Memcon, Kennedy and Italian governmental officials, 1 July 1963, *FRUS, 1961–1963*, 13:884; Carlo Masala, "Deutschland, Italien und die nukleare Frage 1963–1969. Das Problem der nuklearen Mitsprache im Rahmen der Atlantischen Allianz," *Militärgeschichtliche Mitteilungen* 56 (1997): footnote 63.

20. Beatrice Heuser, *NATO, Britain, France, and the FRG: Nuclear Strategies and Forces for Europe, 1949–2000* (Basingstoke: Macmillan, 1997), 148–57, and the special issue of *Revue d'histoire diplomatique* 104, no. 2 (1990).

21. WEU Assembly, Report submitted on behalf of the Committee on Defense questions and armaments by Fred W. Mulley on the state of European security, 147, 30 Oct. 1959, and Recommendation no. 40, *Proceedings WEU Assembly*, 5th session, 2d part, Dec. 1959, III, 58–83 and IV, 36.

22. WEU Assembly, "A NATO Nuclear Force," report submitted on behalf of the Committee on Defence by A. Duynstee, 251, 16 Oct. 1962, and Recommendation no. 83, *Proceedings WEU Assembly*, 8th session, 2d part, Dec. 1962, III, 134–156 and IV, 21.

23. *Die Welt*, 22 Jan. 1963.

24. Beatrice Heuser, "European Strategists and European Identity: The Quest for a European Nuclear Force, 1954–1967," *Journal of European Integration History* 1, no. 2 (1995): 70–72.

25. Maurice Schumann speech at a conference in Cambridge, 20–23 Sept. 1963, Institute of Strategic Study, *The Evolution of NATO* (London: Institute of Strategic Study, 1963), 18–24.

26. Ibid., 41–43.

27. WEU Assembly, "State of European Security. The NATO Nuclear Force," report submitted on behalf of the Committee on Defence by A. Duynstee, 290, 30 Oct. 1963, and Recommendation no. 98, *Proceedings WEU Assembly*, 9th session, 2d part, Dec. 1963, III, 115–48 and IV, 31.

28. Robert Bowie speech to the WEU Assembly, *Proceedings WEU Assembly*, 9th session, 2d part, Dec. 1963, III, 115–28. Bowie referred to a speech by Vice President Lyndon Johnson in Brussels on 8 Nov. 1963, *Department of State Bulletin*, 2 Dec. 1963, 852–54.

29. Multilateral Force working group, *Second Summary*, WG/Document 64/Item 6: Political Control and Annex 1. Central Archives Dutch Ministry of Defence (CAD), Secretary of the Navy (Stasmar), 146.

30. Aufzeichnung des Ministerialdirektors Krapf betr. Gegenwartiger Stand der MLF-Verhandlungen, 15 Nov. 1963; Aufzeichnung des Referats II 7, 17 Dec. 1963, und Aufzeichnung der Politischen Abteilung II betr. MLF, 23 Jan. 1964. *Akten zur Auswärtigen Politik der Bundesrepublik Deutschland (AAPD)*, 1963, III, 414 and 475, 1441–42 and 1650–54; 1964, I, 23, 120–24. Primo Vannicelli, *Italy, NATO, and the European Community: The Interplay of Foreign Policy and Domestic Politics* (Cambridge, Mass.: Center for International Affairs, Harvard Univ., 1974), 19–21.

31. The text of the amendment is quoted in a telegram from the Dutch ambassador. Dutch Embassy Paris tel. to The Hague, Boon N 706, 19 June 1964, Reports of meetings in Dutch Embassy, Paris, tels. to The Hague, Boon N 706, 19 June 1964, Boon N 732, 25 June 1964, and Boon N 841, 16 July 1964, Dutch Ministry of Foreign Affairs (BZ), Secretariat of Atlantic Security (DAV), 538.

32. "Allocation prononcée par Jean Monnet au Congres Européen du Groupe parlementaire social-democrate allemand," Bad Godesberg, 25 février 1964, Fondation Jean Monnet pour L'Europe, Lausanne (FJM), Discours, allocations, interviews, declarations diverses de Jean Monnet (AML), I, 1945–1968, 208/21.

33. Aide mémoire sur la réunion du Comité d'Action pour les Etats-Unis d'Europe à Bonn, le 1er juin 1964, Amendement présenté par monsieur Schmelzer. FJM, Comite d'Action pour les Etats Unis d'Europe (AMK) 16/5/6 et 16/6/202.

34. "Joint declaration 1 June 1964," in Action Committee for Europe, *Statements and Declarations*, 81.

35. Jean Monnet tel. à Cattani, Rome, 546 446, 3 juin 1964, Conversation Jean Monnet avec monsieur Cattani, 15 juin 1964, FJM, AMK C 17/1/107 et C 17/1/109.

36. Staatssekretär Carstens an die Botschaft in Rom, 13 Okt. 1964, Aufzeichnung des Botschafters Grewe, 13 Nov. 1964, *AAPD*, 1964, II, 271 and 330, 1109–11 and 1291–92.

37. Conversations avec Philip Farley, 19 juin 1964, avec monsieur Finletter et monsieur Von Pagenhardt, 17 juillet 1964, et avec monsieur Pagenhardt, 21, 22 et 23 juillet 1964, Lettre de Van Helmont à Monnet, 2 septembre 1964, FJM. Comite d'Action (C.A.), 153, 3. Van

Helmont's draft language was also discussed at a meeting at the State Department. Memorandum re European clause meeting, 22 July 1964, NARA, RG 59, MLF Negotiating Team, box 11, European Clause.

38. Conversation avec monsieur Bowie par Kohnstamm et Van Helmont, le 6 juillet 1964, conversation avec monsieur Bowie par Monnet le 13 juillet 1964, Letter with attached memorandum from Monnet to Bowie on points to be met in the MLF charter and draft provisions, 1 Aug. 1964, Bowie to Monnet, 13 Aug. 1964; FJM, C.A., 153, 2.

39. Bowie to Rusk w. encl. memorandum on approach to the MLF, 31 July 1964, NARA, RG 59, CF 1964–66, DEF (MLF), box 1756, 8/1/64.

40. Conversation avec monsieurs Finletter, Schaetzel, Bowie en Farley le 15 septembre 1964 a Londres, de VH 17 septembre 1964, FJM, C.A., 153, 2.

41. Memorandum de VH, 14 Sept. 1964, FJM, C.A., 153, 2; Finletter to Schaetzel, 22 Sept. 1964; NARA, RG 59, CF 1964–66, DEF (MLF), box 1756, 9/1/64; Memorandum à la suite de la conversation, 20 septembre 1964. FJM, C.A., 153, 2.

42. Finletter tel. to State, Polto 647, 29 Oct. 1964, NARA, RG 59, CF 1964–66, DEF (MLF) 3, box 1758, 7/1/64; Finletter to Rusk, 2 Nov. 1964 w. encl., NARA, RG 59, Office of the Executive Secretariat, MLF documents 1960–1965, box 4, Nov.–Dec. 1964; USRO memorandum on status of issues under discussion in MLF negotiations, 2 Nov. 1964, NARA, RG 59, Office of the Executive Secretariat, MLF documents 1960–1965, box 2, MLF-MLF; Record of conversation U.S. Secretary of State Rusk and Dutch Minister of Foreign Affairs Luns, telegram Washington to The Hague, Schurmann N 88, 8 Nov. 1964; BZ, DAV, 539; "US position on voting formula," encl. to tel. Dutch embassy Paris to BZ, 16 Dec. 1964, BZ, DAV, 539.

43. Jeffrey Giauque, "Offers of Partnership or Bids for Hegemony? The Atlantic Community, 1961–1963," *International History Review* 22 (2000): 101; Christian Hoppe, *Zwischen Teilhabe und Mitsprache: die Nuklearfrage in der Allianzpolitik Deutschlands, 1959–1966* (Baden-Baden: Nomos Verlag, 1993), 109–12.

44. Frank Costigliola, "The Pursuit of Atlantic Community: Nuclear Arms, Dollars, and Berlin," in *Kennedy's Quest for Victory: American Foreign Policy, 1961–1963*, ed. Thomas Paterson (New York: Oxford Univ. Press, 1989), 24–57.

7

Ostpolitik as a Source of Intrabloc Tensions

OLIVER BANGE

Ostpolitik caused friction on a number of different levels: it sparked tensions within Willy Brandt's Social Democratic Party, parliament, and the coalition cabinet, between West Germany and the Western allies, and even within the Eastern bloc. It is the latter two conflicts that this chapter will discuss, arranging documents from various national archives around nine distinct but interconnected arguments. Inevitably, such a *vue d'ensemble* has to start with an explanation of the goals and tactics underlying the new Eastern policy as devised during Brandt's time as foreign minister of the "Grand Coalition" from December 1966 to September 1969 and put into practice during his chancellorship of the social-liberal coalition until 1974 and then onward to the Conference on Security and Cooperation in Europe (CSCE) in Helsinki on 1 August 1975.

One might compare the "*Neue Ostpolitik*" of Willy Brandt and Egon Bahr with a coin: the currency, or ultimate goal, imprinted on it is called "unification." In order to avoid any reminiscence of the original borders of the vanished Reich, Brandt refused to speak about "reunification," preferring the "unification" or "*Zusammenwachsen*" (growing closer) of the two existing German states. The two sides of the coin represent two long-term strategies to achieve unification. Undermining Communism by exposing the people under its rule to Western values and liberties was one side of the coin. But the eventual breakdown of Communism itself would not guarantee German unification. Thus, the other side of the coin was therefore to devise an all-European security system, taking care of the legitimate security concerns of all nations (including the United States and the Soviet Union) concerned by a prospective unification of the two German states. This, and only this, it was argued at the time, could possibly ease the way to unification after an eventual collapse of the regimes in Eastern Europe. Of course, with a secret agenda like this, Brandt and Bahr had to play their cards very close to their chests. For this reason, some of the best evidence for this double-sided strategy is found not in the German archives (for obvious domestic and party political reasons) but in the archives of other Western allies, particularly in Washington and Paris, where this strategy had to be "sold" and defended, and those in Eastern Europe, where the success of the strategy—once it was recognized—became a reason for great concern. The following represents an overview and summary of the arguments deriving from the multiarchival, international research undertaken for the "Ostpolitik and Détente" project at the University of Mannheim.[1]

The "New Ostpolitik" was built upon American and French strategies that were instituted from 1960–61 onward, and particularly on the concept of "ideological competition" first developed in the United States by Secretary of State Dean Rusk during the Kennedy years, then refined by the Johnson administration after 1964.

As a strategic game plan, *Ostpolitik* was an intelligent, early reaction to the new approaches developed under Charles de Gaulle and John F. Kennedy. Seen from Berlin, but not only from Berlin, these approaches offered real alternatives to the prioritization of "Westindung" over reunification by the then Konrad Adenauer government. Within this new strategy, two aspects can be clearly distinguished: one is the search for the holy grail (i.e., a unified Germany) in a new European security system (proposed by de Gaulle as early as 1959–60 and pursued by him with concrete policies from 1961–62); the other is the idea of an intensive ideological struggle through, above, or under the Iron Curtain, conceived perhaps by Kennedy or, much more probably, by the team around Dean Rusk back in 1961.[2]

In the years following the catastrophic summit between Kennedy and Nikita Khrushchev in Vienna in June 1961,[3] Rusk kept on talking to Brandt about the West's ideological superiority, arguing that it would be better to look forward to ideological "competition" than to shy away from it.[4] The most appropriate weapons for that struggle would be human contacts of all sorts, culture, and, above all, the exchange of information. It was only under Johnson that the loose and largely unconnected ideas of Kennedy's men were finally cast into a coherent strategy. Already in January 1964 this strategy became, at least internally, the declared foundation of American policy toward the Eastern bloc. The euphemism used by the Johnson White House to present this strategy to the outside world—"bridge building"—meanwhile served as a cover for its true agenda, a function that Egon Bahr's celebrated contemporary catchphrase of "change by rapprochement" (*Wandel durch Annäherung*, presented first in a famed speech Bahr delivered at Tutzing) provided for the *Neue Ostpolitik*. Despite some rather curious anecdotes, like Johnson's personal ploy to force Brezhnev into accepting a performance of the musical *Hello Dolly* in Moscow,[5] we seem to witness, as presented by Thomas

Schwartz[6]—the beginning of a fundamental revision of Johnson's foreign policy posture, to which more recent research on the interrelationship between Brandt's *Ostpolitik* and Johnson's détente policy can now be added.

Whether the secret agenda behind the bridge-building concept was handed over to the succeeding administration and, if so, to what extent it influenced the Eastern policies of Richard M. Nixon and Henry A. Kissinger is still an open question. Despite the wealth of papers in the Johnson Library[7] that reveal a unique and surprisingly comprehensive transition process between the Johnson and Nixon administrations, the author was unable to locate any documents concerning East-West relations. Nevertheless, within the Nixon Papers in the National Archives in Washington, an important analysis from Henry Kissinger has survived from mid-February 1969 comparing for the newly inaugurated president the approaches taken to East-West relations and détente by his incoming administration with those taken by Johnson's team. Here, Kissinger—himself a former consultant to both Johnson and Rusk—described in detail the goals and strategies of the outgoing administration, only to reject them in the end as a risky strategy of "compartmentalization of our relations with the USSR" and to argue, completely in line with Nixon's own thinking, for a series of pragmatic and interlinked status-quo agreements between the two superpowers.[8]

Given that these concepts were developed under Kennedy and Johnson, there can be very little question that Johnson's speech of October 1966 was not the fundamental shift in policies on Germany as historiography has tended to interpret it.[9] Johnson appears at best to have felt rather less obliged to follow the long-established bilateral terminology, perhaps encouraged by the latest developments in Bonn's own German policy.

French fears of German (re-)unification were at the heart of de Gaulle's all-European security concept and of Georges Pompidou's rejection of any subversive Ostpolitik *tactics.*

In June 1965 a remarkable event took place in the Elysée Palace in Paris: Willy Brandt, then mayor of West Berlin, met almost totally in private with President Charles de Gaulle. This was anything but a meeting between equals, but more a ritualized setting for the exchange of pleasantries and the renewal of French readiness to defend Western liberties in Berlin. Instead of listening politely to the opening address of his visitor, de Gaulle went straight to the heart of things: What kind of policy toward the East, what kind of *Ostpolitik,* would he, Charles de Gaulle, pursue, if he were a German?

What followed can rightly be considered a master plan for exactly the kind of *Ostpolitik* that Brandt would practice from 1969 onward—at least as far as its strategic and security dimensions were concerned. One can only speculate about the reasons behind de Gaulle's extraordinary initiative since comparable conversations with Chancellor

Ludwig Erhard or Foreign Minister Gerhard Schröder were not recorded. On a range of key questions, the confluence of their thinking about security and defense policy questions was almost complete, from the opening up of West Germany's relations with the states in Eastern Europe in distinct phases to the idea of a possible change of the status quo through its acceptance with regard to the Oder-Neisse Line, the GDR as a second German state, and the renunciation of nuclear weapons. Losing no time on thoughts about strategies of undermining or subverting, de Gaulle simply registered the Kremlin's status quo policy in Europe and concluded from it the inevitable breakdown of the Warsaw bloc in the distant future:

> On that basis, perhaps some day Germany might be reunited. On that point, you are not in agreement with us, for, in the final analysis, you are not in agreement with your eastern borders. You are perhaps wrong. You are perhaps right. Nonetheless, that is the way it is and that prevents us from having a common policy on the reunification of Germany.[10]

Pompidou's papers give very clear confirmation of Brandt's and Bahr's tactic of intellectual subversion. During the very first months of his presidency, Pompidou's foreign policy adviser, Jean-Bernard Raimond, wrote three lengthy memoranda on German *Ostpolitik*. The memoranda deemed reunification by ideologically undermining the regimes in the East and by military neutralization—even unification itself—to be incompatible with French national interests, and he therefore advanced appropriate counterstrategies.[11] When compared with the de Gaulle era, Pompidou's hasty reactions are a clear indication that the three most important determinants of France's German and Eastern policy, even of its entire foreign policy, were undergoing a fundamental change. De Gaulle had propagated a concept of German unification in a changed European framework. This meant, at least in the understanding of his contemporaries, that the actual event of unification was deferred to the indefinite future. This was, of course, a clever trick on de Gaulle's part because it defused the potential rift over that question in Franco-German relations.

Now, however, Pompidou, Michel Jobert, and Raimond conceded—after the experiences of the Prague spring and what they perceived as an unduly strong involvement of West German Social Democrats in the Prague events—that the new and more independent German *Ostpolitik* made for a far greater probability of success regarding the unification of East and West Germany. Such a development naturally represented a forthright danger to France's role as a mediator between the governments in Bonn and in Eastern Europe. France also no longer appeared to be in a position to veto British entry into the EEC, at least in the medium term, and, in addition, the latest shifts in the balance of power in—or with respect to—East-West relations seemed to militate strongly against the prolongation of such a Gaullist stance. British entry, however, would weaken France's key position within the EEC and, at the same time, Paris was losing its sometimes illusionary role as a mediator between East and West because of the new focus of the East European states on Bonn. Practical consequences for French policy stemming from that analysis took some time to emerge, however, probably first manifested in Pompidou's deep mistrust of Brandt in 1973 and his initiative for basket III (free movement of persons and information, human rights) within the CSCE process.[12]

Therefore, both of the strategic concepts that constituted the basis of Brandt's and Bahr's new approach to Ostpolitik *were of limited originality, while their combination and instrumentalization for a specific German goal, unification, added a new and controversial dimension to the strategic outlook.*

This assessment, of course, means that Bahr in his 1963 "*Wandel durch Annäherung*" speech merely accepted the realities of a bipolar world and the German need for a protecting power, relating this to the specific conditions and objectives that applied in Berlin and Germany as a whole. Following from this observation, the original contribution of Brandt and Bahr would be twofold: on the one hand, it would be the realization that Germany and especially the SPD were able to play a special role in this Western strategy; on the other, it would consist in a very perceptive connection between the German dream of unification and this Western strategy, as opposed to silent acceptance of the elimination of this goal from the Western agenda. The fact that, for the FDP (the German Liberals), Wolfgang Schollwer also started working on plans to achieve unification within a European security system as early as 1962–63 is further proof of the need to track the origins of the international-system strategy within the new *Ostpolitik* to an earlier date; it is also a further indication of the external influences acting on its makers.[13] After the Social-Liberal coalition was formed, Jürgen Diesel, one of Bahr's closest collaborators in the Planungsstab, the think tank of West Germany's Foreign Office, greeted Schollwer's ideas with utter astonishment, irked "that such a paper could possibly have been written up without any participation of the Planungsstab in the proceedings."[14]

Recent studies have tracked the origins in Brandt's thinking of a strategy of undermining Communism by a multiplication of information and communication to the late 1950s.[15] Arne Hofmann's research points to the mutual impact of Brandt and Kennedy as almost a precondition for the development of this strategy.[16] This must call into question the notion of *Ostpolitik* as a purely endogenous development in German policy. From this perspective, the merits of the creators of Bonn's new Eastern and German policies would instead lie in the early recognition of momentous shifts within the international framework—concerning friends and foes alike—and the rigorous use of these new trends for specific German goals.

The strategies combined in the Neue Ostpolitik *served as both a glue and a catalyst for the breakdown of the Grand Coalition between the conservative CDU/CSU and the SPD—depending on the perspectives of the individuals involved and the various problems to which it was applied.*

So far, the relentless fight within the conservative parties over the eventual candidate for the next general elections (Rainer Barzel, Franz Josef Strauß, Schröder—1969–1974) has continued to be disregarded as a major factor in the course of *Ostpolitik*—and has developed into something of a historiographical blind spot.[17] The obstructive impact of party politics and personal intrigue on West German foreign policy was felt particularly during the negotiations with the Soviet Union over a prospective agreement on the mutual renunciation of force and Bonn's accession to the Non-Proliferation Treaty (NPT). Although these efforts were frustrated by the right wingers within the Grand Coalition while it lasted, the negotiations and meetings with the Soviets also provided Brandt and particularly Bahr with ample opportunity to test the prospective constraints that a new and rigorous Eastern policy would face in the not-so-distant future. Interpreted from this perspective, the negotiations over the renunciation of force (*Gewaltverzicht*), and the developments in conceptual thinking that they triggered in the inner circle of Bonn's Foreign Office, became something of a parallel, if only speculative, foreign policy. It helped create a perception of what could be achieved if the new Eastern policy were no longer to be a prisoner of the constraints of the Grand Coalition and particularly of the forces at work within the CDU and CSU.

Three important events stood at the beginnings of a truly new Eastern and German policy in Bonn. The signing of the NPT cleared away hitherto insurmountable obstacles in the East and the West and ended the domestic blockade in Bonn. The second event of this triptych of détente policy was constituted by the experiences of constructive negotiations and shared responsibility involving both superpowers surrounding the Berlin crisis of the first months of 1969. The third of these events was the ongoing negotiating process over a possible agreement on the renunciation of force between Bonn and Moscow. Without West Germany's accession to the NPT, the agreement on the renunciation of force soon codified in the Treaty of Moscow in the summer of 1970 would not have been feasible, and without such an official treaty progress on all other areas of Bonn's *Neue Ostpolitik*—and quite possibly East-West détente in general—would have been barred for years.[18]

Władysław Gomułka, the head of the Polish Communist Party, saw through the smokescreens provided by Brandt and Bahr, realizing the potential threat of "Social-democratism" to Communism in Eastern Europe that other leaders of the Warsaw Pact often neglected or underestimated.

Perceptions of the *Neue Ostpolitik* varied significantly among the various member states of the Warsaw Pact—dependent upon current political necessities, like East Berlin's thirst for international recognition or the Kremlin's need for large-scale economic cooperation. Yet only the Polish leadership appears to have realized the ambiguity in Brandt's *Ostpolitik* (i.e., the attempt to gain unification through the temporary recognition of the status quo) and to have thought this through to its ultimate consequences.[19] Mieczysław Tomala, a leading thinker behind the making of Polish foreign policy at the time, even lists a number of sources in his memoirs[20] that seem to prove that Gomułka not only knew about the tactic of "Social-democratism"—using a policy of enhanced contacts "to punch holes," "to soften up," and "to undermine" the East—but also actively attempted to counteract it. This offers, in turn, a new perspective on what Western observers once dubbed the "Iron Triangle" among East Berlin, Warsaw, and Prague.[21] In vain, the Sovietologists of the 1960s, often ridiculed as Kremlinologists or astrologists, had attempted to decipher Gomułka's motives.[22] Walter Ulbricht and then Erich Honecker rejected outright the Polish concept of intensified economic integration, because trade with the Federal Republic of Germany, effectively as part of the EEC, clearly offered the prospect of more hard currency. This enabled the GDR to obtain advanced Western technology, which in turn constituted the basis of the GDR's economic preponderance within the Eastern bloc—in Ulbricht's words, the GDR's "model character."

When Gomułka realized the objectives of Brandt's policy, he estimated that the German Democratic Republic would merely survive another ten to fifteen years, accepting at the same time that the work of his life, securing the Western borders of a socialist Poland, was in jeopardy.[23] When talking to the Politbureau of Poland's Communist Party in June 1969, he did not even try to hide his fear that the USSR might neglect vital Polish interests for its own sake and that the GDR's ever-increasing dependence on the West could lead to its complete dissolution: "One can safely assume that the GDR belongs to the EEC-'Six' through its ties with the FRG. . . . In perspective, this might lead not only to economic affiliation, but to rapprochement resulting in [Germany's] unification." He also accused Moscow of pushing for intensified contacts between the Warsaw Pact members and the Brandt administration in Bonn: "Efforts in favour of an intensification of relations with the FRG come from all sides, particularly from the USSR. . . . We have to draw practical conclusions from this. . . . We cannot possibly maintain that we do not care whether or not the FRG recognizes our borders, because our position will be weakened."[24]

When the Soviet Union and the GDR intensified their contacts with Bonn in early 1970, Gomułka had to act. Isolated by his own allies, he had to salvage whatever he could as quickly as possible (be it the Oder-Neisse Line or economic arrangements with the West) and in cooperation with the new Brandt government. This interpretation would also offer a logical explanation for the sudden end of Warsaw's complete lack of official communication in response to the secret approaches made by Egon Bahr.[25] What an irony: the only Eastern European ruler who realized the danger coming from "Social-democratism," and who actively tried to prevent it, had to become a pacemaker for détente.

Seen from the eyes of the leadership in the Kremlin, Bonn's Neue Ostpolitik offered timely leverage for the realization of Soviet-induced détente policies, welcomed within the Kremlin for both domestic and international reasons. Meanwhile, long-term risks connected with Ostpolitik were grossly underestimated.

In an almost cynical twist of events, only the crisis in Czechoslovakia in August 1968, reflecting the temporary predominance of the hawks in the Politbureau, with its catastrophic consequences for the Soviet Union's foreign policy stature both within the Warsaw Pact and in relations with the outside world, gave détente-minded politicians in the Kremlin the opportunity to push their policies through. The armed intervention against the Prague spring had tightened discipline and "solidarity" within the entire Eastern bloc, heightened awareness everywhere of the USSR's dominant position within the Warsaw Pact, opened up the Eastern flank of the second superpower, and led both blocs to the verge of a nuclear and conventional arms race, with unpredictable consequences for all parts of the world.

Only in this highly precarious situation in September 1968 were détente and an ongoing dialogue between the superpowers accepted as guiding principles of Soviet foreign policy.[26] In the meantime, suitable partners in the West had almost vanished. In the last months of his administration, Johnson was a lame duck, not least because of events in Czechoslovakia. Thereafter, Nixon and Kissinger pursued, at least officially, a less compromising course in East-West relations. In Europe, de Gaulle's favorite role as a mediator between the blocs had been discredited by the events of 1968, and he resigned in 1969. The first priority of London's foreign policy was EEC entry and, in Bonn, left- and right-wingers within the Grand Coalition had caused a virtual standstill over foreign policy for the months preceding the general elections.

This situation only changed when the federal German elections in September 1969 brought Willy Brandt to the chancellorship in a new coalition, this time comprising his Social Democrats and the German Liberals, thus giving the Kremlin a unique opportunity that had to be seized.[27] The rapid conclusion of the Moscow Treaty in the summer of 1970 was therefore not only a product of the long-term preparations made on the German side, of the successful probing of each other's room for maneuver, of the skilled tactical game played by Egon Bahr, or of Bonn's renewed interest in moving quickly. It was also a sign of the determination with which the mighty few in the Kremlin were able to exploit the chance offered to them.[28] A selective détente struck with Bonn was the only policy that at the time had a prospect of winning over a hesitant majority in the Politbureau of the Communist Party of the Soviet Union to the merits of the new course. Only by leading a selective détente with Bonn could Moscow prove to its allies that it would safeguard their national interests in the pursuit of this new course, and only by pursuing this selective détente with Bonn before the eyes of a global public could

Moscow hope to tempt the administration in Washington back to the negotiating table. Only after its Western treaties and agreements with the Federal Republic of Germany and the United States were successfully finalized, around mid-1973, did the Kremlin, too, become somewhat more suspicious and warn its own allies to observe utmost caution over Bonn's potentially subversive tactics in their respective and still-ongoing negotiations.

European integration, and particularly the British application to join the EEC, served London, Paris, and Washington as insurance against West German "adventurism" and provided Bonn with a guarantee of a secure "anchoring" in the West ("anchoring" being the term used in Washington, "Westbindung" the term coined in Bonn).

Another crucial aspect—entirely neglected by international historiography until today—is the interrelation between *Ostpolitik* and the British negotiations for entry to the European Economic Community. Notwithstanding the East-West conflict, the British government had poor intelligence on current thinking in Eastern Europe and within the EEC and had to rely on German mediation. If, however, Brandt's *Ostpolitik* was in reality a "*Deutschlandpolitik*," and if "*Deutschlandpolitik*" took priority over other policies (as Brandt himself had maintained), the rift between Britain and the Soviets was an advantageous situation that needed to be exploited or even prolonged. This, in turn, would also offer an explanation for the different approaches taken by Brandt and Kissinger to de Gaulle's European policies. Bonn as a "good European" was also a pledge against any adventurist *Ostpolitik*—something that was made instrumental by Bonn as a kind of guarantee ("*Ostpolitik* starts in the West") and required and even conceptualized by the three Western allies—each in turn with its own national interests and strategy deriving from it.

Other facets of this anchoring concept emerged in the West German defense budget (which jumped to an all-time high during the years of *Ostpolitik* under Social Democratic defense ministers Helmut Schmidt and Kurt-Georg Leber); in the fact that the financing of the EEC's push for further, deeper integration was mostly paid by Bonn (this relates particularly to the French demand of a common agricultural policy); and in Brandt's active support for Kissinger's ill-fated idea of a "Year of Europe." The extent of the acceptance of different treatment for West Germany within Europe also shows, prima facie, the extent to which the European communities were actually designed as an instrument of control over the Germans on both sides of the Wall. British prime minister Harold Wilson told de Gaulle, Nixon, and even Aleksey Kosygin that the real reason for his desire to bring the United Kingdom into the EC was to help the French control the Germans, whose increasing economic success would soon lead to demands for a greater voice in European affairs.[29] None of his interlocutors indicated surprise at this claim, nor did they contradict it. Instead, it was simply accepted.

Partly as a result of a series of spy cases, "solved" under the public gaze, the British remained fairly isolated in the continually intensifying exchanges between East and West in the late 1960s and early 1970s.[30] Neither the French nor the Americans intended to change this situation for the sake of their own objectives with regard to détente. It was only in 1974 that—triggered by the ongoing CSCE process and Wilson's return to power—the first British diplomats realized that "exposure to Western values (could have) a long-term impact upon Eastern Europe."[31] Therefore, instead of leading Western détente, as Anne Deighton has argued, London's Eastern policy might be perceived rather as a latecomer to this new era of East-West relations.

Despite frictions between Washington and Bonn over Ostpolitik, *parallelisms prevailed during the Nixon-Brandt era.*

Frictions between the Nixon and Brandt administrations were manifold and concerned both the personalities involved and the policies they stood for. An important undercurrent was the deeply rooted mistrust in the White House, furthered even under express instruction of the president himself—of the "semi-Communist" in Bonn's chancellor's office, the Palais Schaumburg. When Brandt and Bahr initiated their negotiating offensive toward Moscow in November 1969, there had been no prior consultations with the White House.[32] The unexpected speed of the negotiations was breathtaking, even by American standards, and became an additional factor in the growing alienation between Washington and Bonn. Within the few months between the change of government in Bonn and March 1970, visits by Rainer Barzel, then leader of the conservative opposition in Bonn, became a common sight in the White House. Plans and scenarios were developed on how to overthrow the Brandt government, and in late March 1970 Barzel actually discussed his future cabinet list with Nixon and Kissinger (among other things Barzel inquired whether he should, or could, allow Franz Josef Strauß into the cabinet).[33] The president himself noted on the margins of his briefing papers: "Any non socialist government would be better."[34]

In view of this, one question remains: why was there no early attempt to oust Brandt and his Social Democrats from power? Both Bahr and Kissinger were masters of linkage politics (*Junktimpolitik* in German) and the Americans soon realized that the results of German *Ostpolitik* presented them with powerful leverage in their own pursuit of a bilateral détente with the other superpower. The still-open ratification of the treaties of Moscow and Warsaw (which Barzel wanted to seize upon for a vote of no confidence in the government) and Bonn's unofficial but vital role in the parallel four-power negotiations over a Berlin agreement had become important bargaining tools and constituted a quintessential trump card in the rapprochement between Washington and Moscow. Barzel returned to Washington in April 1971, warning that *Ostpolitik* was a possible source of both nationalism and Marxism in Germany and predicting that the CDU would soon turn against *Ostpolitik* completely. Kissinger simply noted, "This does not fit in our 'game plan' with the Soviet Union at this moment."[35] The change in atmosphere and issues communicated through the top-secret back channel between Kissinger and Bahr mirrored this historic shift of paradigms in intra-allied tactics.[36] In a conversation with the author, Kissinger conceded that he had serious doubts about the wisdom of *Ostpolitik,* adding a concise summary of Washington's options at the time: The U.S. government could lend its open support to the opponents of *Ostpolitik* within the Federal Republic (in other words, help topple the Brandt government), which would have ruined American standing in German politics for a long time to come. Or the Nixon administration could do what it eventually decided, and that was to embrace *Ostpolitik* and its proponents in a friendly manner, thus keeping informed and allowing the United States a chance to steer, if necessary.[37]

For a proper historical understanding of the real friction caused by *Ostpolitik* in American-German relations, it is important to distinguish among personal emotions, idiosyncratic perceptions, ad-hoc reactions, and fundamental national interests.[38] In 1971 and 1972, American and German ideas about détente and *Ostpolitik* quickly intermingled. With the contemporary unfolding of global détente, the U.S. administration's interest in a successful ratification of the *Ostverträge,* Bonn's treaties with the East, increased noticeably. Kissinger knew that it was only the Germans who could deliver to the Soviets what they demanded in return for secure access routes to the besieged city of Berlin. Détente in Europe had become an unofficial prerogative of Moscow, Washington, and Bonn, rather than Paris and London, which were still playing the big power games of long-lost days at the official four-power talks in Berlin. Brandt, Bahr, and Walter Scheel in turn were quick to link a give over Federal presence in West Berlin to the start of negotiations between the West and East German governments and the successful completion of the so-called *Grundlagenvertrag,* the treaty laying the framework for relations between Bonn and East Berlin until 1989. At the end of 1972, an astonished Helmut Sonnenfeldt even praised Bahr as the master of linkage policies to his superior Henry Kissinger.[39]

Despite apparent inactivity on Bonn's side at the beginning of the CSCE negotiations, Helsinki 1975 was a well- and long-planned climax of the Neue Ostpolitik.

The CSCE conference in Helsinki in 1975 provided a natural climax to the *Neue Ostpolitik* as much as for the historical, worldwide era of détente. As far back as 1967, Bahr had drawn up a strategy—labeled by his team and himself as the "timetable"—that was intended finally to result in the multilateralization of *Ostpolitik.* The focal point of this process was a comprehensive conference to lay the basis of an all-European security system.[40] This, it was thought at the time, should aim at reducing tensions along the Iron Curtain, opening the way for the "growing together" of the two German states, ideally leading in the distant future to some kind of confederation and perhaps unification. Outside Bonn, in East and West alike, Helsinki was primarily perceived in the words of John Maresca, head of the American delegation, as an "Ersatz-Peace" over Germany.[41]

Although the Federal Republic played a rather inconspicuous role in the proceedings and results of the conference, it could be argued that West German *Ostpolitik* had been so successfully implemented over the preceding years that by 1975 it had already become a widely accepted basis of détente policies in Europe (at least in the Western Hemisphere). This, in turn, allowed the German "Ostpoliticians," by now widely regarded as renowned and almost elder statesmen, to ease their own efforts and leave the field to the French and other interested parties. This, of course, helped redress the rather strained balance in Franco-German relations while still leading up to exactly the kind of result in Helsinki for which West German policy had long aspired: Basket III.[43] Back in 1969, only days before the general elections, Bahr had written a conclusion to the thoughts developed in his team, which he then considered something of a legacy for whichever party would seize power in Bonn thereafter. This paper gave clear evidence of the interconnection between the conference and the long-term strategy embedded in Brandt's *Neue Ostpolitik:*

European Security Conference
The Warsaw Pact states have tabled their proposal; we now have to try to instrumentalise it for the pursuit of our own interests. The conference offers an opportunity to table proposals aiming at a security system in Europe and at building the defense-political preconditions for a peaceful order. . . . We could also use our readiness to participate at an ESC as a leverage to obtain the inner-German treaty. . . . In all this we should solely be guided by the prospect of an irreversible political process, and we should only retreat from positions which do not offer any better political advantages.[43]

In August 1975 at Helsinki, the most important result of the conference (and yet negotiated predominantly outside the CSCE framework among Washington, D.C., Bonn, and Moscow) was the incorporation of the principles of "peaceful change" and "free[r] movement of persons and ideas" into the Final Act.[44] And exactly these principles were at the heart of the "Helsinki-effect,"[45] which came to dominate the ensuing CSCE process leading up to the events of 1989–90.

Notes

1. This chapter represents an overview of the arguments developed within the research projects "Ostpolitik und Détente," funded by the Thyssen-Foundation, and "CSCE and the Transformation of Europe," funded by the Volkswagenstiftung, both at the Univ. of Mannheim and headed by Gottfried Niedhart (www.detente.de or www.ostpolitik.net and www.CSCE-1975.net).

2. There still exists some controversy about the labeling of this policy. "Bridge building" and "Wandel durch Annäherung" were clearly euphemisms. Johnson later referred to "ideological competition"; Bahr referred to it as "Sozialdemokratismus." Whereas Bahr's term is open to criticism because it originates from Communist sources (depicting their fight against the bourgeois labor movement particularly in Germany), Francis Bator disapproved of the term "competition" or even "liberalization" as implying a "zero-sum strategy." Neither Brandt's *Ostpolitik* nor Johnson's détente was based on static policy models but were aimed at inducing social, economic, and political change. See Francis Bator, "The Politics of Alliance: The United States and Western Europe," in *Agenda for the Nation,* ed. Kermit Gordon (Washington: Brookings Institution, 1971), 335–72.

3. For the different perceptions of the crucial conversation between Khrushchev and Kennedy in Vienna on 6 April 1961—Khrushchev's nuclear threat or his attempt to confront Kennedy with the consequences of nuclear catastrophe—see the American and Soviet protocols. Russian original and (East) German translation in SAPMO: Ulbricht's office files, DY30/3663. LBJL: NSF, Rostow File, vol. 11.

4. This material is well covered in U.S. Department of State, *Foreign Relations of the United States, 1964–1968* (Washington, D.C.: G.P.O., 1996–2001), vols. 11, 14, 15, 17.

5. The musical—and Johnson's ideas for its East European future—was treated as a top-secret issue. LBJL: WHCF, FG105 (Confidential Files from the Department of State), box 24.

6. Thomas A. Schwartz, *Lyndon Johnson and Europe: In the Shadow of Vietnam* (Cambridge, Mass.: Harvard Univ. Press, 2003).

7. The author was able to consult these files in the summer of 2003 at the LBJ Library in Austin, Texas, at the invitation of the Johnson Foundation.

8. Kissinger memorandum to Nixon, "Analysis of Dobrynin Message," 18 Feb. 1969, NARA: Nixon, NSC, Presidential Trip File, box 489.

9. Ernest May, "Das nationale Interesse der Vereinigten Staaten und die deutsche Frage 1966–1972," in *Deutschland in Europa: Nationale Interessen und internationale Ordnung im 20. Jahrhundert,* ed. Gottfried Niedhart, Detlef Junker, and Michael W. Richter (Mannheim: Platinum Verlag, 1997), 271–84. For the true background of Johnson's October 1966 speech, see also Francis M. Bator, "Lyndon Johnson and Foreign Policy: The Case of Western Europe and the Soviet Union," in *Presidential Judgment: Foreign Policy Decision Making in the White House,* ed. Aaron Lobel (Cambridge, Mass.: Harvard Univ. Press, 2001), 41–77. Bator authored the original draft and also served as a coordinator for eventual changes until the final version emerged. Conversation between Francis Bator and the author, 27 Mar. 2004.

10. Conversation between de Gaulle and Brandt, translated from French by Mark Rubin, 2 June 1965, 17–18.10 o'clock, at the Elysée, AN: 5 AG 1/167 (de Gaulle Papers). For Brandt's rather less illuminating account of the meeting, see Willy Brandt, *Berliner Ausgabe,* vol. 3, *"Berlin bleibt frei": Politik in und für Berlin 1947–1966,* ed. Siegfried Heimann (Bonn: Dietz, 2004), doc. 102.

11. Raimond's memoranda for Pompidou, 3 July, 6 Nov., 8 Dec. 1969, 24 Jan. 1970. AN: 5 AG 2/1010 and -/1009 (Pompidou Papers). See also MAE: Série Europe, Sous-Série Republique Fédérale d'Allemagne, vol. 1726.

12. See Marie-Pierre Rey, *La tentation du rapprochment: France et URSS à l'heure de la détente, 1964–1974* (Paris: Publications de la Sorbonne, 1991).

13. See Mathias Siekmeier, *Restauration oder Reform? Die FDP in den sechziger Jahren: Deutschland- und Ostpolitik zwischen Wiedervereinigung und Entspannung* (Köln: Janus Verlag, 1998); Gottfried Niedhart, "Friedens- und Interessenwahrung: Zur Ostpolitik der F.D.P. in Opposition und sozial-liberaler Regierung 1968–1970," in *Jahrbuch zur Liberalismus-Forschung*, vol. 7, Baden-Baden 1995, 105–26. Volker Erhard, "Die Schollwer-Papiere von 1962 und 1967: Meilensteine auf dem Weg der FDP zur neuen Deutschland- und Ostpolitik," in *Deutsch-deutscher Liberalismus im Kalten Krieg: Zur Deutschlandpolitik der Liberalen 1945–1970*, ed. Reinhard Hübsch and Jürgen Frölich (Potsdam: Verlag für Berlin-Brandenburg, 1997), 237–51.

14. Jürgen Diesel to Schollwer, 23 Oct. 1969; AdL: Schollwer Papers, vol. 6960/65.

15. With regard to the concepts elaborated upon by Brandt and Bahr during their time in Berlin, new ground has been charted by a number of recent works: Gerhard Kunze, *Grenzerfahrungen, Kontakte und Verhandlungen zwischen dem Land Berlin und der DDR 1949–1989* (Berlin: Akademie Verlag, 1999); Peter C. Speicher, "The Berlin Origins of Brandt's Ostpolitik, 1957–1966" (Ph.D. diss., Cambridge Univ., 2000); Wolfgang Schmidt, *Kalter Krieg, Koexistenz und kleine Schritte: Willy Brandt und die Deutschlandpolitik 1948–1963* (Wiesbaden: Westdeutscher, 2001); Gottfried Niedhart, "The East-West Problem as Seen from Berlin: Willy Brandt's Early Ostpolitik," in *Europe, Cold War, and Coexistence, 1953–1965*, ed. Wilfried Loth (London: Frank Cass, 2004), 285–94.

16. Arne Hofmann, *The Emergence of Détente in Europe: Brandt, Kennedy, and the Formation of Ostpolitik* (London: Routledge, 2007).

17. Most recent examples include Andrea H. Schneider, *Die Kunst des Kompromisses: Helmut Schmidt und die große Koalition 1966–1969* (Paderborn: Verlag Ferdinand Schöningh, 1999), 202; and Philipp Gassert, *Kurt Georg Kiesinger, 1904–1998: Kanzler zwischen den Zeiten* (Munich: Deutsche Verlags-Anstalt, 2006).

18. See Gottfried Niedhart and Oliver Bange, "Die 'Relikte der Nachkriegszeit' beseitigen: Ostpolitik in der zweiten außenpolitischen Formationsphase der Bundesrepublik Deutschland im Übergang von den Sechziger- zu den Siebzigerjahren," in *Archiv für Sozialgeschichte*, vol. 44 (Bonn, 2004): 415–48. All three themes are treated in detail in the author's forthcoming publication "Détente and *Ostpolitik* in Europe: The Beginnings, 1966–1969," planned for 2008.

19. See Dieter Bingen, *Die Bonner Deutschlandpolitik 1969–1979 in der polnischen Publizistik* (Frankfurt/M: A. Metzner, 1982); and idem, *Die Polenpolitik der Bonner Republik von Adenauer bis Kohl 1949–1991* (Baden-Baden: Nomas, 1998).

20. Mieczysław Tomala, *Deutschland: von Polen gesehen, zu den deutsch-polnischen Beziehungen 1945–1990* (Marburg: Schüren, 2000).

21. The hesitations in Prague over following the Ulbricht-Gomułka line are documented in the briefing papers for Communist leader Antonín Novotný for the meeting of the secretariat on 25 Jan. 1967. See A-ÙV KSC: Antonín Novotný, ČSSR-NSR, box 2/33.

22. For a rich account of the latest research on this context, see the contribution of Douglas Selvage in this volume. See also Wanda Jarzabek, "'Ulbricht-Doktrin' oder 'Gomułka-Doktrin'?

Das Bemühen der Volksrepublik Polen um eine geschlossene Politik des kommunistischen Blocks gegenüber der westdeutschen Ospolitik 1966/67," in *Zeitschrift für Ostmitteleuropa-Forschung* 55, no. 1 (2006): 79–115.

23. Conversation between Gomułka and Brezhnev, Moscow, 3 Mar. 1969. AAN: KC PZPR, teczka 2645, pp. 54–59, printed in Andrezej Paczkowski, ed., *Tajne dokumenty Biura Politycznego: PRL-ZSRR, 1956–1970* (London: Aneks, 1998), doc. 39, 541ff.

24. Gomułka's explanations before the Politbureau, Warsaw, 2 June 1969. AAN: KC PZPR, V/88.

25. AdsD: Egon Bahr Papers, vol. 388. See also Hansjakob Stehle, "Eine vertrackte Vorge-schichte: Zum Warschauer Vertrag: Wie ein Schlüsseldokument verschwand und wieder-auftauchte," in *Die Zeit,* 7 Dec. 1990.

26. Two key documents, Gromyko's memorandum on the USSR's foreign policy from 13 January 1967 and his memorandum "An Estimate of Foreign Policy and Soviet-American Relations," 16 Sept. 1969, can be found in an English translation in the appendix to Anatoly Dobrynin, *In Confidence: Moscow's Ambassador to America's Six Cold War Presidents* (Seattle: Univ. of Washington Press, 2001), 640–43.

27. Soviet directives for the negotiations with Bahr and analysis by Valentin Falin, head of the Foreign Ministry's third European department, 3, 12, 24 Feb. 1969; AVP RF: f.0757, op.14, p.54, d.10, 1.26–30 and f.0757, op.14, p.53, d.5, 1.1–8.

28. The change in Moscow's attitude toward West German *Ostpolitik* was reflected in the communications with East Berlin. Whereas in October 1970 Ulbricht was asked to "sup-port the Brandt government," in May 1973 he received a sincere warning about the "reform agenda and anti-Communism pursued by the SPD." SAPMO: Bureau Ulbricht in the SED-Politbureau, DY 30/3530 and -/3654.

29. See, for example, the Wilson-Kosygin conversations, London and Moscow, 10 Feb. 1967 and 13 Sept. 1971. PRO: PREM 13/1840; Bodleian Library: Wilson Papers, MS. Wilson c.1017. Also Wilson's message to Nixon via Ambassador Bruce in Embtel 1161, London, 11 Feb. 1969. NARA: DoS, RG 59/2563.

30. For the decision to act against the Soviet embassy employees taken under Wilson in September and October 1968, see PRO: PREM 13/2009.

31. Anne Deighton, "Ostpolitik or Westpolitik? British Foreign Policy, 1968–75," *Inter-national Affairs* 74, no. 4 (1998): 893–901. For London's dependency on the much more active German *Ostpolitik* in this era see Gottfried Niedhart, "Auf dem Weg zur Anerken-nung: Die DDR in der britischen Politik 1967–1973," in *Britain and the GDR: Relations and Perceptions in a Divided World,* ed. Arnd Bauerkämper (Berlin: Philo, 2002), 15–172; Luca Ratti, "Brittain, the German Question, and the Transformation of Europe: From Ostpolitik to the Helsinki Conference (1963–1975)," in *Helsinki 1975 and the Transformation of Europe,* ed. Oliver Bange and Gottfried Niedhart (London: Berghahn, 2008). For Wilson's later ap-proach to the CSCE, see PRO: PREM 16/391 and -/392.

32. Henry Kissinger, *White House Years* (Boston: Little, Brown, 1979), 411; Egon Bahr, *Zu meiner Zeit* (Munich: Karl Blessing, 1996), 271. AdsD, Bahr Papers, vol. 439.

33. For the multiplicity of CDU visits and visitors to the White House, particularly in the early months of 1970, see NARA: Nixon, NSC, CF, 683–684; NARA: Nixon, White House Staff File, Conference File, box 6; NARA: DoS, RG 59/2303, -/2304, -/2305.

34. Kissinger memorandum for Nixon, 18 July 1970; NARA: Nixon, NSC, CF 683.

35. Memcon Nixon-Barzel, Washington, 14 Apr. 1971; NARA: Nixon, NSC, President-Kissinger 1025.

36. Bahr informed Brandt on 28 Mar. 1972, after his latest encounter with Kissinger, that "it was the first time that the talks took place in a warm [*herzliche*] atmosphere." AdsD: Bahr Papers, vol. 439/2.

37. Kissinger's conversation with the author, New York, 23 July 2003.

38. White House parlance abusing Brandt, Bahr, Scheel, and others (scandalized by international media in 2004 after the transcripts of Kissinger's telephone conversations became available) is documented both in the "Nixon tapes" and the "Kissinger Telcons." NARA: Nixon Papers, Kissinger Transcripts of Telephone Conversations, and Nixon White House Tapes.

39. Sonnenfeldt memorandum to Kissinger, 7 Nov. 1972; NARA, Nixon, NSC, CF 687. Sonnenfeldt confirmed this in commenting on a paper given by the author at the Woodrow Wilson Center, Washington, D.C., and in an interview, 28 and 29 Apr. 2005.

40. Numerous drafts in AdsD: Bahr Papers, vol. 316. For a detailed account of these West German concepts, see Oliver Bange, "An Intricate Web—Ostpolitik, the European Security System, and German Unification," in Bange and Niedhart, eds. *Helsinki 1975*.

41. John J. Maresca, *To Helsinki: The Conference on Security and Cooperation in Europe, 1973–1975* (Durham, N.C.: Duke Univ. Press, 1987), 211ff. Conversation with the author, Florence, 28 Sept. 2003.

42. Conversation and letter exchange between Barthold Witte, member of the West-German delegation at Helsinki, and the author on the tactics and goals of the Social-Liberal coalition in the CSCE negotiations. See also Wilfried Loth, *Helsinki—1. August 1975—Entspannung und Abrüstung* (Munich: Deutscher Taschenbuch, 1998).

43. Memorandum, "Thoughts About the Foreign Policy of a Future Federal Government," 18 Sept. 1969, including a cover letter from Bahr to Brandt; AdsD: Bahr Papers, vol. 396.

44. Conference for Security and Co-operation in Europe, Helsinki Final Act, 1 Aug. 1975. See www.osce.org/documents/chronological.php, accessed 15 July 2007.

45. Daniel C. Thomas, *The Helsinki Effect: International Norms, Human Rights, and the Demise of Communism* (Princeton, N.J.: Princeton Univ. Press, 2001).

8

The Florentine in Winter

François Mitterrand and the Ending of the Cold War,

1989–1991

CHARLES COGAN

Introduction

The determining role of personalities, and most centrally that of Mikhail Gorbachev, was of course a factor in the way the Cold War ended and German reunification came about. From the time of the fall of the Berlin Wall, there was deep uncertainty as to how the Russians would handle the situation, particularly regarding East Germany. As Pierre Haski has observed, "Let us not forget that [at the time] there were still nearly 400,000 Soviet soldiers on [East German] soil . . . and there was no certainty as to the manner in which the Communist Bloc leaders would conduct themselves in the face of popular unrest in the East, particularly in East Germany."[1] For example, what if German demonstrators attacked Russian troops in their bases? As Robert M. Gates, the former director of U.S. Central Intelligence, stated in a talk at Harvard University in 1992, "Whatever one may think of Gorbachev—and I have criticized him strongly in the past—without his sense of humanity, the end of the Cold War would not have come about in this way."[2]

In this study, the focus is on François Mitterrand during the critical period from the fall of the Berlin Wall in November 1989 through German reunification in October 1990 to the Maastricht Treaty in December 1991: his words, how they changed, how others interpreted them, and how they differed in interpreting them—in short, how Mitterrand handled matters of state in this crucial transition. Mitterrand's role was not comparable in importance to that of George Bush, Mikhail Gorbachev, or Helmut Kohl, but it was a role nevertheless, and one that, with typical French insistence, Mitterrand was constantly seeking to enhance.

This period, Mitterrand's second term of office (1988–95), was not as dynamic

as his first, in part because he was in the process of dying before one's eyes. He
nevertheless retained the sobriquet, in the Paris microcosm, of "le Florentin," for his
sybilline ways, his sense of intrigue, his political sophistication, and his occasionally
opaque way of presenting his thoughts. Quite the opposite of Charles de Gaulle,
who was clear to the point of brutality, who considered Mitterrand incoherent, and
whose nickname for him was "l'arsouille," roughly translated as "the crafty one."

There are almost as many studies of Mitterrand as there are contradictory stories
about how he handled the ending of the Cold War.[3] Despite his later disclaimers,[4]
Mitterrand clearly sought to slow down or otherwise control the process of German reunification, but before long he was compelled to accept it.

Are we to believe Hubert Védrine's formulation that Mitterrand's words varied
but not his acts?[5] Or are we to figure otherwise—namely, that Mitterrand maneu-
vered himself out of a difficult situation after having initially sought to block or at
least put off for long German reunification? The accounts of two of Mitterrand's
aides, Védrine and Jacques Attali, are different in tone and in substance, with Védrine retaining a respect for the former president and Attali repeating the wildest
of Mitterrand's divagations, which probably caused the latter to disown Attali's
third volume (*Verbatim III*), covering the period 1988–91. What we can state with
certainty is that Mitterrand was far more prudent in his public statements than he
appears to have been in private. At one point, when Mitterrand stated on television
that there was a "threshold of tolerance" concerning the presence of foreigners in
France, Attali noted, "It was one of the rare occasions, in the space of 15 years, when
I saw François Mitterrand not express himself with mastery."[6]

It has become a commonplace to criticize Mitterrand, at the fading point of
his life, for shortsightedness in being unable to comprehend in a timely fashion
the irresistible dynamic of German reunification in 1989–90. Overall, it seems to
me that Mitterrand's actions in this transition period were more successful than
is generally assumed. Moreover, his handling of the Gulf War during this critical
period (1990–91) did nothing to discredit France, though it set in motion a long
crisis of confidence for the French military that was to continue through the rest
of the decade, in the Bosnia and especially the Kosovo conflicts.

Above all, Mitterrand managed to keep France's relationship with Germany
on an even keel and, together with Kohl, anchored Germany to the West with
the Maastricht summit at the end of 1991, setting in motion the single currency
(the euro) and laying the foundations for a Common Foreign and Security Policy
(CFSP) and an eventual European Security and Defense Identity. Mitterrand's tactic
was, first, to speed up the timetable for the introduction of the single European
currency, thus assuring Germany's attachment to the West; and, second, to take
the lead in pressing Kohl to declare the Oder-Neisse Line inherited from 1945 as
the definitive eastern border for Germany, and in this manner calm the concerns
of the Poles and the Russians.

With memories of the two world wars still ingrained in the collective conscience, neither Britain nor France had been ready to accept with equanimity a reunified and resurgent Germany. Mitterrand's initial nervousness and hesitancy about German reunification appears to have been based on two considerations. First, he was apprehensive about its possibly destabilizing effect on Europe and particularly on the USSR, even apprehending a threat to the continued existence of the Gorbachev government. (In this respect, Mitterrand was not completely wrong: the failed coup d'état of August 1991 can be seen as a delayed reaction, led by military and intelligence hard-liners, against the policies of Gorbachev.) Second, Mitterrand was concerned about retaining the French *acquis* from the West German settlement of 1954, notably the prohibition against Germany developing nuclear, biological, and chemical weapons on its own soil. Both of these objectives, he seems to have reasoned, could best be served by the four former occupation powers playing a controlling role in the reunification process.

Mitterrand's game was a very delicate one, however. He had also to preserve the *acquis* of the French-German relationship. France had accomplished its post–World War II reconciliation with Germany in a process marked by a series of variously spectacular and symbolic events: the secret negotiations in 1950 between French foreign minister Robert Schuman and German chancellor Konrad Adenauer that resulted in the creation of a European Coal and Steel Community (ECSC), intended by its author, Jean Monnet, to eliminate the possibility of future conflict between the two countries by the pooling of key resources; the invitation by Charles de Gaulle, shortly after his return to power in 1958, to Konrad Adenauer to visit him at his home in Colombey-les-deux-Églises; the signing of the French-German Treaty of Friendship and Cooperation by de Gaulle and Adenauer at the Élysée (presidency) in January 1963, eight days after de Gaulle had brutally and publicly rejected Britain's membership in the European Economic Community (EEC); and the impromptu holding of hands between Mitterrand and Kohl in 1984 at Verdun, the setting of that extended and sanguinary battle in 1916.

Notwithstanding the reconciliation that had taken place between the two blood enemies, Germany and France, it was France that held an ascendant position over Germany throughout the entire postwar period. Not since the pre-Bismarckian era had France enjoyed the luxury of facing a splintered German nation as it did in the period 1945–90. Although France did not hold the area of western Germany in vassalage as it did during the apogee of the Napoleonic era, it exercised a sort of virtual suzerainty over the Federal Republic by means of its manifold attributes: as one of the four postwar occupying powers in Germany; as a permanent member of the UN Security Council; as chief spoiler, if not chief leader, of the European Community; and as a nuclear weapons power vis-à-vis a Germany prohibited from manufacturing such arms on its own soil.

German Reunification

Starting around the middle of 1989, unrest in the satellite countries of Central and Eastern Europe had become palpable. The most singular marking event was Hungary's opening of its borders in September, allowing for large numbers of East Germans to come through the country en route to West Germany. On 9 November 1989, the Berlin Wall came down. On 28 November 1989, German chancellor Kohl announced his own plan for reuniting Germany without having consulted his major allies—Britain, the United States, and France—which were also the former occupation powers in Germany along with Russia—or even his own foreign minister, Hans Dietrich Genscher.

The West, and in particular France, was not expecting such a swift dénouement. As Stanley Hoffmann wrote, "Those who, like de Gaulle, had deemed German unification likely in a world that would have overcome the cold war, expected it to result from an orderly process firmly controlled by Germany's neighbors and by the major powers."[7]

As the decade of the 1990s opened, France was about to lose its favored position in Europe. With the fall of the Berlin Wall in November 1989 and the subsequent reunification of Germany, France's ascendancy over Germany and within the European Union was coming to an end, or at least was about to be profoundly modified. Thus, Mitterrand's actions reflected a strong French desire to contain a future Germany. France's three major wars with Germany over a seventy-five-year time span, and its subsequent alliance relationship with West Germany that had already lasted thirty years, gave France a special interest in making demands on Germany as a condition of its reunification. In addition, France's role as an occupying power, though originally granted almost on sufferance—"out of the goodness of his heart," as Franklin Roosevelt confided to Josef Stalin[8]—gave France the juridical basis for a voice in the future of a reunited German state.

In the aftermath of the fall of the Berlin Wall, Mitterrand, disturbed about Kohl's freewheeling approach to bringing about the absorption of East Germany, touched base all around, with Margaret Thatcher, with Bush, with Kohl, and with Gorbachev, and even going through with a previously scheduled visit to East Germany. The impression that he left was that he wanted to put the brakes on German reunification.

Mitterrand's cautious reaction to German reunification was mild compared to that of Thatcher. The British prime minister was categorically against Kohl's efforts to force the absorption of East Germany, and as Mitterrand gradually muted his own hesitations, Thatcher became angry with him for changing his position.

In a larger sense Britain, unlike France, had never accomplished the necessary epiphany of a reconciliation with Germany. On the geopolitical plane, and quite apart from the average Briton's sense of rancor against the Germans, which remained persistent from World War II onward, London retained its centuries-old concern about an all-powerful nation arising on the European continent. As if to demonstrate the point, the British prime minister brought to a meeting with François Mitterrand on the occasion of a European Council meeting in Strasbourg in December 1989 maps of Greater Germany as it existed on the eve of World War II. She feared that Germany wanted to reconstitute the "Grand Reich" and suggested that there be regular French-British meetings as a counterweight to Germany.[9] According to what Mitterrand related to Pierre Favier and Michel Martin-Roland, the British prime minister was "in a rage. [She] wanted to prevent the reunification. I understood her concerns, but it seemed to me unrealistic to oppose reunification. [It] would be better to concentrate on negotiating the issues."[10]

The day after he met Thatcher in Strasbourg, Mitterrand flew to Kiev to meet with Gorbachev on 9 December 1989. The meeting left the public impression that Mitterrand was trying to counterbalance Kohl's rush toward reunification by evoking the symbols of the historic Franco-Russian alliance. During their meeting, Gorbachev told Mitterrand that if German unity took place, he feared he would be overthrown in a military coup.[11] Mitterrand recognized the importance of Gorbachev's stabilizing role externally as well as the fragility of his position internally, although the latter situation did not become manifest until 1991.

As for George Bush, Mitterrand, who met with the president on 16 December 1989 on the island of St. Martin, described his outlook in the following terms: "[He] couldn't care less about German unity as long as Germany remained within NATO."[12] Mitterrand did not share Bush's preoccupation with NATO, because he considered the military alliances coming out of the Cold War to be *dépassé*.[13]

Although the rapport between Bush and Mitterrand remained good throughout the period—the exception, not the rule, in French-American contacts—the U.S. side was intent on reaffirming its leadership in the post–Cold War era. Secretary of State James Baker later openly admitted in his memoirs that he had gone to Berlin in December 1989 to make a statement on the importance of the U.S. role: "I knew that President Mitterrand was going there the following week, and I wanted to demonstrate American leadership in going there first."[14] (American leadership was in fact quickly asserted in 1990, in large part due to the imperative necessity to react to Saddam Hussein's aggression against Kuwait, starting on 2 August 1990).

Four days after meeting Bush at St. Martin on 16 December, Mitterrand made one trip too many, holding to a previously scheduled visit to East Germany. In doing so, he appeared to be using that failing regime as a counterweight to West Germany. The reality, however, was that discussions on how to handle the future of Germany were being made by the superpowers, and in particular in a meeting between Gorbachev and Bush at Malta on 2 December 1989.

Mitterrand, concerned that Kohl was unilaterally precipitating reunification with East Germany, showed during his visit to East Berlin an undue favoritism toward his hosts. Mitterrand declared on 20 December 1989 that France and the German Democratic Republic (GDR) "still had much to do together."[15]

Documents that surfaced later in the 1990s, after Mitterrand's death, contained the East German version of the talks and were embarrassing to the Mitterrand record. In almost nostalgic terms, François Mitterrand had this to say to East German prime minister Hans Modrow: "A too-rapid pace of events carries with it the risk that the order existing in Europe for the past 40 years could collapse and lead to an unstable situation. . . . It is up to the [GDR] to make the case that its 40 years of existence as a State represents a durable political reality."[16]

As betrayed by Mitterrand's remarks during his visit to East Berlin, France, the chief complainant against Yalta and its division of Europe into two blocs, had come seemingly to regret the stability and ascendancy that this division had afforded it. Moreover, Mitterrand's mindset found it difficult to visualize German reunification given the international situation prevailing at the time. According to Jacques Attali, Mitterrand had observed to him on 2 October 1989, "Those who talk of German reunification understand nothing. The Soviet Union will never accept it. It would be the death of the Warsaw Pact. Can you imagine that? And East Germany is Prussia. It would not want to be placed under the thumb of the Bavarians."[17]

In fact, there was little Mitterrand could do to stop the rush toward German reunification. As Hoffmann noted, "It was not until April 1990 that Mitterrand realized—after the elections that swept the Communists out of power in the GDR— that German unity was a fait accompli for all practical purposes; the problem for France was accommodation, not prevention."[18]

The European Monetary Union

In the 1980s, led by Mitterrand and Kohl, the European Community, after nearly two decades of virtual stagnation, began to take steps toward strengthening itself as an institution. With the passage of the Single European Act of 4 December 1985, a single market was instituted, providing for the free circulation of goods, persons, services, and capital throughout the community by 1993.[19]

The idea of a European central bank and single currency had been proposed by German foreign minister Hans-Dietrich Genscher in a memorandum of 26 February 1988[20] to his eleven counterparts in the European Community. The following April, the report by EC Commission president Jacques Delors set 1 July 1990 as the date of the first phase in the creation of an Economic and Monetary Union (EMU), which was to be part of the free flow of capital. The second and third phases were to be the creation of a European central bank and the institution of single currency.

By the time of the Strasbourg European Council meeting in December 1989, Mitterrand, who held the rotating presidency of the EC at the time,[21] had taken the lead in promoting the single currency. Mitterrand's position was in contrast to that of an initially reluctant Kohl who, though for it in principle, was not eager for electoral reasons to give his countrymen the idea that he was in favor of scrapping the Deutschmark for the euro. Kohl had his eye on the first free elections in East Germany, which were to be held in the spring of 1990. A victory in these elections for his own Christian Democrats would enhance the party's chances in the elections in West Germany scheduled for December 1990.

At Strasbourg, a deal was struck between Mitterrand and Kohl whereby an intergovernmental conference (IGC) would begin before the end of 1990 for the purpose of implementing phases 2 and 3 of the Delors recommendations, in return for which the European Council recognized the right of Germany to recover "its unity through free self-determination."[22] Despite her objections, Thatcher went along with this decision, as she had with the passage of the Single European Act in 1985. As an outgrowth of the IGC, it was agreed at a summit in December 1991 at Maastricht, the Netherlands, to introduce a common currency—what became known as the euro—on 1 January 1999; the euro would become the sole medium of exchange by 2002.

Halting Moves Toward the EU's Political Integration: The CFSP and the European Security and Defense Identity

Mitterrand, together with Delors, had led the campaign for the euro, which Mitterrand saw as a means of anchoring Germany firmly to Western Europe and of reducing France's dependence on the monetary policies of the Bundesbank. Mitterrand was less interested in promoting the political integration of Europe, an idea that had greater appeal for Kohl, who, like most Germans, was ready to sacrifice some sovereignty to achieve a united Europe.

In the European Union context, the French preference is for a union of states and thus for a stronger European Council, which exercises the intergovernmental competencies of the European Union. The German preference is for a union of peoples, and thus for a stronger European Parliament and European Commission, which deliberate and decide on matters of a communitarian nature.

In Mitterrand's view, political integration would naturally flow from an economic and monetary union. The latter was a precondition for the former, Mitterrand declared to the *Nouvel Observateur* on 27 July 1989.[23] With the fall of the Berlin Wall, the impulse toward new political arrangements quickened. In response to a letter from Kohl on 27 November 1989 proposing a succession of intergovernmental conferences over the ensuing years, dealing with economic and monetary union, with institutional reforms, and with an eventual political union, Mitterrand responded, "Like you, I would like, beyond economic and monetary union, a European union."[24]

Most of the EU's forward movement had been inspired by the Franco-German "locomotive," and in the 1980s this was reflected in the effective working relationship between Mitterrand and Kohl. By the spring of 1990, the misunderstandings of the period immediately after the collapse of the Berlin Wall had largely gone away. Following the compromise at Strasbourg in December 1989 on German reunification and the EMU, Mitterrand and Kohl were ready to work closely together again. As Hoffmann has observed, "After the hesitations of François Mitterrand at the end of 1989, the main lines of [French] policy pursued before that date were maintained."[25]

In April 1990, Kohl and Mitterrand agreed that twin intergovernmental conferences should be held at the end of the year: an economic one, to create the mechanism for the EMU, and another one to set in motion an eventual political union.[26] The two made their proposal in a joint letter to their EC colleagues on 19 April 1990 that officially put the idea of a political union of Europe on the public agenda.[27] They stated that it was time to "transform the nature of relations between the member states into a European Union and to give it the necessary means of action." In their letter, the two leaders suggested holding a conference on Political Union—including the CFSP—in parallel with the EC's EMU conference.

The Mitterrand-Kohl proposal was officially endorsed by the European Council meeting at Dublin on 26 June 1990,[28] at which time the twelve nations of the European Community agreed to work toward a "political union," including the progressive unification of their foreign and security policies. The twin IGCs began on 14 December 1990, in the wake of the European Council meeting in Rome.

The results of the political union initiative were meager. The Treaty of Maastricht would bring into being the CFSP and evoked the possibility of an eventual common defense policy, but the vagueness of the language reflected the deep divisions in the now renamed European Union between the federalists (or communitarians), on the one hand, and the intergovernmentalists, on the other. The key passage in the Maastricht Treaty that instituted these political changes is the following: "The Common Foreign and Security Policy shall include all questions related to the security of the European Union, including the framing of a common defense policy, which might in time lead to a common defense."[29] Significantly, the Atlantic Alliance's New Strategic Concept, issued at the time of the Rome NATO Summit (7–8 November 1991), contained language that paralleled that of the EU. The concept endorsed "the development of a European security identity and defence role" while also noting that this would strengthen "the European pillar within the Alliance."[30]

The accompanying Rome Summit Declaration stated, "We welcome the perspective of a reinforcement of the role of the Western European Union (WEU), both as the defense component of the process of European unification and as a means of strengthening the European pillar of the Alliance."[31]

The CFSP, however, has never achieved liftoff. As British defense expert Charles Grant has observed: "The frequently proclaimed objective of the European Union to create an effective 'Common Foreign and Security Policy' remains mal defined. At the beginning of the 1990's the EU did not develop any common line on the Gulf War or on the breakup of Yugoslavia. In recent years, there seemed to be some reason for hope. The EU launched the beginning of a common defense policy, and its diplomacy contributed to maintaining the peace in Macedonia and Montenegro. But in 2003, the EU found itself divided over the Iraq war."[32]

Despite NATO's refusal to disappear in the immediate aftermath of the Cold War, France continued to press for an independent European defense identity. While NATO sought to keep such an identity within the confines of the Atlantic Alliance—recognizing "the development of a European identity in the domain of security,"[33] but not in the area of "defense"[34]—France and Germany secretly went ahead in late 1991 and created a separate Franco-German Corps (later mutating into the Euro-Corps, with Spain, Belgium, and Luxembourg also joining). This move, mainly pushed by the French, may have been caused partly by the way the French considered they were shut out of the play in the aftermath of the Persian Gulf War.

French resentment over the end-of-war arrangements also played a role in the gradual distancing of France from Anglo-American policies toward Iraq over the course of the 1990s and into the twenty-first century, a process that culminated in France leading the opposition within the UN Security Council to American and British moves to win UN backing for an invasion of Iraq in 2003.

Toward the end of the decade of the 1990s, and after a long period of fruitful Anglo-French military cooperation on the ground in ex-Yugoslavia, Britain made a historic decision to allow a defense role for the EU, which it had been resisting for decades. This decision, emerging from the Anglo-French summit at St. Malo in December 1998, paved the way for the creation of a European autonomous defense force that would consist of sixty thousand personnel, deployable within two months and capable of being sustained in place for one year. As worked out in a compromise arrived at in early 2004, this force would have an operational planning staff that would not be separately located but would be inside the headquarters of SHAPE (Supreme Headquarters Allied Powers Europe) at Mons, Belgium. The compromise reflected the continuing contrast between the British vision of the force, which would be complementary to NATO, and the French vision of the force as independent from NATO.

Relations with the Rest of Europe

Initially, Mitterrand appeared to look toward the Conference on Security and Cooperation in Europe (CSCE) as an umbrella organization for a new post–Cold War order in Europe. As Louis Gautier has pointed out, the CSCE was one of three basic choices for a security structure after the Cold War.[35] The other two were NATO, about which France was reticent, and the European Union, which did not have a defense role at that time.

At Kiev on 6 December 1989, Mitterrand proposed to Gorbachev that the CSCE be convened in 1990 in order to guarantee Germany's frontiers as tentatively laid down at Yalta. Gorbachev agreed, advancing the view that if a solution could be found in a pan-European framework, it would guarantee Europe against a cataclysm.[36]

But the Organization for Security and Cooperation in Europe (OSCE), as it came to be known in 1995, was too diffuse to be effective. Decisions had to be taken by unanimity; the organization had no military teeth in it, unlike NATO; and also unlike NATO it did not have forty years of experience as an organization behind it. NATO, by contrast, was more homogeneous. It also had an enforcement capability and an acknowledged, but not always respected, leader, the United States. Most fundamentally, the OSCE did not represent a true community of interests, as NATO and the European Union arguably do.

At the end of the year 1989, Mitterrand came up with a new proposal that betrayed his intention, as Jolyon Howorth characterized it, "of keeping the USA at arms length from the process of *European* transformation."[37] In his New Year's Eve address, Mitterrand proposed the creation of a European Confederation. Mitterrand started out with the observation that "Europe, obviously, will no longer be the Europe we have known during the last half-century. Formerly dependent on the two superpowers, she is, like going back to one's own house, returning to her history and her geography."[38]

But, Mitterrand added, to avoid a return to 1919 and which led to war, the only remedy was the construction of European unity. Instead of proposing a union of Central and Eastern Europe with the twelve nations of the European Community, he proposed an intermediate stage in which all the nations of Europe would come together in a "European Confederation," which "would associate all the States of our continent in a common and permanent organization of exchanges, of peace and of security." Such a confederation, he said, would welcome any state with pluralistic and democratic institutions.[39]

Explaining his point of view to Kohl several weeks later, Mitterrand stated, "I spoke of a possible European confederation, because the countries that have liberated themselves from the Communist yoke should not remain isolated, as this will lead to an unhealthy competition among us. It is necessary therefore to have an institution to which all democratic countries will have access. People say that the CSCE already exists for that [purpose]. But it will be very important, for the dignity of these countries, to have a political institution among Europeans alone."[40]

Mitterrand's idea was to fail at an intended founding meeting held in Prague in June 1991, most particularly because the European Confederation would have comprised both Western and Eastern Europe, including the USSR, but would have excluded the United States and Canada. This was not a welcome proposal for those Central and Eastern European countries struggling to achieve complete freedom from the Soviet Union after forty years of occupation—which looked to the United States to help bring this about. In addition, the proposal was vague. Hubert Védrine, the secretary-general of the Élysée at the time, confided, "We were dumbfounded. We found the idea magnificent, but we wondered what it implied, concretely."[41]

The confederation idea would have sidestepped, or postponed, at any rate, the issue of these countries joining the European Union, at a time when, in the aftermath of the fall of the Berlin Wall and the collapse of the Iron Curtain, their focus was on the European Union. The issue of their joining NATO had not yet arisen as a serious consideration. Here, as was the case in a number of later instances, the EU was to disappoint the westward-looking countries of Central and Eastern Europe. It was the reluctance of certain powers, chiefly Great Britain and France, to extend the European Union to the Visegrad countries[42] that was to lead ineluctably to an intensive look at NATO enlargement, which would have seemed quite improbable at the start of the 1990s.

NATO

With the end of the Cold War, NATO seemed suddenly irrelevant to some observers, while the creation of a stronger European defense entity seemed a logical next step. In the event, however, the United States showed that it had no intention of closing down NATO, which would mean losing its military position on the European continent. Furthermore, rather than prompting the end of NATO, the settlement of the German question brought about the first *expansion* of NATO since the accession of Spain in 1982. East Germany's *Anschluss* with West Germany meant that East Germany would become part of NATO (albeit without any nuclear weapons or non-German troops on its soil). With this new acquisition, NATO began its own peaceful march into Eastern Europe, and its momentum has carried on ever since, as has Eastern Europe's fervent devotion to NATO. As a senior French diplomat characterizes it, "To its members, NATO is like a religion. We [the French] are agnostics."

In France there was the expectation, one might say the hope, that with the end of the Cold War there would be a disengagement of the United States, at least partially, from Europe, or at any rate a loosening of American hegemony represented in the NATO integrated command. As Louis Gautier put it, "The end of the Cold War, because it signified the disappearance of the continental adversary, and also in the long run the disengagement of the American ally, offered France new perspectives for its security."[43]

Mitterrand's view of a new world order was expressed on various occasions in the course of the year 1990. He saw a post–Cold War world developing along the following lines: the Europeans would take charge of their own security; the role of NATO would be continued but remain confined to its traditional geographic zone of Western Europe and North America; the United Nations, free of East-West tensions, would be reactivated as the principal instrument for regulating world order; and France would intensify its role as a champion of peace, democracy, and human rights.[44]

As 1989 drew to a close, and the waning of the Cold War was evident, a redefinition of the strategy of the Western Alliance was inevitable. With the frozen (and stable) atmosphere of the Cold War a thing of the past, the question of who was to be in charge of security in the new Europe now arose.

For the "Europeanists" (1990s style), the reform of NATO was preferably to proceed in the direction of less integration and not more: the eventual strategic goal would be an essentially "bilateral" relationship between a European defense identity on the one hand and the United States on the other.[45] For the "Atlanticists," however, the conjurer's trick for demonstrating the continuing validity of the alliance was to find more missions for NATO rather than less. These two conceptions were to come into sharp dispute.

As the Cold War faded away, French strategists were adamant that the U.S. "veto power" over the West's military activities, stemming from its long-dominant position in NATO through the integrated command structure, must not carry over to an emerging European defense architecture. Wrote Frédéric Bozo, "The Americans must understand that all right of veto on their part regarding European political or military decisions is excluded because it is contrary to the very nature of the plan [for a European strategic identity]."[46]

When wars end, the expectation is that the alliances created to cope with them go away also. This was not to be the case with the end of the Cold War, which, of course, was not a typical war in that there never was a direct military exchange between the principal protagonists. There was a widespread feeling, in France in particular, that the momentous events taking place in 1989–91 meant that Europe was now free to continue on its own. As Mitterrand said in the fall of 1991, after the failed coup in Moscow, "We have just witnessed the deposition of the last empire on our continent. There is no longer an imposed order. Europe is now master of its choices, or it can be."[47] This was to be the mantra of French policy in the 1990s, carried on by Mitterrand and his successor, Jacques Chirac. Indeed, French policy in this regard, remarkable in its consistency despite perceived tactical zigzags, goes much farther back. In the 1990s, with the end of the Cold War, this ambition simply became more pronounced and intense.

While certainly motivations of revenge for past humiliations were never absent from French thinking toward the United States as the Cold War drew to a close, there had been all along a certain logic to French policy that the more pragmatic Americans found difficult to discern, much less accept. Bozo, writing in 1991, laid out France's long-term strategic view: "The affirmation of a European strategic identity has in effect represented for forty years the constant ambition of the diplomatic and strategic action of France, which legitimately believes that the European upheavals of 1989 have increased both its necessity and its possibility."[48]

For the United States, however, the affirmation of a "European strategic identity" did not mean that NATO was going to go away or even confine itself to its traditional role of the collective defense of Western Europe. In a speech in Berlin on 12 December 1989, Secretary of State James Baker closed off any notion that NATO should disappear with the fall of the Iron Curtain. In a speech that some observers found "hegemonistic" in overtones, Baker in effect preempted the debate. He laid out a vision of an alliance not limited to the collective defense of its member states under article 5 of the Atlantic Treaty, but as something more.[49] He proposed, in general terms, a new security architecture for Europe as a whole in which the United States would continue to play a major role.[50] He spoke of a new Atlanticism, and a NATO that was to be more "political." He even suggested a treaty between the United States and the European Community.[51]

President Mitterrand, preoccupied by the necessity of a French role in the determination of the future of the two Germanys, did not at that moment enter fully into a debate over NATO. As Bozo has observed, "The debate over the maintenance of the [Atlantic] Alliance after the cold war virtually never took place."[52]

In fact, there was little the French could do to prevent the continuation of NATO as an organization, if indeed this was a serious intention on their part. Although Mitterrand at that time (the end of 1989) did not suggest that NATO not continue as an organization, he felt firmly that it should be contained. The new vision of NATO, as outlined by Baker in his speech at Berlin on 12 December 1989, of reaching out for relationships with the de-Communizing states of Eastern Europe, was to be met with resistance by the French president. Although there was no public thinking at the time of incorporating new members from Eastern Europe into NATO, there was a juridical basis for doing so: article 10 of the Washington Treaty of 4 April 1949 stated in part, "The parties may, by unanimous agreement, invite any other European state . . . to accede to this treaty."

Mitterrand, like nearly everyone else, was not contemplating in late 1989 an expansion of NATO to the east. Rather, he was focused on making sure that NATO would restrict itself to operating in the zone specified in the Washington Treaty of

1949, which mandated a collective defense of the territory of the alliance's member states. For France, extending the zone of NATO's competence for intervention meant extending the zone of American domination, via NATO's integrated command, to other areas besides Western Europe. Mitterrand preferred a period of pause, a period of waiting: his appraisal was that a U.S. withdrawal from Europe was ineluctable in the long run, and when the U.S. troop level in Europe became significantly reduced the expression of a European identity would take on its full meaning and inspiration.[53]

As to how the alliance should evolve, and the role for France in it, Mitterrand made his point of view known publicly through his foreign minister, Roland Dumas, at a meeting of the North Atlantic Council at Turnberry (UK) on 7 June 1990: "France for its part is ready to participate wholeheartedly in a study (on the evolution of the Atlantic Alliance), based on the respect of the following three principles: there should not be a question of pushing out the lines of competence of the Alliance; France intends to retain its autonomy of decision regarding its own defense; it does not intend to call into question its doctrine of deterrence which is of a defensive character. It is open to discussion on everything else."[54]

In keeping with the Turnberry statement, Mitterrand refused to be bound by the new NATO doctrine sketched out at the North Atlantic Council Summit in London in July 1990—the use of nuclear weapons only as a last resort—because it denigrated the value of the French nuclear deterrent and the doctrine behind it. In a press conference on 6 July 1990, Mitterand stated, "They announce that nuclear weapons will not be used except after the fact, after a conventional war. . . . This seems to be completely antinomic with French strategy, which is not to take the initiative to resort to force, but which keeps the option to use all of its forces at the desired moment, the latter having as much as possible to precede the opening of the conflict."[55]

The next NATO summit, at Rome (7–8 November 1991), promulgated NATO's New Strategic Concept. The French participated in the drafting and accepted the document. The term "last resort" was dropped and in its place appeared the following: "The circumstances in which any use of nuclear weapons might have to be contemplated . . . are . . . even more remote."

The New Strategic Concept stated that in peacetime the Atlantic Alliance could "contribute to the maintenance of the stability and equilibrium in Europe; . . . bring a contribution to dialogue and cooperation in Europe as a whole, in participating in confidence-building measures, including those which increase transparency and improve communication, as well as the verification of arms control agreements; . . . [and] be called upon to contribute to peace and stability in the world by furnishing forces for missions of the United Nations."[56]

The above functions were to be carried out under article 4 of the North Atlantic Treaty, which states, "The parties will consult together whenever, in the opinion of any of them, the territorial integrity, political independence or security of any of the parties is threatened." Article 5 regarding the mission of collective defense and article 6 concerning the territory of the member countries to which it applied were left unchanged, as this would have required a revision of the treaty. The New Strategic Concept's justification regarding article 4 was as follows:

> Any armed attack on the territory of the Allies, from whatever direction, would be covered by Articles 5 and 6 of the Washington Treaty. However, Alliance security must also take account of the global context. Alliance security interests can be affected by other risks of a wider nature, including proliferation of weapons of mass destruction, disruption of the flow of vital resources and actions of terrorism and sabotage. Arrangements exist within the Alliance for consultation among the Allies under Article 4 of the Washington Treaty and, where appropriate, coordination of their efforts including their responses to such risks.[57]

As already mentioned, the French had subscribed to and indeed participated in the elaboration of NATO's New Strategic Concept. Diego Ruiz-Palmer has noted that "once France had subscribed in 1991 to the same Strategic Concept of the Alliance as its allies, and once the distinction between integrated forces and non-integrated forces no longer covered either a political need or a tangible military reality, it became less and less conceivable that France could continue to remain apart from the decision-making bodies of the Alliance."[58] This anomaly of the French position vis-à-vis NATO in the post–Cold War era led to the attempt in the mid-1990s by the incoming French president, Jacques Chirac, to return to the integrated command of NATO. The initiative ran aground over the French request to be given the charge of NATO's Southern Command as a compensation for returning to the integrated military structure of the alliance.

The Balance Sheet

When it comes to assessing the performance of François Mitterrand in the critical years of the transition from the Cold War, and bearing in mind that France is not a superpower (albeit a major power in the European region), the verdict has to be a favorable one. France received an endorsement by NATO of a defense role in the construction of Europe. The French-German Treaty of Friendship and Cooperation of 1963 was preserved despite some turbulence during the transition, as was the French ascendancy over Germany in the nuclear military field. France retained its role from 1917 as one of the Big Three Western powers through its participation in the Gulf War. And France rekindled its historic relationship with Russia, which had originated in 1893.

Notes

1. Pierre Haski, "Mitterrand et la réunification de l'Allemagne," in *Mitterrand et la sortie de la guerre froide*, ed. Samy Cohen (Paris: Presses universitaires de France, 1998), 9–10.

2. From a seminar conducted by Gates at Harvard Univ., 1 May 1992.

3. See in particular Cohen, ed., *Mitterrand et la sortie de la guerre froide*; Hubert Védrine, *Les mondes de François Mitterrand: A l'Élysée, 1981–1995* (Paris: Fayard, 1996); Pierre Favier and Michel Martin-Roland, *La Décennie Mitterrand*. Vol. 3: *Les défis (1988–1991)* (Paris: Seuil, 1996) (hereafter referred to as *DM*, vol. 3); and Jacques Attali, *Verbatim III, 1988–1991* (Paris: Fayard, 1995).

4. François Mitterrand, *De l'Allemagne, de la France* (Paris: Odile Jacob, 1996).

5. Védrine, *Les mondes de François Mitterrand*, 486.

6. Attali, *Verbatim III*, 373.

7. Stanley Hoffmann, "French Dilemmas and Strategies in the New Europe," in *After the Cold War: International Institutions and State Strategies in Europe, 1989–1991*, ed. Robert O. Keohane, Joseph S. Nye, and Stanley Hoffmann (Cambridge, Mass.: Harvard Univ. Press, 1993), 128.

8. Jean Laloy, *Yalta: Yesterday, Today, Tomorrow*, trans. William R. Tyler (New York: Harper and Row, 1988), 72–73.

9. Favier and Martin-Roland, *DM*, vol. 3, 235.

10. Ibid.

11. Ibid

12. Ibid., photo section.

13. Ibid., 218.

14. Ibid., 242.

15. Ibid., photo section.

16. Ibid., 249. The citation is from notes of the conversations taken by a colleague of Modrow and published by *Le Monde* and *Der Spiegel* on 2 and 3 May 1996.

17. Attali, *Verbatim III*, 313.

18. "French Dilemmas and Strategies," 130. The elections had taken place in March 1990.

19. *DM*, vol. 3, 78.

20. Ibid., 182.

21. The European Community became the European Union with the Treaty of Maastricht, concluded on 9–10 Dec. 1991 and signed on 7 Feb. 1992.

22. Christian Lequesne, "Une lecture décisionnelle de la politique européenne de François Mitterrand," in *Mitterrand et la sortie de la guerre froide*, ed. Cohen, 135–37.

23. François de la Serre, "La politique européenne de François Mitterrand," in *Mitterrand et la sortie de la guerre froide*, ed. Cohen, 112.

24. Lequesne, "Une lecture décisionnelle," 139.

25. Stanley Hoffmann, "La France dans le Monde, 1979–1999," *Politique Étrangère*, Feb. 2000, p. 4.

26. Cohen, ed., *Mitterrand et la sortie de la guerre froide*, 51–52.

27. Duquesne, "Une lecture décisionnelle," 154.

28. Ibid., 141.

29. Treaty of Maastricht, Article J.4, paragraph 1, www.hri.org/docs/Maastricht92/mt_titles5.html, accessed 12 July 2007.

30. See NATO New Strategic Concept at www.nato.int/docu/comm/49-95/c911107a.htm, accessed 12 July 2007.

31. See "Rome Declaration on Peace and Cooperation," NATO Press Service, 8 Nov. 1991, p. 3.

32. Charles Grant, "La Grande-Bretagne, la France, et l'avenir de la politique étrangère européenne," in Dominique de Villepin, *Un autre monde* (Paris: Éditions de l'Herne, 2003), 547.

33. Declaration of the North Atlantic Council, London, 5–6 July 1990, www.nato.int/docu/comm/49–95/c900706a.htm, 1, accessed 12 July 2007.

34. As Hubert Védrine wrote, "We always say 'security' and not defense, so as not to alarm the NATO integrationists. But they're already on their guard. The whole problematic of the 1990's is there [in these two terms]." Hubert Védrine, *Les mondes de François Mitterrand*, p. 459.

35. Louis Gautier, *Mitterrand et son armée, 1990–1995* (Paris: Grasset, 1999), 69.

36. *DM*, vol. 3, 222–23.

37. Howorth, "Renegotiating the Marriage Contract: Franco-American Relations Since 1981," in *US-European Interactions Since the End of the Cold War*, ed. Sabrina Ramet and Christine Ingebritsen (Boulder, Colo.: Rowman and Littlefield, 2000), 6.

38. *DM*, vol. 3, 253.

39. Ibid.

40. Attali, *Verbatim III*, 427.

41. *DM*, vol. 3, 255.

42. Poland, the Czech Republic, Hungary, and Slovakia are the so-called Visegrad Four.

43. Gautier, *Mitterrand et son armée*, 11.

44. Ibid., 42.

45. Interview of Jacques Andréani, French ambassador to the United States, with the author on 26 June 1992.

46. Frédéric Bozo, *La France et l'OTAN: de la guerre froide au nouvel ordre européen* (Paris: Masson, 1991), 196.

47. Alain Rollat, "Jeu de patience à l'Elysee," *Le Monde*, 19 Oct. 1991, 9.

48. Bozo, *La France et l'OTAN*, 195.

49. Frédéric Bozo, "De la 'bataille' des euromissiles à la 'guerre' du Kosovo: l'Alliance atlantique face à ses défis (1979–1999)," *Politique étrangère*, Mar. 1999, 593.

50. Howorth, "Renegotiating the Marriage Contract," 6.

51. *DM*, vol. 3, 241, 254, 283.

52. Bozo, "De la 'bataille' des euromissiles," 592.

53. Pierre Favier and Michel Martin-Roland, *La Décennie Mitterrand*. Vol. 4: *Les Déchirements (1991–1995)* (Paris: Seuil, 1996), 162.

54. Gautier, *Mitterrand et son armée*, 65.

55. *Le Monde*, 8–9 July 1990, 5.

56. Bernadette d'Armaillé, *L'Architecture européenne de sécurité* (Paris: CREST, 1991), 114.

57. See www.nato.int/docu/comm/49–95/c911107a.htm, 4–5, accessed 12 July 2007.

58. Diego A. Ruiz-Palmer, "La coopération militaire entre la France et ses alliés, 1966–1991: entre le poids de l'héritage et les défis de l'après-guerre froide," in *La France et l'OTAN, 1949–1996*, ed. Maurice Vaïsse, Pierre Mélandri, and Frédéric Bozo (Brussels: Editions Complexe, 1996), 598.

PART II

The Warsaw Pact

9

The Warsaw Pact

An Alliance in Search of a Purpose

Vojtech Mastny

In the prime of its life, the Warsaw Pact appeared to contemporaries as an effective, even superior, counterpart of NATO. The Communist alliance's enforced cohesion was widely regarded an asset while democratic NATO's contentious pluralism seemed a liability. In retrospect, it has became fashionable to cite the Western alliance's consensual nature as the secret of its longevity and the Warsaw Pact's coercive character as its fatal flaw. This comfortable distinction, however, can hardly explain why the respective alliances functioned or failed to function the way they did. After all, with all its warts, the Communist military grouping lasted for a respectable thirty-six years—no mean accomplishment.

The following discussion links the relations within the Warsaw Pact with its purpose. It argues that there was a crucial difference in the purpose of the two Cold War alliances, which affected decisively their functioning. NATO's purpose—the protection of its member states from perceived Soviet threat—remained clear and constant from its birth in 1949 until the death of its Soviet nemesis in 1991. In contrast, uncertainty about the Warsaw Pact's true, as distinguished from declaratory, purpose was its inauspicious birthmark from its inception in 1955 until it disappeared from the world along with its Soviet progenitor.

The story of the Warsaw Pact is that of a search for its purpose, which kept changing over time. Not even its Soviet managers were always clear in their minds about what they wanted the alliance to be and to do. At issue was not only the distinction between its military and political purposes, whose relative importance fluctuated with the ebb and tide of the Cold War, but also accommodation of the diverse interests and priorities of its unequal members.

The members of the Communist alliance were different in nature from their NATO counterparts. They consisted of self-appointed party elites who represented their national constituencies in name, though not necessarily in reality. They pursued their respective power interests rather than those of their subjects—interests that may or may not have been the same. Moreover, the Soviet Union's junior allies depended on its protection in a way that their Western opposite numbers did not depend on the United States—namely, for internal rather than external survival. This did not mean that their and Soviet interests always coincided or that the pursuit of their particular interests depended entirely on Moscow's fiat. Instead, it was up to the individual Eastern European regimes and their leaders to choose the extent to which they would—or would not—make use of the limited freedom of action they had at any given time.

New evidence from the archives of the Warsaw Pact's former member states shows that, behind the façade of its unity, discord was more rife than outsiders used to suspect. If there was less discord than in NATO, the discord nonetheless threatened the integrity of the alliance more fundamentally than would be the case with its Western counterpart, whose institutions and procedures were tailored to accommodate diversity. Not only did the Communist system require higher standards of uniformity in order to function effectively but uncertainty about the Warsaw Pact's true purpose also was divisive. All this made relations within the Warsaw Pact more muddled than within NATO.

The Redundant Alliance

It has been noted that "alliances which fail to increase [their] partners' security levels almost never form."[1] The Warsaw Pact at its creation was such an alliance. It was superimposed in 1955 on the network of bilateral treaties of "friendship and mutual assistance" that had already bound the Soviet Union and its Eastern European dependencies since the end of World War II. It was not formed in response to the creation of NATO, which had already been in existence for six years, nor was its establishment warranted by any increased military threat that Moscow may have perceived at the time. On the contrary, having concluded that the threat of war had diminished, Soviet leader Nikita S. Khrushchev had successfully initiated at that very time what became known as the "first détente." He proceeded unilaterally to start cutting his country's conventional forces—the forces more usable than the nuclear ones—for the first time since the onset of the Cold War.[2]

Far from presaging the Warsaw Pact's later function as a Soviet instrument for waging war in Europe, its proclamation in the Polish capital was thus a political rather than a military act rooted in the particular circumstances of the time, which was marked by an unexpected and sudden ascendancy of the Western alliance. Although the immediate issue was the forthcoming admission into NATO of West Germany, the eventual contribution of its twelve divisions was of less concern to Moscow than the tilting "correlation of forces" between East and West—the Soviet formula that took properly into account other attributes of power than merely military.

The Soviet Union sought to derail West Germany's entry into NATO by diplomatic and other political means, including the threat to conclude a military alliance with its own dependent states. The Soviet Foreign Ministry, rather than the Defense Ministry, was in charge of the preparations, improvised hastily as the ratification of West Germany's membership in NATO neared completion. Only at a late date, almost as an afterthought, did Defense Minister Marshal Georgii Zhukov receive the assignment to draft a document providing for the establishment of military command of the future alliance.[3]

The alliance's prospective Eastern European members played a negligible role in the process leading to the signing ceremony stage-managed by the Soviet Union in Warsaw on 14 May 1955. The timing of the event nevertheless suggested that their political, if not so much military, relationship with Moscow loomed very much on the manager's mind. Proclaimed the day before the conclusion in Vienna of the state treaty providing for Austria's neutrality and the withdrawal of Soviet troops from the country, the establishment of an alliance binding the Soviet clients more closely with each other as well as with Moscow signaled unmistakably that the enviable neutral status about to be granted Austria was inapplicable to them.

The Soviet concern about a precedent that could implant unacceptable ideas into East European heads was not entirely unwarranted. A few weeks later Emil Bodnăraş, an aide to Romania's Stalinist boss, Gheorghe Gheorghiu-Dej, who was worried about his own vulnerability to the reformist spirit that had been emanating from the Kremlin since Stalin's death, broached with Khrushchev the idea of withdrawing Soviet troops from Romania as well. Khrushchev unceremoniously rejected it.[4]

Preventive consolidation of the Soviet hold on Eastern Europe was secondary to the main purpose Moscow envisaged for the new alliance. The primary objective was to create conditions that would allow for trading the dissolution of the nascent Warsaw Pact for dissolution of the mature NATO. The text of the Warsaw treaty therefore mirrored in important ways the provisions of NATO's founding document. That such a bad bargain had no chance of being entertained by the West did not mean that Khrushchev, with the faith of a true believer in the irresistible advance of Communism, did not think that it could be, provided the capitalists could be compelled to see they had no choice. The documents prepared in the Moscow Foreign Ministry envisaged negotiations leading to a new European security system, with the Soviet Union as its linchpin. Such were the illusions on which the Warsaw Pact was originally being built.

Meanwhile, there was no urgency about giving the alliance military substance and institutional structure, thus justifying its contemporary description by NATO officials as a "cardboard castle . . . carefully erected over what most observers considered an already perfectly adequate blockhouse . . . no doubt intended to be advertised as being capable of being dismantled, piece by piece, in return for corresponding segments of NATO." The first meeting of the alliance's Political Consultative Committee (PCC) in January 1956 was mainly a propaganda exercise during which East European leaders, seconded by "observers" from China and other Asian Communist countries, lambasted in unison Western "imperialism," showing off their support for the Soviet vision of the future European order. Their expressed intention to develop the alliance's institutional structure did not translate into action.[5]

The one tangible accomplishment of the meeting consisted in using that structure as the framework for the creation of East German armed forces. This was something the Soviet Union had been reluctant to do but could no longer afford not to do without creating an impression of trusting "its" Germans less than the Western powers trusted "theirs." Analogous to the status of West Germany's *Bundeswehr,* the East German army was integrated into the alliance in its entirety rather than only in parts, as was the case with all the other member countries. The arrangement not only allowed for closer Soviet supervision but also gave East German leaders an opportunity to exploit shrewdly their extraordinary contribution to the Warsaw Pact in gradually transforming their pariah state into Moscow's most respected ally.

The Warsaw Pact's rudimentary military structure did not supersede the well-established structures employed by the Soviet Union since the Stalin years to put the military potential of its nominal allies at its disposal. For the first five years of its existence, the Warsaw Pact amounted to little more than three meetings of its PCC, used by Khrushchev as a public platform for launching his assorted disarmament initiatives in a vain effort to sow enough discord within NATO to compel the West to negotiate. When in 1956 Eastern Europe erupted in revolt, however, the Warsaw Pact assumed unexpected significance, giving the Soviet leader reasons to ponder the wisdom of having created it in the first place.[6]

The Rise of Dissent

In 1956, the Warsaw Pact became the lighting rod of its members' discontent with the arbitrary Soviet management of their armed forces. Moscow tried to preempt criticism by inserting assurances of a readiness to put military relations on a less unequal footing into its landmark 31 October declaration on proper relations among Communist states. It offered to withdraw the widely resented Soviet military advisers, as well as Soviet troops, from the countries where they were present and to make their future deployment subject to approval by the local governments.[7]

The statement encouraged rather than discouraged the Poles and especially the Hungarians to question the merits of the alliance and its modus operandi.

Reform-minded Polish generals took the lead in trying to redefine its terms in a memorandum that alluded to NATO as a model. Although they did not succeed any better than the Hungarians did in their bolder attempt to leave the Warsaw Pact and proclaim neutrality, at least the Soviet advisers were withdrawn from Poland and the presence of Soviet troops there became formally regulated by status-of-forces agreements that could be invoked against abuses.[8]

Betraying a certain apprehension about his brainchild, Khrushchev did not rely on the Warsaw Pact in crushing the Hungarian revolution or restoring Soviet control in the region afterward. His chosen instrument was rather the Council for Mutual Economic Assistance—COMECON—the Soviet bloc's organization for economic coordination. His aversion to the use of military power as a tool of alliance management, despite its prodigious use in Hungary and perhaps for that very reason, manifested itself in the reversal in 1958 of his earlier opposition to the withdrawal of Soviet troops from Romania. He took them out on his own initiative—a loss of leverage on its devious rulers that his successors would live to regret.[9]

It was only the 1958–61 Berlin crisis that infused blood into the anemic arteries of the Warsaw Pact. This was not what Khrushchev originally intended to do when he provoked the crisis as a diplomatic war of nerves designed to force a solution of the German question on his terms without the risk of war. "Of course there will be a sharpening, there will be blockade," he explained his strategy to the Polish Communists, but "there will be no war."[10] Once the scheme failed to work as intended, however, the risk of a military clash that might arise from his planned conclusion of a separate peace treaty with East Germany, which would have blocked the Western powers' access to Berlin, brought the Warsaw Pact into the picture in a military role for the first time. The prospect served as a catalyst of discord among its members.

Moscow used the alliance to prepare Eastern European armies for a possible military emergency. Although its likelihood depended on Khrushchev's management—or mismanagement—of the crisis, the planning for the worst-case scenario was the responsibility of the Soviet general staff, discharged through the Warsaw Pact's unified command down to the newly created defense councils of the respective party central committees. The substitution of the defensive strategy inherited from the Stalin era with an offensive strategy calling for a deep thrust into Western Europe provided the most important innovation. The change proved a lasting legacy of the Berlin crisis, determining the alliance's strategic posture until 1987.[11]

The prolongation of the crisis offered an example of the power of the weak. It exposed Khrushchev to pressure by his East German client, Walter Ulbricht, whose narrow goal of seizing control of West Berlin did not fully coincide with Khrushchev's larger goal of forcing the Western Allies to negotiate about the future of Germany as a whole. In the end, the Soviet leader had the last word, not allowing the subordinate to be the "tail wagging the dog." By securing Soviet backing for the tottering East German state, Ulbricht nevertheless showed how much bargaining influence, even if not power, he could exercise. This was the kind of leverage the Warsaw Pact's junior members could muster if they cared to try.[12]

When Khrushchev authorized the building of the Berlin Wall, he thought it prudent to spread the risk by formally presenting the operation as a collective undertaking of the Warsaw Pact. At that time, he had not yet ruled out the potentially risky conclusion of a separate East German peace treaty. He did not, however, consult in advance with his allies, several of whom balked at subsidizing the East German state and later expressed resentment about having been driven into a confrontation that might lead to war.[13]

The tension within the alliance had deeper roots in differences about strategy and tactics toward the West, which also underlay the evolving Sino-Soviet split and its subsidiary split between the Soviet Union and Albania. The Warsaw Pact's weakest and strategically least important member was the first to defy Moscow successfully, making good use of its lack of a common border with any of the alliance's other members, but Albania provided no example to emulate because of its isolation and ideological extremism. Its ejection in October 1961 from the PCC at the height of the Berlin crisis nevertheless signaled the Warsaw Pact's unraveling before it was even built. The subsequent exclusion of the disruptive Chinese observers by a Soviet procedural maneuver amounted to further unraveling.[14]

The Warsaw Pact was excluded from Khrushchev's surreptitious moves that provoked the Cold War's climactic crisis over Cuba in October 1962, but the very exclusion further undermined the alliance's cohesion. Only *post factum* did Khrushchev inform the East European leaders, whom he had assembled for a secret briefing, that the outbreak of a nuclear war had been only "a few minutes" away.[15] The prospect of getting embroiled in the crisis without even knowing, much less being able to do anything about it, had the effect of concentrating thoughts, all the more so since Khrushchev's position, shaken by his Cuban adventure, came under growing assault by the Chinese.

Romania went the farthest in secretly offering the U.S. government assurances that, in case of a confrontation between the superpowers, it would remain neutral—an act of alliance disloyalty without parallel in NATO. Other allies—the Poles, Hungarians, even the Czechoslovaks and East Germans—tried in their own ways to promote projects that would place constraints on the use of the doomsday weaponry by either superpower. The Rapacki Plan for a nuclear-free zone in Central Europe was but one example of several such projects originating in Eastern European capitals that elicited only tepid Soviet backing, usually after they had already failed for other reasons.[16]

When Khrushchev in 1963 endorsed a bid for admission into the Warsaw Pact by Mongolia, whose membership would have extended its applicability to the potential battlefield with China, he encountered both Romanian and Polish opposition. On second thought, he withdrew Soviet support, and Mongolia obligingly shelved its application.[17] For the remainder of his stay in office, the alliance languished politically but, regardless of the stabilization of the Berlin situation, continued to grow militarily. This was by Khrushchev's default rather than his design as Soviet generals, increasingly at loggerheads with him, took the leading role in building up the Warsaw Pact's military dimensions. Actions included joint exercises simulating a future European war with prodigious use of nuclear weaponry. The buildup would accelerate after Khrushchev's replacement by the more militaristic Brezhnev leadership.

Crisis and Consolidation

Moscow's hold on its allies weakened after the change of the guard in the Kremlin. The 1965 PCC meeting was the first convened at the initiative of an alliance member, East Germany, rather than that of the Soviets. It was the most contentious meeting to date, riven with disagreements on a host of issues ranging from diplomatic relations with West Germany to NATO's plan for nuclear sharing, the proposed nonproliferation treaty, and support of Third World "national liberation movements," not to mention the rift with China. Moscow and its dependents never saw eye to eye on relations with China.[18]

Distinctive positions of Romania and Poland crystallized more clearly than those of other countries. The Romanians sought to minimize Soviet influence within a weakened Warsaw Pact, preferably transformed into a "discussion club," if not discarded altogether. The Poles wanted to maximize their own influence in a strengthened Warsaw Pact with, rather than against, Moscow, which they considered an indispensable safeguard against what they perceived as the German threat. In their quest for recognition as the Soviet Union's most valuable and respected allies, the Polish Communists competed with their East German comrades, who tried to use the alliance for rallying its members behind their top priority of achieving international recognition of their artificial state.[19]

The nationalist postures adopted by Eastern Europe's party oligarchies did not necessarily conform to the best interests of their peoples. This situation was more obvious in Romania, where the main beneficiaries were Nicolae Ceauşescu and his cronies, instead of their destitute subjects, than in Poland, where the non-Communist majority of the population at least agreed with the proposition, however dubious, that the nation needed Soviet support against a West German menace. No such majority support could be presumed for the East German Communists' ambition to make Germany's division permanent.[20]

Other Warsaw Pact allies, the Soviet Union included, did not have vested interest in underwriting that ambition either. More or less subtle differences of attitude with regard to the German question permeated the alliance. Romania became the first to step out of the line by establishing diplomatic relations with Bonn as early as 1967 and claimed to have been vindicated when others followed suit much later with Soviet permission. All this time, Hungary, another historically Germanophile country, was eyeing the economic benefits of normal relations with West Germany that, according to party leader János Kádár, were in his country's "state interest," albeit not in the interest of "proletarian internationalism."[21] Even Bulgaria, with its ambivalent mixture of Russophile and Germanophile traditions, was not opposed in principle to close relations with both German states. Germanophobe Czechoslovakia remained hostile to Bonn for most of the 1960s for its own reasons, related to compensation claims of its expelled Sudeten German minority, rather than for any love for East Berlin.

Such was the contentious backdrop against which Brezhnev launched in early 1966 the Soviet scheme for the Warsaw Pact's reform and institutionalization from above. Although he had consulted with the allies in advance and expected them to comply expeditiously, the reform plan quickly bogged down and eventually took three years to be implemented. These were the years of the Warsaw Pact's gravest crisis, coincident with NATO's gravest crisis. In both cases, "burden-sharing" with the dominant superpower, including the share in making decisions on vital security issues, was at the heart of protracted disputes. Within NATO, respect for its established institutions and procedures facilitated eventual accommodation; within the Warsaw Pact, accommodation was more difficult because of the lack of such institutions and procedures, aggravated by Communists' habitual disrespect for minority views. The resulting wrangling involved not only the call for a share in decision making in times of peace and war but also safeguards against Soviet interference with national policies, and the Warsaw Pact's very raison d'être.[22]

By the time NATO had overcome its crisis and set its course toward defense-*cum*-détente, as mapped out in its December 1967 Harmel Report, the consolidation of the Warsaw Pact was not yet in sight. Only in the following year did Moscow step up efforts to bring its restructuring plans to fruition, just as the mounting Czechoslovak crisis threatened to test the integrity of the alliance. This was not because of any pressure from Prague's Communist reformers to revamp it radically, much less leave it, as their Polish and Hungarian counterparts had vainly attempted to do in 1956; their critique of it was mild by comparison. Nor was it true that NATO was poised to take advantage of Czechoslovak developments, as Soviet propaganda claimed disingenuously. Instead, the threat to the integrity of the Warsaw Pact came from the Soviets striving to reverse the internal process of democratization in Czechoslovakia.

Unlike in 1956, this time Moscow tried to use the Warsaw Pact's military structures to compel the regime in Prague to mend its ways. But the "Šumava" exercise, which brought Soviet, Polish, and Hungarian troops into Czechoslovak territory to intimidate the reformers, failed to achieve its intended purpose while unintentionally revealing serious tensions between Soviet generals and commanders of the allied forces earmarked for possible intervention in the country. When the intervention finally took place in August 1968, it was therefore not a Warsaw Pact operation. Although token Polish, Hungarian, and Bulgarian troops participated in it—with East Germany allowed to send in only noncombat troops, lest uncomfortable memories of their Nazi predecessors be reignited—the overwhelming majority of the invading forces were Soviet and their commander was an outsider to the Warsaw Pact. The Romanians had not been asked to participate.[23]

According to conventional wisdom, the intervention in Czechoslovakia enabled the Soviet Union to restore discipline in Eastern Europe and consolidate the Warsaw Pact. In fact, there was no such simple connection. Not only did all of Moscow's client regimes, other than that of Romania, welcome the suppression of Czechoslovak reformism, if not necessarily the means used to achieve it, but they had also accepted the main features of the Soviet-inspired reorganization of the alliance before the invasion of Czechoslovakia. Nor had Prague's vaunted "normalization" yet been accomplished when the PCC put the stamp of approval on the Warsaw Pact's reorganization at its Budapest session in March 1969. The committee met under the shadow of the outbreak of fighting between the Soviet Union and China along their disputed border, thus giving Moscow a special reason to take its allies' sensibilities into account.[24]

The reform of the Warsaw Pact was not a simple Soviet diktat. It aimed at offering the East European regimes a greater sense of partnership, thus making the alliance a more reliable Soviet instrument. With an eye on the NATO model, the PCC was made to resemble more the North Atlantic Council, becoming a consultative, even if not decision-making, body. In practice, Moscow increasingly shared information about the policies of its choice with its clients and solicited their views before making decisions, thus extending them the opportunity to influence the outcomes, if they wanted to, as long as the Kremlin remained undecided. This differed from previous practice.

In an attempt to clarify the previously nebulous division of power between the supreme commander and the national governments, the armed forces of the member states were left under their respective national commands in peacetime, whereas the sensitive decision about how they should be commanded in the event of war was delayed. So was the similarly controversial establishment of a committee of foreign ministers, opposed by Romania as restrictive of its foreign policy, as well as the creation of a permanent secretariat with a secretary general, which was delayed indefinitely. The reorganization amounted to a major change since Stalin's or Khrushchev's times by making Moscow's management of its allies' military assets indirect rather than direct. Its effectiveness was nevertheless ensured with the help of new joint institutions: the military council, committee on technology, and committee of defense ministers.[25]

The first group resembled NATO's Military Committee by representing the nations through their chiefs of staff but differed from it by including also the supreme commander as guarantor of Moscow's supremacy. In addition, the Warsaw Pact's Soviet chief of staff, with much expanded personnel at his disposal, provided the council's executive mechanism. The committee on technology oversaw research and development, armaments, and equipment. The committee of defense ministers, which had previously held ad hoc sessions as a group, was now formally constituted as the PCC's advisory body on defense policy, meeting at annual intervals.[26]

After fifteen years of uncertainty about its purpose, the Warsaw Pact was thus at last converted from Khrushchev's "cardboard castle" into a genuine military alliance. For right or for wrong, NATO subsequently treated it as its own legitimate counterpart. Paradoxically, much like the original creation of the Warsaw Pact during the "first détente," its boosting again occurred at a time of diminishing rather than increasing East-West tensions. This underlined the alliance's political significance but left the purpose of its military structures open to doubt.

The Perils of Détente

Defining the Warsaw Pact's mission at the time of incipient détente posed challenges. PCC meetings became the forums where the Soviet Union tried to hammer out common positions on foreign policy issues it considered paramount, such as the project of the Conference on Security and Cooperation in Europe (CSCE), rapprochement with the United States, normalization of relations with West Germany, and the perceived Chinese threat. On none of these issues were the priorities of the allies the same as Moscow's; nevertheless, with the usual exception of Romania, they all considered achieving a common stand to be in their best interest. Their cooperation allowed the Soviet Union to preside over the flowering of détente that culminated in the 1975 Helsinki Accords, hailed by the Brezhnev leadership as a signal success and harbinger of Europe's more congenial new security order.[27]

During this period, the Warsaw Pact's preparations for war not only continued but also accelerated and intensified. The alliance's high-level meetings betrayed an unresolved contradiction between the mainly upbeat tenor of discussion about common foreign policy, especially with regard to the CSCE, and the dire warnings by Soviet generals that the threat of war had not diminished and possibly increased. With Romanian obstructionism effectively contained, the meetings of defense ministers and of the military council were notable for the submissiveness of members to Soviet demands for more military spending and greater military preparedness. The generals' insistence that détente was not to be trusted contrasted with Brezhnev's belief that it was irreversible.[28]

The extent of influence exerted by the Soviet military on the discourse, or lack thereof, within the Warsaw Pact during the rise and fall of détente cannot be reliably determined until the closed records of the Moscow Defense Ministry have been opened. There cannot be a doubt, however, that the influence was both growing and baneful. The progressive weakening of the Kremlin leadership during Brezhnev's "era of stagnation" and the reign of his decrepit successors allowed Soviet generals to exert more influence, by default even if not necessarily by design. Moreover, because the military remained by definition the ideologically most committed as well as the most disciplined segment of the Soviet establishment, the influence was conducive to confrontation rather than accommodation.[29]

The transformation of the Warsaw Pact into an extended arm of the Soviet Defense Ministry redefined the purpose of the alliance in an ominous way. During its numerous exercises, the offensive thrust into Western Europe was now being repeatedly rehearsed in unprecedented detail while practicing defense against NATO's putative aggression became increasingly perfunctory. The actual war plans hatched in the Soviet general staff in deepest secrecy were revealed to select Eastern European officers only to the extent necessary for their intended implementation.

Some of the involved officers later testified how they became more or less willing accomplices in Soviet planning for a catastrophic European war that would have entailed devastation and possible annihilation of the nations that they were nominally responsible for defending. Only a few of those in a position to know have been prepared to discuss this uncomfortable subject candidly; most have been evasive. Significantly for the progressing decadence of the ruling elites, Eastern European party leaders—in a telling contrast to the conduct of their predecessors in the 1950s and 1960s—did not know or want to know the plans bearing on their countries' most vital interests, much less question those plans.[30]

The evanescence of détente since the mid-1970s fostered both military and political tightening of the Warsaw Pact. In 1979, the controversial statute on the command of the alliance in wartime, which granted its Soviet supreme commander vast discretionary powers, was finally accepted after considerable foot-dragging by all the allies save Ceauşescu. He angrily walked out of the PCC meeting, leaving Soviet control of Romania's armed forces in abeyance. The resulting document also left unclear the crucial question of how much authority the supreme commander would have in relation to the chief of the Soviet general staff; the respective incumbents happened to be on poor terms at the time. The allies had agreed more readily to the creation in 1976 of the committee of foreign ministers that promised to deal more effectively with the unexpected consequences of détente as well as its baffling decline.[31]

In trying to forge the Warsaw Pact's common stance against the "enemies of détente," Moscow dwelt on the importance of what it called "military détente" but never clarified what this really meant. At the one international forum where the two alliances were negotiating about reducing their military confrontation, the Mutual and Balanced Force Reduction (MBFR) talks in Vienna, the Soviet Union blocked substantive discussion. With Romania already absent, the negotiations excluded Hungary, next in line in desiring better relations with countries of the other alliance.[32]

The Warsaw Pact's political tightening reflected the common interest of its members in resisting growing pressure on their human rights records brought to bear through "Basket Three" of the Helsinki agreement, the unwanted child carelessly fathered by the Soviet Union that now threatened the foundations of their repressive regimes. As Moscow took the lead in battling Western advocacy of human rights at the CSCE's follow-up meetings, the alliance came full circle. It was regaining its earlier primary function of coordinating diplomatic and propaganda activities aimed at weakening the West's political cohesion, as it had done during the Khrushchev years.[33]

Rather than challenging Moscow's supremacy, its junior partners, other than Romania, assisted it with different degrees of enthusiasm in its various Third World ventures. They did so individually and not on behalf of the alliance. East Germany's preeminence in such projects marked its success in the competition with Poland for the distinction of the Soviet Union's most valued ally. The East Germans were not only willing to take the responsibility for projects others shunned but also proved more capable of delivering results. In snatching NATO's secrets, in particular, East German spies surpassed all others.[34]

The 1980–81 Solidarity crisis in Poland presaged the end of Soviet domination and of Communist rule in Eastern Europe, but it posed no immediate threat to the integrity of the Warsaw Pact. Its supreme commander, Marshal Viktor Kulikov, retrospectively testified that he had not been worried about the safety of the vital Soviet supply lines through Poland to East Germany, even if a Solidarity-led government had come to power in Warsaw. Self-serving though his testimony was, it conformed to the desire of Solidarity leaders to eschew anything that might cast doubt on their country's loyalty to its Warsaw Pact obligations and thus provoke a possible Soviet military move against them.[35]

As events in Poland began to spin out of control, Moscow's instinctive first reaction was to ready itself for a repetition of the 1968 Czechoslovak scenario. It gathered loyal Warsaw Pact forces for an exercise aimed at prompting the demoralized Polish party leadership to crack down on the opposition, or else prepare for an intervention to install a substitute leadership. The political cost of such an operation, however, kept growing, while its feasibility seemed to be diminishing. The increasingly fainthearted Kremlin leaders eventually put their hopes on cajoling the Soviet-trained Polish military to suppress the opposition on its own responsibility, and the gamble worked.[36]

The imposition of martial law on 13 December 1981 by General Wojciech Jaruzelski and his cohorts routed the opposition without Soviet matériel or even moral support and represented a major accomplishment for the Warsaw Pact as it had been built up since 1969. The generals' success attested to the emergence in Eastern Europe of a dedicated core of indigenous officers, most of them alumni of Soviet military academies, who owed their primary allegiance to the alliance rather than to their own people. In pulling off a virtually bloodless military coup in the region's most anti-Soviet nation, they proved capable of acting effectively in their own self-interest, which coincided also with Soviet interest.

Concurrently, the feat showed how much Moscow, in maintaining its grip on the alliance, came to depend on willing collaboration by subordinates, whom it did not fully control. Moreover, a military dictatorship on behalf of the party was an uncomfortable novelty for the Kremlin. The generals, however, proved inept in running the country, never trying hard enough to gain the confidence of the majority of its people, and their accomplishment eventually turned hollow.

Decadence and Demise

The Warsaw Pact's Eastern European regimes, including Ceaușescu's increasingly despotic Romania, shared with the Kremlin the desire to maintain themselves in power. With détente turning into a "second cold war" after the Soviet invasion of Afghanistan, however, their cooperation on controversial security issues could no longer be taken for granted. The Romanians kept throwing monkey wrenches into the alliance's operations by demanding reductions of both nuclear weapons and conventional forces as well as defense budgets—as Khrushchev had clamored for in his days. Ceaușescu also donned Khrushchev's mantle by calling for the dissolution of both Cold War alliances and the withdrawal of both U.S. and Soviet forces from Europe. Raising a lonely voice with his condemnation of the Afghanistan adventure, more as a mistake than a crime, the contentious Romanian leader seemed bent on "confrontation with the foreign policy line of the USSR and other Warsaw Treaty nations."[37]

Other allies sought to avoid such a confrontation. They went along when Moscow used the Warsaw Pact for conducting its campaign against the deployment of the "Euromissiles" that NATO intended to install in response to the already deployed Soviet intermediate-range missiles targeted on Western Europe. Nor did the allies balk when the Soviet Union convened a PCC emergency meeting once the campaign failed, leaving the Kremlin with the awkward choice of either making good on its threat to "counter-deploy" additional missiles on their territories or suffering a serious loss of credibility. But when the missiles started arriving in East Germany and Czechoslovakia, these otherwise model allies signaled their unmistakable displeasure.[38]

None other than Erich Honecker, East Germany's militaristic leader, took the lead in campaigning for "damage limitation," invoking shared "special responsibility" with

West Germany to ensure that war would never again come from German soil. He took it upon himself to lecture the unhappy Konstantin Chernenko, the senescent Soviet party chief, that what he was doing was in the best interest of the Soviet Union and the alliance as a whole. The missile controversy produced briefly a novel kind of rapprochement between East Germany and Hungary, the Warsaw Pact's least and most tolerant states, on the basis of their proclaimed commitment to the pursuit of national interests compatible with the common ones. In a more old-fashioned display of assertiveness, East Germany confronted Poland by claiming territorial waters at its expense.[39]

Moscow's junior allies had gone farther than the Soviet Union in trying to redefine the purpose of the alliance by downplaying its military functions by the time Mikhail Gorbachev came to power in 1985. To contemporaries, the new leader appeared to be dedicated to reasserting Soviet control over the Warsaw Pact as he presided over its extension for another twenty-five years against Romanian opposition. In hindsight, though, he has been credited with the opposite intention by having supposedly made it clear to its members that from then on they were on their own. Either reading of Gorbachev's initial impact on intra-alliance relations is incorrect.[40]

The Soviet return to the Geneva negotiations on intermediate-range nuclear forces and Gorbachev's subsequent initiatives for both nuclear and conventional cuts temporarily invigorated the alliance, as its members praised his effort to defuse the armed standoff in Central Europe. Feeling vindicated, Honecker again took the lead, this time by encouraging further reductions of Soviet troops in the area. Poland and Czechoslovakia chimed in with their own proposals for reductions of both conventional and unconventional armaments. The Soviet Union and its nominal partners now began to act as real partners for the first time—unwitting collaborators in the Warsaw Pact's demise as well as their own.[41]

The historic change of the Warsaw Pact's military doctrine from offensive to defensive, proclaimed by Gorbachev at the PCC's Berlin meeting in May 1987, dealt a mortal blow to the alliance as a military instrument. As its established structures, designed for an offensive against Western Europe, were dismantled in conformity with "new thinking" on security without being replaced by new ones, the Warsaw Pact became effectively paralyzed. It was symptomatic of its redundancy that no one raised a voice in protest.[42]

The Soviet military had just been shaken by the humiliation of West German pacifist Matthias Rust's flight of his light plane through the formidable Soviet defenses, landing in the heart of Moscow. Military passivity was ensured by the interpenetration of the military and party establishments in the Soviet system, which deprived the generals of an independent power base. Nor did the East European leaders, none more confident of the future than Honecker, object to the reduction of the Warsaw Pact's military functions. They saw in a politically revitalized alliance a better safeguard against the creeping "soft power" of the West.[43]

Yet once the challenge of Gorbachev's liberal experiments began to complement the impact of what Honecker termed Western "human rights demagogy," the Warsaw Pact's alarmed conservative partners placed their hopes in its transformation into a mutual rescue association. Gorbachev, hoping to salvage rather than to discard the Soviet system, abetted the idea. The year 1988 witnessed the extraordinary reunion of the Warsaw Pact's most steadfast upholder and its notorious wrecker, Honecker and Ceauşescu. No longer keen on dissolution of the alliance, Romania proposed strengthening it by "democratizing" its institutions and procedures. With Soviet support, Bulgaria countered an alternative proposal for bolstering it by giving its members a greater say without too much tampering with its structure.[44]

Neither proposal had gotten off the ground before the rush of events climaxed in the collapse of the Berlin Wall in November 1989, making both of them—but not the Warsaw Pact as such—irrelevant. Ironically, the end of the Cold War gave the alliance a new lease on life by making it serve for the first time a clear and constructive purpose—namely, the dismantling of the outsized conventional forces and armaments that remained the Cold War's legacy. The two alliances successfully negotiated their drastic reduction, after the sterile MBFR talks had been merged into the fecund CSCE during its final round in 1987–90. The resulting agreements, which placed limits on military deployments in different parts of the Continent, became the cornerstone of Europe's unique security "architecture" on which its peace has been resting ever since.[45]

The Warsaw Pact did not collapse under pressure from its enemies. Both NATO and Eastern Europe's post-Communist governments, as well as the Soviet Union, were notably reluctant to push for its abolition. Even the dissident Václav Havel, as the new president of Czechoslovakia, initially saw merit in keeping both alliances in place. Non-Communist Polish leaders were temporarily under the illusion that they might need the Warsaw Pact as leverage to achieve full recognition of their country's western border by a reunited Germany. Hungary, alone, made clear early on its desire to get rid of the relic, though eventually Havel took the decisive step to rally Polish and Hungarian colleagues into an action forcing Gorbachev to yield. In the end, the Warsaw Pact faded away with a whimper rather than a bang in June 1991—a fitting end of a creature that had never managed to prove sufficiently its worth.[46]

The Warsaw Pact's trajectory reflected unresolved tension between its military and political purposes. Apart from the interventions against its own members, its military functions were always potential and hypothetical. In the event of a European war, Moscow never relied on it in the manner Washington relied on NATO. Expendable to the Soviet Union, the alliance was not indispensable to its other members either, except, perhaps, to East Germany in its drive for recognition as Moscow's premier ally.

The more important function of the Warsaw Pact as the forum on which political disagreements between the Soviet Union and its clients played themselves
out was not so much superfluous as skewed. There was something esoteric about
disputes involving self-appointed guardians of national interests bound together
by diminishing ideological affinities and uncertain dependence on Soviet support.
East Germany's former defense minister, Heinz Kessler, recalled the last gathering of
Warsaw Pact protagonists that he had attended in 1989 as an "assembly of ghosts."[47]
Their quarrels proved notably irrelevant to the manner in which the Cold War and
the Soviet Union came to an end after the ghosts themselves had vanished into the
proverbial rubbish heap of history.

The superfluous alliance's search for a purpose presents a cautionary tale for
NATO. All of the Warsaw Pact's former Eastern European members, except Albania, and the Baltic republics, from among the Soviet Union's successor states,
have since become members of the Atlantic alliance. They joined it after they had
already become more secure than they ever were in their history, as had NATO's
other members as well. The enlarged alliance's search for a purpose after the Cold
War had been won has thus far been inconclusive. Until its new purpose has been
found and clearly defined, NATO will be courting the fate of its former rival.

Notes

1. Michael F. Altfeld, "The Decision to Ally: A Theory and Test," *Western Political Quarterly* 37 (1984): 523–44, at p. 538.

2. On the origins of the Warsaw Pact, see Vojtech Mastny, "The Soviet Union and the Ori-
gins of the Warsaw Pact in 1955," in *Mechanisms of Power in the Soviet Union,* ed. Niels Erik
Rosenfeldt, Bent Jensen, and Erik Kulavig (New York: St. Martin's Press, 2000), 241–66. Also on
PHP website, www.php.isn.ethz.ch/collections/coll_pcc/into_VM.cfm, accessed 8 July 2007.

3. Resolution by Soviet Party Central Committee, 1 Apr. 1955, 06/14/54/4/39, Foreign
Policy Archives of the Russian Federation, Moscow.

4. Dennis Deletant, *Communist Terror in Romania: Gheorghiu-Dej and the Police State,
1948–1965* (London: Hurst, 1999), 273–74.

5. "Cardboard castle" quoted in Robert Spencer, "Alliance Perceptions of the Soviet
Threat, 1950–1988," in *The Changing Western Analysis of the Soviet Threat,* ed. Carl-Christoph
Schweitzer (London: Pinter, 1990), 9–48, at p. 19. Records of the PCC meeting, 27–28 Jan.
1956, www.php.isn.ethz.ch/collections/colltopic.cfm?lng=en+id=17116+navinfo=14465,
accessed 8 July 2007.

6. For records of the PCC's second and third meetings, see www.php.isn.ethz.ch/collections/
colltopic.cfm?lng=en+id=17117+navinfo=14465 and www.php.isn.ethz.ch/collections/colltopic.
cfm?lng=en+id=17118+navinfo=14465, both accessed 8 July 2007.

7. Declaration on relations with socialist states, 30 Oct. 1956, in *Documentary Study of
the Warsaw Pact,* ed. Jagdish P. Jain (Bombay: Asia Publishing House, 1973), 168–71.

8. "Memorandum on the Warsaw Treaty and the Development of the Armed Forces of the
People's Republic of Poland," 10 Jan. 1957, in Vojtech Mastny, "'We Are in a Bind': Polish and

Czechoslovak Attempts at Reforming the Warsaw Pact, 1956–1969," *Cold War International History Project Bulletin* 11 (1998): 230–50, at pp. 236–38.

9. Ioan Scurtu, ed., *România: Retragerea trupelor sovietice, 1958* [Romania: The Withdrawal of Soviet Troops, 1958] (Bucharest: Editura didactică și pedagogică, 1966), 273–83; Gheorghe Vartik, "Odsun sovětských vojsk z Rumunska: Vítězství Bukurešti nebo rozhodnutí Moskvy?" [The Withdrawal of Soviet Troops from Romania: Bucharest's Victory or Moscow's Decision?], *Historie a vojenství* [Prague], 2003, nos. 3–4: 687–92.

10. Excerpt from minutes of Khrushchev-Gomułka conversation, 10 Nov. 1958, *Cold War International History Project Bulletin* 11 (1998): 201–3, at p. 202.

11. The change is referred to in "Materiály k otázce Spojeného velení" [Materials Concerning the Issue of Unified Command], undated [early 1966], GŠ-OS 0039042/1, Central Military Archives, Prague [hereafter VÚA]. Resolution by Military Defense Committee, 2 Sept. 1961, 18/4, VKO, VÚA.

12. Michael Lemke, *Die Berlinkrise 1958 bis 1963: Interessen und Handlungsspielräume der SED im Ost-West-Konflikt* (Berlin: Akademie, 1995), attributes to Ulbricht less actual leverage than does Hope Harrison, *Driving the Soviets Up the Wall: Soviet-East European Relations, 1953–1961* (Princeton, N.J.: Princeton Univ. Press, 2003).

13. Joint Declaration of the Warsaw Treaty States on the Berlin Wall, 13 Aug. 1961, in *Documents on International Affairs, 1961*, ed. Donald C. Watt et al. (London: Oxford Univ. Press, 1965), 343–45. Matthias Uhl, "Storming on to Paris: The 1961 *Buria* Exercise and the Planned Solution of the Berlin Crisis," in *War Plans and Alliances in the Cold War: Threat Perceptions in the East and West,* ed. Vojtech Mastny, Sven G. Holtsmark, and Andreas Wegner (London: Routledge, 2006), 46–71. Sălăjan to Ceaușescu, 9 May 1966, V2, file 4/34, 124–25, Romanian Military Archives. Also in *Romania and the Warsaw Pact, 1955–1989,* ed. Mircea Munteanu, vol. 1 (Washington, D.C.: Cold War International History Project, 2002), 273–81, at p. 280.

14. For documents on Albania, see Vojtech Mastny and Malcolm Byrne, eds., *A Cardboard Castle? An Inside History of the Warsaw Pact, 1955–1991* (New York: Central European Univ. Press, 2005), 108–15; on China, "China and the Warsaw Pact Under Mao and Khrushchev," www.php.isn.ethz.ch/collections/colltopic.cfm?lng=en+id=16034, accessed 8 July 2007. Also Douglas Selvage, "Poland and the Sino-Soviet Rift, 1963–1965," www.wilsoncenter.org/index.cfm?topic_id=1409&fuseaction=topics.publications&doc_id=43898&group_id=13349, accessed 8 July 2007.

15. Report by Novotný to Czechoslovak party central committee, 2 Nov. 1962, Archives of the Central Committee of the Communist Party of Czechoslovakia, Prague (hereafter AÚV KSČ) 01/98/85, Central State Archives, Prague (hereafter SÚA).

16. Raymond L. Garthoff, "When and Why Romania Distanced Itself from the Warsaw Pact," *Cold War International History Project Bulletin* 5 (1995); Piotr Wandycz, "Adam Rapacki and the Search for European Security," in *The Diplomats, 1939–1979,* ed. Gordon A. Craig and Francis L. Loewenheim (Princeton, N.J.: Princeton Univ. Press, 1994), 289–317, at p. 301.

17. Tsedenbal to Cyrankiewicz, 15 July 1963, and Khrushchev to Gomułka, 15 July 1963, Central Committee of the Polish United Workers' Party (hereafter KC PZPR), XIA/103, k. 523–26, Modern Records Archives, Warsaw, www.php.isn.ethz.ch/collections/colltopic/cfm?lng=en+id=16340+navinfo=16034 and www.php.isn.ethz.ch/collections/colltopic/cfm?lng=en+id=16341+navinfo=16034, both accessed 8 July 2007. Report by Kádár to Hungarian politburo, 31 July 1963, MOL-M-KS-288.f.5/309. őe, National Archives of Hungary, www.php.

isn.ethz.ch/collections/colltopic.cfm?lng=en+id=17907+navinfo=14465, accessed 8 July 2007. See also Sergey S. Radchenko, *The Soviets' Best Friend in Asia: The Mongolian Dimension of the Sino-Soviet Split*, Working Paper no. 42, Cold War International History Project, wwics. si.edu/topics/pubs/ACF4CA.pdf, accessed 8 July 2007.

18. Records of the PCC meeting, 19–20 Jan. 1965, www.php.isn.ethz.ch/collections/colltopic.cfm?lng=en+id=17127+navinfo=14465, accessed 8 July 2007.

19. Naszkowski to Rapacki, 17 Feb. 1966, KC PZPR 2948, 58–69, at p. 68, Modern Records Archives, Warsaw. Vojtech Mastny, "Détente, the Superpowers and Their Allies, 1962–64," in *Europe, Cold War and Coexistence, 1953–1965*, ed. Wilfried Loth (London: Cass, 1964), 215–35, at pp. 229–30.

20. Dennis Deletant and Mihail Ionescu, *Romania and the Warsaw Pact, 1955–1989*, Working Paper No. 43, Cold War International History Project, 71–101, www.php.isn.ethz.ch/collections/coll_romania/documents/CWIHP_WP_43.pdf?navinfo=15342, accessed 8 July 2007.

21. Minutes of the Crimea meeting of party first secretaries, 31 July 1972, DY/30/J/IV/2/201, SAPMO, www.php.isn.ethz.ch/collections/colltopic.cfm?lng=en+id=16044+navinfo=16037, accessed 8 July 2007.

22. Vojtech Mastny, "Learning from the Enemy: NATO as a Model for the Warsaw Pact," in *A History of NATO: The First Fifty Years*, ed. Gustav Schmidt, vol. 2 (New York: Palgrave, 2001), 157–77, 393–401, at pp. 163–70, also at www.isn.ethz.ch/publihouse/details.cfm?q51=holdregger+lng=en+id=53, accessed 8 July 2007. Mihail E. Ionescu, "Rumunsko a vojenská reforma Varšavské smlouvy (1964–1968)" [Romania and the Military Reform of the Warsaw Pact], *Historie a vojenství* [Prague], 2003, nos. 3–4: 699–705.

23. Vojtech Mastny, "Was 1968 a Strategic Watershed in the Cold War?" *Diplomatic History* 29, no. 1 (2005): 149–77.

24. Record of the Romanian politburo meeting, 16 Mar. 1969, CC PCR, folder 16, National Central Historical Archives, Bucharest, English translation in Munteanu, *Romania and the Warsaw Pact*, vol. 1, 445–68.

25. For records of the 18 Mar. 1969 PCC meeting, see www.php.isn.ethz.ch/collections/colltopic.cfm?lng=en+id=17125+navinfo=14465, accessed 8 July 2007.

26. Christian Nünlist, "Cold War Generals: The Warsaw Pact Committee of Defense Ministers, 1969–90," www.php.isn.ethz.ch/collections/coll_cmd/introduction.cfm?navinfo=14565, accessed 8 July 2007.

27. On disputes about priorities, see memorandum by Erdélyi, M-KS-288.f. 5/501.ő.e., 18 Oct. 1969, Hungarian National Archives, English translation in Mastny and Byrne, eds., *A Cardboard Castle?* 347–49.

28. Grechko at meeting of committee of defense ministers, 22 Dec. 1969, AZN 32855, 18–28, Military Division of the Federal Archives, Freiburg (hereafter BA-MA). English in Mastny and Byrne, eds., *A Cardboard Castle?* 356–57. Report on meeting of Warsaw Pact Committee of Ministers of Defense, 2–3 Mar. 1971, DVW 1/71027, BA-MA, also at www.php.isn.ethz.ch/collections/colltopic.cfm?lng=en+id=21376+navinfo=14565, accessed 8 July 2007.

29. On theories of party-military relations, see William E. Odom, *The Collapse of the Soviet Military* (New Haven, Conn.: Yale Univ. Press, 1998), 218–22.

30. "Warsaw Pact Generals in Polish Uniforms: Oral History Interviews," www.php.isn.ethz.ch/collections/colltopic.cfm?lng=en+id=20611+navinfo=15708, accessed 8 July 2007.

31. "Grundsätze über die Vereinten Streitkräfte der Teilnehmerstaaten des Warschauer Vertrages und ihre Führungsorgane (für den Krieg)," 18 Mar. 1980, AZN 32854, 85–120,

BA-MA, also at www.php.isn.ethz.ch/collections/colltopic.cfm?lng=en+id=20408+navinfo =15708, accessed 8 July 2007. Interviews with generals Skalski and Jasiński, in "Warsaw Pact Generals in Polish Uniforms," www.php.isn.ethz.ch/collections/colltopic.cfm?lng=en+id=2066 5+navinfo=15708, pp. 23–24, and www.php.isn.ethz.ch/collections/colltopic.cfm?lng=en+id =20668+navinfo=15708, p. 6, both accessed 8 July 2007. Anatoli Gribkow, *Der Warschauer Pakt: Geschichte und Hintergründe des östlichen Militärbündnisses* (Berlin: Edition Q, 1995), 46–47.

32. On military détente, record of the meeting of Warsaw Pact deputy foreign ministers, 8–9 July 1980, MR C-20 I/4–4570, SAPMO. For a study of the Warsaw Pact's positions at the MBFR, voluminous documentation is available in Polish, Czech, and other former Soviet bloc archives.

33. Anna Locher, "Shaping the Policies of the Alliance: The Committee of Ministers of Foreign Affairs of the Warsaw Pact, 1976–1990," www.php.isn.ethz.ch/collections/colltopic. cfm?lng=en+id=20668+navinfo=15708, accessed 8 July 2007. Daniel C. Thomas, *The Helsinki Effect: International Norms, Human Rights, and the Demise of Communism* (Princeton, N.J.: Princeton Univ. Press, 2001).

34. Agreement on principles of military assistance to developing countries, 11 Apr. 1980, AZN 32854, 119–31, BA-MA. "Stasi Intelligence on NATO," www.php.isn.ethz.ch/collections/ colltopic.cfm?lng=en+id=15296, accessed 8 July 2007.

35. Interview with Kulikov, Piotr Jendroszczyk, "Układ" [The Pact], *Rzeczpospolita* [Warsaw], 7 Nov. 1997.

36. Vojtech Mastny, "The Soviet Non-Invasion of Poland in 1980–1981 and the End of the Cold War," *Europe-Asia Studies* 51, no. 2 (1999): 189–211, also at www.wilsoncenter.org/ topics/pubs/ACFB35.pdf, accessed 8 July 2007.

37. Report for the Czechoslovak Party Presidium on the 14–15 May 1980 PCC meeting, 27 May 1980, AÚV KSČ 02/1/8349/24, SÚA, also at www.php.isn.ethz.ch/collections/ colltopic.cfm?lng=en+id=18296+navinfo=14465, accessed 8 July 2007.

38. Record of the Moscow meeting of Warsaw Pact leaders, 28 June 1983, MR C-20 I/3–1950, SAPMO. Record of the Budapest meeting of committee of foreign ministers, 19–20 Apr. 1984, MR C-20 I/3–2033, SAPMO. Also at www.php.isn.ethz.ch/collections/colltopic.cfm? lng=en+id=16518+navinfo=15699, accessed 8 July 2007.

39. Minutes of Honecker-Chernenko meeting, 17 Aug. 1984, DY-30/2380, SAMPP, English translation in Mastny and Byrne, eds., *A Cardboard Castle?* 496–99. Ronald Asmus, *East Berlin and Moscow: The Documentation of a Dispute* (Munich: Radio Free Europe, 1985). On the East German-Polish dispute, Kessler to Axen, 2 July 1987, and summary of Kessler-Siwicki conversation, 12 Aug. 1987, VA-01/32676, BA-MA, and record of Honecker-Jaruzelski meeting, 16 Sept. 1987, ZK SED, J IV/893; DY 3/2479, SAPMO.

40. Record of the Warsaw Pact summit in Warsaw, 26 Apr. 1985, 8696/24, AÚV KSČ, SÚA. Raymond L. Garthoff, *The Great Transition: American-Soviet Relations and the End of the Cold War* (Washington, D.C.: Brookings Institution, 1994), 571–72.

41. Vojtech Mastny, "Did Gorbachev Liberate Eastern Europe?" in *The Last Decade of the Cold War: From Conflict Escalation to Conflict Transformation,* ed. Olav Njølstad (London: Cass, 2004), 402–23.

42. Records of the 28–29 May 1987 PCC meeting in Berlin at www.php.isn.ethz.ch/ collections/colltopic.cfm?lng=en+id=17112+navinfo=14465, accessed 8 July 2007. English translations in Mastny and Byrne, eds., *A Cardboard Castle?* 562–71.

43. Records of the 15–16 July 1988 PCC meeting in Warsaw, at www.php.isn.ethz.ch/collections/colltopic.cfm?lng=en+id=17113+navinfo=14465, accessed 8 July 2007. English translations in Mastny and Byrne, eds., *A Cardboard Castle?* 615–17.

44. Speech by Honecker at the PCC meeting in Bucharest on 7–8 July 1989, DC20/I/3/2840, p. 80, SAPMO, Berlin, also at www.php.isn.ethz.ch/collections/colltopic.cfm?lng=en+id=19032+navinfo=14465, accessed 8 July 2007. Record of Honecker-Ceauşescu meeting, 17 Nov. 1988, J IV/939, SAPMO. Romanian proposal, 4 July 1988, copy in Fond 1b, opis 35, a.e. pp. 88–108, Central State Archives, Sofia. Bulgarian proposal, 14 June 1989, 60p/161/63, Archives of the Ministry of Foreign Affairs, Sofia. English translations of the proposals in Mastny and Byrne, eds., *A Cardboard Castle?* 600–601, 636–41.

45. Richard A. Falkenrath, *The Origins and Consequences of the CFE Treaty* (Cambridge, Mass.: MIT Press, 1995).

46. Records of the 6–7 June 1990 PCC meeting in Moscow, at www.php.isn.ethz.ch/collections/colltopic.cfm?lng=en+id=17115+navinfo=14465, accessed 8 July 2007. Jaroslav Šedivý, *Černínský palác v roce nula* [The Palais Czernin in Year Zero] (Prague: Železný, 1997), 124–30.

47. Heinz Kessler, *Zur Sache und zur Person: Erinnerungen* (Berlin: Edition Ost, 1996), 244.

10

Polish–East German Relations, 1945–1958

SHELDON ANDERSON

*"There are no good Germans. . . . A German communist is always and above all
a German who places German interests above the international solidarity of the
proletariat." —The Polish West Institute in Poznań*

Franz Sikora, *Sozialistische Solidarität und nationale Interessen*
[Socialist Solidarity and National Interests]

There is an old Polish saying that *"Jak świat światem, nie będzie Niemiec Polakowi
bratem"* [As long as the world is whole, no German will be a brother to a Pole].[1] This
filial reference is an apt metaphor for East German–Polish relations after World War
II. The East Germans and Poles were like siblings born into the Soviet family; no
matter how much they quarreled, they could not leave it. They curried favor with
the paternal center while pursuing conflicting national interests. The result was a
cold war of misunderstanding and distrust. Like the Cold War between the Soviet
Union and the United States, there were times of détente and times of crisis, but in
the end East German and Polish Communist parties had irreconcilable national differences. Furthermore, the illegitimacy of the East German and Polish Communist
governments precluded an honest reconciliation between their peoples.

Several issues were particularly contentious: the dispute over Poland's administration of German territories east of the Oder and Western (Lusacian) Neisse border;
policy toward the West, especially toward West Germany; and East Germany's
rearmament in 1956. These and other disagreements intensified during and after
the Polish October in 1956.

The Oder-Neisse Border

The primary obstacle to better relations between the Polish and German Communists after World War II was the loss of German territories to Poland. The
equivocation of the Communist Party (KPD) and the Social Democratic Party

(SPD) on recognizing the permanence of the Oder-Neisse border undermined Polish confidence in the German Left from the start.

In September 1945, the Polish Workers' Party (PPR) organ *Głos Ludu* wrote that "all Poland is of the opinion that there is no place for the Germans in these territories, and that they should be expelled from them as soon as possible." The newspaper even criticized the government for not deporting them faster.[2] Party leader Władysław Gomułka eschewed proletarian internationalism by declaring that "we must expel all the Germans because countries are built on national lines and not on multinational ones."[3] When he promised that no "enemy or foreign" elements would be allowed to live in Poland, he meant the Germans.[4] As for Poland's borders, Gomułka declared that "Poland no longer wants to be a soccer ball that is kicked around from place to place."[5]

After the Socialist Unity Party (SED) was forged out of the KPD and the SPD in the Soviet zone in April 1946, the PPR hoped that Wilhelm Pieck and Walter Ulbricht would prevail upon the party to recognize the Oder-Neisse border. But the SED adopted a position that more closely reflected the SPD's blunt revisionism. Although the SED could not promote national interests as openly as the Poles, the party's stubborn opposition to the new Polish-German border confirmed what the Polish Communists feared most—that the ghost of Rapallo and the Nazi-Soviet Pact would return in the form of a deal between Stalin and the SED at Poland's expense.

Although it is not clear to what extent the Soviets pressured the SED to accept the Oder-Neisse Line, the SED leaders undoubtedly drew their own conclusions from the breakdown of allied cooperation in Germany.[6] In 1948, the SED cast its lot with the other East European Communist parties, which after the Czechoslovak Communist coup in February controlled all of the governments in the region. The SED had to accept the present border as final.[7] The Poles still had lingering doubts about the SED's sudden change of heart because they suspected that the Soviets had ordered an end to the SED's revisionism. They were fully aware that many SED members did not accept the party's official position. The Polish-German border remained a recurring source of friction between the Poles and East Germans, long after the creation of the GDR in October and its formal recognition of the Oder-Neisse Line in 1950.

The SED refused to recognize Poland's historic rights to German territory. The Poles suspected that the SED wanted to keep the option open for a border revision if Germany was reunified. Polish officials were repeatedly angered about the East Germans' persistent references to the GDR as "Middle Germany," as though Poland's western territories constituted "East Germany." In May 1959, Ulbricht used the term in *Neues Deutschland*.[8] At first East German ambassador Stefan Heymann told Polish diplomat Leon Szybek that it was an editorial error and that he was "surprised and perplexed" by the mix-up, but when Szybek later showed him a copy of the speech, Heymann tried to explain that Ulbricht was referring to a workers' revolt near Halle in the 1920s that had been called the "middle German uprising."[9] The Poles remained unconvinced. The Polish Foreign Ministry advised Ambassador Roman Piotrowski to inform the East German Foreign Ministry that Polish public opinion was strongly opposed to the term.[10]

Polish officials suspected that the SED referred to the GDR as "Middle Germany" to pander to the East German settlers from Poland, many of whom still expected to get their land back. A functionary in the SED's propaganda section, Horst Heinrich, told Polish diplomat Stanislaw Kopa that "the view is rather widespread of the necessity to revise the border drawn in the Potsdam agreement. . . . Recognition of the right of Germans to return to these areas is justified mainly by the difficulties Poland has had in administering them."[11]

The tenth anniversary of the 1950 Görlitz agreement recognizing the Oder-Neisse border offered an opportunity to trumpet the solidarity of the two peoples, but differences immediately surfaced over the site of the celebration. Polish foreign minister Adam Rapacki proposed a summit and a large demonstration at Zgorzelec in support of the Oder-Neisse border, but the East Germans told the Poles that they wanted to avoid giving the West the impression that Poland and the GDR needed to reconfirm their recognition of the border. In reality, the East German Communists wanted no part of a big public show of support for a border that was still highly unpopular among the East German people. Furthermore, the SED wanted to keep any celebration under tight control. East German foreign minister Lothar Bolz recommended a modest ceremony in Magdeburg that would be devoted in large part to condemning West German revanchism. There was symbolic importance for the East Germans to hold the commemoration on the Elbe and not on the Oder, because they wanted tacit Polish agreement that an attack on the GDR's western border would be considered an attack on Poland.[12] Polish ambassador Roman Piotrowski reluctantly agreed to the Magdeburg demonstration.[13] The controversy resurfaced in June 1961 when the Poles criticized Ulbricht for adhering to the old SED line that Hitler had merely gambled away the eastern territories, while ignoring any reference to Poland's historical claims.[14] A year later the East German government issued a document that made a positive reference to German general Hans von Seeckt's support of the Treaty of Rapallo between Weimar Germany and the Soviet Union in 1922. The document cited Rapallo as part of the tradition of friendly Soviet-German relations—which the GDR was now perpetuating—and blamed German monopoly capitalists and large landowners for fighting Hitler's war and losing German territory.[15]

For years Polish officials had expressed their strong objection to any positive references to Rapallo, which they interpreted as precedent to the Nazi-Soviet Pact of 1939. They were especially angered by this document because von Seeckt was a confirmed enemy of Poland.[16] Gomułka cited as proof von Seeckt's declaration that "the existence of Poland is intolerable, irreconcilable with the conditions of the life of Germany. Poland must disappear and will disappear."[17] East German diplomats explained that the publication was for West German consumption, but one Polish official responded that the price for this kind of propaganda was too high: "Poland feels hit on the head by it. Whom does that help?"[18]

The document added to Polish perceptions that, if a German confederation became a reality, East Berlin would work with Bonn to revise the Oder-Neisse border. Speaking to a crowd in Gdańsk in July 1962, Gomułka intentionally cited Poland's historical presence along the Baltic Sea, and in Gdańsk specifically, to justify Polish claims to the former German territories.[19]

The Polish October

The coerced normalcy that Stalin brought to Communist Party relations in the early 1950s broke down after his death in 1953. In addition to their greater political autonomy, the satellites soon began to reassert their economic interests as well. As the political and economic fault lines dividing Europe weakened somewhat, the Polish government reassessed the benefits of its trade with the Soviet bloc. Many Polish Communists grumbled about the SED's blind obedience to Stalinist orthodoxy, while the SED distrusted the PZPR (Polish United Workers' Party) for its alleged social democratic, capitalist, and bourgeois tendencies. East Berlin was especially critical of Warsaw's tolerance of the Polish Catholic Church and lack of collectivized agriculture.

These rifts bubbled to the surface after Khrushchev's de-Stalinization speech in February 1956. In October, Gomułka returned to power on a platform that directly challenged the tenets of Stalinism. Gomułka's election set a dangerous precedent for the Stalinists in the other Communist parties, and Ulbricht was one of them. Gomułka's national brand of socialism posed a direct challenge to the SED's orthodox Marxist-Leninist-Stalinist policies. When the PZPR had purged Gomułka in 1949, the SED had obediently echoed the Kremlin by condemning Gomułka's mistakes. Ulbricht had often lumped Tito and Gomułka together, castigating them for various "criminal activities."[20] An East German Foreign Ministry official told Polish diplomat Jan Pierzchała that "the imprisonment and earlier removal from the party permanently compromises comrade Gomułka and his present election to First Secretary reflects badly on [your] CC [Central Committee]."[21]

The SED's sharp condemnation of Gomułka's allegedly un-Marxist and nationalist policies, and the Polish Communists' equally vituperative criticisms of Ulbricht's unrepentant Stalinism, soon erased what little goodwill the two parties had developed over the past decade. The SED suppressed all news reports coming out of Poland. *Trybuna Ludu* alluded to Gomułka's expulsion from the party and arrest in 1949, but the East German press made no mention of Gomułka's past or the frank public discussions going on in Poland about the party's past errors.[22] East German Ministry of Security official Richard Schmöing told Polish diplomats that "things are not going well in Poland if everyone can say what they please, because that does not strengthen the power of the state authorities."[23]

In the two weeks between Gomułka's election on 20 October and the Soviet suppression of the Hungarian revolt, the SED leadership was clearly placed on the ideological defensive. One PZPR member asked an East German journalist, "Well, when are you [the SED] going to oust the Stalinists?"[24] The SED's propaganda apparatus geared up for a new defense of the party's policies. Condemnation of the "counterrevolution" in Hungary dominated the pages of *Neues Deutschland* at the end of October, and the SED Politburo boasted that it had taken steps to avoid the kind of upheaval taking place in Poland and Hungary.

The Politburo tried to keep the party rank and file ignorant of developments in Poland and Hungary. Even Central Committee members were not informed. Alfred Neumann, the head of the SED in Berlin, specifically told East German journalists in Berlin not to ask the party about Gomułka.[25] At the end of October the SED Politburo notified the Central Committee that it had restricted access to news from Poland because of the uncertain situation within the PZPR. The Politburo cautioned that the Polish Communists were making statements with too many "false formulations."[26]

The Ulbricht regime had good reason to censor reports coming in from Poland. Ulbricht knew that there was widespread support among the East German populace and in the SED itself for Polish-style reforms. Many party members wanted the GDR to embark on its own road to socialism. East German official Anton Ackermann told Pierzchala confidentially that some party members had removed all signs connecting them with the SED for fear of reprisals from the German people if the party fell from power.[27] According to Pierzchała, East German security officials were monitoring a rise in anti-Soviet attitudes in East Germany. He reported that "almost everyone is making comparisons between [the] June 17 [1953 uprising] in Berlin and the present events in Poland. . . . Everyone has much sympathy for Poland. The general attitude [is] against Ulbricht."[28] Bruno Baum, who headed the SED district office in Potsdam, told a West German journalist that the East German people were whispering that "we need a German Gomułka, a German Nagy."[29]

On 25 October the editor of *Neues Deutschland,* Hermann Axen, and the editor of *Trybuna Ludu,* Artur Kowalski, met in East Berlin. Their heated exchange reflected how deep the ideological divide between the SED and the PZPR had become. Axen knew Kowalski personally from the Spanish Civil War and from their imprisonment together in the concentration camp at Vernet, France, during World War II. Axen deemed him to be an experienced and loyal Marxist, but Axen expressed his disappointment in Kowalski's "nationalist and anti-Soviet conceptions." Axen reflected that "this is even more troubling when one considers that comrade Kowalski sincerely loves the Soviet people and the CPSU." Axen also criticized Kowalski and his comrades for blaming Poland's economic difficulties on Soviet economic advisors. He argued that the GDR had experienced successful economic growth by following the Soviet economic model and that the mistakes in Poland's industrialization program resulted from nationalistic policies, not bad Soviet advice. Axen was shocked that Kowalski had accused Khrushchev of meddling in Polish affairs by flying to Warsaw on 20 October. When Kowalski charged the CPSU with anti-Semitism, Axen retorted that it was more likely that the PZPR was nationalist and anti-Semitic. Axen concluded, "We think it is very dangerous that comrades with such—gently put—ambiguous and anti-Soviet ideas travel around here. He got from us a cup of coffee and otherwise just ideological fireworks."[30]

Gomułka's attempt to make the PZPR more reflective of workers' interests also challenged the SED's Leninist view of the party's leading role in building socialism. Gomułka rejected the notion that all workers' protests in a people's democracy were inherently antisocialist, including the Poznań demonstrations that summer. Gomułka declared in his speech to the Eighth Plenum, "The workers in Poznań, when they went out on the streets of the city, were not protesting against People's Poland, [or] against socialism. They were protesting against the ills which had vastly multiplied in our social system, which had also painfully affected them, [and] against the warped fundamental principles of socialism."[31] East German officials, such as Hanna Wolf, the director of the SED's party schools, termed Poznań "a failed fascist putsch."[32]

The SED and the PZPR were clearly headed in different ideological directions in 1956. Intense debates ensued that fall between reformers in the PZPR and hard-liners in the SED. Polish and East German officials made unprecedented public denunciations of each other—the Poles chiding the East German Communists for their blind devotion to Stalinist political, social, and economic policies, and the East Germans lecturing the PZPR for deviating from orthodox Marxist-Leninist principles.

The Oder-Neisse issue also resurfaced during the unrest in Poland in 1956. After ten years as the dominant party in the Soviet zone, the SED had made little headway in convincing East Germans to accept the border. Often East Germans openly expressed their dissatisfaction with Poland's occupation of German territories. They doubted whether Poland could make efficient use of the territories the way Germany had before the war.[33] East German officials admitted that many of their compatriots characterized the Poles' alleged lack of initiative and hard work as typical of the "Polish economy," an old slur that had long offended Poles.[34]

Some East German officials insinuated that the border could be revised. In November, Politburo member Karl Schirdewan warned Polish Communists who had raised the possibility of regaining Poland's lost eastern territories: "Poles alluding to the problem of their eastern border—ought not to forget about the western [border] as well."[35] Schirdewan's statement elicited a storm of protest from the PZPR, as did his attribution of the Polish and Hungarian revolutions to "bourgeois ideologues and their collaborators." Schirdewan vehemently rejected suggestions from some PZPR members that the SED should adopt similar reforms.[36]

On 29 January 1957, the *New York Times* broke the story that during the succession crisis in Poland the previous October, the East Germans had informed the PZPR that Poland's political development could influence their position regarding the border. Although Schirdewan had suggested exactly that, *Neues Deutschland* issued an angry reply: "This report of the American newspaper *The New York Times* is invented and false from A to Z."[37] Publicly the PZPR also denounced the article. *Trybuna Ludu* ran a series of front-page articles supporting the SED and blamed American journalists and West German foreign minister Heinrich von Brentano for trying to drive a wedge between Poland and the GDR.[38]

Nonetheless, Gomułka was concerned with the *New York Times* report. He had not forgotten that Ulbricht and the rest of the SED had officially rejected the border in 1946. Repeating propaganda that the PPR had used right after the war, the PZPR stressed its partnership with the other Slavic Communist parties as the main guarantors of the Oder-Neisse border. The Polish press even lauded China as an important contributor to the security of the border, while downplaying the role of the GDR.[39]

Gomułka and Ulbricht met in Berlin in June 1957. The atmosphere surrounding the talks was, in the words of one East German official, "stiff and reserved."[40] It was immediately apparent that the two sides were far apart in their conceptions of socialism. The Poles asked the East Germans to declare their agreement with the resolutions of the Eighth and Ninth Plenary Sessions of the PZPR Central Committee, but the East Germans refused on the grounds that the resolutions were not based on Marxist-Leninist principles.[41] The Poles baited Ulbricht and the other East German hard-liners by asking them whether there was really a "fully free and unconstrained atmosphere" in the SED, in contrast to the democratization of the PZPR. The East Germans thought that Gomułka was naively underestimating the dangers of class conflict in Poland and that his policies were not promoting Marxist-Leninist social, economic, and political development. They were particularly critical of Gomułka's agricultural policies and toleration of the "reactionary and counterrevolutionary" Polish Catholic Church.[42]

A sharp exchange ensued when Ulbricht accused the Poles of passing top-secret East German documents to Western governments. Gomułka called it a "serious reproach" and asked for proof of the allegations. Ulbricht replied that some Poles, who had inside information on the GDR, had fled to the West. Polish premier Józef Cyrankiewicz reminded Ulbricht that many East German officials had defected as well.[43] Ulbricht was also deeply dissatisfied with Warsaw's trade policies, which he blamed for jeopardizing key elements of the GDR's economic plan.[44] East German negotiators called the Poles "obstinate" and accused them of betraying the principles of socialist solidarity.[45]

The Ulbricht-Gomułka summit clearly failed to normalize relations. The SED's year-end report on relations with Poland reiterated earlier criticisms of the PZPR for ignoring ideological and political propaganda, underestimating the dangers of German imperialism and militarism, and a half-hearted campaign against revisionism. Although the GDR had established diplomatic relations with Yugoslavia in October 1957, the report criticized Warsaw for favoring connections to Belgrade and the West over ties to the Soviet bloc countries. The East Germans also faulted the Poles for refusing to declare that the Soviet Union was the "first and the mightiest" socialist state. According to the report, the Polish Communists not only were reluctant to recognize the leading role of the Soviet Union but also misjudged the "role and character of the GDR." In contrast to the cooperative attitude of the Czechoslovak Communists, the East Germans found it virtually impossible to conduct ideological discussions with the Polish Communists on the basic foundations of Marxism-Leninism. The East Germans even accused the Poles of being arrogant, though it was usually the East Germans who displayed an air of superiority about their supposedly more advanced economic and political development.[46]

The Problem of West and East German Rearmament

In the early 1950s, Western Europe contemplated the formation of a West German army. West German rearmament threatened the entire postwar settlement in East Central Europe. The Poles worried that any change in the status quo would jeopardize the Oder-Neisse border, while the East Germans feared that the Soviets might sacrifice the GDR to prevent the FRG from entering NATO.

In the fall of 1954 representatives of the Czechoslovak, Polish, and East German parliaments met in Prague to discuss West Germany's entry into NATO and Central European security issues in general.[47] The head of the SED's Department of Foreign Affairs, Peter Florin, complained that the Poles did not show any particular interest in strengthening cooperative diplomatic efforts against West German revanchism and militarism. Florin concluded that the Poles needed to be better informed about the serious threat that the Bonn government posed to the GDR and to peace in Europe.[48] Ambassador Heymann was convinced that Warsaw was ignoring East German interests in favor of better ties to the West.[49]

When the Soviet Union declared an end to the state of war with East Germany in January 1955, Poland dutifully followed suit. In the original draft of Poland's declaration was a warning that if the Western powers and the West German government ratified the Paris treaty to rearm Germany, "the People's Republic of Poland will further strengthen its relations with the GDR and take any measures with the other peace-loving states which will guarantee the security of Poland and other nations."

There was no special mention of the GDR in the final declaration, however, which left Heymann noticeably disappointed: "This deletion has a significant political meaning. I see in this incident more proof that right now the Polish government is still not very enthusiastic about concluding a tripartite pact between the GDR, Poland, and Czechoslovakia."[50]

West Germany joined NATO in 1955, and Moscow went ahead with plans for an East German army. It was a controversial subject in the Soviet Union, as well as in Poland, for as Soviet foreign minister Vyacheslaw Molotov argued, "Why should we fight the West over the GDR?"[51] Poles, with fresh memories of the German attack and brutal five-year occupation, vehemently opposed an East German army.[52] Bolz assured Warsaw that the East German people would fight alongside Poles to defend the Oder-Neisse border,[53] but few Poles trusted an East German army whose existence depended on Soviet power. The Polish government was so concerned about people's reaction to East German rearmament that during one special simultaneous radio broadcast from factories in Warsaw, Prague, and East Berlin in 1955, Polish officials asked the East Germans not to play any marching or martial music.[54] Heymann speculated that Polish officials had canceled a tour of East German musicians to Poland that summer for fear that their concerts would be disrupted by demonstrations against the creation of an East German army. The Poles also denied an East German request for a performance of a Quartered People's Police (KVP) band at the fifth anniversary celebration of the Oder-Neisse agreement on 6 July 1955.[55] The Poles rejected any unified high command with East German army officers and surprised the East Germans with a plan for a joint Polish-Czech command of an army group "north."[56]

The Polish government recognized that, if war broke out with NATO, it would be virtually impossible to ask Polish soldiers to sacrifice their lives in defense of the East German state. Embarrassing confrontations punctuated relations between the East German and Polish militaries, such as a particularly rancorous meeting between East German sailors and the crew of the Polish ship *Baltik* at Sassnitz in May 1957. The head of the East German navy, Vice Admiral Waldemar Verner, was shocked at the Poles' "negative and hostile attitude" toward the Soviet Union, as well as their attacks on socialism in general. To his surprise, they interpreted the Poznań strikes in June 1956 as a genuine workers' revolt rather than a fascist provocation. The Polish officers claimed that Poles had lived much better under capitalism before the war. They said that Soviet concentration camps were much worse than Hitler's and that Stalin was a criminal who had exploited the Polish economy. The Poles were proud of the fact that they had removed Soviet advisors and political officers from the Polish army in 1956. One Polish sailor concluded that socialism was "shit." The Polish sailors also had some particularly unflattering things to say about the GDR. They told Verner that the East German government was "too Communist" and merely aped Moscow's policies. They called Ulbricht a "Stalinist" and wondered why he and Prime Minister Otto Grotewohl had not been removed from power.[57]

The Polish sailors displayed no signs of the politically correct behavior that the East German Communists had come to expect from their Warsaw Pact partners. According to the East Germans, the Polish sailors did not address each other as "comrade" and seemed more concerned with finding prostitutes than holding "friendship meetings" to discuss Marxism. The Poles made fun of the SED's strict control over Western influences, such as the party's ban on "rock 'n' roll" dancing. They boasted that they could smoke American-made Lucky Strike and Camel cigarettes whenever they liked.[58]

The East German officers took from this confrontation real doubts about the loyalty and fighting capability of the Polish armed forces. One concluded that the Poles had no interest in the Warsaw Pact and that an East German soldier sitting in a foxhole with a Pole had better be ready "to get a knife in the ribs." Another officer observed that if high-ranking Polish officers behaved in such a way, Poland was not an asset to the Warsaw Pact. One East German officer called the Polish officers "a very reactionary bunch" and accused them of "spitting on the Warsaw Pact." He said that if the East Germans had known what a bunch of "Heinis" the Polish sailors were, they would have beaten them up.[59] A Polish visitor to the GDR's "East Sea Week" in July 1958 typified the Polish attitude in this question to an East German official: "Won't your sons, who will serve in the army some day, turn their weapons around and want to reconquer the former German territories?"[60]

Gomułka was reluctant to allow the East German army to participate in Warsaw Pact maneuvers in Poland, for he knew that Poles would shudder at the sight of a German army marching around the countryside and German military convoys rolling down Polish highways. Gomułka asked Ulbricht why East German soldiers had to wear uniforms so similar to the old Wehrmacht issue. Ulbricht admitted that it was a sop to East German feelings of nationalism: "We give the people their uniforms, [which is] perhaps a compromise, but in this way we win them over and can more easily raise them to be good Communists."[61]

Polish officials chided the East Germans for allowing nationalist and anti-Polish elements to play a significant role in East German military, political, and economic affairs and for coddling former Nazi and neofascist elements in the army, party, government, and intelligentsia.[62] Polish officials even told the East Germans that they were glad that the Soviet army was stationed in the GDR.[63] A year after the Berlin Wall went up in 1961, party functionaries were still telling the East Germans that the Polish people feared that the decision to divide Berlin might lead to war.[64]

In 1957, the North Atlantic Treaty Organization began serious deliberations on stationing nuclear weapons in West Germany. U.S. president Dwight D. Eisenhower hoped to extricate American troops from Europe and even considered putting nuclear forces under West German control.[65] The idea sent shock waves through the Polish and East German regimes. Grotewohl dusted off his 1952 proposal for a confederation of the two German states, this time with a provision that neither would station or produce atomic bombs. The FRG and GDR would end obligatory military service and exit NATO and the Warsaw Pact, and all foreign troops would leave German soil. Bonn immediately rejected the plan.[66]

Although the former Polish ambassador to the GDR, Jan Izydorczyk, told the Polish parliament that a confederation was a just and sensible solution to the German problem,[67] the Polish government did not throw its full diplomatic weight behind Grotewohl's proposed confederation; most Poles warily viewed any united German state, regardless of its composition. Furthermore, any change in the status quo could result in a revision of the Oder-Neisse border.[68]

Warsaw's foreign policy options regarding the German question were limited, but the Gomułka regime was determined not to wait for the Soviet Union or the GDR to dictate Poland's foreign policy toward West Germany.[69] Instead of fully supporting East Berlin's démarche, the Polish government developed its own plan to preempt the nuclearization of Central Europe. The idea for a nuclear-free zone in Germany, Poland, and Czechoslovakia first appeared in the Polish journal *Świat a Polska* in the spring of 1957. The Polish plan bore the name of Foreign Minister Adam Rapacki. After receiving formal approval from the Warsaw Pact, Rapacki and Czechoslovak foreign minister Vaclav David presented the plan to the United Nations on 2 October.[70]

The Poles were clearly proud of their initiative. As the editor of the weekly journal *Polityka*, Mieczyslaw Rakowski, wrote, "[The Rapacki Plan was] a good testimonial of her diplomacy. . . . [Poland] had worked out the idea contained in the plan to the minutest detail. Among the many projects put forward by various states in the initial phase of European détente, Poland's initiative for many years occupied the chief place. . . . The discussion of the Rapacki Plan helped make Poland known throughout the world."[71]

The East German Foreign Ministry immediately informed Stanisław Kopa that the Rapacki Plan "makes an important contribution to solving the German problem,"[72] and on 6 October *Neues Deutschland* carried a big article on the proposal, including Bolz's telegram to the United Nations declaring the GDR's support.[73] The East Germans, however, were reluctant to let Poland play a key role in German affairs. After the 6 October issue *Neues Deutschland* virtually ignored the Rapacki Plan, choosing instead to publicize the Soviet Union's disarmament proposals.[74] One East German diplomat recalled that the Soviet Union and the GDR reacted to the plan with "great mistrust and did everything to let the initiative peter out."[75]

The East German leaders expressed indifference to the Rapacki Plan in part because it did not include any guarantees for the continued existence of the GDR.

East Berlin preferred bilateral negotiations with Bonn on any issues affecting the fate of East Germany. Grotewohl demanded that the two German states sign a nuclear-free agreement, which of course would have meant the FRG's recognition of the GDR.[76]

The East Germans remained in the dark about the details of the negotiations on the Rapacki Plan. In December, Rapacki finally informed East German ambassador Josef Hegen about Poland's ongoing talks with Great Britain, France, Austria, and Sweden. Rapacki said that the latter two neutral countries were very supportive of the proposal.[77] Czechoslovak diplomats in Warsaw sensed that the Rapacki Plan was contributing to tensions between East Berlin and Warsaw. They asked East German diplomats about it at a reception at the East German Embassy for the eighth anniversary of the founding of the GDR.[78] Offended that neither Cyrankiewicz nor Gomułka had bothered to attend, Hegen replied that he still had serious doubts about Poland's political and economic stability.[79]

Official West German sources alleged that Ulbricht told Soviet ambassador Puschkin that "the Rapacki Plan is endangering the 'GDR's' fight against 'West German imperialism' and the stationing of atomic weapons there, and therefore is weakening the solidarity of the 'socialist camp.'"[80] According to another West German source, the Soviets gave the Poles a free hand to pursue the Rapacki Plan, which "purposely went around the 'GDR.'"[81] During the Warsaw Pact meetings in Moscow in November, the other Communist parties rebuked the SED for its harsh criticism of the PZPR in the past year, and for the failure of its propaganda campaign against the FRG.[82]

In early February 1958, East German Foreign Ministry officials tried to seize the diplomatic initiative by proposing a trilateral East German–Czechoslovak–Polish disarmament plan for Central Europe. In an obvious attempt to loosen West Germany's ties to NATO, Otto Winzer suggested that the four nuclear-free states (Poland, Czechoslovakia, and East and West Germany) would pledge not to develop any weapons in cooperation with other countries. The Poles rejected the idea, arguing that a joint proposal with the GDR would reduce the Rapacki Plan's chance of gaining acceptance in the West. The Poles told Winzer that Poland had to regard the interests of countries other than Germany, not just Germany itself.[83]

That the East Germans would not recognize the Rapacki Plan as a Polish idea incensed the Poles.[84] The East Germans characterized it instead as a joint East German–Czechoslovak–Polish proposal.[85] At the end of 1958, the Polish Foreign Ministry observed that "for a long time the 'Rapacki Plan' was presented as an initiative of the GDR, 'subsequently supported by Czechoslovakia and Poland.'" The ministry noted that the East German press had not paid much attention to the plan and, when it did, emphasized the "key role" of the GDR. *Neues Deutschland* refused to call it the "Rapacki Plan," a stance that Polish diplomats blamed on its chief editor Hermann Axen, who had been a vigorous critic of the Gomułka regime from the start.[86] When the chief editor of *Trybuna Ludu*, Artur Kowalski, asked *Neues Deutschland* correspondent Karl Krahn point blank whether the GDR was ignoring the Rapacki Plan because it was a Polish proposal, Krahn had no answer.[87]

The Rapacki Plan, however, was never seriously considered as a basis for addressing the escalating arms race in Central Europe. The Western alliance went ahead with plans to station nuclear missiles in Western Europe, including West Germany. The United States was unwilling to bargain away its NATO partner for a politically and militarily nonaligned German state. Furthermore, Bonn was opposed to leaving NATO and the recently constituted European Common Market.

The next meeting with Gomułka in Warsaw in December 1958 did not alleviate Ulbricht's doubts about the reliability of the PZPR, especially in regard to the German question. Although Gomułka eventually proved to be a loyal Warsaw Pact partner and even supported the military intervention into Czechoslovakia in 1968, Ulbricht never forgot that Gomułka was the product of a potentially dangerous reform movement.[88]

The strained East German–Polish relationship after World War II provides further evidence that the Communist parties of Eastern Europe could not supplant national loyalties with Marxist internationalism. Even the leadership and the rank and file of the SED and the PZPR remained staunchly nationalist.

The inability of the SED and the PZPR to resolve their ideological differences, or to bring understanding and trust between their two peoples, posed a serious problem for Warsaw Pact cohesion on its strategic western front. The reliability of the East German and Polish soldier to the common defense of the two countries was highly questionable.[89] Given the strategic importance of East Germany and Poland to the Soviet Union, the Kremlin could not allow the problems in East German–Polish relations to develop into an open break. It almost came to that in 1956. Left on their own, there is little doubt that relations between the East German and Polish Communists would have gone the way of the Tito-Stalin split in the late 1940s, or the Sino-Soviet break in the early 1960s.

Notes

1. Quoted from Ines Mietkowska-Kaiser, "Zur brüderlichen Zusammenarbeit zwischen polnischen und deutschen Kommunisten und Antifaschisten nach dem Sieg über den deutschen Faschismus (1945–1949)" [On the Fraternal Cooperation Between the Polish and German Communists and Anti-Fascists After the Victory over German Fascism, 1945–1949], *Jahrbuch für Geschichte der sozialistischen Länder Europas* [Yearbook for the History of the Socialist Countries of Europe] 23, no. 1 (1979): 51.

2. *Głos Ludu* [Voice of the People], 16 Sept. 1945, 3.

3. Quoted in Norman Naimark, *The Russians in Germany: A History of the Soviet Zone of Occupation, 1945–1949* (Cambridge, Mass.: Harvard Univ. Press, 1995), 146.

4. *Głos Ludu*, 1 Jan. 1946, 12–13.

5. Władysław Gomułka, *O problemie Niemieckim* [On the German Problem] (Warsaw: Książka Wiedza, 1971), 105.

6. See Ralf Badstübner, "Die sowjetische Deutschlandpolitik im Lichte neuer Quellen" [The Soviet Policy Toward Germany in Light of New Sources], in *Die Deutschland Frage in der Nachkriegszeit* [The German Question in the Postwar Period], ed. Wilfried Loth (Berlin: Akademie Verlag, 1994), 114–23.

7. "Agricultural Policy in the New Poland," from the SED Press Service, 11 May 1948, SED ZK, Otto Grotewohl Papers, NL 90/483, Records of the Central Committee of the Socialist Unity Party, Stiftung Archiv der Parteien und Massenorganizationen der DDR im Bundesarchiv [Archive of the Party and Mass Organizations of the GDR in the Federal Archive], Berlin.

8. Piotrowski to Łobodycz, 17 May 1959, MSZ, 10/383/42, Archiwum Ministerstwa Spraw Zagranicznych [Archive of the Ministry of Foreign Affairs], Warsaw.

9. Leon Szybek notes of discussions with Heymann on 19, 27, 29 May 1959, MSZ, 10/383/42.

10. Łobodzycz to Piotrowski, 18 May 1959, MSZ, 10/383/42.

11. Kopa notes of meeting with Horst Heinrich, 11 Feb. 1959, MSZ, 10/346/38.

12. Bolz to Ulbricht, 11 June 1960, SED ZK, Walter Ulbricht Papers, NL 182/1250.

13. Grunert notes of meeting between Bolz and Piotrowski, 22 June 1960, SED ZK, Walter Ulbricht Papers, NL 182/1250.

14. Röse to the GDR Foreign Ministry, 25 Sept. 1961, SED ZK, microfilm FBS 339/13496.

15. Mieszław Tomała notes of a meeting with Helmer, undated, ca. Apr. 1962, PZPR KC, 237/XXII-1103, Records of the Central Committee of the Polish United Workers' Party, Archiwum Akt Nowych [Archive of Newer Records], Warsaw.

16. Stenographic summary of a meeting with East German officials on the issue of the GDR and the future of Germany, 16 May 1962, PZPR KC, 237/XXII-1103.

17. Observations on the document "The History of the GDR and the Future of Germany," undated, ca. May 1962, PZPR KC, 237/XXII-1103.

18. Hilmar Schumann report, 22 May 1962, SED ZK, microfilm FBS 339/13496.

19. GDR Embassy report on the state holiday in Poland on 22, 31 July 1962, SED ZK, microfilm FBS 339/13496.

20. Dietrich Staritz, *Geschichte der DDR, 1949–1985* [History of the GDR, 1949–1985] (Frankfurt/Main: Suhrkamp Verlag, 1985), 24.

21. Pierzchała to the Polish Foreign Ministry, 26 Oct. 1956, PZPR KC, 237/XXII-822.

22. *Trybuna Ludu*, 20 Oct. 1956, 1.

23. Czechoń notes of a meeting with Richard Schmöing, 20 Oct. 1956, MSZ, 10/378/42.

24. Suzanne Drechsler report, 9 Jan. 1957, SED ZK, Walter Ulbricht Papers, NL 182/1249.

25. Kopa notes of meeting of the PZPR POP [Basic Party Organization] on 24, 25 Oct. 1956, MSZ, 10/378/42.

26. SED Politburo letter to the members and candidate members of the Central Committee, SED ZK, Politburo Draft Protocol No. 54, 30 Oct. 1956, J IV 2/2A/528.

27. Pierzchała notes, cited in Kopa to the Polish Foreign Ministry, 9 Nov. 1956, MSZ, 10/378/42.

28. Pierzchała to the Polish Foreign Ministry, 26 Oct. 1956, PZPR KC, 237/XXII-822.

29. Nasielski notes, cited in C. Urbaniak (Polish Military Mission) to Łobodycz, 26 Oct. 1956, MSZ, 10/378/42.

30. Notes of a meeting between Hermann Axen, Georg Hansen, and Artur Kowalski on 25, 29 Oct. 1956, SED ZK, Hermann Axen Office, IV 2/2.035/43. See also Pierzchała notes, cited in Kopa to the Polish Foreign Ministry, 9 Nov. 1956, MSZ, 10/378/42. The SED had the same problems in overcoming anti-Soviet attitudes in the GDR. Pierzchała noted a definite distaste among East German students for studying Russian.

31. *Trybuna Ludu,* 21 Oct. 1956, 3.

32. See "Notes on Current Events and Relations Between Poland and the GDR," unsigned, 8 Dec. 1956, MSZ, 10/378/42.

33. Kopa notes of a meeting with Grünberg, 28 Sept. 1956, MSZ, 10/378/42.

34. Report on obtaining visas to Poland, unsigned, 28 Sept. 1956, SED ZK, microfilm FBS 339/13488.

35. Kupis notes of his visit to Karl Marx Univ. from 13 Oct. to 12 Nov., 16 Nov. 1956, PZPR KC, 237/XXII-822.

36. Polish Foreign Ministry report, unsigned, 30 Nov. 1956, MSZ, 10/378/42.

37. *Neues Deutschland,* 6 Feb. 1957, 1.

38. *Trybuna Ludu,* 6 Feb. 1957, 1; ibid., 9 Feb. 1957, 1.

39. See Franz Sikora, *Sozialistische Solidarität und nationale Interessen,* 147.

40. Kopa notes of meeting with Haid on 2, 4 July 1957, MSZ, 10/379/42.

41. Florin to Grotewohl, 20 June 1957, SED ZK, Otto Grotewohl Papers, NL 90/483.

42. Report of the Polish and GDR government and PZPR and SED party meetings, 20 June 1957, SED ZK, microfilm FBS 339/13423.

43. Record of the discussions of party and government delegations in Berlin from 18–20, 29 June 1957, MSZ, 10/309/36.

44. König notes on Gomułka's visit to Moscow, 31 May 1957, SED ZK, Otto Grotewohl Papers, NL 90/485.

45. Grotewohl to Schmidt, 4 June 1957, SED ZK, Otto Grotewohl Papers, NL 90/485.

46. Report on the results of cooperation between the regional offices of the SED and counties in Poland, undated, ca. Dec. 1957, SED ZK, IV 2/20/31.

47. See the documents on this conference in MSZ, 10/466/48.

48. Florin to Ambassador Koenen in Prague, 5 Jan. 1955, DDR MfAA, Warsaw Embassy, A3670, Politisches Archiv des Auswärtigen Amtes, Bestand Ministerium für Auswärtigen Angelegenheiten der DDR [Political Archive of the Foreign Office. Holdings of the Ministry of Foreign Affairs of the GDR], Berlin. See also Werner Hänisch, *Aussenpolitik und internationale Beziehungen der DDR, 1949–1955* [The Foreign Policy and International Relations of the GDR, 1949–1955] (Berlin: Staatsverlag der DDR, 1972), 248. As usual, East German

historians such as Hänisch claimed that the conference proceeded without acrimony: "Characteristic for this closer cooperation was the fraternal solidarity of the governments, the parliaments, and the people of Poland and Czechoslovakia with the GDR."

49. Heymann to Florin, 1 Feb. 1955, DDR MfAA, Warsaw Embassy, A3670; and Heymann to the GDR Foreign Ministry, 7 Feb. 1955, DDR MfAA, Warsaw Embassy, A3670; see also Heymann notes on the meetings in Warsaw between Polish representatives and an East German government delegation (led by Bolz), 7 Mar. 1955, DDR MfAA, Warsaw Embassy, A3579.

50. Heymann to Florin, 1 Feb. 1955, DDR MfAA, Warsaw Embassy, A3670.

51. Quoted in Nikita Khrushchev, *Khrushchev Remembers: The Glasnost Tapes,* trans. Jerrod L. Schecter (Boston: Little, Brown, 1990), 70.

52. See Peter H. Merkl, *German Foreign Policies, West and East: On the Threshold of a New European Era* (Santa Barbara, Calif.: ABC-Clio Press, 1974), 99.

53. Izydorczyk to Warsaw, 31 Dec. 1953, PZPR KC, 237/XXII-518.

54. Heymann to Grosse, 9 Apr. 1955, SED ZK, microfilm FBS 339/13492; and Grosse to Heymann, 25 June 1955, DDR MfAA, Warsaw Embassy, A3670.

55. Heymann to the GDR Foreign Ministry, 2 July 1955, DDR MfAA, Warsaw Embassy, A3670.

56. Berlin Office of the BRD Foreign Ministry to Bonn, 21 Mar. 1955, BRD AA, Department 7, vol. 84, Bundesarchiv, Auswärtigen Amtes der BRD [Federal Archive, Foreign Office of the Federal Republic of Germany], Bonn.

57. Verner to Stoph, 9 May 1957, SED ZK, Walter Ulbricht Papers, NL 182/1249.

58. Ibid.

59. Ibid. "Heini" is a derogatory term for a soldier, or an "ass."

60. Rostock office to Ulbricht, 25 July 1958, SED ZK, Walter Ulbricht Papers, NL 182/1250.

61. Quoted in Franz Sikora, *Sozialistische Solidarität und nationale Interessen,* 161.

62. PZPR evaluation of the situation in the GDR, unsigned, undated, ca. fall 1961, PZPR KC, 237/XXII-1102.

63. Püschel notes of meeting between Reissig and Wichlacz et al., on 11, 16 Jan. 1962, SED ZK, microfilm FBS 339/13496.

64. Tönnies report on his visit to Poznań from 13–15, 23 Aug. 1962, SED ZK, microfilm FBS 339/13422.

65. See Marc Trachtenberg, *A Constructed Peace: The Making of the European Settlement, 1945–1963* (Princeton, N.J.: Princeton Univ. Press, 1999), 185–88.

66. Polish Embassy report from 15 Mar.–31 Aug. 1957, MSZ, 10/371/41. See also Andrei Gromyko, *Memories* (London: Hutchinson, 1989), 196.

67. Izydorczyk speech to the Polish parliament, undated, ca. Nov. 1957, PZPR KC, group Izydorczyk, file 473/6.

68. Lobodycz to Naszkowski, 3 Sept. 1957, MSZ, 10/359/39.

69. Heymann to the GDR Foreign Ministry, 29 Oct. 1957, DDR MfAA, HA/I Secretariat, A38.

70. See Sikora, *Sozialistische Solidarität und nationale Interessen,* 151–52.

71. Mieczysław Rakowski, *The Foreign Policy of the Polish People's Republic* (Warsaw: Interpress Publishers, 1975), 164.

72. Kopa notes of a meeting with Beling on 11, 16 Oct. 1957, MSZ, 10/379/42.

73. *Neues Deutschland,* 6 Oct. 1957, 1.

74. Ibid., 13 Oct. 1957, 1.

75. Horst Grunert, *Für Honecker auf glattem Parkett: Erinnerungen eines DDR-Diplomaten* [For Honecker on the Smooth Parquet: Memoirs of a GDR Diplomat] (Berlin: Edition Ost, 1995), 118.

76. Douglas Selvage, "Introduction" to "Khrushchev's November 1958 Berlin Ultimatum: New Evidence from the Polish Archives," *Bulletin: Cold War International History Project,* no. 11 (winter 1998): 200.

77. Hegen notes of a meeting with Rapacki on 10, 11 Dec. 1957, SED ZK, Otto Grotewohl Papers, NL 90/485.

78. Memorandum of a meeting with Koudela, Tomasek, and Cerny (Czechoslovak Embassy diplomats), unsigned, 10 Oct. 1957, DDR MfAA, Warsaw Embassy, A3771.

79. Łobodycz notes of meeting with Koudela (Czechoslovak Embassy) on 9, 10 Oct. 1957, MSZ, 10/380/42.

80. Report on the political development in the Soviet zone of Germany in December, 1957, BRD BfGDF, B137/1473, Records of the Federal Ministry for All-German Questions, Bundesarchiv [Federal Archive], Koblenz.

81. Report on the political development in the Soviet zone of Germany from 1 Jan.–28 Feb. 1958, BRD BfGDF, B137/1473. See also James G. Richter, *Khrushchev's Double Bind: International Pressures and Domestic Coalition Politics* (Baltimore: Johns Hopkins Univ. Press, 1994), 114. Richter writes that Moscow lobbied hard for the Rapacki Plan by announcing troop reductions and a moratorium on nuclear testing.

82. Report on the political development in the Soviet zone of Germany, Nov. 1957, BRD BfGDF, B137/1473.

83. Record of negotiations between Ogrodzinski and Piotrowski et al., and Handke and Winzer et al., 7–8 Feb. 1958, DDR MfAA, HA/I Secretariat, A14759; Polish Embassy political report from 1 Sept. 1957–28 Feb. 1958, Mar. 11, 1958, MSZ, 10/371/41.

84. Polish Embassy report from 1 Nov. 1957–28 Feb. 1958, MSZ, 10/371/41.

85. Piotrowski to Łobodzycz, 2 Jan. 1958, MSZ, 10/371/41.

86. Polish Foreign Ministry report on the GDR press, undated, ca. Dec. 1958, MSZ, 10/464/48.

87. Karl Krahn to Hermann Axen, 17 Feb. 1958, SED ZK, microfilm FBS 339/13489.

88. Winzer to Ulbricht, 12 Feb. 1959, SED ZK, Walter Ulbricht Papers, NL 182/1250.

89. Kopa notes of meeting with Colonel Grünberg, 10 Apr. 1959, MSZ, 10/346/38.

11

The Warsaw Pact and the German Question,

1955–1970

Conflict and Consensus

DOUGLAS SELVAGE

During the Cold War, political scientists engaged in a debate about the nature of the Warsaw Pact. Was it a transmission belt for Soviet directives, an alliance, or something in between?[1] Argument over the nature of the Warsaw Pact, it turns out, was not limited to the realm of Sovietology; it was also an active subject of discussion within the Warsaw Pact itself. This was particularly true concerning the pact's policy on the German question: whether Germany was to be unified, and if so, in which borders and under what political system. Debates within the Warsaw Pact over the German question from 1955 to 1970 quickly became entwined with the question of how the body should function in the political realm.

This chapter traces the debates within the Warsaw Pact from 1955 to 1970 over the German question and discusses their relationship to differences with regard to the pact's functioning. The three main protagonists in the Warsaw Pact's debates over the German question were Poland, the German Democratic Republic (GDR), and the Soviet Union. The GDR—even more than the Soviet Union—believed that the Warsaw Pact should serve as a transmission belt for Soviet directives. From the GDR's perspective, the transmission belt, in turn, was to convey foreign policy directives to the other socialist states aimed at bolstering the GDR's international position. In contrast, the People's Republic of Poland, under the leadership of "national Communist" Władysław Gomułka, pushed for the pact's transformation into more of a consultative body that would protect the security interests of all socialist states, not just the GDR. Gomułka's position derived in large part from the fact that Communist Poland could not obtain Western recognition of the Oder-Neisse Line on its own, and the Soviet Union was not interested in putting the border issue at the top of the pact's agenda. Poland could push for recognition of its border only through general pact initiatives with regard to West Germany. So Gomułka resisted granting the GDR and its demands a special status within the Warsaw Pact. Instead, he favored a unified, coordinated policy on the German question that would take into account both the GDR's and Poland's security interests. Even though the Soviet Union's leaders preferred the transmission-belt approach, Moscow proved to be more open to Poland's ideas than the GDR; it often played the role of arbiter between the GDR and Poland until Leonid Brezhnev moved to reassert Moscow's authority over the pact at the end of the 1960s.

The debate over the German question and the functioning of the Warsaw Pact from 1955 to 1970 can be divided roughly into three periods. In the first period, 1955–63, Moscow sought first and foremost to use the Warsaw Pact as a transmission belt for Soviet foreign policy initiatives. During this period, Soviet policy initiatives within the Warsaw Pact focused on obtaining Western—and especially West German—recognition of the GDR and preventing West German access to nuclear weapons. Indeed, the justification for the Warsaw Pact's very existence lies in the German question: the alliance was allegedly established in response to West Germany's joining NATO. In January 1956, Moscow distributed a foreign policy paper to all the socialist states announcing that one of the "most important foreign policy tasks of our countries" was the "struggle to consolidate the international position of the GDR." Soviet leader Nikita S. Khrushchev followed up on the paper at a meeting of the leaders of the socialist states later that month; individual socialist states, he maintained, might come forward with foreign policy initiatives as part of the coordinated policy of the entire Soviet bloc. Khrushchev was not talking about independent foreign policy initiatives; rather, there might be tactical advantages, he said, for states other than the Soviet Union to propose coordinated initiatives that would subsequently receive the backing of Moscow and the other socialist states.[2]

It was against this backdrop that East German leader Walter Ulbricht, following up on an initiative by the Warsaw Pact, proposed in February 1956 that the two German states negotiate an agreement prohibiting the stationing or production of nuclear weapons on German soil.[3] The East German initiative ostensibly sought to counter NATO's plans, announced in December 1955, to equip the armed forces of all its members, including the West German Bundeswehr, with tactical nuclear weapons.[4] For the GDR, however, the initiative had a second and more important goal. If Bonn signed an agreement with the GDR, it would constitute de facto recognition of the GDR. In talks with Polish diplomats, the East German ambassador to Poland made clear that the second goal, international recognition of the GDR, took priority over disarmament.[5] Thus, the GDR, which benefited the most from Moscow's German policy line, supported Moscow's use of the Warsaw Pact as a mere transmission belt for foreign policy directives to the other socialist states. This was especially the case during the Berlin crisis of 1958–62, when all the foreign policy efforts of the socialist bloc ostensibly focused on obtaining some form of Western recognition of the GDR.

Already in the spring of 1956, Communist Poland diverged from East Germany in its interpretation of Khrushchev's announcement and began to work on its own proposal for a nuclear weapon–free zone in Central Europe, the Rapacki Plan.[6] After Gomułka returned to power in the "Polish October" of 1956, the proposal increasingly became linked with a Polish policy of "national self-assertion."[7] In October 1956, Gomułka escaped the fate of Soviet intervention in Poland by swearing to Khrushchev his absolute fealty to the Polish-Soviet alliance. In light of West Germany's refusal to recognize the Oder-Neisse Line, Poland, he said, needed the alliance with Moscow even more than Moscow needed an alliance with Poland.[8] Despite Gomułka's oath of loyalty, Khrushchev subsequently used the Polish border issue in private discussions as a "leash" to keep Communist Poland in line.[9] Gomułka thus sought to obtain Western recognition of the border.[10] Such recognition, however, would come only from Poland's own efforts or as part of a larger package of demands put forward by the Warsaw Pact. Because the Western powers were unwilling to break with West Germany over the border issue, the Polish Communists sought to preserve the border by isolating the FRG internationally, preventing it from gaining the weapons necessary to influence or change the borders (that is, nuclear weapons), and raising Poland's international stature in the West. The Rapacki Plan, finally approved by the Soviet Union in October 1957, served all three goals. Despite Moscow's approval and the official support of the Warsaw Pact, the plan ran into opposition from East Germany, which sought to keep the focus on recognition of the GDR and its own nuclear proposal.[11] Poland's consultations with Moscow, Czechoslovakia, and the GDR over the initiative suggested a different interpretation of what the Warsaw Pact might be—that is, more of a consultative body than a transmission belt. The brief interlude of multilateral consultation within the Warsaw Pact ended in November 1958 when Khrushchev issued his Berlin ultimatum, sparking the Berlin crisis, during a visit by Gomułka to Moscow.[12] The ultimatum marked a return to Moscow's use of the pact as a transmission belt for Soviet directives—directives aimed at gaining the GDR's recognition. Nevertheless, Poland had set an example of multilateral consultation within the Warsaw Pact to which it would later return.

The next turning point in the veiled debate over the functioning of the Warsaw Pact came in 1963–64 and coincided, once again, with a shift in Soviet policy on the German question. Khrushchev began to move away from the alliance's common policy of 1955–62, based on preventing West German access to nuclear weapons and strengthening the GDR and gaining its recognition. In 1963, Khrushchev began to speak openly about the possibility of a modus vivendi with Bonn or a "new Rapallo."[13] In October 1963, Moscow informed its allies of plans to conclude a nuclear nonproliferation treaty with the United States that did not explicitly forbid NATO's planned multilateral force (MLF). Previously, the Warsaw Pact had strenuously opposed the MLF as a dangerous scheme to grant West Germany access to nuclear weapons. Gomułka vociferously opposed Khrushchev's plans and demanded that Khrushchev call a Warsaw Pact meeting for consultations. Khrushchev refused. The final straw for both Gomułka and Ulbricht was the visit of Khrushchev's son-in-law, Alexei Adzhubei, to Bonn in the summer of 1964. In some of his private conversations, the famous son-in-law hinted that Moscow might compromise on West Berlin, the Polish border, and the issue of humanitarian improvements in the GDR. The announcement after Adzhubei's return to Moscow that Khrushchev was planning a visit to West Germany only served to heighten Polish and East German fears. Both Gomułka and Ulbricht protested to Moscow about Adzhubei's behavior, and Khrushchev's enemies used a Polish transcript of Adzhubei's conversations to help justify Khrushchev's removal from power in October 1964.[14]

Khrushchev's "Rapallo policy" ushered in a period of increased militancy on the part of both Gomułka and Ulbricht with regard to the Warsaw Pact and the German question. In this second period, from 1964 to 1968, Ulbricht and Gomułka largely succeeded in dominating the Warsaw Pact's agenda with their anti–West German demands.[15] Gomułka, for his part, pushed the Soviet Union and the other Warsaw Pact states to return to the hard line toward West Germany of the 1955–63 period. Gomułka's anti–West German line within the Warsaw Pact met with the GDR's support and approval. Concurrently, East Berlin's continued insistence that its allies put the GDR's recognition first—a unilateral dictate that East Berlin sought to impose through bilateral negotiations—undermined Gomułka's efforts to transform the Warsaw Pact into a body for multilateral policy coordination. Gomułka's efforts to revamp the alliance body also met with Romania's active opposition. Bucharest not only opposed any effort at multilateral policy coordination as an infringement upon its sovereignty; it also sought to improve its own relations with Bonn without any preconditions. From 1964 to 1968, or at least until the Prague Spring, the Soviet Union largely played the role of arbiter within the pact. Its greatest concern was preserving a façade of unity against the backdrop of the Sino-Soviet rift. On the one hand, this worked to Gomułka's advantage. Moscow became a somewhat reluctant patron of Gomułka's multilateralism regarding West Germany. On the other hand, Moscow's desire for an outer show of unity led it to seek compromise with Romania; this often led to a moderation of the pact's position on relations with the FRG, to the chagrin of both Warsaw and East Berlin.[16]

The first meeting of the Political Consultative Committee after Khrushchev's fall from power, held in Warsaw in January 1965, revealed the fault lines within the pact over policy coordination and the German question. On the surface, the meeting appeared to be a victory for Gomułka's hard line against Khrushchev's Rapallo policy. The East Germans presented a draft nonproliferation treaty, prepared in close consultation with Moscow, that banned alliance nuclear forces such as the MLF. Brezhnev went so far as to declare that Adzhubei's trip to West Germany had occurred without the knowledge or permission of the Soviet Politburo, which, in Soviet parlance, amounted to an apology.[17] Gomułka followed up on his victory with the demand, in effect, that the Warsaw Pact should become more of a true alliance. To prevent a return to Khrushchev's Rapallo policy, the Soviet Union, he suggested, should have to submit its more important foreign policy initiatives to the allies for approval, either bilaterally or within the Warsaw Pact. To this end, Gomułka supported a Soviet proposal, submitted by the East Germans, to amend the statute of the Warsaw Pact to provide for regular meetings of the alliance's foreign ministers. Periodic foreign ministers' meetings, he said, were "necessary for the sake of working out a common line. For example, Khrushchev did not consult with us about his desire to go visit the FRG. And after all, that affected all of us."[18]

Romania, however, opposed both the draft nonproliferation treaty and the proposed amendment to the Warsaw Pact's founding statute. Citing China's opposition and Bucharest's sovereignty, Romanian Communist leader Gheorghe Gheorghiu-Dej effectively vetoed presentation of the draft nonproliferation treaty to the United Nations as a Warsaw Pact document. He also refused to entertain any change in the Warsaw Pact's founding statute: any consultation of the alliance's foreign ministers would have to occur on an ad hoc basis. Dej suggested that regular foreign ministers' meetings would infringe upon the sovereignty of the individual states by dictating their foreign policy. Thus, Gomułka's efforts to protect Poland's sovereign interests, including its security, through regular consultations of the Warsaw Pact met with the opposition of Romania, which sought to preserve its sovereignty by avoiding regular consultations. The Soviet Union, seeking to preserve a façade of unity, did not try to compel Romania's compliance. Instead, it submitted the draft nonproliferation treaty to the United Nations as a Soviet draft, and all the other Warsaw Pact states, except Romania, backed it.[19] Even worse from Gomułka's standpoint was the Bucharest meeting of the Warsaw Pact in July 1966. The final document, the Bucharest Declaration on European security, represented a compromise between the hard-line position of Poland and the GDR toward West Germany and the desire of Romania and the other socialist states to improve economic and political relations with Bonn. One section harshly condemned Bonn for its unwillingness to recognize the status quo in Europe and for its alleged drive to obtain nuclear weapons. Another section, in keeping with the stance of Romania and at least Hungary, emphasized the Warsaw Pact's desire to improve cultural, economic, and political relations with Western Europe, including the FRG.[20] By December 1966, Poland and the GDR faced the prospect of isolation within the Warsaw Pact. All the other socialist states sought to improve economic and political relations with Bonn, up to and including diplomatic relations. Romania was poised to establish diplomatic relations with Bonn without any preconditions, and the other socialist states were poised to follow.[21] How would the GDR, Poland, and the Soviet Union react?

From 1964 to 1968, the GDR lined up with Poland in all its skirmishes within the Warsaw Pact over the German question; it sought the hardest possible line on relations between its allies and Bonn. Over and beyond this, however, it sought to force through its own traditional unilateral demand that all the socialist states place recognition of the GDR above all else in their foreign policy agendas. Because the Warsaw Pact no longer functioned as a transmission belt, Ulbricht appealed directly to Moscow for bilateral support. The Soviets replied in January 1967 that Moscow could not prevent the other socialist states from establishing diplomatic relations with Bonn; all it could ask was that they follow Moscow's example from 1955 and declare that such a move did not affect their stance on Germany as a whole.[22] For the GDR, the "Moscow 1955 model" was unacceptable, so at the end of January 1967 East Berlin submitted its own memorandum to the Warsaw Pact states asking that they make certain public declarations and take certain diplomatic steps to affirm the existence of two German states if they established diplomatic relations with Bonn.[23]

Gomułka found East Germany's bilateral approach unacceptable; even more unacceptable were the stances of Romania and the Soviet Union. The Polish leader demanded that Moscow call a meeting of the Warsaw Pact to prepare a coordinated response to Bonn's *Ostpolitik*. By the end of January 1967, it became clear to him that the Soviets were trying to sneak an initiative past Poland and the GDR permitting the other socialist states to establish diplomatic relations with the FRG. During a meeting with Brezhnev, Premier Aleksey Kosygin, and the Soviet Politburo in eastern Poland at the end of January 1967, Gomułka launched into a bitter tirade against the disunity within the Warsaw Pact and Moscow's failure to counter it. The situation, he said, was beginning to remind him of what Khrushchev had accused Lavrenty Beria of doing in 1953: selling out the GDR. He dismissed the "Moscow 1955 model" and repeated Warsaw's three conditions for diplomatic relations with the FRG: Bonn's recognition of the Oder-Neisse Line, its de facto recognition of the GDR, and its renunciation of access to nuclear weapons in any form. He was particularly unnerved that Moscow had put in writing that it was not opposed to diplomatic relations with Bonn. When Brezhnev protested that there was nothing else that Moscow could do, Gomułka accused the Soviets of secretly favoring the movement within the alliance toward diplomatic relations with Bonn. "The Warsaw Pact," Gomułka declared, "is dissolving." If the Soviets could not stop the other socialist states from establishing diplomatic relations with Bonn on their own—and indeed wanted to stop them, Gomułka implied—a Warsaw Pact meeting was all the more necessary. By the end of the gathering, a chastened Brezhnev promised to call a meeting of Warsaw Pact foreign ministers in a matter of days, preferably in East Berlin.[24] Yet before the meeting, which was rescheduled for Warsaw on 6–8 February 1967, could be held, Romania established diplomatic relations with Bonn.

The meeting of the pact's foreign ministers in Warsaw in February 1967 marked the high-water mark of Gomułka's multilateralism vis-à-vis West Germany. The assembled foreign ministers, under pressure from Moscow, Warsaw, and East Berlin, agreed to adopt Warsaw's preconditions for diplomatic relations with Bonn, dubbed the "Warsaw Package." The GDR was so grateful to Poland that Ulbricht agreed to closer economic and political cooperation with Warsaw and the other socialist states. The GDR's firm economic integration within the Soviet bloc had long been a desideratum for Gomułka; it would help seal Germany's division and preserve Poland's western border.[25] The GDR, it seemed, was moving away from its bilateral approach to German policy—through the transmission belt from Moscow.

Although the Warsaw Package held—the remaining socialist states did not establish diplomatic relations with Bonn—both the GDR and the Soviet Union dashed Gomułka's hopes for multilateral policy coordination. In the fall of 1967 the GDR reneged on an agreement for closer economic cooperation with Poland. East Berlin also put forward its own bilateral initiative to West Germany: a draft treaty for the normalization of relations. The draft treaty made no mention of the need for Bonn to recognize the Oder-Neisse Line. Once again, the GDR was placing its own recognition ahead of the other socialist states' security interests. After the Poles complained in Moscow, the Soviets intervened and demanded that East Germany revise its proposal to include the entire Warsaw Package. The GDR did so, and Bonn promptly rejected the East German initiative.[26]

More dangerous to Gomułka's nascent multilateralism than the East German initiative were Moscow's own talks with Bonn and its new Social Democratic foreign minister, Willy Brandt, over renunciation of force. In April 1967, Gomułka had made his own proposal on the matter, calling for a multilateral renunciation of force as part of a European security conference.[27] Bonn's recognition of the status quo in Europe at a European security conference would have had the advantage of "unwrapping" the entire Warsaw Package at once. Bonn would recognize the Oder-Neisse Line at the same time as it recognized the GDR de facto. A multilateral renunciation of force would have also given the demands of Poland, the GDR, and the Soviet Union equal billing and thus have underlined the sovereignty of Poland and the GDR.[28] In contrast, the Soviets preferred to move ahead with their own bilateral negotiations with Bonn over renunciation of force, in which they claimed the power to negotiate on behalf of their "allies."[29] If Moscow concluded a bilateral renunciation-of-force agreement with Bonn on behalf of the entire Warsaw Pact, it would reconfirm Moscow's sphere of influence in East-Central Europe. The GDR, for its part, also preferred bilateral negotiations with Bonn over renunciation of force, but for a different reason: if Bonn concluded the first renunciation-of-force agreement with the Warsaw Pact with the GDR, it would have further enhanced the GDR's international stature.[30] It was for this very reason that Bonn preferred to negotiate with Moscow first.

The invasion of Czechoslovakia in 1968 temporarily concealed the differences between Poland, the GDR, and the Soviet Union over renunciation of force. Moscow broke off its dialogue with West Germany and joined Poland and the GDR in publicly linking the "counter-revolution" in Czechoslovakia to alleged "infiltration" by West Germany. While Ulbricht and Gomułka hoped the developments in Czechoslovakia would lead the Soviets to return to a hard line toward West Germany, for Moscow, the invasion was a mere "traffic accident on the road to détente." In October 1968, Soviet foreign minister Andrei Gromyko informed Brandt of Moscow's willingness to renew the Soviet–West German dialogue over renunciation of force.[31]

Gromyko's offer to Brandt ushered in a third stage in the debate over the functioning of the Warsaw Pact and the German question. In the wake of the invasion of Czechoslovakia, Brezhnev sought to return the alliance body to its original purpose as a transmission belt for Soviet directives. In conjunction with the process of "normalization" in Czechoslovakia, Brezhnev sought to "normalize" relations within the Warsaw Pact.[32] Given Moscow's simultaneous desire to normalize relations with West Germany, the greatest obstacles to Brezhnev's plans were the GDR and Poland. Both entered into their own bilateral negotiations with Bonn, thereby conflicting with the Soviet leader's goal of subordinating the other socialist states to the multilateral discipline of a reinvigorated Warsaw Pact.

Ulbricht had been pressuring the Soviet Union ever since Moscow had entered its dialogue with Bonn in the fall of 1967 to make a FRG-GDR renunciation-of-force agreement a precondition for any such agreement between Bonn and Moscow.[33] When Moscow broke off its talks with Bonn in July 1968, it cited Bonn's alleged refusal to conclude a similar, legally binding agreement with the GDR. Ulbricht and the East Germans picked up where the Soviets left off; during the summer and fall of 1968, East Berlin offered to enter into negotiations with Bonn on a variety of issues, including renunciation of force.[34] The East Germans, it seems, had seen the writing on the wall; the Soviets were interested in bilateral negotiations with Bonn, so East Berlin needed to move quickly if it wanted to obtain concessions from West Germany. In December 1968, the GDR startled both Poland and the Soviet Union by concluding a long-term trade agreement with West Germany that provided for an unprecedented increase in inter-German trade, fueled by West German loans.[35] Gomułka warned the Soviets of a potential "economic reunification of Germany," which was a security threat to the entire Warsaw Pact. He demanded that the Soviets take action to compel the GDR to integrate itself economically with the rest of the Soviet bloc.[36] Gomułka's tool to this end was Poland's long-standing proposal to reform the COMECON through the introduction of a common currency. A

COMECON summit meeting in April 1969 rejected Gomułka's proposal due to Moscow's lukewarm support and the outright opposition of Romania and the GDR.[37]

This final rebuff to Gomułka's efforts at multilateralism in the German question led the Polish leader to undertake his own bilateral initiative toward West Germany. In a public speech in May 1969, he offered to conclude a treaty with Bonn providing for recognition of the Oder-Neisse Line. Gomułka did not make his offer conditional on Bonn's recognition of the GDR or the other Warsaw Package conditions.[38] The East Germans protested to Moscow that Gomułka's offer violated the Warsaw agreement.[39]

In the wake of Gomułka's speech, the Soviet Union moved to restore order within the Warsaw Pact, lest the initiatives of its allies undermine its own bilateral efforts to normalize relations with Bonn. In September 1969, Gromyko forcefully told the East Germans that Moscow did not want the GDR to enter into bilateral negotiations with Bonn over a renunciation-of-force agreement or a normalization treaty. Moscow, he said, had the power of attorney to negotiate on behalf of the entire Warsaw Pact. The East Germans replied that they accepted Moscow's position, as long as it applied to all the socialist states, including Poland.[40] Later the same month, Moscow informed the East Germans of its intention to push for the convocation of a European security conference during the first half of 1970 in Helsinki. Moscow's immediate goal in convening such a conference, the Soviets said, would be to obtain de facto recognition of the GDR. Moscow's only precondition to the West for such a conference would be the participation of the GDR. The first agenda item for such a conference, they said, would be a general renunciation-of-force treaty among all the European states. Such a multilateral renunciation of force, Moscow suggested, would substitute for bilateral agreements between the individual socialist states and Bonn. Other issues, including normalization of relations between all the European states and recognition of the existing borders in Europe, would have to wait for a later session of the security conference.[41] Thus, the Soviet Union would proceed with its own bilateral negotiations with Bonn over renunciation of force, and the other socialist states would have to wait their turn until the convocation of a European security conference.

Moscow's stance was completely unacceptable to Poland, which would no longer settle for a mere multilateral renunciation-of-force agreement at a European security conference; in the wake of Gomułka's speech, it was demanding West German recognition of Poland's borders. In May 1969, the Polish delegation to a Warsaw Pact deputy foreign ministers' meeting had presented a "maximalist program" for a European security conference in the form of a draft Treaty for Collective Security, in which all the participants would not only renounce force in their mutual relations but also recognize all the existing borders in Europe.[42] It was clear that the Soviets had the Polish proposal in mind when they told the East Germans that such matters would have to wait until a later stage of the European security conference.[43] Matters came to a head at an October 1969 meeting of the Warsaw Pact foreign ministers in Prague. The Soviets presented the foreign ministers with only two draft proposals for consideration at a European security conference: a draft treaty on renunciation of force and a treaty on economic, scientific, and technical cooperation. The Polish foreign ministry initially rejected Moscow's proposals as a violation of the previous Warsaw Pact resolutions on European security. The Poles tried to present their own counterproposal at Prague: a "treaty on collective security and cooperation in Europe," which would have provided for recognition of existing borders. The Soviets blocked any discussion of the Polish document, which forced the Poles to settle for the inclusion of a mere phrase in Moscow's draft multilateral agreement on renunciation of force: "recognition and respect for the territorial integrity of European states." The assembled foreign ministers approved Moscow's draft proposals.[44] The outcome of the conference only served to strengthen Poland's desire to pursue its own bilateral negotiations with Bonn on recognition of the Oder-Neisse Line.

It was not until Gomułka visited Moscow at the beginning of October that the Polish Communists learned of Moscow's intention of substituting a European security conference for bilateral negotiations between the other socialist states and Bonn. The Soviets insisted on omitting a passage from Poland's draft communiqué expressing support for Gomułka's bilateral initiative toward Bonn. Moscow wanted to substitute a passage favoring a European security conference instead.[45] At the same time, the Soviets had been turning the economic screws on Poland. In the run-up to the meeting, they had announced plans to freeze their exports to Poland, including much-needed raw materials, at existing levels. Gomułka balked. When Brezhnev reaffirmed Moscow's trade plans, Gomułka abruptly called a recess in the meeting and withdrew with the Polish delegation to its residence. In the end, the Soviets conceded an increase in raw-material exports to Poland in return for the omission of the disputed phrase from the Polish communiqué.[46] The Soviets and East Germans tried to pressure Gomułka once again to drop his plans for bilateral negotiations with Bonn at a meeting of the Political Consultative Committee of the Warsaw Pact in Moscow in December 1969, but Gomułka steadfastly refused.[47] So the GDR could save face, Moscow agreed to permit East Berlin to make its own proposal for bilateral negotiations to Bonn in the form of a draft normalization treaty, but Brezhnev compelled the East Germans to demand recognition in international law, a demand completely unacceptable to Bonn. This would permit the Soviets to move ahead in their negotiations with Bonn while the inter-German talks stalled.[48]

In the end, the Soviets could not overcome Gomułka's bilateralism. Moscow concluded the first treaty with Bonn, the Moscow Treaty, in August 1970 which provided for Bonn's de facto recognition of the existing borders in Europe, including the Oder-Neisse Line and the border between the two German states. Poland followed in December 1970 with its own bilateral treaty with Bonn, the Warsaw

Treaty. Although the Polish–West German treaty also provided for Bonn's de facto recognition of the Oder-Neisse Line, in a bid to underline their nation's sovereignty, the Polish Communists successfully insisted on different language than in the Soviet–West German treaty.[49] In the end, Gomułka's resistance meant that Brezhnev had to wait until the Warsaw Pact's normalization of relations with Bonn was already under way to "normalize" the situation within the Warsaw Pact. The Soviet leader did so by withdrawing support for Gomułka during the riots in Poland in December 1970, riots that provided a pretext for Gomułka's removal from power.[50] Then, in May 1971, Brezhnev agreed to Ulbricht's removal as first secretary of the SED.[51] Brezhnev's "normalization," it turned out, would require personnel changes outside of Czechoslovakia.

Notes

The views contained herein are purely the views of the author; they do not necessarily reflect the views of the U.S. Department of State or the U.S. government.

1. For works that consider the Warsaw Pact to be more of a transition belt, see Malcolm Mackintosh, "The Warsaw Treaty Organization: A History," in *The Warsaw Pact: Alliance in Transition?* ed. David Holloway and Jane M. O. Sharp (Ithaca, N.Y.: Cornell Univ. Press, 1984), 42; Andrzej Korboński, "The Warsaw Pact After Twenty-five Years: An Entangling Alliance or an Empty Shell?" and Jorg K. Hoensch, "The Warsaw Pact and the Northern Member States," in *The Warsaw Pact: Political Purpose and Military Means,* ed. Robert W. Clawson and Lawrence S. Kaplan (Wilmington, Del.: Scholarly Resources, 1982), 18–19, 48; Robert L. Hutchings, *Soviet–East European Relations: Consolidation and Conflict, 1968–1980* (Madison: Univ. of Wis. Press, 1983), 4; and Richard Löwenthal, "Vormachtkontrolle und Autonomie in der Entwicklung des Sowjetblocks," in *Der Sowjetblock zwischen Vormacht-kontrolle und Autonomie,* ed. Richard Löwenthal and Boris Meissner (Cologne: Markus Verlag, 1984), 11. For works that consider the Warsaw Pact to be on the path to something of a true alliance, see Zbigniew K. Brzezinski, *The Soviet Bloc: Unity and Conflict,* 2d rev. and enl. ed. (Cambridge, Mass.: Harvard Univ. Press, 1967), 433; J. F. Brown, "Relations Between the Soviet Union and Its Eastern European Allies: A Survey," *Rand Report* R-1742-PR (Nov. 1975), 11–12; Robin Alison Remington, *The Warsaw Pact: Case Studies in Communist Conflict Resolution* (Cambridge, Mass.: MIT Press, 1971), 6, 8; and David Holloway, "The Warsaw Pact in Transition," in *The Warsaw Pact,* ed. Holloway and Sharp, 19.

2. Beate Ihme-Tuchel, *Das "nördliche Dreieck": Die Beziehungen zwischen der DDR, der Tschechoslowakei, und Polen in den Jahren 1954 bis 1962* (Cologne: Verlag Wissenschaft und Politik, 1994), 119–20.

3. Jacek Ślusarczyk, *Układ Warszawski: Działalność polityczna, 1955–1991* (Warsaw: ISP-PAN, 1992), 72; Karl Bittel, *Atomwaffenfreie Zone in Europa* ([East] Berlin: Kongress-Verlag, 1958), 21; M. Łobodycz, "Notatka z rozmowy Wiceministra Spraw Zagranicznych M. Nasz-kowskiego z Ambasadorem NRD S. Heymannem w Ministerstwie Spraw Zagranicznych dn. 22.II.1956r," marked 6 Mar. 1956, in Archiwum Ministerstwa Spraw Zagranicznych (AMSZ), Z. 10, t. 361, w. 39, pp. 12–16.

4. On NATO's decision, see Helga Haftendorn, *Abrüstungs- und Entspannungspolitik*

zwischen Sicherheitsbefriedigung und Friedenssicherung: Zur Außenpolitik der BRD 1955–1973 (Düsseldorf: Bertelsmann Universitätsverlag, 1974), 112.

5. Łobodycz, "Notatka z rozmowy."

6. Piotr Wandycz, "Adam Rapacki and the Search for European Security," in *The Diplomats, 1939–1979*, ed. Gordon A. Craig and Francis L. Loewenheim (Princeton, N.J.: Princeton Univ. Press, 1994), 295.

7. G. Markscheffel, "Gespräch mit Außenminister Rapacki im Warschau am 7. Jan. 1959 von 17,00 bis 19,15 Uhr im Außenministerium: Vertraulicher Bericht für Erich Ollenhauer, Herbert Wehner, Waldemar von Knoeringen," n.d., Archiv der sozialen Demokratie der Friedrich-Ebert-Stiftung (AdSD), Bestandteil G. Markscheffel, sig. 23.

8. L. W. Gluchowski, "Poland, 1956: Khrushchev, Gomułka, and the 'Polish October,'" *Cold War International History Project Bulletin* (henceforth, *CWIHP Bulletin*) 5 (spring 1995): 41; Mark Kramer, "New Evidence on Soviet Decision-Making and the 1956 Polish and Hungarian Crises," *CWIHP Bulletin* 8–9 (winter 1996/1997): 361–62.

9. Andrzej Korzon, "Rozmowy polsko-radzieckie w maju 1957 roku," *Dzieje najnowsze* 25 (1993): 121–30. A transcript of the Polish-Soviet talks has also been reprinted in Paczkowski, ed., *Tajne dokumenty Biura Politycznego, 1956–1970*, 31–72. It was Gomułka who dubbed Moscow's potential change of stance on the Oder-Neisse Line a "leash" around Poland's neck; see Mieczysław Rakowski, *Dzienniki Polityczne, 1969–1971* (Warsaw: Iskry, 2001), 175–77.

10. "Słowo końcowe tow. Wiesława na spotkaniu z dziennikarzami dnia 5.X.57," 5 Oct. 1957, Archiwum Akt Nowych (AAN), KC PZPR, 237/V-255.

11. See Douglas E. Selvage, "Poland, the German Democratic Republic, and the German Question, 1955–1967" (Ph.D. diss., Yale Univ., 1998), chap. 2.

12. Douglas E. Selvage, "Khrushchev's Berlin Ultimatum, Nov. 1958: New Evidence from the Polish Archives," *CWIHP Bulletin* 11 (summer 1999).

13. On Khrushchev's frequent discussion of "Rapallo," see, for example, Averell Harriman tel. from Moscow to the Department of State, 27 July 1963, in U.S. Department of State, *Foreign Relations of the United States, 1961–1963* (Washington, D.C.: G.P.O., 1994), 15:540; Jaszczuk (Moscow) tel. to Naszkowski, 11 July 1963, in AMSZ, Zespół depesz, w. 94, t. 604. Also see Gomułka's speech to the II Plenum of the PZPR in Nov. 1964 in "Stenogram II Plenarnego Posiedzenia Komitetu Centralnego Polskiej Zjednoczonej Partii Robotniczej," 20–21 Nov. 1964, in AAN, KC PZPR, sygn. 1265, pp. 337–39.

14. For a more detailed discussion of the nonproliferation issue in its Warsaw Pact context, see Douglas Selvage, "The Warsaw Pact and Nuclear Nonproliferation, 1963–1965," *Cold War International History Project Working Paper* 32 (Jan. 2001). On Khrushchev's "Rapallo policy," also see Daniel Kosthorst, "Sowjetische Geheimpolitik in Deutschland? Chruschtschow und die Adschubej-Mission 1964," *Vierteljahrshefte zur Zeitgeschichte* 44 (1996).

15. Brown, "Relations Between the Soviet Union and Its East European Allies."

16. See Selvage, "Poland, the German Democratic Republic, and the German Question," chaps. 4–6.

17. "Rede des Genossen L. I. Brehsnew [sic], Erster Sekretär des ZK der KPdSU, auf der Tagung des Politischen Beratenden Ausschusses des Warschauer Vertrags," 19 Jan. 1965, in Stiftung Archiv der Parteien und Massenorganisationen der ehemaligen DDR im Bundesarchiv (SAPMO BA), IV 2/1–321, pp. 78–79.

18. "Notatka z rozmów szefów delegacji, które przybyły do Warszawy na posiedzenie Politycznego Komitetu Doradczego państw-uczestników Układu Warszawskiego," n.d. AAN, KC PZPR, sygn. 2662, p. 187.

19. Selvage, "The Warsaw Pact and Nuclear Nonproliferation," 16–18.

20. For the final version of the Soviet bloc's declaration, the so-called Bucharest Declaration, see "Deklaration der Teilnehmerstaaten des Warschauer Vertrages über die Festigung des Friedens und der Sicherheit in Europa," 5 July 1966, in *Dokumente zur Deutschlandpolitik (DzDP)* IV/12: 1061–71. For the Soviet draft from June 1966, along with Romania's proposed amendments, see "Entwurf: Deklaration über die Festigung des Friedens und der Sicherheit in Europa [Draft: Declaration on the Consolidation of Peace and Security in Europe]," n.d., in SAPMO BA, J IV 2/202–258.

21. See, for example, "Bericht über die wissenschaftliche Konferenz zu Fragen der europäischen Sicherheit vom 7.—10.12.1966 in Warschau," 12 Dec. 1966, in SAPMO BA, NL 182/1301, pp. 179–87; "Informacja o międzynarodowej konferencji naukowej na temat 'Bezpieczeństwo europejskie i współczesne koncepcje Zachodu' /Warszawa, 8–10 grudnia 1966r./," n.d., in AAN, KC PZPR, p. 125, t. 87.

22. "Vermerk über die Unterredung zwischen Genossen Walter Ulbricht und Genossen W.S. Semjonow, Stellvertreter des Ministers für Auswärtige Angelegenheiten der UdSSR (17.1.67)," n.d., SAPMO BA, J IV 2/201–1094.

23. "Protokoll Nr. 3/67 der Sitzung des Politbüros des Zentralkomitees am 24. Januar 1967," SAPMO BA, J IV 2/2–1.095, pp. 1–7; "Denkschrift," 25 Jan. 1967, in SAPMO BA, J IV 2/202–79.

24. "Protokół ze spotkania przywódców Polskiej Zjednoczonej Partii Robotniczej i Komunistycz-nej Partii Związku Radzieckiego /18 stycznia 1967 roku—Łańsk," n.d., AAN, KC PZPR, sygn. 2642.

25. Douglas Selvage, "Polska-NRD. 'Doktryna Ulbrichta' w świetle dokumentów," *Rocznik polsko-niemiecki* 3 (1994).

26. Douglas E. Selvage, "The Treaty of Warsaw (1970): The Warsaw Pact Context," in *Bulletin of the German Historical Institute, Supplement 1: American Detente and German Ostpolitik, 1969–1972,* ed. David C. Geyer and Bernd Schafer (Washington, D.C., 2004), 70–72.

27. See the excerpts from Gomułka's speech to the Conference of Communist and Workers' Parties in Karlový Varý on 24 Apr. 1967 in *DzDP* V/1: 1015–23.

28. In May 1967, Gomułka objected to a draft renunciation-of-force agreement that Moscow was planning to present to Bonn because the Soviets had included in it a commitment by Bonn not to use force in its relations with the GDR. Such a clause, Gomułka wrote Brezhnev, would imply that the GDR was an object, not a subject, in international law and would thus undermine the GDR's sovereignty. The Polish leader did not point out, but it was undoubtedly on his mind, that a similar clause with regard to Communist Poland in a bilateral Soviet–West German agreement would undermine Poland's sovereignty. Gomułka to Brezhnev, 23 May 1967, in AAN, KC PZPR, sygn. 2632, pp. 301–6.

29. Oskar Fischer, "Vermerk über ein Gespräch des Ministers für Auswärtige Angelegenheiten der DDR, Otto Winzer, mit dem Außenminister der UdSSR, Andrei Gromyko, am 1.9.1969 in Moskau," 3 Sept. 1969, SAPMO BA, J IV 2/202–81.

30. In 1967–68, the GDR demanded that the Soviet Union make Bonn's conclusion of a renunciation-of-force agreement a precondition for a Soviet–West German agreement and that Moscow break off its talks with Bonn over renunciation of force so that Bonn would be compelled to negotiate with the GDR. "Stenografische Niederschrift: Verhandlungen der Partei- und Regierungsdelegation der DDR und der UdSSR am 11. Dezember 1967 in Moskau," 11 Dec. 1967, SAPMO BA, J IV 2/201–76.

31. Douglas Selvage, "Papírháromszög: Lengyelország, az NDK és Csehszlovákia," *Külpolitika* [*International Affairs: Budapest*] 1–2 (2001): 184–87.

32. Timothy Garton Ash has argued the existence of a strong link between the normalization of relations between East and West during the late 1960s and 1970s and the internal "normalization" in Czechoslovakia after 1968—that is, reaffirming Moscow's sphere of influence by returning Czechoslovakia to Soviet norms after the Prague Spring. Timothy Garton Ash, *In Europe's Name* (New York: Vintage Books, 1993), 15–16.

33. See note 29.

34. "Aide-mémoire der Sowjetregierung an die Regierung der Bundesrepublik Deutschland vom 5. Juli 1968," *Politik des Gewaltverzichts,* 36–46; "Stellungnahme der Regierung der DDR zu Problemen des Gewaltverzichts," *DzDP* V/2: 1019.

35. U.S. embassy in Bonn, tel. 6 Dec. 1968, in NARA, RG 59, Central Files, 1967–69, FT GER E—GER W.

36. "Protokół ze spotkania przywódców PZPR I KPZR w Moskwie, 3–4 marca 1969 r.," n.d., AAN, KC PZPR, p. 114, t. 33, pp. 28–90.

37. See Gomułka's handwritten notes during the Twenty-third Extraordinary Session of the COMECON in Moscow, 24–26 Apr. 1969, in AAN, KC PZPR, p. 110, t. 16.

38. For relevant excerpts from the speech, see Hans-Adolf Jacobsen and Mieczysław Tomala, eds., *Bonn-Warschau, 1945–1991* (Cologne: Verlag Wissenschaft und Politik, 1992), 184–89.

39. Oskar Fischer, "Vermerk über ein Gespräch des Ministers für Auswärtige Angelegenheiten der DDR, Otto Winzer, mit dem Außenminister der UdSSR, Andrei Gromyko, am 1.9.1969 in Moskau," 3 Sept. 1969, SAPMO BA, J IV 2/202–81.

40. Ibid.

41. Oskar Fischer, "Vermerk über ein Gespräch des Ministers für Auswärtige Angelegenheiten der DDR, Genossen Otto Winzer, mit dem stellvertretenden Außenminister der UdSSR, Genossen W.S. Semjonow, am 25. Sept. 1969," 25 Sept. 1969, SAPMO BA, J IV 2/201- 1104.

42. Dr. Scholz (gez. Fiszer), "Bericht über die Beratung der Stellvertretenden Außenminister der Staaten des Warschauer Vertrages am 20. und 21. Mai 1969 in Berlin," 22 May 1969, SAPMO BA, J IV 2/202–265.

43. See note 39.

44. "Stenografische Niederschrift: Beratung der Außenminister der Warschauer Vertragsstaaten am 30. Oktober 1969 in Prag," n.d., SAPMO BA, J IV 2/202–266; "Protokoll Nr. 45/69 der Sitzung des Politburos des Zentralkomitees am 18.11.1969," n.d., SAPMO BA, J IV 2/2/1253, pp. 43–50.

45. Projekt, "Komunikat o wizycie partyjno-rządowej delegacji Polskiej Rzeczypospolitej Ludowej w Związku Radzieckim," n.d., AAN, KC PZPR, p. 114, t.33. pp. 308–18.

46. Jan Ptasiński, "Moje rozmowy z Władysławem Gomułką w latach 1960–1970," 1992, cz. 1; PII/7a, k. 358, Instytucji Dokumentacji Historycznej Polskiej Rzeczypospolitej Ludowej (IDH-PRL), pp. 42–44.

47. "Przemówienie tow. Gomułki na spotkaniu z I sekretarzami KW i kierownikami wydziałów KC w dniu 12 grudnia 69r.," n.d., AAN, KC PZPR, 237/V-911, pp. 5–32; Rakowski, *Dzienniki polityczne,* 177–78.

48. M. E. Sarotte, *Dealing with the Devil: East Germany, Détente, and Ostpolitik, 1969–1973* (Chapel Hill: Univ. of N.C. Press, 2001), 30–35.

49. During negotiations in October 1970, the Polish foreign ministry successfully resisted the efforts of West German diplomats to weaken the border formulation in the draft Polish–West German treaty to conform to the Moscow Treaty between the USSR and the

FRG, signed two months earlier. See "Gespraech des Staatssekretaers Frank mit dem sow-jetischen Botschafter Zarapkin," 27 Oct. 1970, and "Staatssekretaer Frank, z.Z. Warschau, an das Auswaertige Amt," 3 Nov. 1970, in *Akten zur Auswärtigen Politik der Bundesrepublik Deutschland* 1970/III: 1850, 1902–5.

50. P. E. Shelest, *Da ne sudimy budete: Dnevnikovye zapisi, vospominaniia chlena Politbiuro TsK KPSS* (Moscow: Izdatel'stvo "Kvintessentsiya," 1995), 21, 460–62.

51. Sarotte, *Dealing with the Devil,* 109–10.

12

The Warsaw Pact and Southern Tier Conflicts, 1959–1969

JORDAN BAEV

The years immediately following the mid-1950s witnessed an evident increase in self-confidence on the part of the Soviet Union's leadership. Its practical expression came in the ambitious twenty-year program for securing Soviet superiority over the United States, triumphantly proclaimed by Nikita Khrushchev at the Twenty-second Communist Party Congress in October 1961. Soon after the Soviet military intervention in Hungary in November 1956, the situation in Eastern Europe appeared stabilized and fully under Moscow's control, despite the feeble attempts of Polish leader Władysław Gomułka to express a personal view on key European issues and East German leader Walter Ulbricht's strong call for hardening the Soviet bloc's position toward West Germany.

Political conditions in the Warsaw Pact's southern tier also appeared favorable for Soviet interests. For more than a decade Romania had remained a Soviet stronghold in the Balkans. Shortly after the Stalin-Tito conflict flared up in the early summer of 1948, Cominform headquarters moved from Belgrade to Bucharest, followed by a number of related moves. It was by no means accidental that the notorious secret fund "Moscow," which was designed to finance scores of leftist radical parties and organizations in Western European and Third World countries (with average annual expenditures of more than $10 million), bore the official name International Trade-Union Fund for Assistance of Left Labor Organizations at the Council of the Romanian Trade-Unions. The Romanian leadership displayed energetic support for the Soviet military intervention in Hungary and after the uprising's suppression kept the detained Hungarian leaders under arrest for nearly two years on Romanian territory until their executions. Nor is it accidental that the first two meetings of the multilateral Warsaw Pact Intelligence Services were held in Bucharest in 1955 and 1958, initiated by General Alexander Dragici, Romania's minister of the interior.[1]

In the late 1950s, Albania also appeared to be a trustworthy Soviet outpost in the Mediterranean area. After Nikita Khrushchev's triumphal visit to Tirana in 1959, Moscow signed auxiliary military agreements providing for access to the Albanian naval base of Vlorë by Soviet warships and for submarines to sail under the Albanian flag as a cover. In Bulgaria, traditionally friendly toward Russia, there was little reason to suspect even a trace of anti-Soviet feelings. In addition, the Bulgarian Communist leader, Todor Zhivkov, had assumed power with Khrushchev's personal support and successfully managed in the early 1960s to oust systematically all his old rivals and to establish extremely close relations with his Kremlin patron.

Within several years, however, this relatively harmonious region for Soviet interests dramatically changed. Albania would transform itself into the most fervent opponent of "Soviet revisionism," and Romanian leaders would express hard-line opposition to Soviet initiatives within the Warsaw Treaty Organization (WTO). In 1965, Zhivkov's security services uncovered plans for a military coup, in what would be the most serious challenge in his thirty-five years of authoritarian personal rule. Coup organizers, members of the Communist leadership, and army generals would be branded as supporters of Maoist China. Thus, in the span of just a few years, the Balkans turned from the most secure and loyal area of the Soviet domain into a thorny region for Moscow's interests. Notwithstanding these problems, the Kremlin did not send its troops against Albania or Romania, as it had with other Eastern European states. Unlike the policy Stalin had utilized to challenge Tito, the Soviets now initiated no serious covert actions to unseat Enver Hoxha or Nicolae Ceauşescu.

Since the demise of the Communist regimes, Eastern European archives have disclosed much specific information on the decision making of individual leaders and their governments during the Cold War years. In contrast, Soviet policy and estimates, apart from crisis years (1953, 1956, 1968, 1980–81), have been rather scantily studied. Consequently, although it will be difficult to answer a good number of questions as long as there is insufficient access to the Moscow archives, it is nonetheless appropriate to discuss them on the basis of available archival documentation, the objective of this chapter.

During the Soviet bloc's first postwar "Stalinist" decade, the Kremlin established total control over Eastern Europe and had access to fairly complete and reliable intelligence on conditions in the region. Reports sent through diplomatic, party, and military channels and the information supplied by KGB agents in the Eastern European states clearly support this evaluation.[2] The new Soviet leader, Nikita Khrushchev, received summary reports on the situation in each country. For example, several months after the events in Poland and Hungary, in March and April 1957, KGB chairman Alexandr Shelepin submitted reports to Khrushchev on the state of affairs in Romania, Bulgaria, and Albania. In the early 1960s, the new KGB chairman, Vladimir Semichastny, forwarded similar analyses.[3] In addition, the Soviet leader had many opportunities for confidential contacts with his colleagues in Eastern Europe.

The development of conflicts within the Warsaw Pact's southern flank cannot be attributed simply to Khrushchev's personality and his impulsive improvisations or exclusively to variants of "national Communism." The uniform solidity of the system obviously splintered from the processes of "de-Stalinization," the intensification of the ideological dispute between the Soviet Union and China, and the subsequent new round of behind-the-scenes intraparty struggles among the Eastern European elites. For Romania's Gheorge Gheorghiu-Dej and Zhivkov, "de-Stalinization" turned into a most convenient background for settling personal accounts and eliminating old opponents. Though they had taken an active part in the Stalinist repressions of the late 1940s and had had active roles in the trials against Lukretiu Patrascanu and Traicho Kostov, respectively, at the end of the 1950s and the beginning of the 1960s, both systematically displaced a number of their colleagues (e.g., Ana Pauker and Iosif Chisinevski in Romania; Vulko Chervenkov and Anton Yugov in Bulgaria) who were branded "incorrigible Stalinists."

At the peak of Cold War confrontation in the late 1940s and early 1950s, the Balkans occupied a relatively significant place in Soviet policy, primarily because of the ongoing Stalin-Tito split, the expansion of NATO into southeastern Europe with the addition of Turkey and Greece into its ranks, and the announcement of a formal Balkan Pact among Greece, Turkey, and Yugoslavia in February 1953. But even as early as the Korean War, the Balkans had begun losing the strategic importance that it had at the time of the Truman Doctrine. There is no doubt that this de-emphasized role accordingly influenced Soviet policy toward its Balkan allies. The rearmament of the Soviet armed forces with modern weapons by the end of the 1950s and the appearance of strategic ballistic missiles had an important effect on the capabilities of the Warsaw Pact. From the mid-1950s until the end of the Cold War the Balkan theater became a secondary front in relation to the primary theater of confrontation for the two blocs in Central Europe.

Although the Kremlin leadership focused chiefly on Central and Western Europe in the 1960s, the geostrategic position of the Balkans as a key factor for securing control of the approaches to the Mediterranean and the Near East still remained operational. Reflective of this orientation, two annual reports from the British Legation in Sofia clearly describe the role assigned to Bulgaria in Soviet plans and considerations. The 1960 account affirmed: "The Russians, we must assume, regard Bulgaria as the most reliable of their European satellites. She has a stable government, a good army, and a docile population. She also occupies a key sector in the front line facing NATO. It seems clear that the Russians are building up the pressure against Greece and Turkey; and here Bulgaria has an important role to play." The 1964 report included remarks on "Bulgaria's considerable strategic importance to the Soviet Union, both as a buffer against attack from the South and as a springboard for any offensive to the Mediterranean."[4]

Regardless of their unvoiced discontent with the course of "de-Stalinization" and with the attempts for improving relations with Tito until the summer of 1960, Albanian leaders outwardly demonstrated eagerness for the closest possible cooperation within the boundaries of the Soviet bloc. The twenty-day visit of Enver Hoxha to Bulgaria in August–September 1959 and the reciprocal official visit of Todor Zhivkov to Tirana in October offered no hints for the drastic shift in relations that would occur in June 1960. At the Third Congress of the Romanian Workers Party in Bucharest, as well as at the international Communist conference in Moscow in November, Albanian leaders proved much more vocal than even the Chinese representatives in their attacks against the USSR.

Initially, the Romanian Communist Congress was considered an appropriate setting for an international Communist meeting, consequent to the Moscow meeting of 1957. The Chinese stance at the International Trade Unions conference on 6 June 1960 and the visible disagreements at the Sino-Soviet talks in Moscow on 17 June, however, caused the postponement of a broader meeting. On the eve of the Bucharest Congress, the CPSU on 21 June distributed to the other Eastern European ruling Communist parties an extensive sixty-page memorandum dealing with the Chinese position, thus placing this complicated issue on the agenda of a proposed international consultative meeting during the Romanian Communist Party Congress. At the international discussion in Bucharest on 24 June a lower-ranking official from the Albanian Politburo, Husni Kapo, instead of its leader, Enver Hoxha, headed the delegation. The Albanian representative initially postponed his own statement and finally rejected discussion of the Sino-Soviet discord, defining the Bucharest meeting as "quite premature."[5]

During Nikita Khrushchev's visit to New York in September 1960 for the 15th UN General Assembly session, Eastern European leaders took the opportunity to discuss the budding conflict. Significantly, Albanian prime minister Mehmet Shehu did not attend consultations on the sensitive issue. Husni Kapo reiterated the Albanian position at an organizational meeting in October, which preceded the Moscow meeting of eighty-one Communist parties in November 1960.[6] At the Moscow meeting Gheorghiu-Dej and Zhivkov emerged as the most severe critics of Hoxha's pro-Chinese position. Soon after a sharp four-hour speech by Hoxha, the Bulgarian delegation denounced his stance, and, again, in a 24 November statement, Zhivkov characterized the Albanian position as "provocative," "infamous," "scandalous," "abusive," and "rowdy." Hoxha then declined a bilateral meeting with Zhivkov because of the latter's perceived offensive and personal attacks against him. Nevertheless, in a report before a CC BCP Plenary meeting on 10 December

1960 after returning from Moscow, Zhivkov declared: "We shall continue to fulfill henceforth our obligations according to our bilateral agreements with Albania and to render our possible assistance to the Albanian people."[7]

But in December 1960 Soviet state policy toward Albania underwent drastic change, with Moscow leveling direct accusations of Albania's incorrectness and animosity toward Soviet military personnel in the Adriatic port of Vlorë.[8] Moscow subsequently summoned its experts home and soon afterward discontinued Soviet economic and military aid for Albania, very much as it had the preceding year with China and more than a decade earlier with Yugoslavia.

Why did Moscow so easily sacrifice an ally and the maintenance of its naval base in the Mediterranean area, described later by Nikita Khrushchev in his memoirs as the "superb strategic location" of Albania? It must be pointed out in this context that Albania was the only Eastern European Communist country Stalin did not invite to participate in the constitutive meetings of the Cominform in September 1947 and of COMECON in January 1949. In a conversation with Mao Zedong in August 1958, Khrushchev pointed out that, in discussions during the spring of 1955 for the establishment of the Warsaw Pact, Soviet foreign minister Vyacheslav Molotov was initially reluctant to propose including Albania in the Eastern European military alliance.[9] Could it be that Moscow considered the burden of economic and military assistance for that small and poor Balkan country incommensurable with its limited geostrategic importance? Concurrently, the Soviet regime provided enormous aid to a large number of far more problematic Arab and African regimes of countries in which it had military bases (e.g., Egypt, Syria, Somalia, Ethiopia).

In part, the increasing tensions in the relationship with Albania resulted from intelligence reports about the active propaganda and confidential efforts of Albanian embassy personnel in Eastern Europe to recruit supporters among local party functionaries and officer corps. An initial indicator of such actions came in a top-secret KGB report to Sofia in December 1960. According to a KGB agent of Greek origin (code-named "Pavlos") in a communication following his visit to Bulgaria, some middle-rank officers of the Bulgarian army shared the pro-Stalinist views expressed by Hohxa at the Moscow conference in November 1960.[10] In 1965 the chairman of the Bulgarian State Security Committee, General Angel Solakov, informed the CC BCP of the "subversive activity" of Albanian embassy staff in Sofia since 1963, which resulted in the establishment of "anti-party" groups in Sofia, Pernik, Yambol, and other Bulgarian cities. The most dangerous case was the plot, discovered in April 1965, against the Zhivkov regime involving the participation of a few army generals and Central Committee members. In January 1966 for the first time the BCP Politburo approved a proposal for initiating intelligence and counterintelligence measures against China and Albania. Soon after the exposure of a new pro-Chinese conspiracy in 1968, the Bulgarian government expelled seven Albanian diplomats as "persona non grata."[11]

The split with Albania seriously affected Tirana's participation in the WTO. The final involvement of Albania in a Warsaw Pact activity came in a session of the Political Consultative Committee (PCC) in March 1961, and the delegation's attitude was defiant and provocative. Albania subsequently refused invitations to participate in any joint sessions of the organization's bodies.[12] Under these circumstances, Todor Zhivkov took the initiative to have Albania expelled from the Warsaw Pact. In a special letter for Nikita Khrushchev on 10 June 1961 he proposed "to refer the matter concerning the behavior and actions of the Albanian leaders to the PCC [Warsaw Pact Political Consultative Committee] for consideration and relevant conclusions."[13] At that time, however, the Albanian leadership declined any further participation in the organization, although the country continued to be formally considered a member until as late as September 1968.

Romanian alienation from the Kremlin manifested itself after the split with Albania in 1961. Certain publications claim that such a pattern could have been detected as early as 1958, or perhaps even earlier in 1955.[14] Actually, the withdrawal of Soviet troops from Romania in 1958 resulted from an independent Soviet decision as part of the package of Khrushchev's initiatives for the reduction of Soviet forces in Eastern Europe. As early as 1958 Moscow withdrew 41,000 troops from East Germany and 17,000 from Hungary. During Khrushchev's August 1958 conversation with Mao, mentioned earlier, the Soviet leader informed his Chinese counterpart that he had suggested a full withdrawal of Soviet troops from Hungary to Janos Kadar. In his speech at the Moscow meeting of Warsaw Pact leaders on 4 February 1960, Khrushchev once again pointed out that Soviet military units might be withdrawn from Hungary and Poland. This move, however, never did develop.

The position that the Soviet-Romanian controversy started because of differences on the economic division of labor among the socialist countries, which came up at the CMEA conference in August 1961, also seems exaggerated and interpreted from the vantage point of events subsequent to the split. A careful study of shorthand minutes of the CMEA meetings reveals that, unlike Warsaw Pact meetings, they were a battlefield of conflicting interests among the member-states throughout CMEA's entire existence. Each "partner" sought to win as favorable a position as possible under existing circumstances. For example, in a critical report to Nikita Khrushchev on 5 May 1963, Mihail Lesechko, the Soviet representative to CMEA, described in detail the claims and expressions of discontent of some Eastern European countries regarding economic cooperation with the USSR and inside CMEA. The report disclosed many facts regarding Poland, the GDR, Czechoslovakia, Hungary, and Bulgaria, but mentioned Romania only incidentally.[15] One can surmise, then, that economic rifts offered only one of many causes for Romania's alienation from Moscow. Significantly, after the August 1961 CMEA conference, at the Twenty-second CPSU Congress two months later, as well as at a Party Plenary Session in December of that same year, Romanian leaders maintained their strong support for Soviet criticism of Albania and China.

Major differences initially found expression in a letter of the CC of the RWP addressed to Moscow on 15 March 1963 and became quite clear in the discussions between the Romanian leadership and the secretary of the CC of the CPSU, Yuri Andropov, on 3 April 1963.[16] If one bears this sequence in mind, it can be hypothesized, and probably with greater certainty, that a key factor in the drastic change in Romania's behavior was the impact of the Berlin Wall and the Cuban missile crises.[17] During the first months of its disputes with the Romanian leadership, the Kremlin adopted a more moderate and conciliatory tactic. Since Gheorghiu-Dej declined an invitation to visit Moscow, only two weeks after receiving on 7 June 1963 another letter from the CC of the RWP, Khrushchev traveled to Bucharest. Most probably, the first rumors and informal comments within Eastern European circles regarding possible disagreements with Romania started circulating during the second half of 1963. Included in confidential information on Bulgarian public reactions to Zhivkov's talks with Khrushchev in Moscow was the supposition that divisions with the Romanian leadership on the relationships within the international Communist movement motivated such a visit.[18]

In further letters of 13 January and 25 March 1964 Romanian leaders persisted in their position, which was made public at the Plenary Session of the CC of the RWP in April. Talks in Moscow between representatives of both countries in June as well as the visits of Nikolai Podgorni in July and Anastas Mikoyan in August to Bucharest did not contribute to settling the differences. Neither did the meeting with the new Soviet leader, Leonid Brezhnev, in November 1964 bring about any serious change in the positions of both sides. It only served as a setting for subsequent clarification of the Romanian position, which was additionally provided in writing on 4 January 1965, in response to a 24 November 1965 letter of the CC of the CPSU.[19]

The first actual step stemming from Romanian alienation came in the form of a specific request for the withdrawal of Soviet advisers from the Romanian security services. Initially, the Romanian side refused to participate in the conference of the deputy ministers of foreign affairs held in Warsaw in December 1964 but then yielded only because of the "persistent intervention" of the meeting's convenor, Walter Ulbricht.[20] At the Warsaw Pact summit in the Polish capital in January 1965, the Romanian delegation officially opposed some important Soviet proposals (e.g., on the Nuclear Test Ban Treaty and the reorganization of the pact's structure) and declared its position for the dissolution of both military blocs.[21] The election of the new Romanian party and state leader, Nicolae Ceaușescu, after the death of Gheorghiu-Dej in March 1965, actually witnessed a hardening of the Romanian line. For the next twenty-five years Romania permanently played the part of the "lonely internal dissident" in the Warsaw Pact.

Ceaușescu's policy had an impact not only on Romania's relations with the Kremlin but also on certain aspects of its contacts with the other Eastern European states. For example, Soviet-Romanian discord contributed to the renewal of the dispute with Hungary over Transylvania.[22] The East German government fiercely attacked Ceauşescu for Bucharest's unilateral decision to establish diplomatic relations with West Germany. The Romanians irritated the Poles for obstructing their initiatives for collective security in Europe and their idea of seeking a negotiated peaceful outcome of the Vietnam War.[23] Paradoxically, President Josip Broz Tito of nonaligned Yugoslavia attended the meeting of Warsaw Pact leaders in June 1967 in Moscow dealing with the Six-Day Middle East War, while Ceauşescu did not even receive an invitation to the gathering.

Archival documentation unambiguously shows that in the latter half of the 1960s and in the 1970s, Leonid Brezhnev assigned to Bulgaria's Zhivkov a confidential role of "negotiator" with the task of turning Ceauşescu around by restraining and influencing him. Concurrently, the two Balkan Communist rulers continued to compete with each other in trying to cultivate more influence and greater prestige in the region and among the Third World states. The condition of Bulgarian-Romanian relations in several categories also offers insights into the state of Soviet-Romanian relations. Since both regimes were similarly authoritarian Communist, bilateral party and social relations at different levels were maintained. Adverse exchanges appeared in the official media, but confidential information bulletins contained explanations from party functionaries on the ideological and foreign policy differences.

In the six months after he came to power in March 1965, Ceauşescu met with Zhivkov four times, twice in Romania (March and July) and twice in Bulgaria (August and September). In a BCP Politburo meeting after his talks with Ceauşescu and Romanian prime minister Ion Gheorghe Maurer in September, Zhivkov elaborated on the necessity for improving and developing Bulgarian-Romanian relations. He argued that the differences between the leaderships of these neighboring countries should not be "exaggerated" or "dramatized" but must nonetheless be "overcome." Despite no evident agreement on some issues (e.g., China, reorganization of Warsaw Pact structures, the nuclear disarmament process), Zhivkov characterized his personal relations with Ceauşescu as "very close, and almost intimate and friendly."[24] The comments following bilateral talks between the two leaders on 17–19 April 1967 in Bucharest typified the essence of their relationship: Each leader announced his own positions but also stressed the positive results of bilateral cooperation between both countries. In a government meeting soon after these talks, Zhivkov underlined again: "We are pursuing a very patient policy of friendship and cooperation with Romania . . . and this is one of our opportunities to influence their leaders." The Bulgarian prime minister, however, brought a significant issue to the attention of his colleagues, that of "Romanian obligations as a Warsaw Pact member country in a case of war." He had posed a direct question to Ceauşescu and Maurer about the implementation of Romania's allied obligations in case of an attack against Bulgaria. Despite Ceauşescu's positive response, Zhivkov concluded: "I have doubts of their effective military support since their army is undeveloped, and their defense budget was reduced two times."[25]

Romania would discontinue its field cooperation within the Warsaw Pact not long after the August 1968 invasion of Czechoslovakia. The initial signs of mutual suspicion and misunderstanding had been noticed two years earlier. In an account of a joint Warsaw Pact military exercise in October 1966, which took place both on Romanian and Bulgarian territory, the chief of Bulgarian Military Counter-Intelligence described "some new revealing tendencies in the behavior of many Romanian high commanders." According to the report, one of the Romanian officers had expressed the view that "these kinds of military exercises were too expensive and that it was quite needless to maintain such large armies in peacetime."[26] A number of differences between Romania and the other allies surfaced during the Warsaw Pact meeting in Sofia in March 1968. Romanian leaders would not be invited to subsequent Eastern European consultations regarding the tense conditions in Czechoslovakia on the eve of the Warsaw Pact invasion.

The last joint Soviet-Romanian-Bulgarian military exercise occurred in March 1969. Romania participated with naval ships and troops in the exercise, after which the Bulgarian navy's commander in chief noted in his 12 March report that

> In the course of the exercise the Romanian Naval Command demonstrated . . . ᵥ its strong inclination toward independent actions within its own operational zone and limited operational interaction with allied fleets. The creation of joint formations of all allies' naval forces was subject of their open adversity and such formations were only made up after endless persuasions and strong persistence on my part. . . . During my visit to Mangalia the High Command of the Romanian Navy definitely rejected the idea of carrying out joint analysis under the pretext that such analyses are not of much use.

At the end of his report, Vice-Admiral Ivan Dobrev directly suggested: "Taking into consideration the existence of a certain reluctance for closer cooperation on the part of the Romanian Naval High Command, some solutions to problems should be found better bilaterally between the Bulgarian Navy and the Soviet Black Sea Fleet."[27] Only in 1973 did Romania again attend a joint naval Black Sea exercise with seven warships, and from 1975 on with troops and staffs.

Bulgarian-Romanian cooperation survived the longest between their intelligence, security, and police services. Following the implementation of a new agreement for collaboration between the Bulgarian and Romanian security services, signed on 1 June 1968, they exchanged a significant amount of intelligence for about two years, a period when Romania reduced its political contacts with other Warsaw Pact allies.[28] Extensive Romanian-Bulgarian intelligence sharing continued into 1971, although during that year military and diplomatic cooperation decreased to basic levels. In mid-1971, for example, General Jon Stanescu, chairman of the Romanian State Security Council, delivered to Sofia some valuable information on NATO's Political Committee session, the structure and activity of Turkish security services,

Israeli intelligence actions in the Balkans, U.S.-Turkish relations, and U.S.-Greek differences.[29] Most probably, the termination of Bulgarian-Romanian collaboration in late 1971 resulted from direct (or indirect) KGB pressure, even though some exchanges of important information continued until 1975. In a December 1971 letter to KGB chairman Yuri Andropov, the new Bulgarian minister of the interior, General Angel Tzanev, described as one of the major "faults" of his predecessor "the establishment of quite close relations with the Romanian Secret Services without any kind of vigilance." In another letter to Andropov in January 1972, the Bulgarian minister of the interior reported on "the Albanian, Yugoslav and Romanian intelligence activity against Bulgaria." And finally during the talks with Andropov in March 1972, General Tzanev reported that Bulgarian State Security Committee contacts with the Romanian State Security Council had been "frozen."[30]

A number of scholars have debated the issue of a possible attack on Romania by Warsaw Pact forces after the invasion of Czechoslovakia in August 1968. Western sources held a lively discussion on the matter, proposing that such a possibility existed not only in the second half of 1968 but also at the beginning of 1969. The general conclusion has been that not enough reliable information exists to confirm that the Soviet Union ever had such intentions. Until now no direct or indirect evidence has surfaced to support even the theoretical proposition that any scenarios for armed intervention in Romania had ever been discussed. Since almost all Russian documentation covering that period is still unavailable, it is not possible to provide a definitive position on the subject. Nonetheless, it is still instructive to refer to three major differences in the situations in Czechoslovakia and Romania. The first is the Ceauşescu regime's embodied orthodox Communism with repressive authoritarian rule (i.e., it had never directed any ideological initiatives to transform or erode the existing model for monopolistic Communist rule); in contrast, "Communism with a human face" and the "Prague Spring" posed a distinct challenge to this paradigm. Second, Romanian leaders advanced the position that both NATO and the Warsaw Pact should be dissolved, but they neither insisted that the pact be dissolved unilaterally nor proposed that Romania should leave the pact; contrariwise, the first public appeals for breaking with the Warsaw Pact were aired in early July 1968 in Czechoslovakia. And third, Romania found itself bordering on four "friendly socialist" states.

Similar to the Cyprus dispute involving two contentious Balkan NATO allies, the controversies between Moscow and two of the four Balkan Communist states in the 1960s decisively influenced and blocked any plans for multilateral regional cooperation. Compounding this problem, the Kremlin appeared to be less worried about what NATO did in the region and more concerned about the spreading of Chinese influence in the Balkans and the establishment of an "anti-Soviet" Balkan bloc among Yugoslavia, Romania, and Albania. Such a position constituted a rather fanciful concern created by the conservative mood prevalent in the Soviet Foreign Ministry, headed by Andrei Gromyko.

The serious disputes within the Warsaw Pact during the 1960s, which resulted in the departure of one ally, the alienation of another, and multilateral armed intervention in the internal affairs of a third, delayed but did not stop the process of transformation in the military and political structures of the organization. Coincidentally, the interstate conflicts in the pact stimulated Western authorities, such as Zbigniew Brzezinski, to start talking about "desatellization" and "heterogenization" of the Soviet bloc.[31] Such projections also brought about considerable change in U.S. policy in the direction of a more "differentiated" approach toward each of the Eastern European states.[32] Regardless of the "stagnation" and "slump" during the second decade of Brezhnev's rule and the predominance of the "limited sovereignty" doctrine, the Warsaw Pact's southern tier was never to be as strongly united or unproblematic for Soviet interests as it had been in early 1960.

Notes

1. Archive of the Ministry of the Interior (AMVR), Sofia, Fond 2, Record 1, File 1345.

2. *Vostochnaya Evropa v dokumentah rossijskih arhivah* [Eastern Europe in the Russian archival documents], v. 1, *1944–1948* (Moscow: Novisibirsk, 1997); v. 2, *1949–1953* (Moscow: Novisibirsk, 1998); *Sovetskij factor v Vostochnoj Evrope* [Soviet Factor in Eastern Europe], v. 1, *1944–1948* (Moscow: Rosspen, 1999); v. 2, *1949–1953* (Moscow: Rosspen, 2002).

3. See documentary collections at the Russian State Archive of Contemporary History (RGANI), Fonds 5, 89; Basil Kontis, Natalia Tomilina et al., eds., *KPSS I formirovanie sovetskoj politiki na Balkanah v 1950-h—pervoj polovine 1960-h godov* [CPSU and the formulation of the Soviet policy in the Balkans: 1950s–early 1960s] (Thessaloniki: Russian Federal Archives Services and Institute for Balkan Studies, Paratiritis, 2003).

4. Cited in D. Dimitrov, *Soviet Bulgaria. From the Foreign Office Records,* Book 1, *1956–1963* (London: BBC World Service, 1994), 67; Book 2, *1964–1966* (London: BBC World Service, 1999), 66.

5. Central State Archive (CDA), Sofia, Fond 1-B, Record 5, File 433—CC BCP Plenary Meeting, 13 July 1960.

6. Ibid., File 438—CC BCP Plenary Meeting, 2 Nov. 1960.

7. Ibid., File 442—CC BCP Plenary Meeting, 10 Dec. 1960, pp. 10, 53–55, 201, 204, 217–18, 221.

8. See Vojtech Mastny and Malcolm Byrne, eds., *A Cardboard Castle? An Inside History of the Warsaw Pact, 1955–1991* (New York: Central European Univ. Press, 2005).

9. Vladislav Zubok, "The Mao-Khrushchev Conversations, 31 July–3 August 1958, and 2 Oct. 1959," *CWIHP Bulletin,* issue 12/13 (2001): 260.

10. AMVR, Sofia, Fond 2, Record 3, File 19, pp. 5–8.

11. CDA, Fond 1-B, Record 6, File 6576, pp. 3–4; Record 8, File 7732, pp. 4–10; Record 34, File 52; Record 64, File 345, pp. 1–10; AMVR, Fond 2, Record 4, File 84, p. 2.

12. Aside from purely conceptual differences, the Albanian leadership refuses to share information with the WP member states. In his report delivered at a conference of Bulgarian diplomats in the beginning of June 1961 Bulgarian foreign minister Karlo Lukanov argued that the Albanian leaders failed to inform the Allied Armed Forces' Unified Command of

very important matters of military political nature, though according to the provisions of the Warsaw Treaty the other members of the organization were obliged to provide military support to Albania in case of aggression against it. See CDA, Fond 1-B, Record 33, File 662, p. 63.

13. Ibid., Record 6, File 4490—Letter from 10 June 1961, pp. 1–3.

14. See Sergiu Verona, *Military Occupation and Diplomacy: Soviet Troops in Romania, 1944–1958* (Durham, N.C.: Duke Univ. Press, 1992); Vladimir Tismaneanu, "Gheorgiu-Dej and the Romanian Workers Party: From De-Stalinization to the Emergence of National Communism," CWIHP Working Paper No. 37 (Washington, D.C., May 2002); Dennis Deletant and Mihail Ionescu, "Romania and the Warsaw Pact, 1955–1989," CWIHP Working Paper No. 43 (Washington, D.C., 2004); Mark Kramer, "Soviet-Romanian Relations and the Warsaw Pact: Repercussions from the Czechoslovak Crisis," in *NATO, the Warsaw Pact and the Rise of Détente, 1964–1972* (Stanford, Calif.: Stanford Univ. Press, forthcoming).

15. National Security Archive (NSA), Washington, D.C., RADD Collection, Box 1960–1964—"About the necessity of further improvement of our economic relations with the CMEA countries," Moscow, 5 May 1963.

16. See Deletant and Ionescu, "Romania and the Warsaw Pact."

17. For the first time Dr. Raymond Garthoff exposed the hypothesis of the "nuclear war scare psychosis" as a basic motive for such a drastic move, explaining it as a reaction to the Cuban missile crisis. See Garthoff, "When and Why Romania Distanced Itself from the Warsaw Pact," *CWIHP Bulletin* 5 (1995): 111.

18. CDA, Fond 1-B, Record 5, File 585—Plenary Meeting, 31 July 1963, p. 4.

19. Ibid., Record 51, File 429—Letter from CC RWP to CC CPSU, 4 Jan. 1965, pp. 1–10.

20. Ibid., File 52—Letter from W. Ulbricht to CC BCP, 28 Nov. 1964, p. 8.

21. Ibid., Record 34, File 1—Joint CC BCP—Ministerial Plenary meeting, 26 Jan. 1965, pp. 20, 26, 29–30.

22. Constantin Botoran, Mihaj Retegan, and Alesandru Dutu, *Transylvania and the Romanian-Hungarian Relations. A New Approach* (Bucharest: Institute of Military History and Theory, 1993), 113.

23. The dispute between Gomułka and Ceaușescu flared up at the Warsaw Pact summit in Bucharest in July 1966. See CDA, Fond 1-B, Record 34, File 39—CC BCP Plenary meeting, 12 July 1966, pp. 112, 126; CDA, Fond 378-B, Record 1, File 177, pp. 1–19—Verbatim Record of the Warsaw Pact summit plenary discussions, Bucharest, 4–5 July 1966.

24. CDA, Fond 378-B, Record 1, File 152—Information on Nicolae Ceaușescu visit in Sofia and his talks with Todor Zhivkov, 20 Sept. 1965, pp. 2, 19–20.

25. Ibid., File 732—Todor Zhivkov Report at a Joint CC BCP and Ministerial Plenary meeting, 31 July 1967, pp. 29–31.

26. AMVR, Fond 3, Record 4, File 282—Report from 4 Nov. 1966, pp. 1–2.

27. Central Military Archive, Veliko Turnovo, Fond 1027, Record 13, File 13, pp. 59–60.

28. AMVR, Fond 1, Record 10, Files 749, 1532.

29. Ibid., Files 837, 1660.

30. Ibid., File 879—Information on the talks with Yuri Andropov, 5 Mar. 1972.

31. See Zbigniew Brzezinski, *The Soviet Bloc: Unity and Conflict* (Cambridge, Mass.: Harvard Univ. Press, 1967).

32. Answering a question by NATO secretary general Manlio Brosio regarding the forthcoming surprise visit to Bucharest by President Richard Nixon in July 1969, Dr. Henry Kissinger ststed that "the U.S. does not recognize one Communist country over another—

which would tend to lend support to the Brezhnev doctrine. . . . It would be absurd now to assert that the U.S. was jeopardizing East-West, particularly US-USSR, relations by a visit to Romania. The U.S. does not want now, on this account, to be accused of reverse linkage." General Records of the State Department, RG 59, Central Foreign Policy Files, 1967–1969, Box 1581, DEF-NATO, SYG Brosio's Discussion with Mr. Kissinger, 3 July 1969, National Archives II, College Park, Md.

13

The Sino-Soviet Conflict and the Warsaw Pact, 1969–1980

Bernd Schaefer

Introduction

Institutional links between the Warsaw Pact and the People's Republic of China (PRC) were already severed by 1961. Eventually differences over support of North Vietnam in its ongoing war with the United States, in conjunction with the launching of the "Great Proletarian Cultural Revolution" in the PRC, terminated what was left of party and other bilateral relations between Beijing and all Warsaw Pact member states except Romania.[1] Frosty political nonrelations were sometimes interrupted by incidents involving respective embassies and individual citizens in Beijing, Moscow, and Eastern Europe.[2] From 1969 onward, however, China's policies became the most serious challenge that the Soviet Union believed it faced from across its borders since World War II. As an opponent, China seemed to be of more relevance to the Warsaw Pact than during its time as an ally. At the least, it deserved significantly more attention.

Maturing from an intrasocialist ideological split into a global conflict, aggravated tensions between Moscow and Beijing became prominent issues at multi- and bilateral gatherings of the Soviet Union and its Eastern European allies for more than a decade. Despite mutual signs to differentiate between the USSR, on the one hand, and Hungary, Poland, Czechoslovakia, Bulgaria, and the GDR, on the other, the overarching conflict spilled over into bilateral relations between the PRC and individual Warsaw Pact members. Moscow defined this Chinese policy in 1971 as a two-stage approach—beginning with "Romanization" to neutralize socialist countries vis-à-vis the USSR, and eventually culminating in "Albanization" to mold them into the Chinese model.[3] In private, and outside protocol, Eastern Europeans repeatedly expressed reservations against Soviet "hegemony" and ideological rigidity. With the exception of Romania, however, dependent socialist party leaderships of Eastern Europe had to share Moscow's perspective, in spite of all nuances and uneasiness about origins and patterns of the Sino-Soviet conflict.[4]

Polemics and clashes with the PRC had begun as an intrabloc conflict but soon developed into intrasocialist ideological battles. After 1972, they became part of the familiar bloc confrontation between East and West, with a formerly "Eastern" country now considered part of the Western-led capitalist camp. Only insofar as it concerned intrasocialist debates with PRC sympathizers of varying degrees, like Romania or certain Western European Communists ("pro-Maoist opportunists" and "neutralists" in Soviet diction), did the Chinese question still figure as an element of intrabloc conflicts. From the Soviet perspective, the domestically driven Chinese journey from a member of Moscow's bloc all the way to the "antisocialist camp" was unprecedented in the history of Marxist movements and "an entirely new phenomenon."[5]

By 1980, China had become, in Moscow's view, more dangerous than ever as it continued to "side with imperialism" as a de facto ally of the three "capitalist centers"—that is, the United States, Western Europe, and Japan. Such thinking constituted the exact fulfillment of Soviet internal predictions from as early as the fall of 1969.[6] Participating in a "conspiracy" to alter global "correlations of power" with capitalist economic and military support, the PRC, according to Soviet phraseology, advanced into "great-power-chauvinism with expansionist intentions."[7] It almost looked as if Moscow had inadvertently created a fictitious mirror image of its own behavior.

1969–1972: Intrasocialist Ideological and Military Clashes

Besides individual incidents, before 1969 the acrimonious polemics between Beijing and Moscow had not crossed the line to armed conflict. Nonetheless, suspicions existed within the Warsaw Pact concerning how China might intentionally increase "adventurism" to avert attention from domestic crises. A Polish delegate verbalized such sentiments in January 1969 in Berlin during a multilateral gathering of representatives from the International Departments of Communist Parties of the "fraternal countries" (USSR, Czechoslovakia, GDR, Bulgaria, Hungary, Poland, Mongolia).[8] Those internal meetings on China ("Interkit"), first convened in December 1967 in Moscow, became the regular Warsaw Pact forum in which views on developments in Chinese domestic and foreign policy were raised and propagandistic measures were supposed to be coordinated. The Soviet Union drafted "protocols" in advance for each participating delegation to sign at the end of the meeting. Discussion was mostly stifled during the formal sessions, but informally there was at least some maneuvering room to address nuances in perspectives and search for generally acceptable compromise language. Next to the steamrolling Soviet delegation and its faithful Mongolian followers, the East Germans most eagerly participated in discussing and editing final documents of such meetings. Their results were supposed to be forwarded and approved by each national politburo.

Participants in the 1969 Berlin meeting concurred that, for the PRC, "Soviet revisionism" appeared more dangerous than the United States. Meeting participants maintained that Maoism aspired to become the "third ideological force" in international affairs besides capitalism and socialism and the new "center of world revolution." Such an assessment was anything but beyond the point. Except for the tightly controlled countries from the pro-Soviet socialist camp, there was indeed a steady rise in fascination with Maoism to observe in leftist movements and groups all around the globe.[9]

Meanwhile in Washington, the Nixon administration had just come into power and harbored only distant dreams about future rapprochement with Beijing. Still, Warsaw Pact representatives at the 1969 Berlin Interkit took an upcoming Chinese understanding with the United States almost for granted, provided Washington would disengage from Vietnam. To avoid such developments, the Soviets still employed the wishful thinking that the "Mao Group's current hold" on the PRC might turn out to be only temporary.

Several Sino-Soviet clashes at the eastern border on 2 and 15 March 1969, and some follow-ups in both east and west until 13 August 1969, changed the equation forever against Soviet interests. From everything that has become known thus far, small-scale "provocations" might have started from the Chinese side without any orchestrated strategy from the top (interestingly enough, coinciding with similar incidents along the Chinese–North Korean border in the same month).[10] But it was Moscow's massive military response with two battalions and rocket launchers attacking up to seven kilometers deep into PRC territory, resulting in heavy Chinese casualties, which exacerbated the incidents beyond proportion. While the Soviet media hailed the "heroes of Damansky island," this significantly increased Mao's paranoia about a looming attack from the north[11] and eventually furthered Beijing's moves toward rapprochement with the United States in due course.[12]

Although China was eventually not mentioned in the final communiqué, the situation in the Far East completely overshadowed the PCC meeting in Budapest on 17 March 1969.[13] Convened to implement institutional reform in the Warsaw Pact and issue an appeal for a European Security Conference, participants assembled at the verge of a Sino-Soviet war. Unbeknownst to them, while traveling to the Hungarian meeting by train, Leonid Brezhnev had personally ordered the devastating rocket attack on China two days earlier during a stop.[14] Now Eastern Europeans faced the prospect of becoming involved in a conflict by Moscow's invocation of military assistance. Nicolae Ceauşescu's vivid account of his nightly discussions with Brezhnev and Kosygin provides the dramatic background.[15] Because of Romania's stubborn refusal to sign a joint statement containing any language on China, all Eastern European alliance members were actually saved from being drawn into a potential conflict.

After the shock over an ideological battle's bloody turn in early 1969 and another step toward the brink of conflict in August of that year, both Beijing and Moscow grew eager not to have the situation escalate into an all-out war. Conversely, both sides constantly expected the other to prepare for battle and fueled domestic hysteria by incendiary pieces in the party-controlled media and internal alert measures. Mao's exploitation of the clashes even exceeded Moscow's paranoid actions in this regard: the 1968 military intervention in Czechoslovakia was ever more considered as a test case for the PRC. Afraid of a preemptive Soviet decapitation strike against the Beijing-concentrated Chinese leadership, Mao ordered evacuations and scattered most of them, beginning in late October 1969, over various places in the Chinese provinces. Preceding these actions, his anointed successor, Vice Chairman Lin Biao, had issued on 17 October an emergency directive "Strengthen War Readiness Against a Surprise Enemy Attack," the so-called Order Number 1.[16] It served as a convenient pretext to send hundreds of bewildered low-level functionaries and cadres from cities into provinces, allegedly for their own safety, but in fact to continue and further the Cultural Revolution.[17] The meeting between prime ministers Zhou Enlai and Andrei Kosygin at Beijing Airport on 11 September 1969 might have relaxed to some extent immediate military-related tensions by freezing the status quo,[18] but the paranoid faction in the Chinese leadership soon prevailed again in setting the agenda. At least the airport conversation temporarily opened some bilateral talks—if one prefers to use such a term for two years of fruitless, and rancorous, Sino-Soviet border negotiations held in Beijing. Despite Kosygin's request and Zhou's possible inclinations, Mao refused to stop public polemics against the USSR. Though the latter did suspend anti-Chinese propaganda for about three months, China had to continue it by the chairman's decision. "Nobody will die from polemics," Mao philosophically remarked. "The fish will continue to swim in the water; the women will further give birth to children." In the mid-1960s the PRC leader had famously quipped that hostilities would last for ten thousand years; however, recent quotations by the Great Helmsman now reduced this figure to eight thousand.

During this period the Soviet Union constantly informed leaders of the "fraternal" Warsaw Pact countries (that is, except Romania) through secret information and internal meetings about Soviet-Sino relations, border negotiations, and Moscow's alleged efforts to mend fences. Despite detailed elaborations on self-righteous Soviet claims over disputed areas, dating back to the Russian-Sino Treaty of 1861, even the fraternal allies seemed to have problems deciding who was "right" on the border issue. Chinese maximalist positions seemed likewise unacceptable. Above all, the PRC intended to thwart any kind of agreement, or, to quote Zhou Enlai, there would be no border agreement in "10, 20, or 30 years."[19] Talks in Beijing moved on because, for the moment, nobody wanted to call them off first and also because they might have helped both sides to gather some intelligence on the intentions of the other side.

Guided by Mao's vaunted insights, China remained on a countrywide war footing and stayed on alert to fight off alleged Soviet military attacks ("All Mountains and Valleys: A Single Military Camp" or "Make 700 Million People into 700 Million Soldiers"). Because these fears had no basis according to Soviet declarations, assumptions still cannot be corroborated from any insights into Moscow's secret military planning vis-à-vis China during this period. An offer for a mutual non-aggression treaty with the PRC, linked to a border agreement on Soviet terms in 1970 (while omitting this condition in 1971), partially countered such rumors. For Beijing, such a treaty was out of the question and viewed as insulting: from the Chinese perspective it placed both countries on the same level, assumed potentially aggressive intentions and preparations on both sides, and asked for mutual containment similar to patterns of U.S.-Soviet relations.

As far as Moscow's fraternal allies were concerned, they clearly were highly critical of Maoism's ideological underpinnings, but they also were not entirely pleased with Soviet positions. The majority of participants attending an international conference of Communist parties between 5 and 17 June 1969 in Moscow had condemned China on a broad scale by signing onto USSR positions. Though the final joint declaration was much vaguer, the Soviets considered the meeting as a binding statement issued by the "majority" of the global Communist movement. What the convention actually failed to convey, Moscow subsequently attempted to make up by relentless propagandistic exploitation of the meeting's pro-Soviet statements. Still, for achieving true socialist unity even the USSR's closest allies would have preferred a sincere search for ideological compromise over constant propagandistic "unmasking." The Soviet position continued to raise global curiosity about China's course and Maoism and made it easy for Beijing to equate both hostile "superpowers" and claim the mantle of "Third World" leadership.

Maverick Romania was a special case, neither having positive influence in the Warsaw Pact nor carrying enough weight to act as an honest broker between Moscow and Beijing. Ceaușescu vacillated in many directions, in turn, sometimes behaving in accordance with expectations, while other times counteracting from protocol, drawing the wrath of Brezhnev and other leaders. Brezhnev knew the idiosyncratic "*Conducător*" all too well: "Ceaușescu is no hero. If he feels pressure, he retreats."[20] By courageously blocking any joint resolutions on China merely by its presence at meetings, however, Romania objectively limited military implications of Sino-Soviet tensions to the two antagonists themselves. This relieved other Eastern European states skeptical of certain Soviet postures and positions from raising their own criticism during Warsaw Pact meetings. Moreover, it saved them from signing up for unintended consequences for potential military engagement in Asia.

Whereas the actual date of Sino-U.S. rapprochement in 1971–72 might have surprised Moscow and its allies, the long-expected fact itself did not. Still, it was difficult for the USSR to swallow when it eventually occurred. Developments ran parallel with the PRC's admission into the United Nations at the expense of Taiwan, a move that the Warsaw Pact had always advocated and consequently supported in October 1971. The sheer extent of Soviet diplomacy with Washington alone made it impossible for Moscow to deny the PRC the right to normalize its relations with the United States and break out of its long years of international isolation. Preventing, or even publicly denouncing, the rapprochement between Beijing and Washington was no option for the USSR. In retaliation, Brezhnev wanted to "counter" the Sino-U.S. opening by establishing closer ties with Vietnam at Beijing's expense. "We must continue to be cold-blooded and vigilant at the same time," explained the Soviet leader in August 1971 on Crimea Island to his fellow general secretaries from the Eastern European fraternal countries.[21] Otherwise, Moscow put on a brave face in an unfavorable development. Rather haplessly, it sought to downplay the significance of the February 1972 Chinese-U.S. summit in Beijing,[22] presenting the May 1972 meeting between Brezhnev and Nixon in Moscow as actually the much more important encounter for shaping global policy.

Until late 1972, the Sino-Soviet conflict still remained within the framework of traditional intrasocialist dispute over ideology and hegemonic theories. Both protagonists addressed the global socialist camp and accused opponents of being "revisionists," thus attacking them from "leftist" positions. In quantitative terms of numerical adherence among Communist parties, this battle was to Beijing's loss despite some scattered successes in several countries on almost all continents. China worked hard to achieve and prove ideological parity with the Soviet Union: in 1970, the PRC counted around eighty Maoist groups in fifty different countries,[23] with the fiftieth anniversary of the CCP in 1971 registering thirty-five congratulatory letters from major groupings worldwide.[24] With his globalist rhetoric of "antihegemonism" directed against Moscow and Washington alike, Mao aspired for China to be the leader of "medium and small countries." Beijing's leftist course of the early 1970s was also indicative of, for instance, its evaluation of détente and Eastern responsiveness to German *Ostpolitik*. From the beginning of talks between Bonn and Moscow, the Soviets were accused of irresponsible accommodation and "dirty business" with capitalist West Germany, "betrayal" of socialism, and selling out the GDR and Eastern Europe.[25] In the long run, however, China had to adapt its own "Westpolitik" in Europe according to the new Soviet approach on that continent.

1972–1980: China's "Rightist Turn" and Change of Sides

At a time when the "antihegemonic" course seemed to gain some global ground and credibility, Mao began to confuse friend and foe with a gradual switch to "rightist" foreign policies when he sensed, in his perception, unprecedented attention to his country and his personal leadership from all across the "capitalist" world. Losing the "Cultural Revolution ally" of Chinese resources–draining Albania seemed quite bearable in this context. In the aftermath of its accession to the United Nations and the Sino-U.S. rapprochement, China was swept by Westerners lining up to establish diplomatic relations, business ties, and cultural exchanges. Still driven by manic fear of Moscow's intentions, the PRC used this opportunity to admonish, and lecture, Western visitors to be more firm against Soviet aggressiveness. According to Zhou's talk with West German foreign minister Walter Scheel in October 1972 on the occasion of the establishment of diplomatic relations between Beijing and Bonn, the USSR wanted the Conference on Security and Cooperation in Europe and détente on the continent only to have its hands free for aggression against China. The West German government and other Western Europeans, however, did not give heed to Chinese calls and were eager to continue détente vis-à-vis the Soviet Union and its Eastern European allies. "We are not going to replace our 'Eastern policy' (*Ostpolitik*) by a 'Far Eastern policy' (*Fernostpolitik*)," Bonn famously quipped. As a result, Chinese policy literally turned further to the "right." PRC leaders openly allied China with causes of Western opponents of détente like Franz-Josef Strauss in West Germany[26] and, in Moscow's words, the "émigré scum" and "the renegade Solzhenitsyn."[27]

By early 1973, a point of no return into the global socialist movement had been reached. Gradually, the PRC's policies became out of sync with almost any government line in the East and West. In ideological terms, China now relied mostly on fiercely anti-Soviet conservatives, scattered sectarian Maoists, and a few adherents in the "Third World." Otherwise, Beijing's course and China's potential were open for pragmatic use by the Western alliance. Its representatives seized opportunities to establish diplomatic and other ties with the PRC, listening along the way to Chinese exhortations to bolster their military forces against the USSR. Attention was reciprocal; between January and July 1973 alone about two dozen articles about various NATO activities appeared in the Chinese press.[28] Perceptions about peculiar Chinese obsessions notwithstanding, Western interests in China remained unchanged. Leaders from NATO countries and elsewhere were particularly eager to have a personal meeting with Mao Zedong as a highlight of their visits to the PRC. Because they were aware of the chairman's exhortations, Mao commented upon the unveiled skepticism of his conversation partners with self-irony.[29]

Since early 1974, another revival of domestic preoccupation with cultural revolution campaigns ("Criticism of Lin Biao and Confucius"),[30] actually launched also against Zhou Enlai and impairing his decision making, threw China's foreign policy conduct into disarray. Human mortality further exacerbated the situation: both

Mao and Zhou were ailing, and the jockeying for leadership positions after their foreseeable deaths in the near future had considerable impact. Some Western sympathizers became temporarily confused, and fresh converts to Maoism were hardly won, but vilification of the Soviet Union remained constant. The latter persisted in its efforts to "unmask Maoism as a parasite to Marxism's healthy body," following Lenin's prophecy that a "correct theoretical decision" will guarantee "permanent success of agitation."[32]

In Moscow's perception, China under Mao had become a "dangerous, devious, and persistent opponent" with powerful potential.[32] For the USSR this meant more than ever that it had to "prepare a significant part of its economic and military potential for protection against the adventurist actions of the Mao Group."[33] This quote actually comes from the Third Interkit Meeting in Warsaw back in March 1970, but gradually such sentiments became ever more prevalent. Moscow expected China to strive for nuclear forces matching the two superpowers: the PRC would willfully ignore disarmament talks, instead promoting its own nuclear testing (eighteen atomic tests between October 1964 and January 1976, two of them underground). By 1976, the Soviets internally talked about a danger of war with the PRC in similar terms as in 1969. Chinese policy and propaganda proceeded in kind. It is still unclear as to what Moscow had actually planned in terms of possible preemptive strikes against China's nuclear potential.

The Sino-Soviet border measured around 7,500 kilometers in length. Including the Mongolian-Chinese frontier, it amounted to 12,500 kilometers. According to Soviet counts from December 1972, China amassed more than two million troops along these borders and fortified the hinterland. Soviet satellite reconnaissance identified in 1973 more than 70 percent of Chinese ground forces concentrated in this area. More than 50 percent of the PRC's air force with more than a thousand aircraft were spotted in border regions. The USSR appeared to panic and mirrored Beijing's conspiracies: "From Soviet perspective, the danger from the West does not exceed the threat from the East."[34] In 1977, Moscow had more expenditures for defending the 12,500-kilometer border with China against its now three million troops there than for the entire Warsaw Pact combined. Moscow seriously feared that Chinese forces would attack, launching an all-out war.[35]

Mao's death on 9 September 1976 and the removal of some Cultural Revolution leaders ("Gang of Four") raised slight hopes in the Warsaw Pact for modification of China's foreign policy course. East Germany's politburo issued a decree on 26 October 1976 voicing hopes for rapprochement between Beijing and Moscow and normalization and improvement of relations with all countries of the Warsaw Pact: "It goes without saying that such a development would work to the advantage of the cause of peace and socialism."[36]

According to a conversation involving an East German representative in the CPSU Central Committee's International Relations Department on 13 December 1976, the Soviet leadership held three different opinions concerning Beijing's future course:

(1) Same regime, same policy, just a different helmsman; (2) sincere change of the regime, de-Maoization, return to the path of socialism; (3) partial de-Maoization pertaining to Cultural Revolution exaggerations, keeping major patterns of regime, saving Mao's face by portraying "Gang of Four" as exclusive scapegoats.[37]

Overall skepticism prevailed and dire Soviet predictions were soon confirmed. The anti-Soviet legacy of Mao's rule, as well as Moscow's behavior, had long-term repercussions and resulted in Beijing's continuation of the same foreign policy regarding the Soviet Union. The Chinese side refused even to receive substantial Soviet communication, as when it rejected Moscow's telegrams on the occasions of Mao's death and Hua Guofeng's appointment as chairman.

Besides maintaining friendly relations with Romania, Yugoslavia, and North Korea, China increasingly displayed sincere respect toward Moscow's close Eastern European allies. The PRC considered them as involuntarily suffering under Soviet domination. The Soviets raised their vigilance level to watch, and thwart, bilateral contacts between China and Warsaw Pact members, which they considered Beijing's attempts toward "selective normalization"[38] for undermining the Moscow-oriented socialist camp. It became increasingly difficult for the Soviets to hold the allies in check with regard to economic cooperation, however, once China had begun to follow the path of "modernization."

At the same time, the USSR remained deaf to any Eastern European suggestions to modify policies toward the PRC and exclusively blamed the latter for antagonism and acrimony in bilateral relations. From Moscow's vantage point, it was China's responsibility to change its course and move toward the orthodox ideology of the Soviet Union. The USSR leadership thought there was nothing innovatively required on its side but to appeal, closely study Beijing's behavior and actions, and hope for Chinese conversion and repentance to happen. Quite revealing after 1980, exasperated Eastern European partners no longer jointly signed Soviet, preformulated China-denouncing "protocols" of Interkit meetings.

In general, the Soviet-Sino confrontation deteriorated to a level where China became economically, politically, and militarily closer to the West than would ever had been imaginable during the life of Mao Zedong. Whereas the volatile factions of infighting functionaries in Beijing, attempting to lead the PRC in the aftermath of Mao's death, continued, and preserved the Great Helmsman's anti-Sovietism, they substituted his skepticism toward capitalist Western nations for their open embrace of modernizing China. From the Soviet perspective this was tantamount to the West's arming of the PRC for territorial conflicts in Asia and along the border with the USSR. The leading China specialist in the CPSU's Central Committee, Oleg Borisovich Rachmanin, told his Eastern European colleagues on 25 May 1978, "It's important to explain to the world openly and convincingly: Maoism—that's war, that's revision of the status quo. Increasingly we must emphasize territorial questions in the wake of our confrontation."[39]

At the regular Warsaw Pact PCC meeting on 22 November 1978 in Moscow, Leonid Brezhnev lashed out against China and called it a "quite attractive ally of imperialism." The PRC would be propped up with Western arms in order to be encouraged to hostile actions against socialist countries, as had happened in 1938 with Hitler through the Munich Agreement: "[NATO's] economic and military cooperation with China . . . becomes ever more real. Who does not get this, has little understanding of the current international situation."[40] The Tenth Interkit meeting, convened in Havana from 11 to 13 December 1978, heeded Brezhnev's call and accused Beijing's "warmongering" policy of creating acute and present dangers in a reckless alliance with the United States. A "united front between Chinese social-chauvinism and the imperialists" would represent "the most grave danger of our times."[41] At his reception for the Interkit delegations at the end of the meeting, Cuban leader Fidel Castro repeated Brezhnev's comparison and outlined a scenario where the imperialist powers were stimulating China's belligerency in the same vein as the Western powers allegedly did with Hitler in 1938 at the Munich conference.[42]

Whereas "Munich" had eventually resulted in the beleaguered Soviet Union's 1939 signing of a nonaggression treaty, including a secret protocol on Poland, with Hitler's Germany, this time there were no Soviet intentions to appease the opponent. Moscow felt highly challenged by the full normalization of relations between Washington and Beijing in January 1979 and became paranoid over worldwide anti-Soviet conspiracies. China had not even bothered to declare the 1950 Sino-Soviet treaty terminated; it expired three months after China established diplomatic relations with the United States. By the summer of 1980, the world seemed to become "ever more dangerous" for Moscow, now with the United States, NATO, Japan, and the PRC allegedly in one boat and "ever more intensively advancing militarily in Asia, from the eastern Indian Ocean to the Persian Gulf, and in Africa."[43] Détente with the West, on a sickbed for quite some time, finally died in 1979 with the Soviet military intervention in Afghanistan. It hardly occurred to the USSR leadership how their own actions had played a role in those developments or, for that matter, how the USSR's China policy since 1969 could serve as the epitome for misreading other nations out of high-handed ideological convictions. Accusations of Beijing striving "to become a world power by 2000," a political center bound to "international hegemony," domestically based on nationalism and "superpower-chauvinism," seemed rather odd, or ironic, when coming from the Moscow of the 1970s and early 1980s.[44] In Brezhnev's Soviet Union there was not even a slight chance for a self-reflective debate over "who lost China."

Notes

I want to thank German Historical Institute interns Liz Benning and Helmut Strauss for their valuable assistance with this essay.

1. See Chen Jian, *Mao's China and the Cold War* (Chapel Hill: Univ. of N.C. Press, 2001), 205–37; and Qiang Zhai, *China and the Vietnam Wars, 1950–1975* (Chapel Hill: Univ. of N.C. Press, 2000), 130–75.

2. See, for example, documentation on incidents involving the PRC and the German Democratic Republic (GDR) in 1967: Werner Meissner, ed., *DDR und China bis 1990: Politik-Wirtschaft-Kultur. Eine Quellensammlung* (Berlin: Akademie Verlag, 1995), 163–75.

3. Report on an Internal Meeting of Delegations from International Departments of the Central Committees in Sofia, 15–18 Feb. 1971, Foundation Archive of GDR Parties and Mass Organizations in the Federal Archive, Berlin, Germany (SAPMO-BA), DY 30, IV A 2/20/1152, p. 3.

4. Xiaoyuan Liu and Vojtech Mastny, eds., *China and Eastern Europe, 1960s–1980s: Proceedings of the International Symposium "Reviewing the History of Chinese–East European Relations from the 1960s to the 1980s"* (Zurich: ETH Forschungsstelle für Sicherheitspolitik, 2004).

5. China after the Tenth CCP Party Congress and the Adoption of Maoist Constitution (Current Problems of PRC Domestic and Foreign Policy at the Current Stage), June 1975 (Soviet Material for Eighth Interkit Ulan-Bator). SAPMO-BA, DY 30, IV B 2/20/588 (p. 73).

6. SED Central Committee, Department of International Relations, 6 Oct. 1969 (Meeting between Oleg Borisovich Rachmanin and Bruno Mahlow of 2 Oct. 1969), SAPMO-BA, DY 30, 3613.

7. Leonid Brezhnev's Speech at PCC Meeting in Warsaw on 15 May 1980, SAPMO-BA, DY 30, 2351, pp. 214–15. See also the Web site of the Parallel History Project on NATO and the Warsaw Pact (PHP): www.isn.ethz.ch/php/documents/collection_3/PCC_meetings/coll_3_PCC_1980.htm, accessed 20 June 2004.

8. Stenographic Transcript of Internal Consultation about the Situation in the PRC and the Policy of the Mao Group at the Current Stage, 28–31 Jan. 1969, Political Archive of the Foreign Office, Ministry for External Affairs of the GDR, Berlin, Germany (PolAA, MfAA), C 601/77.

9. For West Germany, see Gerd Koenen, *Das Rote Jahrzehnt. Unsere kleine deutsche Kulturrevolution 1967–1977* (Cologne: Kiepenheuer & Witsch, 2001).

10. Bernd Schaefer, "North Korean 'Adventurism' and China's Long Shadow, 1966–1972," Cold War International History Project Working Paper no. 44 (2004).

11. Yang Kuisong, "The Sino-Soviet Border Clash of 1969: From Zhenbao Island to Sino-American Rapprochement," *Cold War History* 1, no. 1 (2000): 21–52; William Burr, "Sino-American Relations. 1969: The Sino-Soviet Border War and Steps Towards Rapprochement," *Cold War History* 1, no. 3 (2001): 73–112; Lyle J. Goldstein, "Return to Zhenbao Island: Who Started Shooting and Why It Matters," *China Quarterly* 168 (2001): 985–97. See also "New Evidence on Sino-Soviet Relations," *Cold War International History Project Bulletin* 11 (winter 1998): 155–75.

12. Chen Jian, "The Path Toward Sino-American Rapprochement, 1969–1972," in *American Détente and German Ostpolitik, 1969–1972*, ed. David Geyer and Bernd Schaefer (Washington, D.C.: Bulletin of the German Historical Institute/Supplement 1, 2004), 26–52; James Lilley, *China Hands: Nine Decades of Adventure, Espionage, and Diplomacy in Asia* (New York: Public Affairs, 2004), 135–68; William Burr, ed., *The Kissinger Transcripts: The Top-Secret*

Talks with Beijing and Moscow (New York: New Press, 1999); James Mann, *About Face: A History of America's Curious Relationship with China* (New York: Alfred A. Knopf, 1999); John Holdridge, *Crossing the Divide: An Insider's Account of the Normalization of U.S.-China Relations* (Lanham, Md.: Rowman & Littlefield, 1997).

13. See in particular the Romanian and Hungarian documents on this Mar. 1969 meeting at www.isn.ethz.ch/php/documents/collection_3/PCC_docs/1969/1969_10_transl.htm and www.isn.ethz.ch/php/documents/collection_3/PCC_docs/1969/1969_12_transl.htm, both accessed 20 June 2004.

14. Tatjana Moullec-Zazerskaja, "Fighting Maoism: Soviet Isolation of China, 1964–1974." Paper presented at the conference "NATO, the Warsaw Pact, and the Rise of Détente, 1965–1972," Dobbiaco, Italy, 26–28 Sept. 2002, 9.

15. Ibid. (www.isn.ethz.ch/php/documents/collection_3/PCC_docs/1969/1969_10_transl. htm, accessed 20 June 2004). Stenographic Record of the Meeting of the Executive Committee of the Central Committee of the Romanian Communist Party, 18 Mar. 1969.

16. Deng Rong, *Deng Xiaoping and the Cultural Revolution: A Daughter Recalls the Critical Years* (Beijing: Foreign Languages Press, 2002), 106–7. See also "New Evidence on Sino-Soviet Relations," *CWIHP Bulletin* 11 (1998).

17. Wang Shu, *Maos Mann in Bonn. Vom Journalisten zum Botschafter* (Frankfurt/Main: Societaets Verlag, 2002), 30.

18. Mikhail Stepanovich Kapitsa, *Na Raznykh Parallelakh. Zapiski Diplomata* (Moscow: Kniga i Biznes, 1996), 81–92.

19. Stenographic Transcript of Friendship Meeting with Leading Representatives of Communist and Worker's Parties of Socialist Countries on 31 July 1972 [Leonid Brezhnev's Speech]. SAPMO-BA, DY 30, J IV 2/201/923, p. 32.

20. Leonid Brezhnev's Speech at the Crimea Meeting on 2 Aug. 1971 [of "fraternal" socialist leaders]. SAPMO-BA, DY 30, J IV 2/201/1570, p. 42.

21. Ibid. (quotation from p. 39).

22. See from the eve of Nixon's visit to China the internal "Presentation by Soviet Ambassador Comrade Tolstikov at the 'Club' of heads of fraternal diplomatic representations on 7 Feb. 1972 (proofread and revised according to a manuscript made available in Russian)." SAPMO-BA, DY 30, IV B 2/20/580. In English, wwics.si.edu/index.cfm?topic_id=1409&fuseaction=library.document&id=63651, accessed 20 June 2004.

23. Numbers according to Soviet material "The Chinese Problem after the IX Party Congress of the PCC," Mar. 1970 (German translation), SAPMO-BA, DY 30, IV A 2/20/1151, p. 82.

24. Numbers according to Soviet material "International Policy and Domestic Situation in the PRC in Current Conditions," July 1972 (German translation), SAPMO-BA, DY 30, IV B 2/20/580, p. 30.

25. Joachim Schickel, ed., *China—Deutschlands Partner? Politik-Kultur-Wirtschaft* (Frankfurt/Main: S. Fischer, 1974), 260–65 (translation of articles from "Renmin Ribao/People's Daily"). See also Brezhnev's Speech at PCC Meeting in Prague on 25 Jan. 1972, SAPMO-BA, DY 30, J IV 2/202/526, p. 24. Also documented in www.isn.ethz.ch/php/documents/collection_3/PCC_meetings/coll_3_PCC_1972.htm, accessed 20 June 2004.

26. Wang Shu, *Maos Mann in Bonn*, 167–73; Franz-Josef Strauss, *Die Erinnerungen* (Berlin: Siedler, 1989), 466–69; Friedrich Voss, *Den Kanzler im Visier: 20 Jahre mit Franz Josef Strauss* (Mainz/Munich: von Hase und Koehler, 1999), 350–84.

27. Confidential CPSU Information [to Warsaw Pact leaders], "On Soviet-Sino Relations," Mar. 1974, SAPMO-BA, DY 30, IV B 2/20/127, p. 4.

28. According to Soviet count. Secret CPSU Information [to Warsaw Pact leaders], 9 July 1973, SAPMO-BA, DY 30, J IV 2/202/542.

29. Wang Shu, *Maos Mann in Bonn,* 186; Helmut Schmidt, *Menschen und Maechte* (Berlin: Siedler, 1987), 362.

30. Joachim Schickel, ed., *Konfuzius: Materialien zu einer Jahrhundert-Debatte* (Frankfurt/ Main: Insel Verlag, 1976).

31. Speech by Oleg B. Rachmanin at Seventh Interkit in Budapest, 25 Mar. 1974, SAPMO-BA, DY 30, IV B 2/20/586, p. 45.

32. Confidential CPSU Information [to Warsaw Pact leaders], "On Soviet-Sino Relations," Mar. 1974, SAPMO-BA, DY 30, IV B 2/20/127, p. 7.

33. Report on Internal Meeting of Representatives from International Departments of the Central Committees in Warsaw, 10–13 Mar. 1970, SAPMO-BA, DY 30, IV A 2/20/1151, p. 2.

34. Memorandum on a conversation [of GDR politburo member Hermann Axen] with Comrade O. B. Rachmanin (deputy of a CPSU Central Committee Department), on 28 Feb. 1973 in Moscow, SAPMO-BA, DY 30, IV 2/2.035/55, pp. 20–21.

35. Memorandum of a conversation of Hermann Axen with Comrade O. B. Rachmanin on 17 June 1977 in Berlin, SAPMO-BA, DY 30, IV B 2/20/126, p. 3.

36. SED Politburo, Information about Events in the PRC, Decree of 26 Oct. 1976, SAPMO-BA, DY 30, IV 2/2.033/61.

37. Helmut Peters, Memorandum of a conversation in Department IV of CC of CPSU on 13 Dec. 1976, SAPMO-BA, DY 30, IV B 2/20/126.

38. [Secret CPSU] Information [to Warsaw Pact Leaders] about the Situation in China and the Policy of the PRC's New Leadership, 17 Jan. 1977, SAPMO-BA, DY 30, J IV 2/202/543.

39. GDR Institute for Foreign Relations/Helmut Peters, Memorandum on Remarks by Comrade O. B. Rachmanin, Candidate of the CPSU's Central Committee and First Deputy of the International Relations' Department Chairman, during the Conference of the International Commission of Socialist Countries for Far Eastern Problems on 25 May 1978 in Moscow, SAPMO-BA, DY 30, IV B 2/20/126.

40. Leonid Brezhnev's Speech at PCC Meeting in Moscow on 22 Nov. 1978. See www.isn. ethz.ch/php/documents/collection_3/PCC_meetings/coll_3_PCC_1978.htm, accessed 20 June 2004.

41. Protocol of the Tenth Internal China Meeting. SAPMO-BA, DY 30, IV B 2/20/592.

42. GDR Embassy Havana, Telegram to Honecker/Axen, 14 Dec. 1978, SAPMO-BA, DY 30, IV B 2/20/592.

43. Leonid Brezhnev's Speech at PCC Meeting in Warsaw on 15 May 1980. See www.isn. ethz.ch/php/documents/collection_3/PCC_meetings/coll_3_PCC_1980.htm, accessed 20 June 2004.

44. [Secret CPSU] Information [to Warsaw Pact Leaders] about the Situation in China and Beijing's Current Course of Foreign Policy, 12 Apr. 1977, SAPMO-BA, DY 30, J IV 2/202/543. It is interesting to note that the Soviets internally predicted that in 2000 China would reach the economic standard of the 1975 USSR and the 1959 USA. In 1977, Moscow identified China's state of science and technology with the Soviet Union of 1952–54.

14

Why Was There No "Second Cold War" in Europe?

Hungary and the East-West Crisis Following

the Soviet Invasion of Afghanistan

Csaba Békés

Belatedly Informed Soviet Allies

On 28 December 1979 Soviet ambassador Vladimir Pavlov forwarded a highly confidential communication on the Soviet intervention in Afghanistan to the Hungarian Communist Party leadership. Its closing sentence was meant to be an excuse for the total lack of preliminary communication between Moscow and its Warsaw Pact allies concerning the Soviet policy decision: "Our friends will naturally also understand that the development of events did not make a preliminary exchange of opinions possible for us." Although the Hungarian "friends" never made it public, they did not at all understand why they had to be informed about an event of such importance from the news.[1]

In fact, in the years following the 1962 Cuban missile crisis, the invasion of Afghanistan was the first and only case when the East-Central European allies had to face a fait accompli concerning Moscow's unexpected initiative in a serious international crisis. In 1962, too, the Hungarian leadership had been disconcerted about that humiliating situation. János Kádár, first secretary of the Hungarian Socialist Workers' Party (HSWP) and prime minister, did not hide his frustration when, during a meeting with Nikita Khrushchev in July 1963, he warned the Soviet leader, "The point is that there should not occur such a situation when the Soviet government publishes different declarations and the other governments read them in the newspaper. . . . I have thought of preliminary consultation. . . . According to our experiences it is better to quarrel before rather than after the events." To avoid similar situations and to compel Moscow to inform its allies regularly about its intentions, Kádár suggested the establishment of a council of foreign ministers for the Warsaw Pact.[2]

Although the Hungarian proposal was turned down at the meeting, deputy foreign ministers of the Warsaw Pact member states, now on Soviet initiative, began to meet regularly from early 1964, often several times annually, and other forums of consultation gradually developed. Eventually, a more or less functional mechanism for Moscow to inform its East-Central European allies regularly on important international issues evolved at the meetings of the Warsaw Pact Political Consultative Committee from 1965, the Warsaw Pact Council of Defense Ministers from 1969, and the Council of Foreign Ministers from 1976. There were also consultations for the ruling parties' Central Committee secretaries for foreign affairs starting at the end of the 1960s.

Reflecting on earlier crises inside the Soviet bloc, Hungarian leaders believed that it would not have been impossible for Moscow to consult with its allies even on very short notice. Just before crushing the Hungarian revolution in 1956, Khrushchev and his associates personally visited the heads of five countries (Poland, Czechoslovakia, Bulgaria, Romania, and Yugoslavia) at four locations in the course of only two days.[3] A half-year-long series of very intensive bilateral and multilateral consultations preceded the invasion of Czechoslovakia by the Warsaw Pact states in August 1968. That precedent was especially significant for the Hungarian leadership since Kádár personally played a prominent role in mediating between the Soviet and Czechoslovak leaders.[4] During the Vietnam War, too, Moscow regularly informed its East-Central European allies about the current Soviet position. The Conference for Security and Cooperation in Europe (CSCE) process, starting in 1969 and culminating in the signing of the Helsinki Final Act in 1975, just four years before the invasion of Afghanistan, resulted in extensive efforts for cooperation and harmonization of joint positions with the Soviet bloc. The Eastern European states played a key role in the process that was unprecedented in the bloc's history.[5]

As far as the situation in Afghanistan was concerned, Moscow regularly provided confidential information to its allies following the "revolution" in April 1978. This policy suggested that Moscow seriously considered the allies in its planning and that they therefore had every reason to believe that an important initiative, such as the invasion of Afghanistan, would not be launched without preliminary consultation with the members of the alliance. It is now known that the Communist Party of the Soviet Union (CPSU) Politburo decision on the invasion was taken on 12 December 1979,[6] so in fact there was sufficient time for such consultation.

First Reactions

Because Hungary was a committed member of the group of "closely cooperating socialist countries"—defined as the Warsaw Pact members minus Romania—there was little to do other than accept the Soviet explanation and follow the general line of the bloc in areas of propaganda. Initially, this did not seem to cause too much trouble, because Hungary's main concern was to maintain its good political and, above all, economic relations with the West, especially dynamically developing links with Western Europe since the mid-1970s.

Unlike the case of the Warsaw Pact's intervention in Czechoslovakia in August 1968, Hungary would not be directly involved as a participant in the international crisis concerning Afghanistan. According to the official Hungarian position developed in the first weeks following Moscow's intervention, Soviet support for the Afghan revolutionary forces constituted not an internal affair of the Warsaw Pact but rather a bilateral issue between the Soviet Union and Afghanistan.[7]

Initially, the Hungarian leadership did not foresee that the Afghan crisis might have serious consequences for East-West trade and economic relations, crucially important for Hungary. In terms of precedents, there had been no Western economic retaliation even after 1968, when Hungary participated in the harshly condemned invasion of Czechoslovakia. In fact, quite the opposite resulted as the dynamic phase of the CSCE process commenced scarcely six months after the crushing of the Prague Spring: in March 1969 the Warsaw Pact had issued its well-known Budapest Declaration for the convening of an all-European security conference. Although it took some time for the West to adjust its policies to the new challenge coming from the East, the serious intention to pursue Realpolitik was clearly illustrated in the recently discovered initiative of President Lyndon B. Johnson to ask Leonid Brezhnev to organize a summit meeting in the Soviet Union as early as September 1968.[8]

It therefore did not seem improbable for Hungary to maintain its main foreign policy objectives, even under the circumstances of the crisis—Hungary would work to preserve and develop its dynamically improving and balanced political and economic relations with the West and Western Europe, in particular, while sustaining its status as a loyal, reliable, and predictable partner in the Eastern bloc. As a result, the reaction of the Hungarian leadership to the crisis was initially rather enervated.

The political leadership first discussed the situation in an official party forum only on 8 January 1980,[9] about two weeks after the Soviet intervention in Afghanistan, and even then, as an issue among the so-called miscellaneous topics.[10] Moreover, Kádár, on holiday at that time, did not return to his office even after hearing the news, and Prime Minister György Lázár was also absent from the meeting. They evidently did not consider the situation too alarming from Hungary's vantage point. In spite of this general response, several participants in the session of the political committee evaluated events critically, even expressing their concern that inadequate consideration of the crisis might have a long-lasting negative effect on East-West relations. Former prime minister Jenő Fock ventured to compare the situation in Afghanistan with the intervention in Czechoslovakia in 1968. He postulated that there had then been no one to ask for Moscow's help legally and that this time, too, the new government was formed only after the Soviet invasion. Moreover, in this instance it became obvious for everyone that official propaganda, following the Soviet line, had initially labeled Hafizullah Amin[11] a friend of the Soviet Union in a rather misleading way, but now he became an adventurer who had been killing honest Communists.

Károly Németh, similarly pessimistic about the situation, argued that Western Europe had been divided concerning the issue of Euromissiles,[12] and in the West, too, relevant social forces stood up defiantly against the deployment of missiles. Owing to the Soviet intervention in Afghanistan, however, this favorable situation would change in a negative direction for the Eastern bloc, and the crisis would pose serious problems in the international workers' movement as well. Finally, as if foreseeing the dangerous consequences of the escalation of the crisis for Hungary, he formulated his main concern in the following manner: "We should do our best in the field of politics, in international relations to prevent—that is, the socialist countries should not provoke—such mutual pressure, stoppage, rigidity, refusal in international life as 'unless you deliver corn, we will not deliver oil.' This does not exclude the necessity of such a step. But to try to maximally avoid it is also in the interest of the socialist world."

At the end of the debate, the political committee undertook one specific task relating to Afghanistan: to approve the text of the government declaration published on 10 January 1980. Political committee members agreed that the document should express Hungary's solidarity with the new Afghan leadership but that the Soviet intervention should be mentioned in the most reserved tone possible. At the same time, the closing sentence stated the Hungarian leadership's undiminished resolution to preserve the achievements of détente, a statement that went beyond a mere obligatory reference in the post-Helsinki international discourse. This was probably the most important message of the declaration, the delivery of which they did not leave to chance.

The Horn Mission in the United States and Canada

Although many people worried about the effect of the harsh American reaction to the invasion on the future of East-West relations, for the Hungarian leadership it was reassuring that both the Soviet leaders (Brezhnev in his speech of 16 January) and most key politicians in Western Europe, including West German chancellor Helmut Schmidt, made it clear that there was a strong joint interest in maintaining the results of détente.

Gyula Horn, then deputy head of the HSWP Central Committee International Department, conveyed this Hungarian hope during a special mission to the United States and Canada in January 1980.[13] He was officially designated as a "diplomatic courier" to visit party organizations preparing for the impending HSWP congress, but the Hungarian embassies in Washington and Ottawa informed the diplomatic services about the presence of the Hungarian official, which then resulted in meetings.[14] Leading State Department officials stressed that by 1979 the general balance of power in the arms race of the two superpowers had shifted in favor of Moscow and that the Soviet Union's military intervention in Afghanistan had caused a distinctly qualitative change in East-West relations. The United States therefore had to take the necessary military steps to ensure the protection of its basic interests. These developments, they warned, could be expected to set back greatly the process of détente.

The Hungarian ambassador organized a session for Horn in New York with "leading representatives of great financial and economic monopolies and religious organizations," who warned that the Soviet Union had to "prepare for an extremely hard fight" and indicated that the Soviet Union's intervention in Afghanistan meant the removal of the last barriers on the road leading to increasing the defensive capabilities of the United States and its allies. At the same time, they also predicted that for the execution of this program a stronger leader than Jimmy Carter was required as the winner of the upcoming presidential elections.[15]

Regarding bilateral relations, State Department officials emphasized that the United States still followed a discriminating approach in its policy concerning the East-Central European countries. They emphasized that in the pending difficult period with an anticipated deterioration in Soviet-American relations these states would acquire an important role and could ensure continuity in maintaining the policy of détente. They called the Hungarian leadership's attention to the fact that U.S.-Hungarian economic relations and, specifically, the most-favored-nation status achieved just two years earlier in 1978 as the result of several years' hard work now hinged on Hungary's positions toward the United States.[16] American officials urged the Hungarian side not to take a step backward in the field of bilateral relations and placed great importance on the upcoming visit to the United States by a parliamentary delegation headed by the speaker of parliament and HSWP Political Committee member Antal Apró.

The Horn mission also confirmed the Hungarian leadership's belief that the estrangement of the superpowers would not necessarily lead to the narrowing of the country's Western relations. On the contrary, it seemed that under the circumstances, besides Poland, Hungary had the greatest chance for using the situation to its advantage.

The Soviet Union, János Kádár, and His "Little Lousy Country"

The real shock for the Hungarian leadership came in the form of Soviet pressures in late January 1980, which "requested" that Hungary freeze its high-level contacts with the West immediately. This unexpected Soviet demarche stemmed from Moscow's revamped position on the international crisis. The Kremlin had originally anticipated a certain level of criticism from the West but basically projected that, after a short interlude, the fait accompli would be accepted by the world community and that the critical objective of maintaining the momentum of détente would overshadow the problem of Afghanistan. The West, and especially the United States, however, reacted differently. They rightly interpreted the situation as the first instance since 1945 that the Soviet Union militarily occupied a country that did not fall within the Soviet sphere of influence. While at the time of the East-Central European crises of 1953, 1956, and 1968 the West reluctantly acknowledged the Soviet Union's right to restore order within its bloc, it now considered the Soviet invasion of Afghanistan to be a unilateral and aggressive expansion of the Soviet sphere. With this initiative, Moscow had breached the tacit agreement that formed the basis of European status quo policy and that had functioned well since the end of World War II. Yet considering Afghanistan's geostrategic location, the acquisition of that territory violated only potential Western interests. As a result, the severity of the international crisis generated by the Soviet aggression ultimately did not attain the levels of the Berlin and Cuban crises at the beginning of the 1960s.

American countermeasures announced at the beginning of 1980 (e.g., restricting the sale of fodder grain to the Soviet Union, freezing of cultural and economic relations, banning the transfer of developed technologies) had not yet caused too great a trauma for Soviet leaders. Similarly, these measures did not initially effect any essential changes in their policy when the UN Security Council placed the Afghan question on the agenda on 5 January 1980 and when a special General Assembly session condemned the Soviet action. Although the possibility of the UN keeping the Afghan question permanently on the agenda might later have contributed to the reinforcement of the confrontational trend within the Soviet leadership, Brezhnev's speech of 16 January unambiguously emphasized the need for the maintenance of cooperation. Concurrently, however, on 20 January, President Carter called on all countries to boycott the Olympic Games scheduled for Moscow during the summer. Since these Olympics were to be the first in a Communist country, this event loomed importantly for the international prestige of the Eastern camp.

At the end of January 1980, the situation became even more critical. Although most Western European countries were not unambiguously and in all areas joining the American campaign aimed at the "punishment" of the Soviet Union, the question of European security was now viewed in a completely new light as a result of the Afghan intervention. On the basis of NATO's "double resolution," passed at the beginning of December 1979, it was still quite possible that, in the case of successful East-West talks, the deployment of the so-called Euromissiles would not take place in Western Europe. Under the new circumstances, however, it became more and more obvious that the NATO member states could not be dissuaded from the deployment of the missiles aimed at the strengthening of their security. Moreover, they now did not have to confront higher levels of popular resistance, which had earlier become an important political factor in a number of countries.

Thus, in late January 1980, after the announcement of the Olympic Games boycott and especially when it became clear that the Soviets could not convince the Western European countries to reject the deployment of the "Euromissiles," an offended Moscow decided to take countermeasures. During this campaign, Moscow ordered the cancellation of imminent high-level talks with Western politicians. Two visits of West German politicians—Foreign Minister Hans Dietrich Genscher to Prague and Chancellor Helmut Schmidt with Erich Honecker in Berlin—were subsequently called off. Although the Bulgarians did not have upcoming meetings with Western politicians, they, too, received warnings against planning such steps.

These measures caused a serious clash of interests between the Soviet Union and the Eastern European Communist states, since at this juncture all of these countries, in varying degrees and in different ways, remained interested in developing their relations with Western Europe. Further research will show exactly how this conflict affected the relations of the individual states with Moscow. To be sure, for Hungary this Soviet move caused one of the most serious crises since 1956, both within the Hungarian leadership and in Hungarian-Soviet relations. In the case of Hungary, the Soviets "requested" that the visit of Hungarian foreign minister Frigyes Puja to Bonn, scheduled in less than a week, be canceled and, similarly, that the visit of a parliamentary delegation to the United States be postponed. At the 29 January meeting of the HSWP Political Committee, one of the most dramatic in its history, the Hungarian leadership came the closest to making a political decision that openly defied the Soviet will. During a heated debate several Politburo members, including hard-liners like Apró, Dezső Nemes, and Németh, proposed that, taking into consideration the extremely short notices and the country's economic interests, the Soviet request should be disregarded. There seemed to be a clear majority for this position.[17]

Perhaps for the first time since 1956, the HSWP's first secretary, in an issue involving relations with the Soviet Union, always considered overriding, assumed a position contradicting that of the party's main operative body. During the debate Kádár, who had always strived to play a centrist role, found himself defending the policy considered to be the only realistic option, basically as a "leftist" deviator. Kádár adhered to the customary routine of carefully listening to members of the body and at the session's end of summing up the debate's essence in his own speech. He then proclaimed the resolution, which had worked well for decades but now brought its own punishment. In his rather confused and curse-filled speech, revealing his state of great agitation, Kádár argued that "we are again in a situation when we have the choice of two evils." In an anticipated conclusion, he announced that the high-level visits to Bonn and Washington had to be canceled. He considered that Hungary would not lose anything by obeying Moscow, and, at the worst, he,

Kádár, would be called "a Soviet satellite" in the West. "Some presumed advantage may only be hoped for, the negative effect is immediate" warned the experienced party leader to the members of the political committee, referring to the fact that by forfeiting the trust of the Kremlin's leaders, Hungary might lose much. Kádár proceeded to outline the basically determined character of Hungarian foreign policy: "At present Hungary has a certain reputation concerning its international policy, . . . this started . . . by our boycott by NATO, and we have reached a certain position, recognition with much effort, but at the same time never permitting to question that we were the allies of the Soviet Union. We have acquired this . . . and this is in the long-term interest of the nation. By another type of prestige we could obtain only short-term, sham advantages, eventually our people would be losers, believe me." To enlighten those who still might have had illusions concerning the nature of the Soviet request, he added, "What do you think, how long will they be polite to us? Why with us . . . excuse me for the phrase, with our little lousy life and country . . . how long will they behave politely toward us?"

This desperate declaration of the veteran Hungarian party leader offers perhaps the most blunt and drastic representation of the true nature of Hungary's relations with the Soviet Union in the whole Kádár era. From the debate's course it seemed that the members of the political committee did not perceive adequately the radical change in the political situation, and that is why they insisted on their position, worked out at the beginning of January, which emphasized the priority of cooperation with the West. Now, however, after Kádár's revealing speech, several of them rushed to point out that if the situation was as described, nothing was left to be done. In spite of this interpretation, Ferenc Havasi expressly indicated even afterward that, as a result of the planned step, the country might experience very serious economic difficulties, since Budapest had to take out a $1.7 billion Western loan to survive 1980. The two states concerned, the United States and the Federal Republic of Germany (FRG), could therefore make the situation rather difficult for Hungary.

But after Kádár's dramatic speech, the possible options withered, and the political committee finally passed a resolution on the cancellation of both visits. At the same time, in a confidence-building measure toward the West, the political committee requested that the Soviets postpone for a later date the joint Soviet-Hungarian military exercise originally scheduled for the western section of Hungary between 11 and 16 February.[18]

In some respects, this political committee session began the process leading to Kádár's political downfall. Although at this juncture the veteran party leader still succeeded in imposing his will upon his comrades, it can be stated that he might have won the battle but would ultimately lose the war. A few years later, because of Hungary's increasingly difficult economic situation, this conflict significantly contributed to an unfolding situation in which even his closest colleagues wanted him to step down from his leadership position.

Successful Crisis Management: A "Hungarian" Decision in the Kremlin

The two visits were canceled.[19] Paradoxically, the humiliation that Kádár had to suffer in this instance eventually contributed to the development of positive processes for his country. It resulted from a series of diplomatic maneuvers aimed at exerting pressure on the Soviets to change their position, on the one hand, and at explaining Hungary's difficult situation to Western partners, on the other. At that same Politburo session in late January, Hungary's leaders also decided that Moscow should be asked urgently to hold a multilateral consultative meeting on the impact of the situation in Afghanistan on East-West relations. A special envoy, András Gyenes, the central committee secretary for foreign affairs, was immediately dispatched to Moscow with a letter from Kádár to Brezhnev. The message articulated a firm Hungarian position: in the present situation the allies must be consulted regularly on joint policy for the Soviet bloc in international politics, and the results of détente must be preserved. Only by maintaining and strengthening the relations of the Eastern European countries with Western Europe would this be possible. Kádár concluded that this approach would deflect the spread of American influence in those countries.

With Brezhnev chronically ill, internal fights intensified among factions within the Soviet leadership. It was under such circumstances that Hungary's urgent call for consultation arrived in Moscow. Foreign Minister Andrei Gromyko replied to the suggestion nervously, because he did not understand what the Hungarians wanted to discuss.[20] Nonetheless, the Soviets accepted the Hungarian proposal for consultation and summoned a meeting of the central committee secretaries for foreign affairs of the "closely cooperating socialist countries" in Moscow on 26 February 1980. At the conference, Boris Ponomarjev, CPSU Central Committee secretary for international affairs, not only adopted the above-mentioned Hungarian position but also put forward this thesis *as the current CPSU line,* emphasizing that "the socialist countries should make the maximum use of the possibilities contained in existing relations with the Western European countries to counterbalance the United States's foreign policy line."[21]

This proved to be an important victory for Hungarian diplomacy.[22] First, Budapest received a green light for continuing efforts to develop its Western relations, so crucial for the country's economy at that time; freezing these relations in 1980 would have blocked Hungary's acquisition of a critical $1.7 billion Western loan in 1980, which, it is now known, would have led to the country's insolvency.[23]

From a historical perspective, it is even more important to point out that Kádár's firm personal intervention and the effective Hungarian diplomatic initiatives eventually helped liberal forces in the Soviet leadership—mostly key members of the central committee apparatus interested in maintaining détente—overcome their adversaries, led by Gromyko, who advocated a more belligerent attitude toward the West. As Vadim Zagladin, first deputy head of the International Department of the CPSU Central Committee, told Gyula Horn on 16 July 1980, "for several months in the CPSU Politburo, there had been heated debates about the Soviet Union's specific foreign policy steps, the general evaluation of the international situation and the situation of the Communist movement."[24] He emphasized that in this debate comrade János Kádár's message to the Soviet leadership played an important role.[25]

Parallel with the letter for Brezhnev, Kádár forwarded explanatory messages to Social Democratic Party chairman Willy Brandt and West German chancellor Helmut Schmidt. In these communications, he apologized for the cancellation of the visit of the Hungarian foreign minister on such short notice and subtly explained the difficult situation for the Hungarian leadership. He also stressed that his country was strongly committed to maintaining the results of détente and to fostering East-West cooperation. Helmut Schmidt, who in 1979 was the first German chancellor to visit Hungary, formulated in his reply the historical challenge confronting European states: it now depended on these states "whether they let themselves be drawn into the Cold War instigated by the two superpowers or not! Neither the FRG nor any other Western or Eastern European country can keep out of this [Cold War] alone. This is possible only with the collaboration of all states concerned."[26] It is evident that by the beginning of the 1980s, Hungary, while remaining a loyal member of the Warsaw Pact, felt compelled by its economic interests to move even closer to this virtual European community.

The resolution of this internal crisis can be regarded as an informative lesson concerning the limits of small-state diplomacy in the Warsaw Pact, or, stated otherwise, the opportunity for a small state, belonging to the "closely cooperating" group, to exert pressure on the Soviet leadership in order to achieve certain political goals. While it turned out to be impossible for Hungary to defy Soviet will openly, subsequent diplomatic maneuvers and Kádár's personal intervention could be successful, by extension, in affecting internal debate in the Kremlin, thereby influencing the outcome of events according to the crucial interests of the country and, in fact, of the international community.

This interlude contributed to conditions that averted the aggravated deterioration of East-West ties, as had occurred in U.S.-Soviet relations following the invasion of Afghanistan. It can be inferred that, consequently, there was no "Second Cold War," as many term these years, in Europe. Thus, the invasion of Afghanistan, in which the Warsaw Pact states were not involved, in fact helped amplify the notion of an East-Central Europe with a special identity significantly different from that of the Soviet Union. All these patterns, paradoxically, contributed to the gradual establishment of a common European consciousness, which had been evolving since the late 1960s.

During this period of serious tension at the superpower level—from the invasion of Afghanistan to the rise of Mikhail Gorbachev in 1985—Hungary served as a model case by demonstrating how a small state, driven by its economic interest, while a "closely cooperating" member of the Warsaw Pact, could maintain and advance the policy of détente as if nothing had happened between the United States and the Soviet Union. In fact, these years brought a dynamic and prosperous era in developing the country's economic and political relations with the West. In 1982, Hungary was able to join the International Monetary Fund and the World Bank.[27] Moreover, as early as 1981 exploratory talks had already begun concerning a potential agreement between Hungary and the European Community. These overtures stalled not from Moscow's pressure but because of Chancellor Helmut Schmidt, who worried about the potentially negative effect such a step might have on his own country's relations with the Soviet Union. The German chancellor explicitly talked Kádár out of this plan on his visit to Bonn in April 1982.[28] This period witnessed a general intensification of high-level relations with Western states. Kádár paid visits to Bonn and Rome already in 1977, to Paris in 1978, to Bonn again in 1982, and to London in 1985. In turn, Budapest received visits from French prime minister Raymond Barre in 1977, Chancellor Helmut Schmidt in 1979, French president François Mitterrand in 1982, Vice President George Bush in 1983, and Helmut Kohl, Margaret Thatcher, and Bettino Craxi in 1984. Since Poland lost the sympathy of the Western states after the introduction of martial law in 1981, as did Romania due to its repressive policy, Hungary become the favorite in the eyes of the West as the most respectable country of the Eastern bloc.

With Gorbachev's rise to power in the Soviet Union, the new Soviet leadership became the primary advocate of dialogue between East and West. The initiating and moderating nature of Hungarian foreign policy remained but would now assume secondary importance in dramatically unfolding developments.[29]

Notes

1. Magyar Országos Levéltár [Hungarian National Archives] (hereafter: MOL), M-KS-288.f.5/ 790. ő.e., in Csaba Békés, "Miért nem lett második hidegháború Európában? A magyar pártvezetés és az 1979. évi afganisztáni szovjet intervenció. Dokumentumok. [Why Was There No "Second Cold War" in Europe? The Hungarian Party Leadership and the Soviet Invasion of Afghanistan in 1979. Documents]," in Évkönyv 2003. Magyarország a jelenkorban, 1956-os Intézet. Szerk. János M. Rainer, Éva Standeisky, Budapest, 1956-os Intézet, 2003, 232–33. The English translation of the document was published as part of a collection of Hungarian archival sources on the Soviet intervention in Afghanistan in Csaba Békés, "Why Was There No 'Second Cold War' in Europe? Hungary and the Soviet Invasion of Afghanistan in 1979. Documents from Hungarian Archives," *Cold War International History Project Bulletin* 14/15 (winter 2003–spring 2004): 204–19.

2. János Kádár's account on his visit to Moscow at the 31 July 1963 meeting of the HSWP Political Committee, MOL, M-KS-288.f.5/ 309.ő.e. A similar proposal was already made by Hungarian diplomacy as early as 1958, but then it did not cause any reaction on the Soviet side. Following Khrushchev's fall, at a meeting with the new Soviet leadership Kádár warned Brezhnev that, whatever the Soviet leadership does, it had an important effect on the other socialist countries as well. Magyar–szovjet csúcstalálkozók, 1957–1965 [Hungarian–Soviet summit meetings], Évkönyv, 6. 1998 /szerk. György Litván (Budapest: 1956-os Intézet, 1998): 171.

3. Csaba Békés, Malcolm Byrne, and János M. Rainer, eds., *The 1956 Hungarian Revolution: A History in Documents* (Budapest: Central European Univ. Press, 2002), xli–xlii.

4. On the invasion of Czechoslovakia see *The Prague Spring 1968*, comp. and ed. Jaromir Navratil with Antonin Bencik, Václáv Kurál, Marie Michálková, and Jitka Vondrová (Budapest: Central European Univ. Press, 1998).

5. For an account of Hungary's role and activity in the Warsaw Pact, see Csaba Békés, "Hungary in the Warsaw Pact, 1954–1989. Documents with an Introduction," Parallel History Project on NATO and the Warsaw Pact, 2003: www.isn.ethz.ch/php, accessed 12 Dec. 2003, and Csaba Békés, *Hungary and the Making of the CSCE Process, 1965–1970*, in *The Helsinki Process: A Historical Reappraisal*, ed. Carla Meneguzzi Rostagni (Padova, Italy: CEDAM, 2005), 29–44.

6. Odd Arne Westad, "Concerning the Situation in 'A': New Russian Evidence on the Soviet Intervention in Afghanistan," *Cold War International History Project Bulletin* 8–9 (winter 1996/1997): 131.

7. Bulletin for the members of the Political Committee and the Secretariat on the talks of the deputy head of the HSWP Central Committee International Department in the United States and Canada; 23 Jan. 1980; MOL M-KS 288 f. 5/ 791.ő.e.

8. President Johnson suggested the discussion of the following topics at the planned summit: Vietnam, the Middle East, and the issue of antimissile systems. Moscow agreed to the proposal and the meeting was to be held in Leningrad in October 1968, but it was eventually canceled. See Csaba Békés, *Európából Európába: Magyarország konfliktusok kereszttüzében, 1945–1990*. [From Europe to Europe: Hungary in the crossfire of conflicts, 1945–1990] (Budapest: Gondolat, 2004), 236; see also Anatoly Dobrinin, *Confidence: Moscow's Ambassador to Six Cold War Presidents* (New York: Random House, 1995), 189–95.

9. Minutes of the HSWP Political Committee meeting on 8 Jan. 1980; MOL, M-KS-288.f. 5/790.ő.e.

10. Between 17 Dec. 1979 and 14 Jan. 1980, there was no meeting of the HSWP Secretariat either, so the operative bodies of the party did not discuss this issue before January 8. In spite of this, members of the top leadership must have talked about it unofficially at ad hoc meetings. It is most likely that the text of a telegram welcoming the new Afghan leadership right after the Soviet intervention was accepted at such a meeting.

11. Hafizullah Amin was foreign minister following the "revolution" in Apr. 1978; in Sept. he became prime minister. He was killed during the Soviet invasion on 27 Dec. 1979.

12. At the meeting of the NATO Council on 12 Dec. 1979 a so-called double resolution was adopted. On the one hand, it was decided that 108 Pershing 2 missiles and 464 ground-based robot planes would be deployed in Great Britain, the FRG, Belgium, Italy, and the Netherlands. On the other hand, the Soviet Union was called upon to start negotiations on the limitation of medium-range nuclear missiles. According to the resolution, in case such talks are not completed successfully by the end of 1983, the deployment of the Western missiles would be started.

13. Horn's report on his mission, as part of a collection of documents on Hungarian archival sources on the Soviet intervention in Afghanistan, was published in Békés, "Why Was There No 'Second Cold War' in Europe?" 209–11. Later Gyula Horn was foreign minister (1989–90) and prime minister (1994–98).

14. Information bulletin for the members of the Political Committee and the Secretariat on the talks of the Deputy Head of the International Department in the United States and Canada; 23 Jan. 1980; MOL M-KS 288 f. 5/ 791.ő.e.

15. At the elections on 4 Nov. 1980, Republican candidate Ronald Reagan was elected president.

16. The status of most favored nation was granted to Hungary in a way that it had to be renewed by the U.S. Congress annually.

17. Minutes of the session of the HSWP Political Committee on 29 Jan. 1980; MOL, M-KS-288.f. 5/791.ő.e. The full text of the verbatim minutes, pertaining to this topic as part of a collection of documents on Hungary and the East-West crisis following the Soviet intervention in Afghanistan was published in Békés, *Miért nem lett második hidegháború Európában?* 234–50.

18. The Soviets approved the suggestion and postponed the military exercise to a later date, to July 1980.

19. Hungarian foreign minister Frigyes Puja eventually visited Bonn between 10 and 12 Sept. 1980.

20. Memorandum of conversation between János Kádár and Leonid Brezhnyev, 4 July 1980; MOL, M-KS-288. f. 47/764.ő.e. Kádár emphasized, at this meeting, too, the great importance of preliminary consultation, while reminding the Soviet leader about the events that had taken place about half a year earlier: "At that time, the Afghan question was rather acute and we cancelled our visits to the West. At the time of the signal of the Soviet Union, there was only one week left before the date of our foreign minister's visit to the FRG. The FRG did not get offended by the cancellation, they came to the conclusion: 'it is clear, the Soviet Union has blocked everything.' However, we could have spared this in case of a more operative co-ordination. The conference of 'the six' is useful for avoiding such situations, too. We understand every word that makes sense, but we require consultation, otherwise we walk blindfolded, and this we cannot afford. If we coordinate our policies in time, no one could embarrass us."

21. Memorandum of conversation between Vadim Zagladin, first deputy head of the International Department of the CPSU Central Committee, and Gyula Horn, deputy head of

the HSWP Central Committee Department of Foreign Affairs, on debates inside the Soviet leadership on issues of international politics; [16 July 1980]; MOL M-KS 288 f. 47/ 764.ő.e.

22. On the history of Hungarian foreign policy in this period see Békés, *Európából Európába* and "Hungarian foreign policy in the Soviet alliance system, 1968–1989," *Foreign Policy Review* (Budapest) 3, no. 1 (2004): 87–127.

23. Minutes of the session of the HSWP Political Committee on 29 Jan. 1980; MOL., M-KS-288.f. 5/791.ő.e., in Békés, *Miért nem lett második hidegháború Európában?* 234–50.

24. For the substance of these debates see memorandum of conversation between Vadim Zagladin, first deputy head of the International Department of the CPSU Central Committee, and Gyula Horn, deputy head of the HSWP Central Committee Department of Foreign Affairs, on debates inside the Soviet leadership on issues of international politics; [16 July 1980]; MOL M-KS 288 f. 47/ 764.ő.e. The English translation of the document was published as part of a collection of Hungarian archival sources on the Soviet intervention in Afghanistan in Békés, "Why Was There No 'Second Cold War' in Europe? 214–15.

25. Békés, "Why Was There No 'Second Cold War' in Europe?" 214.

26. Information bulletin for the Political Committee and the Secretariat concerning the oral reply of Chancellor Helmut Schmidt to the message of János Kádár; 14 Feb. 1980; MOL, M-KS-288. f. 11./4512.ő.e.

27. Hungary made an attempt to join the International Monetary Fund and the World Bank as early as 1967 but at that time this move was blocked by Moscow.

28. István Horváth, István Németh, . . . *És a falak leomlanak: Magyarország és a német egység (1945–1990)* [And the walls come down: Hungary and German Unity (1945–1990)] (Budapest: Magvető Kiadó) 1999, 173–76. Eventually the contract was made in 1988 and official relations between Hungary and the EEC were established.

29. Csaba Békés, "Back to Europe: The International Context of the Political Transition in Hungary, 1988–1990," in András Bozóki, ed., *The Roundtable Talks of 1989: The Genesis of Hungarian Democracy* (Budapest: Central European Univ. Press, 2002), 237–72.

Contributors

SHELDON ANDERSON is professor of history and international studies at Miami University in Oxford, Ohio, where he specializes in early Cold War diplomacy and Eastern European history. He has published two books using declassified documents in Polish and East German archives: *A Dollar to Poland Is a Dollar to Russia: United States Economic Policy Toward Poland, 1945–52* (1993), and *A Cold War in the Soviet Bloc: Polish–East German Relations, 1945–1962* (2000). His current project examines several of the most important myths about European diplomatic history in the twentieth century and the way foreign policy makers have used them to make decisions.

JORDAN BAEV is associate professor of contemporary history and senior research fellow of security studies at the Rakovski Defense College. He has been visiting professor of international relations and conflict studies at New Bulgarian University and the Diplomatic Institute to Bulgarian Foreign Ministry in Sofia. He has published four monographs, seven documentary volumes, and numerous articles based on recently declassified documents dealing with Bulgaria and the Warsaw Pact states during the Cold War.

OLIVER BANGE is on the faculty of the University of Mannheim. He received his Ph.D. in international history from the London School of Economics and has published extensively on the history of European integration, the Cold War, country images, and Willy Brandt's *Ostpolitik*. He held scholarships of the German Historical Institute in London, the European University Institute, and the University of London. He published *The EEC Crisis of 1963: Kennedy, MacMillan, de Gaulle, and Adenauer in Conflict* (2000) and is currently working on a major work on *Ostpolitik* and détente in Europe.

CSABA BÉKÉS is founding director of the Cold War History Research Center (Budapest), senior research fellow of the Institute for the History of the 1956 Hungarian Revolution (Budapest), and member of the international editorial boards of the journals *Cold War History* and *Journal of Cold War Studies*. During the academic year 2001–2002, he was a center fellow, Project on the Cold War as Global Conflict, International Center for Advanced Studies, New York University. His main field of research is Hungary's international relations after World War II and the role of East-Central Europe in the Cold War.

CHARLES COGAN served for thirty-seven years in the CIA (including as Paris station chief) and most recently is an affiliate at Harvard University's Center for European Studies, an associate at the John F. Kennedy School of Government, and an associate at the John M. Olin Institute for Strategic Studies at the Weatherhead Center for International Affairs. Among his many publications is *French Negotiating Behavior: Dealing with "La Grande Nation"* (2003), which has also appeared in an updated French version (2005).

WINFRIED HEINEMANN, PH.D., is a colonel in the German army and director of East German and Warsaw Pact military history at the German Military History Institute at Potsdam. He has published extensively on the history of NATO, including a dissertation on "Vom Zusammenwachsen des Bündnisses. Die Funktionsweise der NATO in ausgewählten Krisenfällen, 1951–1956" (1998), and on the military resistance against Hitler.

MARY ANN HEISS, a specialist in the history of U.S. foreign relations, is an associate professor of history at Kent State University. She is the author of *Empire and Nationhood: The United States, Great Britain, and Iranian Oil, 1950–1954* (1997), and coeditor of books on the future of NATO and U.S. relations with the Third World since 1945. Her current research focuses on the international aspects of decolonization.

JOHN O. IATRIDES was educated in Greece, the Netherlands, and the United States and is Connecticut State University Professor Emeritus of International Politics. During the 1950s he served as NATO liaison officer for the Greek National Defense General Staff and information officer of the prime minister's office. His publications include *Balkan Triangle: Birth and Decline of an Alliance Across Ideological Boundaries* (1968), *Revolt in Athens* (1972), *Ambassador MacVeagh Reports: Greece, 1933–47* (1980), *Greece in the 1940s: A Nation in Crisis* (1980), and *The Aegean Sea After the Cold War: Security and Law of the Sea Issues* (2000).

LAWRENCE S. KAPLAN is University Professor Emeritus and the Lemnitzer Center's founding director at Kent State University. More recently he has been teaching at Georgetown University. His numerous writings include *The Long Entanglement: NATO's First Fifty Years* (1999), *Thomas Jefferson: Westward the Course of Empire* (1999), *NATO and the United States: The Enduring Alliance* (1994), *NATO Divided, NATO United: The Evolution of an Alliance* (2004), and *The McNamara Ascendancy, 1961–1965* (2006).

ANNA LOCHER is senior researcher at the Center for Security Studies at the ETH Zurich. Her specialization is NATO's political history in the 1960s, the role of small states in international relations, and the history of Finland. She is coeditor of *Transatlantic Relations at Stake* (2006) and *Transforming NATO in the Cold War* (2007). She is currently completing a monograph on the management of intrabloc dissent in NATO in 1963–66.

INE MEGENS is a lecturer in contemporary history at the University of Groningen. Her research focuses on NATO, European defense cooperation, and Dutch foreign and defense policy. Her publications include *American Aid to NATO Allies in the 1950s: The Dutch Case* (1994).

VOJTECH MASTNY is project coordinator of the Parallel History Project on NATO and the Warsaw Pact, based at the Center for Security Studies of the Swiss Federal Institute of Technology in Zurich. He has been professor of history and international relations at Columbia University, the University of Illinois, Boston University, and the Johns Hopkins University School of Advanced International Studies. His books include *The Helsinki Process and the Reintegration of Europe* (1992), *A Cardboard Castle? An Inside History of the Warsaw Pact* (2005, with Malcolm Byrne), *Russia's Road to the Cold War* (1979), *The Cold War and Soviet Insecurity* (1996), and several coedited volumes, most recently *War Plans and Alliances in the Cold War: Threat Perceptions in the East and West* (2006).

CHRISTIAN NUENLIST is senior researcher at the Center for Security Studies at ETH Zurich. His research focuses on the evolution of political consultation in NATO, the history of détente, and Swiss foreign policy during the Cold War. He is the author of a political biography of McGeorge Bundy in the Kennedy years (1999) and coeditor of *Transatlantic Relations at Stake* (2006), *Transforming NATO in the Cold War* (2007), and *Origins of European Security* (2008). He is currently completing a monograph on NATO's reactions to Khruschchev's foreign policy from 1955 to 1964.

S. VICTOR PAPACOSMA is professor of history and director of the Lemnitzer Center at Kent State University. He has published extensively on Balkan issues, particularly on twentieth-century Greek politics and security issues. He has co-edited six volumes of Lemnitzer Center conference proceedings, including *NATO after Fifty Years* (2001), *Limiting Institutions: The Challenges of Eurasian Security Governance* (2003), and *EU Enlargement and New Security Challenges in the Eastern Mediterranean* (2004). He is currently serving as executive director of the Modern Greek Studies Association.

BERND SCHAEFER has been a research fellow at the German Historical Institute in Washington, D.C., and is a Senior Scholar with the Cold War International History Project at the Woodrow Wilson Center. He received his M.P.A. from Harvard University and his Dr. Phil. from Martin Luther University Halle. His recent research has concentrated on East Asian Communism during the Cold War. Among his publications are *North Korean "Adventurism" and China's Long Shadow, 1966–1972* (2004) and *The GDR in German Archives: A Guide to Primary Sources and Research Institutions on the History of the Soviet Zone of Occupation and the German Democratic Republic, 1945–1990* (2002).

DOUGLAS SELVAGE is assistant professor of history at Embry-Riddle University, specializing in modern German and Polish history and the history of international relations. Previously, he worked for five years as a documentary editor for the *Foreign Relations of the United States* series in the Office of the Historian at the U.S. Department of State. He has received numerous awards, including a Fulbright Scholarship to Germany, a Mellon Fellowship in the humanities, and a two-year Collaborative Research Grant from the National Endowment for the Humanities. He has published widely on the history of the Cold War in U.S. and international publications.

Index

NATO and the Warsaw Pact:

Text and jacket was designed and composed by Darryl ml Crosby in

10/13.5 Minion Pro; printed on 55# Natures Natural stock

by Thomson-Shore, Inc., of Dexter, Michigan;

and published by

The Kent State University Press

Kent, Ohio 44242